On *the* CONTRARY

Thomas O. Sloane

On *the*

CONTRARY

The

Protocol of

Traditional

Rhetoric

The Catholic University of America Press

Washington, D.C.

Copyright © 1997
The Catholic University of America Press
All rights reserved
Printed in the United States of America

The paper used in this publication meets the minimum requirements of
American National Standards for Information Science—Permanence of
Paper for Printed Library materials, ANSI Z39.48-1984.
∞

Library of Congress Cataloging-in-Publication Data

Sloane, Thomas O.
   On the contrary : the protocol of traditional rhetoric / Thomas O.
Sloane.
      p.   cm.
   Includes bibliographical references and index.
      1. Rhetoric.   2. Humanism.   I. Title.
PN175.S59   1997
808—dc20
96-26257
ISBN 0-8132-0879-3 (alk. paper)

For All Speech Teachers, Wherever You Are

A perfect orator is a skilled debater.
(neque perfectus orator sine hac
virtute [altercatione] dici potest)
Quintilian, *Inst. orat.* VI.iv.3

Humor works.
(est plane oratoris movere risum)
Cicero, *De orat.* II.lviii.236

Epistle Dedicatory

To a late teacher of Elocution

Emerson College was your background (my parents had checked), and although you were familiar with Del Sarte's teaching you preferred the less Catholic-trinitarian and far more liberal approaches of Tassin and Alexander. And you had spent a year in Glasgow in the voice choirs of Marjorie Gullen. How could my parents miss, then? Their purpose, after all, was to give an unruly little boy a "cultured manner" (your phrase), which he neither came by naturally nor was likely to acquire from his companions.

You died before the Fifties were barely out. But I can see you still, with your heavily made up face, that tiara, the expressive feather boa, and the occasional chiton. "Let the gesture begin with the elbow and flow out to the finger tips." I recall your doomed efforts to give me a pliable pose: "Feel the fatigue, the tiredness, of the ploughman as he homeward plods his weary way." I recall, too, your equally doomed efforts to soften my Midwestern twang: "Not 'charractur.' *Cha'ahktah.* Not 'coss-toom,' *coz-tiume.*" "Pear-shaped tones, Tommy, pear-shaped tones." Later, I was disappointed to find that "How now, brown cow?" is not, as I had assumed *(ass-siumed)*, from Shakespeare.

Though I was meant to learn "culture," what I actually acquired were certain ideas, certain attitudes which you simply took for granted, and now hardly anyone does. Nowadays these ideas and attitudes seem atavistic. And "culture" no longer means what you took it to mean. Recalling these matters, these assumptions, I've dedicated this book to you. And to your wayward descendants and neglected progenitors.

Through you I was put in touch with an ancient tradition, something simpler and deeper than the "wondrous strange" results of your lessons. I mean simpler and deeper than the exaggerated acting of silent movies, or the florid orotundity of stump speakers, replete with jumbled retrievals from a literary trash heap. Partly it was a sense of something that had been passed down not through letters but through, well, spirit. Let me try to be specific. I learned from you and from other speech teachers doctrines whose patent obviousness has been almost willfully ignored of late: that discourse is an instrument of the body as well as of the mind, that a word is nothing unless spoken by someone to someone with some clear intention, that language—as a critic I came to admire said—is gesture. It was from you, too, that I learned why teachers are important and why it is that we are right to call a good education a "sound" education.

Who would have guessed, back then, that fifty years later some of these simple matters would become side-stepped in heated intellectual controversies, all arising from our frantic concerns about the nature of language? The metanovel, born of fears that the novel is no longer possible; deconstruction, born of fears that words really are tossed into a void; new historicism, born of fears that poststructuralism has pulled the rug out from under "English Studies"; political correctness, born of fears on the one hand and hopes on the other that education just might be indoctrination after all. It was healing to return, not to elocution, but to the mother of elocution, Rhetoric, and read again Cicero on the synergetic nature of spoken language: speech takes at least two people, he said, and the other person is partly going to determine not just what you say but what you think. And when dealing with people, he said, don't forget your sense of humor. Humor works, in a variety of ways.

I can yet recall your story about the wittiness of your old actor friend, Roger Bonifield. Roger rose to the top of the heap in an actors' studio exercise, one of the early efforts to inject "realism" into the theatre: A waterfront was to be depicted on stage. The hero was to enter and find the heroine's gloves, purse, and parasol on the peer and assume that she's jumped in. Whipping off his coat, he was to jump in too, to rescue her (to the sound effects of splashing water). On the day of the exercise, however, the pad which was to have been placed at the end of pier to soften the hero's dry plunge had been removed. Roger, alas, discovered its removal only when he was in midair. But with perfect aplomb, following the noise of the crash—which drowned out the other sound effects—he pulled himself together and, lifting his bruised head over the end of the pier, faced the class to say, "Well I'll be damned, the lake's frozen over."

Resourcefulness, you said, was the point of the story. Traditional rhetoricians, I learned later, called this kind of resourcefulness *copia*. It was part of their lesson not simply about humor but about linguistic strategies, irony, and illusion.

As a teacher of performance you had a career as a writer staked out for me. The irony of the lesson escaped me at the time. But another kind of illusion-making became my love—teaching, another subject now much in the news.

And it has been for the better part of this century. I am speaking of university teaching. About the time you entered Emerson, we can see now, there was a revolution going on in university education. We began to adopt a scientific model for all knowledge while we also crazily instituted softly unscientific courses aimed simply at training people to live harmoniously in modern society. The university has become "a motley social organism," Barzun in his latest book says contemptuously, "dedicated to the full life." Other critiques, of variable reputability—Bloom, Hirsch, Sykes, Lehman, D'Souza, Kimball, Cheney—all but drown out older voices like Dewey's or newer ones like Graff's and make even John Searle seem reactionary. Searle ends his long essay on education in the *New York Review of Books* (1990) calling for a return to of all things a core curriculum. We had given up on core curricula thirty years ago, back in the 1960s when we decided that students might be less disaffected if they had a role in governing the university—and their first action was to get rid of most required courses. Searle's core curriculum—he probably wouldn't call it that—restores the idea that there are certain kinds of skills, among them proficiency in writing and speaking, that we should expect an educated person to have.

Alas, not only have we given up on the core curriculum, we seem also to have given up on any clear idea about what an educated person is. "Nobody denies that most students entering most colleges write badly, read little, speak in puzzling fragments, and hence in effect *think* badly or not at all," laments Wayne Booth. "They then enter 'programs,' most of which require little writing, scant reading (and then only of an undemanding kind, the predigested pablum of most textbooks), no disciplined speech, and 'thinking' only of whatever kind is useful in practicing a given specialty."

You, too, for that matter, were involved in this fragmentation, the kind that began soon after the turn of the century. The year you graduated from Emerson, 1915, was also the year when the speech and English disciplines split forever. And Speech has now split further into something like the division between "hard" social science and "soft" humanities. Your own literary education was centered in elocution, but you eagerly turned that, elocution, into a specialty—that is, into a profession, which (as George Bernard Shaw had said) was like all professions a conspiracy against the public.

In all this fragmentation, which has continued its long division for over seventy-five years, we have lost something important and it's conditioned our view of rhetoric. We've lost the very heart of the rhetorical creative process. Little wonder that we think of rhetoric as, at best, the writing of expository prose for an only vaguely sensed audience or, at worst, purple prose and specious reasoning for a very definite, targetted audience. Or that those who do think of it as training in argumentation actually give a truncated view of its intellectual procedures.

Although you were part of the fragmentation, you nonetheless held onto a certain wholeness, which was whatever you seemed to mean by "culture." Whatever you meant, I know your ideas would change the very matter at issue in modern quarrels over education. "There can't be good speaking," you said, "unless there is good listening, too."

There was even a certain wholeness in your comic instruction based on *oppositions*: when one rises from a chair, you taught, one should locate the center of gravity in the chest, not in the "bum" where it tries to be; and thus when one rises from a chair, one had to consider both the chest as well as the "bum." (Was this the Alexander method?) The doctrine parodies an intellectual habit I'll describe in this book. Your point, like Henry Higgins', was transformation. Mine is access. But we are linked in our view of language: it is, au fond, more than words.

Berkeley, CA
Fall, 1995

Contents

Figures

Acknowledgements

My title is meant to echo a certain cliche used by debaters formally and informally. It also echoes the opening of Eusebius's speech quoted in chapter 1. For some readers it may recall philosophical documents of old, e.g., On the Soul *(De anima)*, On Oratory *(De oratore)*, and On the Writing of Letters *(De conscribendis epistolis)*. I hope, too, that for some readers it will recall a title used by that contrarian writer Mary McCarthy (1961).

For support, encouragement, knowledge, friendship, and often all of the above, I heartily thank Joel Altman, Art Quinn, Leonard Nathan, Adrienne Miller, Felipe Gutteriez, Kirsten Andersen, Susan Dobra, Amy Seltzer Tick, John McVitty, Karalee and John Harding, all at The University of California at Berkeley; Virginia Renner at the Huntington Library and Tony Bliss at the Bancroft Library; Jean-Francois Vallee, Jim Pearce, Tim McGee, and John Tinkler; William Kennedy of Cornell University, Richard Schoeck of the University of Kansas, Heinrich Plett of the University of Essen, and an anonymous reviewer for the Catholic University Press. I wish also to acknowledge the splendid editorial work of Susan Needham and Philip Holthaus, of The Catholic University of America Press.

Above all, deep and lasting thanks as ever to Barbara, who for over four decades has—and in many more ways than one—mooted for me the question *An ducenda sit uxor.*

These are the stars. The book's faults, dear Brutus, are not in them.

On *the* CONTRARY

1. Issues

The great Roman lawyer of antiquity, L. Licinius Crassus (in Cicero's *De oratore,* a dialogue much loved by Renaissance humanists), has just discussed the ideal rhetorical education, in response to a request from his houseguests. He concludes in the following way:

> We must also read the poets, acquaint ourselves with histories, study and peruse the masters and authors in every excellent art, and by way of practice praise, expound, emend, criticize and confute them; we must argue every question on both sides, and bring out on every topic whatever points can be deemed plausible; besides this we must become learned in the common law and familiar with the statutes, and must contemplate all the olden times, and investigate the ways of the senate, political philosophy, the rights of allies, the treaties and conventions, and the policy of empire; and lastly we have to cull, from all the forms of pleasantry, a certain charm of humour, with which to give a sprinkle of salt, as it were, to all of our discourse.[1]

Crassus offered his ideal as something of an opening sally in a dispute. Consciously controversial in its extremities ("every question," "all the forms"), his concluding remarks nonetheless sound the themes—major as well as minor—of the book you are now reading:

1. *De oratore* I.xxxiv.158–9, trans. E. W. Sutton and H. Rackham (Cambridge, Mass., 1929), 109.

literary criticism as a mode of argumentation, disputation as a mode of reasoning and analysis, a lawyerly logic, antiquarianism, rhetoric as training for statesmanship, and the humane importance of humor.

All of these themes will find their center in the following argument: the play of ideas in pro and con disputation (chapter 2), the mainstay of traditional Western education (chapters 3 and 4), undergirds certain writings of the English Renaissance (chapters 5 and 6) and may deserve renewed consideration by modern teachers of composition (passim, but especially chapter 7). So put, the argument is only an anatomy of this book. For the educational feature I wish to describe involves more than simply requiring students to argue both sides of the question. It involves, among other things, a literally controversial and no longer fashionable view of language. Further, it will become obvious that the purpose and nature of my work is mainly historical and that, while my argument has implications for contemporary pedagogy, it is not intended to provide suggestions for classroom practice. Although I wish mainly to search the past for what is missing in our modern revival of rhetoric, I will make excursions into the modern university classroom primarily by way of substantiation, clarification, and contrast. But in my final chapter, 7, I shall try to look a little more directly at modern rhetorical education.

As this brief review of my argument has suggested, there is a cluster of ideas which centers on contrarianism in education. I shall use that cluster as a kind of prism both to catch lights from certain Renaissance texts and to play against contemporary theory and practice. To explain the range of that cluster, the facets of the prism, we shall center on the educational theories of that great preceptor of northern European humanism, Erasmus. Erasmus, too, will help me pursue my argument that what's missing in modern revivals of rhetoric is that they give too little thought to thinking. Modern revivals of rhetoric fail to help us understand the kind of thinking you have to do as a rhetorician—or at least the kind of thinking traditionally understood as the kind of thinking you have to do as a rhetorician. That was a matter about which Erasmus was very sharp and very clever.

Erasmus will prove useful as a foil for my study of Thomas Wilson, in which we shall get a clearer glimpse of the "real" world beyond the groves of academe or the pillars of the Church. With Wilson we shall examine the work of a Renaissance statesman and rhetorician who put the Erasmian ideals to the service of English politics and personal ambition. Wilson, moreover, set forth the clearest theoretical explications of two arts central to our study, logic (or dialectic) and rhetoric. I have paraphrased these theories and placed them in Appendix A for whoever might want a brief review of them. By contrast, Erasmus, for important reasons which we shall attempt to uncover, was an opaque theorist.

I could have entitled this book *The Contrarian Impulse and its Importance in Rhetorical Paedaia*. But that would have put off, I'm afraid, the very audience I seek. And it would have misnamed the kinds of ideas I'm hoping to midwive. I write not necessarily for students of the Renaissance but for humanists of all stripes. I wish to talk about a part of their/our heritage—the opposing part, the part that is always detached from the status quo, and that infiltrates, or should infiltrate, what we seem to mean by "critical thinking." Contrarianism is of the essence in rhetoric, and was of the essence in careers of traditional rhetoricians such as Erasmus and Thomas Wilson. Understanding that contrarianism should help us understand what it means to think like a rhetorician.

Moreover, contrarianism is of the essence in traditional rhetorical education. Here I must tip my full hand. A critique of modern education is already suggested in my dedicatory epistle. A critique of modern rhetoric is pandemic in this book. Rhetoric, as I understand it, is decidedly not at home in modern education, as I understand it. For the conditions of the latter work against the contrarian protocol of traditional rhetoric and so make impossible a full revival of the central organ in rhetorical thinking, "invention."

Many modern educationists will dislike the view of rhetoric I offer. For it is ostensibly based on antagonism, hostility, strife, competitiveness, indeed all those objectionably male-oriented qualities modern education is seeking to "go beyond." When skillfully applied, I shall argue, rhetoric too actually seeks to go beyond those qualities. For rhetoric at certain points abandons antagonism and enters into an intellectual process that the rhetoric-hater Socrates calls *maieutic,* midwifery, a role women have traditionally performed.[2] It

2. In his dialogue *Theaetetus,* Socrates identifies himself as the son of a midwife and as one who practices midwifery. This famous dialogue, which pursues the nature and meaning of knowledge but which is one of the most inconclusive of all Socratic

is Erasmus, I shall argue, who provides an important conceptual link between rhetoric and maieutic discourse. If my book ultimately fails to make rhetorical invention, as I understand it, attractive, perhaps it will at least help us understand the nature of prose created under some of those superficially male-oriented conditions I have just enumerated, which would include much of the prose created by the great English humanists of the sixteenth century. But, to repeat, I shall further argue that, although created under the conditions of strife and anatagonism, certain complicated examples of that prose did not seek to perpetuate those conditions at all; they sought, rather, to serve as midwives, to assist the readers to give birth to ideas in their own heads. After all, as Erasmus said in his great work on rhetoric, "One should not write so that everyone can understand everything, but so that people should be compelled to investigate and learn some things for themselves."[3] The passage is a key to my argument.

Let me admit—to, I think, no one's surprise in view of my stated purpose—that my work has far more than a tinge of antiquarianism. I am an antiquarian rhetorician but only in the way that Michael Billig is an antiquarian psychologist, someone who digs up relics from the past, "delighting to find odd bits and pieces." Of course, these forays into the past have more than delight as their object. "Unconvinced that modernity is wholly satisfactory," says Billig, "antiquarians venture upon their raids in the hope of preserving relics of the past, and displaying them alongside modern possessions."[4] When I juxtapose the past with the present, it is the incompleteness, the insufficiency, of the present that I would call attention to. We have not fully recovered the educational richness, or for that matter the humanity, of the rhetorical tradition.[5]

---

dialogues, is surely aimed at demonstrating the efficacy of "midwifery" itself, not simply in philosophical dialogue, or even disputes, but also in the general world of "critical thinking." For an excellent analysis of how maieutic discourse works, see Joel B. Altman, "'Prophetic Fury': *Othello* and the Economy of Shakespearean Reception," *Studies in the Literary Imagination* 26 (1993), 85–113.

3. *De copia,* cap. XVIII; trans. Betty I. Knott, *Collected Works of Erasmus* 24 (Toronto, 1978), 336.

4. Michael Billig, *Arguing and Thinking: A Rhetorical Approach to Social Psychology* (Cambridge, England, 1987), 3.

5. Peter Mack's *Renaissance Argument* (Leiden, 1993) is a noteworthy exception. His long and excellent discussion of, as his subtitle puts it, "Valla and Agricola in the Traditions of Rhetoric and Dialectic," ends with the possible application of his

Ironically, the discovery of traditional rhetoric outside the humanities seems richer of late than ongoing revivals of rhetoric within the humanities: compare, for example, the work of Billig, or Buchanan in design, or McCloskey in economics, with, say, the attempted revivals and stunted defenses of rhetoric by DeMan or Vickers.[6] The former emphasize rhetoric as an intellectual method (or, better, habit), the latter dredge up the old figures of speech as new ways of naming the ostensible styles or effects of a discourse. The former try to extend rhetoric into new venues; the latter only demonstrate rhetoric's dislocation from its oldest venues.

Too, I must note that it is my interest in antiquity that accounts for the peculiarly digressive structure of this book. "Digression" used to be an acceptable rhetorical tactic, with a meaning all its own. In my effort to juxtapose the past with the present, I have abandoned the usual scholarly discuss-a-subject-until-it's-exhausted manner. Consequently, to some readers my discussion might seem a jumbles in its back-and-forth, here-a-bit there-a-bit movement. But I have accepted that risk. To those readers who stick with me, I think I may be able in this process to make patent some of the reasons those other antiquarians, the humanists who are the subject of this book, rejected orderliness and seemed to abhor methodology. As a container of either truth or wisdom, they believed, form is at best an illusion.

Moreover, it is noteworthy that in *his* antiquarianism, Billig has reviewed the origins of rhetoric and found not merely argumentation at its center; he has also found that pro-con argumentation is at the very core of rhetoric's conceptual identity. Further, in Billig's view the Sophists are the originators of rhetoric, and Protagoras is the Ur rhetorician par excellence. Unfortunately, the evidence available for a resuscitation of the Sophists is too scanty to prove all that we might wish it to prove.[7] Nonetheless, it is clear that the Sophists originated

---

findings to modern education (372–4). But with my interest in protocol, I am somewhat more narrowly focussed than Mack's more generalized observations.

6. Richard Buchanan, "Declaration by Design: Rhetoric, Argument, and Demonstration in Design Practice," *Design Discourse: History/Theory/Criticism,* ed. Victor Margolin (Chicago, 1989) , 91–109. Donald N. McCloskey, *The Rhetoric of Economics* (Madison, Wis., 1985). Paul De Man, *Allegories of Reading* (New Haven, Conn., 1979) and *The Rhetoric of Romanticism* (New York, 1984). Brian Vickers, *In Defense of Rhetoric* (Oxford, Eng., 1988).

7. Harold Barrett, *The Sophists* (Novato, Calif., 1987); Kathleen Freeman, *An-*

the educational practice of requiring students to debate both sides of the question. And it's equally clear that the Sophists were utterly defeated by their ancient antagonists, the philosophers, a defeat celebrated in our continual use of *sophistry* as a pejorative—the counterpart, perhaps, of Erasmus's word "foolosophy" for the other side. Apart from those observations and a few written fragments, we have little firm ground on which to explore ancient Sophistry. Cicero was the chief conduit from the ancients to the humanists I most admire; but whether we also endorse Cicero's antiquarianism and actually call that rhetoric Sophistry is not vital to my argument. More important, for Billig's point and for my own, is his position that "From a developmental point of view, learning to argue may be a crucial phase in learning to think" (111). The reverse is equally true, whether we call the process *inventio* as the ancient rhetoricians called it or "critical thinking" as modern educators call it. My intention is to controvert the rhetorical myopia we have inherited and to show that the past offers us a certain useful protocol.

A contemporary development that deserves some amplification is Stanley Fish's recent posture as a rhetorician. Few scholars have managed to stay in fashion as long as Fish has, and few have shown more flexibility and sensitivity to change. In many respects—two in particular, his hatred of formalism and his dislike of theory—Fish has always been a rhetorician *malgré lui*. But in his famous *Self-Consuming Artifacts* (1972), he rejected rhetoric in favor of dialectic; partly because he offered the two as nominal counterparts but actual opposites. In his *Doing What Comes Naturally* (1988), he has revised the line-up. Rhetoric is now equated not only with anti-formalism but also with "anti-foundationalism" or "anti-essentialism." Rhetoric

---

cilla to the pre-Socratic Philosophers (Oxford, Eng., 1948); William K. Guthrie, *The Sophists* (Cambridge, Eng., 1971); G. B. Kerferd, *The Sophistic Movement* (Cambridge, Eng., 1981); Mario Untersteiner, *The Sophists,* trans. Kathleen Freeman (Oxford, 1954). See, too, Bernard Knox, *The Oldest Dead White European Males* (New York, 1993). For a creative interpretation of Sophistic rhetoric, see Mark Backman, *Sophistication: Rhetoric and the Rise of Self-Consciousness* (Woodbridge, Conn., 1991). For Sophists in early attic education, see Thomas Cole, *The Origins of Rhetoric in Ancient Greece* (Baltimore, 1991), esp. chapter 5. I am convinced by Cole's argument that rhetoric originated in collections of written commonplaces and oratorical formularies. My point, however, is that rhetoric *ab initio* was associated with disputation, a contention that appears substantiated by parts of Cole's work; see e.g. 99–100.

is now, for Fish, a way of living and thinking in a consciously constructed way. Thereby it has become the very opposite of certain Neoplatonic views that insist that language and thought should mirror a pre-existent reality or perhaps a truth accessible to philosophers (and, in our age, scientists). On the contrary, Fish claims, rhetoric offers us the knowledge "that our convictions are unsupported by anything external to themselves" (552). Whatever we take for reality or truth is simply the currently most persuasive, and profoundly linguistic, construct.

Although Fish in his most recent book appears now to be deep within rhetoric (an essay in the book has been reprinted as the entry for "Rhetoric" in an important handbook of critical terms[8]), he is at a far remove from Erasmus, whose desolation did not actually extend to the shocking and, ostensibly, utterly Sophistic view Fish has now adopted concerning the linguistic nature of truth. Why, then, if as I say Fish's view is deep within rhetoric, turn to Erasmus? Erasmus's unique forte is that he gives us not only a practical but also a clever entrance to rhetoric. He shows us how to teach it and he offers a protocol—a revived, Ciceronian protocol. He loved Skepticism, but he was no skeptic, not so far as revealed Truth was concerned. His contrarianism was aimed not at Truth so much as at *moral choices,* at how one in the midst of this Truth actually must live in this world. Although he had a revulsion for abstraction, formalism, and theory that is almost the equal of Fish's, he also had a practical how-to-do-it bent far exceeding anything in Fish or, for that matter, in any other modern rhetorician I've read. Erasmus would probably prefer teaching undergraduates.

Let me further explain my recurrence to Erasmus in the face of this resurgent interest in rhetoric—not only by Fish but also by other scholars, particularly those in that vaguely denominated group, "secular humanists."

I realize that in focussing on Erasmus, I am focussing on a Christian optimist who, however much he was chastized for his "paganism," clearly tried to sanctify Ciceronian humanism. Cicero's rhetoric was for training statesmen, as Erasmus so well and wisely knew, who were meant to become public bulwarks against tyranny. But

8. Frank Lentricchia and Thomas McLaughlin, ed. *Critical Terms for Literary Study* (Chicago, 1990), 203–22; see *Doing,* 471–502.

Erasmus also believed that the immanence of Christ would be substantiated by the revival of the classics, especially those classics that
seemed so clearly to adumbrate or yearn for Christianized virtue and
salvation. He was an antiquarian, then, but of a certain, obviously
highly religious sort. Educating men to be bulwarks against political
tyranny is a counterpart of educating them to be resistant either to
an un-Christian dogmatism or to any denial of that more abundant
life which Christ claimed would be his legacy. Further, like his friend
Budé, Erasmus believed that the world, once unified by humanist
learning, could become a political entity with a common learning
and culture, an entity that just might once and for all end war. The
ideals, of course, came to a dead end in the religious and political
upheavals of the later sixteenth century—upheavals which made Erasmus exemplary of a movement impugned in Shakespearean drama
and parodied in Cervantes (e.g., Hamlet is paralyzed by pro and con
thinking, and Don Quixote's antiquarianism is a form of madness).

Why Erasmus, then? The question could be answered simply in
terms of the history of education. If the logician/dialectician Boethius was "the schoolmaster of medieval Europe,"[9] the rhetorician
Erasmus was the schoolmaster of Renaissance "high humanism,"
and my interest centers in the English Renaissance largely because
certain ideals and problems of that age deserve to be reconsidered in
our own. And my further, antiquarian point is that when we abandoned the "high humanism" Erasmus represents, we threw out too
much of it. We rejected survivable features which depend upon neither religion nor optimism for their life. We need to go back to that
point and make a new start. Our rhetoric will be the better for it.

A lesson I find deep in the core of Erasmian humanism is the *via
diversa,* the doctrine that (small-*t*) truth is so complex—and maybe
in its variety so ungraspable—that one has to approach it through
different, untried, and even multiple avenues (*diversa* means both
different and various, "divers" the Renaissance Englishman would
say, "diversity" we moderns all too hollowly pray). Concepts like
"method" or "theory"—or "system" for that matter—too easily
lead to a *via una;* therefore let us be suspicious of these but let us not
simply toss them out either. This is the very attitude which marked

9. R. W. Southern, *The Making of the Middle Ages* (London, 1987; first pub.
1953), 167.

the "high humanism" of the Renaissance and was one reason why its "methods" or "theories" are so difficult to uncover and why its textbooks are so slim. It is also the reason some humanist writing appears so chaotic to the serious thinker—a litmus test, perhaps: Are you a "homo seriosus" or a "homo rhetoricus?"[10]

Take a look at this dialogic fragment from Erasmus's "The Godly Feast," one of the many Renaissance dialogues which, like Cicero's *De oratore,* echoes—or, better, plunders—Plato's *Phaedrus* in order to controvert part of the Platonic lesson and reassert the importance of rhetorical protocol. Here I am interested in the movement of Eusebius's mind as he grapples with the problem of pagan literature for Christian audiences and more or less rejects (without condemning "entirely") Duns Scotus. (The Scholastic Duns, recall, was so opposed to the revival of classical learning that humanists made his name forever synonymous with ignorance.)

CHRYSOGLOTTUS: If I weren't afraid my chatter would interfere with your eating, and if I thought it lawful to introduce anything from profane writers into such religious conversation, I'd present something that didn't puzzle but delighted me extremely as I was reading it today.

EUSEBIUS: *On the contrary,* whatever is devout and contributes to good morals should not be called profane. Sacred Scripture is of course the basic authority in everything; *yet* I sometimes run across ancient sayings or pagan writings—even the poets'—so purely and reverently and admirably expressed that I can't help believing their authors' hearts were moved by some divine power. And *perhaps* the spirit of Christ is more widespread than we understand, and the company of saints includes many not in our calendar. Speaking frankly among friends, I can't read Cicero's *De senectute, De amicitia, De officiis, De Tusculanis quaestionibus* without sometimes kissing the book and blessing that pure heart, divinely inspired as it was. *But when, on the other hand,* I read these modern writers on government, economics, or ethics—good Lord, how dull they are by comparison! And what lack of feeling they seem to have for what they write! So that I would much rather let all of Scotus and others of his sort perish than the books of a single Cicero or Plutarch. *Not that* I condemn the former entirely; but I perceive I am helped by reading the latter, whereas I rise from the reading of those others somehow less en-

---

10. For these terms, see Richard Lanham, *The Motives of Eloquence* (New Haven, Conn., 1976), esp. chapter 1.

thusiastic about true virtue, but more contentious. So don't hesitate to present it, *whatever it is*.[11]

The to-fro, pro-con movement of Eusebius's mind reveals something of the protocol by which Erasmus links rhetoric with maieutic discourse, the *via diversa*.

But the humanist lesson itself, whether secular or religious, can be plainly stated: whatever truth is available through any one path is partial and therefore diverse paths should be pursued in the pilgrim's progress. Conversely, one should be equally wary of too rapidly rejecting any singular argument. The lesson shocked some Christians in the Renaissance: Luther, for instance, became so upset at Erasmus's all-inclusiveness that, although he was disputing in Latin, he slipped into his mother tongue to shout, *"Das ist zu viel!"*—"that is too much!" The lesson about wariness, about too rapidly throwing anything out, survives in our modern regard for "contingency" in science, economics, and now in rhetoric's ancient antagonist philosophy.[12] It reaches back to the medieval conflict between *realists* and *nominalists* and into our contemporary obsessions with "made" as opposed to "found" truth. In this respect, the track of Eusebius's mind is something of a nonexclusionary ideal.

The point I am leading to, however, is that we have neglected rhetoric as an intellectual pursuit. As an intellectual pursuit rhetoric is anchored in contingency and bases its conclusions on such non-objective and circumstantial forms of proof as the response of the audience and the often self-fashioned character of the speaker.[13]

11. Trans. Craig R. Thompson, *The Colloquies of Erasmus* (Chicago, 1965), 65 (emphases mine).

12. Even in the Renaissance rhetoric had made some inroads into early scientific modes of inquiry. See Jean Dietz Moss, "Dialectic and Rhetoric: Questions and Answers in the Copernican Revolution," *Argumentation* 5 (1991): 17–38. See also Moss's "The Interplay of Science and Rhetoric in Seventeenth Century Italy," *Rhetorica* 7 (1989): 23–44; and in that same issue William A. Wallace, "Aristotelian Science and Rhetoric in Transition: The Middle Ages and the Renaissance," 7–22. For rhetorical inroads into economics, see Billig (footnote 3 above). For the relation of rhetoric and philosophy, the *locus classicus* remains Chaim Perelman and L. Olbrechts-Tyteca, *The New Rhetoric,* trans. John Wilkinson and Purcell Weaver (Notre Dame, In., 1969).

13. As Stephen Greenblatt observes, "Rhetoric . . . offered men the power to shape their worlds, calculate the probabilities, and master the contingent, and it implied that human character itself could be similarly fashioned, with an eye to audience and effect"; *Renaissance Self-Fashioning* (Chicago, 1980), 162.

These, we shall note, were not allowable in its ancient counterpart, dialectic—or, for that matter, in any other effort to scientize or objectify the protocols of inventing arguments. As Erasmus knew, rhetoric matched the diversity of truth with a *via diversa* protocol of its own.

The first principles of whatever might be considered rhetoric's intellectual habit stem from the discipline's openness to contrari- anness, even to perversity, and from the ancient dialogic practice of generating arguments on both sides of the question. This is the po- sition that—though I've put it in the technical terms of rhetoric—I find central to the great documents of humanism. It is put in equally technical terms in Cicero's dialogues *De oratore, De finibus,* and *De officiis.* We shall examine its terms primarily in Erasmus, for reasons which I have tried to enumerate, and to which I shall add one more, a certain Erasmian paradox. Erasmus was himself a lover of peace and concord, the very "sum and substance" he called it of his reli- gion. Yet his educational theories are based on verbal combat. He insists upon the practice of writing recantations and of reasoning *in utramque partem,* on both or for that matter all sides of the question. Yet he warned against the hazards of overcontroversializing.[14] The debating contest is not his goal. Neither was, simply, "critical think- ing." But few writers offer quite so clear and balanced a route to that end. At the very least, he kept a wise perspective: "life," he said, speaking of his so-called philosophy of Christ, "means more than debate."

Nonetheless, the argument remains, that debating is educationally valuable. The argument, moreover, crops up in virtually any great humanist document in which truth is regarded as something frag- mented, diverse, or difficult to apprehend—like Milton's argument for the freedom of the press, or John Stuart Mill's in behalf of liberty. Not surprisingly, both of the documents I just mentioned are in the form of a Ciceronian oration.

If Milton's *Areopagitica* deserves rereading by any literate person with the slightest tendency toward book-burning, Mill's "On Lib- erty" should be studied by anyone in search of "a controversy-

14. On the hazards of overcontroversializing see, for example, Erasmus's letter to Carondelet (5 January 1523); available in the selected writings edited by John C. Olin, 3rd ed. (New York, 1987), note esp. 190 and 199. The quoted passage appears in the *Paraclesis;* see Olin, 104.

oriented approach to the theory of knowledge."[15] Part of the very point of Mill's essay lies in the simple but too easily overlooked and avoided procedure (the basis of the protocol I shall describe), pro and con argumentation. For Mill, only the person who has submitted his thought to that procedure has "a right to think his judgment better than that of any person, or any multitude who have not gone through a similar process." The society Mill envisions is one in which all truth is open for question: "The beliefs which we have most warrant for, have no safeguard to rest on, but a standing invitation to the whole world to prove them unfounded." And the method of questioning is clear:

> The greatest orator, save one, of antiquity, has left it on record that he always studied his adversary's case with as great, if not with still greater, intensity than even his own. What Cicero practised as the means of forensic success, requires to be imitated by all who study any subject in order to arrive at the truth. He who knows only his own side of the case, knows little of that. His reasons may be good, and no one may have been able to refute them. But if he is equally unable to refute the reasons on the opposite side; if he does not so much as know what they are, he has no ground for preferring either opinion.

Significantly, it is not Cicero's Latinity that is prized in the documents I regard central to my own case but his role as a thinker. Actually argue the opposing side? Cicero practiced it, Erasmus advocated it. Likewise Mill:

> Unless opinions favorable to democracy and to aristocracy, to property and to equality, to co-operation and to competition, to luxury and to abstinence, to sociality and individuality, to liberty and discipline, and all the other standing antagonisms of practical life, are expressed with equal freedom, and enforced and defended with equal talent and energy, there is no chance of both elements obtaining their due; one scale is sure to go up, and the other down. Truth, in the great practical concerns of life, is so much a question of the reconciling and combining of opposites, that very few have minds sufficiently capacious and impartial to make the adjustment with an approach to correctness, and it has to be made by the rough process of struggle between combatants fighting under hostile banners.

15. The quoted phrase is Nicholas Rescher's subtitle: *Dialectics* (Albany, N.Y., 1977); see too xiii–iv.

Reason—for Milton, for Mill—lies in conscious choosing. But the approach in our minds to the constituents of that choice can be a "rough process." Absent that "rough process," however, the social ground is fertile for demagoguery: *"[A]rgumentum ex ignorantia,"* said Kristeller, is "a powerful argument when the readers and listeners are as ignorant of the contrary evidence as the speakers and writers."[16] Indeed, the very sort of society liberals are trying to avoid, according to the liberal philosopher Richard Rorty, is one in which there would be general agreement "that certain questions were *always* in point, that certain questions were prior to certain others, that there was a fixed order of discussion, and that flanking movements were not permitted," a society in which "'logic' ruled and 'rhetoric' was outlawed."[17] Unfortunately, as Lanham has so forcefully pointed out, the "[d]econstructionists have made of the binary oscillation central to Western *decorum* [and humanist rhetoric] a desperate affair. It is not a desperate affair; it is an error-checking operation."[18] For if anything the very combativeness of rhetoric is an antidote to political correctness—the former at least keeps the debate alive.[19]

16. Paul Oskar Kristeller, "A Life of Learning," *American Scholar* 60 (1991): 339.

17. Richard Rorty, *Contingency, irony, and solidarity* (Cambridge, Eng., 1989), 51. The terms *logic* and *rhetoric* are here used almost uniquely (for Rorty) in the sense in which I employ them in my own book, a sense that requires Rorty to place them in quotation marks.

18. Richard A. Lanham, "Twenty Years After: Digital Decorum and Bistable Allusions," *Texte* 8/9 (1989): 98.

19. In a decidedly nonpartisan review of *Doing What Comes Naturally*, Michael Neth has taken Fish to task not simply for being repetitive and somewhat uninteresting (the review is entitled "Johnny One-Note") but also for being unSophistic; *American Scholar* 60 (1991): 608–13. The final charge considers Fish mainly as a public orator, in his role as Chair of Duke's English Department. In that role Fish has irascibly taken certain stances that seem to preclude debate: his use of name-calling and popular buzz-words to silence opposition and disallow further talk would clearly seem to be unrhetorical in the sense used by Fish himself (and me), just as it clearly seems to be in the best sense unSophistical. But Neth's shot if not exactly cheap is a little misdirected. A self-confessed adherence to Sophistry does not make advocacy impossible. The teachings of Protagoras, Fish's new hero, that "there are contrary arguments on every subject" (W. G. Guthrie in *The Sophists,* quoted by Neth, 613) were actually designed to make one a better advocate. As Victoria Kahn has noted, "while the orator or prudent man must be able to argue on both sides of a question, he will in any particular case choose one side or another"; "Humanism and the Resistance to Theory," in *Literary Theory/Renaissance Texts,* ed. Patricia Parker and

"In this course," one of my students announced at the end of my lecture, "all arguments have two sides. Except the argument that all arguments have two sides." The point of my lecture was blunted by the student's cleverness in simplifying my intention. Let me therefore conclude this digression with a kind of prolepsis and, recalling my student, a kind of *réponse d'escalier* as well. Two-sided debate—such as the "Affirmative" and "Negative" of American collegiate debating—is only a simplified version of the intellectual method I find at the heart of humanist rhetoric. For that matter, so too are the prosecution and defense of the criminal trial, the very conceptual model Cicero used to explain his own rhetoric. By these simplified procedures (debate and trial), by these rough processes, all truth is challenged. *All* truth.[20] "One can argue equally well on either side of any question," Protagoras once ventured, "including the question itself whether both sides of any question can be argued."[21] To probe and challenge—that's the point. Debate and the criminal trial are about as useful conceptually as the neutron and proton of an atom. Something *must* be visualized, a procedure *must* be offered. But the phenomenon is ultimately complex, and its destination variable and uncertain. Like atoms. Like, the humanists I love might say, good conversation. Or the maieutic discourse of Erasmian concordists. Or the case for pro-con combat which Mill offers in a smoothy progressing Ciceronian oration. The protocol is not only complex but ancient. So too are the controversies surrounding it.

Recently an essayist observed that Prime Minister John Major "reveals none of the insecurities of the self-educated except, perhaps, his ultramethodical habit of drawing a line down a yellow pad and listing the pros and cons of any question as he thinks or talks."[22] Another putdown ("meiosis," rhetoricians would call it), another

---

David Quint (Baltimore, 1986), 376. Thus Neth's hit was a little wide of the mark. For Fish, like any Sophist, may be put down not for being an advocate but for using the wrong tactics, for being a little too obviously correct politically—to the extent, that is, that his audience includes Neth.

20. Erasmus would exclude Truth, of course. Other kinds of truth may be situationally excluded, like those the framers of our Constitution held to be "self-evident." But without articulated, apriori, agreed upon exclusions, the protocol itself does not stop. No wonder the Skeptics loved it, holding even that they must be as diffident of their doubts as they are of their beliefs.

21. Rosamond Kent Sprague, *The Older Sophists* (Columbia, S. C., 1972), 13.

22. Peter Jenkins in the *New York Review of Books* (April 25, 1991): 43.

simplified version of an intellectual protocol that I believe deserves revival. Let me rebegin.

"Begin at the beginning," the judge advised a witness in one of the strangest trials in English literature, "and go on till you come to the end: then stop." Let us rebegin, then, at the very beginning, with a dialogue that echoes like a deeply known poem through all the Renaissance documents I shall examine.

Plato's *Phaedrus*

One day, over two and half millenia ago, an unusually homely middle-aged man went out for a walk when he encountered a handsome young acquaintance.[23] Both were outside the walls of ancient Athens, and thus on the margins of a culture that prized physical beauty. Socrates, a no-neck, snub-nosed man with protruding eyes, had already gained some fame through criticizing that culture and, not surprisingly, insisting that true beauty lay within. Such beauty was the object of what he called a "philosophical" quest for truth. Phaedrus by contrast had a certain callow ordinariness, often disregarded in favor of his philosophically troubling, outward beauty.

The younger man had just come from Lysias, one of Athens' foremost teachers, who like certain other educators of the time styled himself a "Sophist," a "wise one." Sophists built their fame and wealth upon their skills in argumentation, a discipline known as "rhetoric," or public speaking. For a fee, they taught others those same skills or—probably for an even larger fee—employed them in writing speeches for others and in pleading cases at law.

We, too, might call Lysias a "sophist," because he seemed to be more interested in pursuing tricks of argument than in pursuing the truth. We can't be sure, though, because very little of his work has survived.[24] Cicero obviously admired Lysias (see *Brutus*) and described him as someone "able to hold his own famously in forensic causes" (*Orator,* ix.30). But, alas, our view of Lysias, like our view of most Sophists, tends to depend not upon Cicero but upon Socrates's hardly unbiased vision. After all, what looks like speciousness

23. The text followed in this description and quoted from is the one translated by R. Hackforth and reprinted in *Plato: The Collected Dialogues,* ed. Edith Hamilton and Huntington Cairns (Princeton, N. J., 1961), 475–525.
24. See K. J. Dover, *Lysias and the Corpus Lysiacum* (Berkeley, Calif., 1968).

or trickery from one angle, Socrates's say, could be seen from another, Cicero's perhaps, as an effort to stimulate one's students or challenge the case brought against a client. Making the "worse" appear the "better" reason (as I note in chapter 4) has itself at least one favorable meaning. Let us begin by calling the Sophist Lysias a teacher of rhetoric and a lawyer, whose reputation suffered the bewilderment and suspicion those two professions still arouse. Let us also note that he was someone who had achieved fame and fortune in a culture whose materialism Socrates despised.

Phaedrus had just heard Lysias read an oration on love, and he was on his way out to the countryside with the manuscript of the speech, where he planned to read it aloud for himself and re-experience its eloquence. Like the teacher-lawyer combination, here is another strange mixture, in this case an oxymoron: speechwriting. Sophists were the first to write speeches for others to deliver before a court or a deliberative assembly, or as classroom exercises, or as advertisements for their schools of rhetoric. They thus were among the first to take advantage of writing as a medium of communication, almost a mass medium. Those Athenians who could read could not read silently. Thus they, and others around them, would eventually *hear* the speech. Oxymoron resolved, perhaps. Nonetheless, the practice of *writing,* particularly something as oral in nature as a *speech,* drew Socrates's ire—along with, of course, his anger over the wealth and the fame of the Sophists and their evident glibness, or resourcefulness, and toying with the truth. For Socrates was convinced that truth itself was available, though seldom in written documents. He was convinced that speech between a few, ideally two, minds is the means of exploring truth. Sophists were only further prostituting an already debased culture.

Upon hearing that his young friend has a copy of an eloquent oration by Lysias, Socrates urges him to read it—aloud, naturally. After all, Socrates says, you know that I am a lover of discourse and would delight in hearing Lysias's skill. What's his argument?

Phaedrus replies that the Sophist cleverly argues that it's preferable to have sex with a nonlover than with a lover.

Great, answers Socrates. I hope he will continue to pursue this line of reasoning. Perhaps he will go on to argue that the young and beautiful should have sex with the old, the poor, the outcast (and the ugly?). How democratic!

Phaedrus calls Lysias's manner "clever." Therein lies an important principle of disputation, one that we shall see at work several times in the discourses examined in the present book: Lysias's manner could very well be the manner of the sally, verbal foray, or deliberately provocative opening argument, a rhetorical tactic later rhetoricians will teach young students through such contrarian exercises as disputations, recantations, and writing themes on disagreeable subjects. A proposal is laid before the house, then discussants take sides; therefore the more attention-getting and controversial the proposal the better. Attitudinally perverse, the sally offers a speaker a stance which can be assumed at any time he desires to incite argument. Such, at least, the debater might find the nature of Lysias's manner. He has laid a proposition on the line. Arguments pro and con will soon thereupon follow—ad infinitum, perhaps, ad nauseum. But Socrates has another take on the speech.

Socrates and Phaedrus sit down in the shade of a plane tree.

Isn't this the place, Phaedrus asks, where Boreas raped Orithyia?

No, it was about a quarter of a mile from here, Socrates replies. And at any rate, I don't know what to make of these stories about the gods, whether they are true or not. The most important knowledge, it seems to me, is that enjoyed by the sibyl at Delphi: "Know thyself." All other matters seem to me extraneous. And in order for me to know myself, I always turned to the speech of other men. Therefore (here the irony becomes patent) read me Lysias's speech while I lie down here in the shade.

The speech is indeed clever, as Phaedrus promised. The (perhaps fictive) audience is only one person, a handsome boy. The speaker is the nonlover himself. The speech is in fact more like the declamations which became schoolroom exercises in later, well established schools of rhetoric, set speeches (usually written to be read aloud) of advice which could be addressed to one person, to oneself, or to an assembly, and they were often a kind of argumentative excursion, or sally. (The relation between the *suasoria,* or suasive declamations, and the sally is one I shall attempt to explore and to link with educational disputation in chapters 4 and 5.)

The nonlover marshals a catalogue of reasons why sex with him is preferable. He has no craving, which inevitably ends when satisfied. He has no jealousy, no compulsion to possess. The relationship is based not on erotic passion but on friendship, which is sure to be long-lasting and selfless if seemingly indifferent in some matters. By contrast, the lover is mad. Only the nonlover is sane.

A fine and thrilling speech, exclaims Socrates. But I confess I took my cues more from your response as an oral interpreter of the text than from the text itself. It's only a piece of rhetoric after all, and I doubt that Lysias himself would find it truly exemplary of his prowess. He only did the standard thing: praised the nonlover while putting down the lover—a sort of journeyman labor at pro-con reasoning. We should therefore applaud Lysias's arrangement, not his invention. (Again, Socrates is being ironic and willfully provocative: the arrangement is difficult to praise since it's only a catalogue.) I know I've heard better reasoning, and I could even do better reasoning on the subject myself, he says.

Well, if so, Phaedrus replies, let's hear it.

Socrates at last agrees, though first he will cover his head. He's concerned that in the midst of this pretence—his attempt to outdo Lysias—he will catch a glimpse of the audience and break down for shame. Having covered his head and appealed to the Muses, Socrates begins with a story about how once upon a time there was a handsome youth who had a host of lovers, one of whom had the wiliness to attempt to distinguish himself from the others by making a move on the boy in the guise of a nonlover. Thus Socrates dons a mask to rip the mask off the implied speaker and audience: Phaedrus is the "real" audience of Lysias's argument, Lysias himself apparently the "real" speaker. Lysias, for all his apparent cleverness, is making a shoddy attempt at real persuasion.

Unlike Lysias's speech, Socrates's is tightly organized—an arrangement, therefore, more deserving of praise by the speaker's own criteria. What he's seeking to do is to beat the Sophists at two of their own games: not only the game of the sally, of effectively arguing an outrageous proposition, but also the game of arguing on both sides of the question. Because Socrates is leading up to the second game, he plays the first very carefully.

He has already partly destroyed Lysias's speech by suggesting that it is a real effort at seduction—that it is not simply a rhetorical exercise, in spite of what he had said about it originally when he impugned its arguments for being the usual stock-in-trade. (As we shall see in chapter 4 in our examination of Erasmus's epistle to Mountjoy, the question of whether something is or is not a rhetorical exercise seems always to trouble, if not actually give the advantage to, the literalist, the *via una* pursuer of truth.) Lysias uses stock arguments all right, Socrates claims, but in behalf of actually trying to seduce Phaedrus. Therefore for the sake of the insincere role he believes *he* must play, Socrates covers his head. You really shouldn't argue like this, he implies, but if you're going to do it, here's how to do it well.

Recall, too, that Socrates has already impugned not only Lysias's arguments but his arrangement of material as well. In the role of arguing the case of the nonlover, Socrates sets up his position in good dialectical fashion. First we must *define* what it is we're talking about. (The traditional function of dialectical protocol, to be echoed centuries later by Thomas Wilson, are first definition and then division.) Love is a kind of desire. Then the definition is divided. There are actually two kinds of desire, one rational, the other irrational. Love is the irrational sort. Therefore the lover is indeed mad, for he is dominated by an irrational desire. The remainder of the argument falls easily into place: the lover, enslaved to his passion, can only wish to keep his loved one in thrall. Socrates presents, in orderly fashion, the means and manner of the lover's destructive hold over his loved one. But then he suddenly breaks off his discourse with the aphorism, "As a wolf to a lamb, so a lover to his lad."

But, Phaedrus protests, I thought you were only half finished.

Ah, why go on with it? asks Socrates, somewhat impatiently. You can see where I'm going. To complete the argument, all you have to do is find a good quality on the nonlover's side which matches the evil I've already detailed on the lover's side. So why waste words? I'm going home before you get me involved in any further foolishness.

Don't take off in the heat of the day, Phaedrus pleads.

Well, all right, Socrates responds. After all, perhaps I should first expiate my sin. Something in my mind deeply troubled me as I delivered those arguments. If Love is a god, he will have been terribly offended by these two speeches, Lysias's and the one you compelled me to deliver. So before I leave I should first purify myself.

With these playful moves, Socrates—who has unveiled his head, there now being no risk of either shame or insincerity—has led up to the second part of his performance. Now he will show that he can beat the Sophists at yet another of their games, arguing on both sides of the question. Now he will argue, apparently from the heart, in praise of the lover.

The ensuing speech is the longest one in the entire dialogue. It is a bravura performance, containing most of the ideas in Socratic (or Platonic) moral philosophy. And the *con* perfectly matches the *pro*. For the speech is not exactly directed at refuting Lysias's position. Rather, it begins by controverting the initial definition in Socrates's immediately preceding speech: not all madness is evil. In fact, the madness of love is a blessing. (Therein Socrates has also followed what Erasmus would later describe and teach as the educationally effective practice of recantation.)

For proof, Socrates argues, we must understand the nature of the soul. Of course, only a god can tell us *that*. But we can at least approach that knowledge by means of resemblances. Let us imagine that the soul is like a charioteer with a pair of steeds, one of which is noble and good, the other the opposite. The charioteer's task is therefore extraordinarily difficult. Each time the soul sees true beauty, which is always a remembrance of the beauty of the gods, it seeks to ascend in its chariot and stand in that place beyond the heavens where all true knowledge resides. (Socrates is speaking of "true" beauty, though the question is still open about which sort Phaedrus has. Whatever it is, it has proved to be upsetting.) But because of our two steeds—because our immortal soul is not simply a light and winged and holy thing but here on earth is compounded of mortality—the way is fraught with dangers. Only a memory of the gods—true knowledge, true beauty—keeps the soul's plumage in flying trim. (The metaphors, carefully elided in the original, seem more than a little mixed in paraphrase.) But dragged down by the ignoble steed, the soul no longer feeds on memory but resemblance, and the wings are in danger of being broken.

When that soul is no longer able to follow a godly vision, it becomes reborn upon the body's death into beings increasingly farther removed from the possibilities of ever having its wings restored: that is, in descending order, first "a seeker after wisdom or beauty, a follower of the Muses and a lover," then the lawful king, the statesman, the athlete, the prophet, the poet, the farmer, the Sophist, and finally the tyrant. (The Sophist's place on this scale is, of course, highly significant. So too is the lover's, who virtually shares first place with the "seeker" or philosopher.) Each one of these has seen less and less of the Truth. A soul that sees none of the Truth or has long forgotten about it descends into a beast's body. Only that soul which has seen the Truth, has beheld the gods, enters a human being. As that soul remembers more and more of the Truth, holds fast to its vision of the gods, it begins to recover its wings. Therefore it stands to reason that the philosopher by virtue of his divine vision is the most blessed of all creatures and stands the best chance of fully standing in the very presence of Truth itself.

But the lover is close. For he is touched by a kind of madness— that madness earlier called a blessing—in the presence of beauty, which for him is a remembrance of the beauty of the gods. The lover's soul wishes constantly to be in the presence of the beloved, to continue that vision. Each lover will behave toward his beloved as his soul did in its heavenly existence in the train of a particular god, praising, adoring, and exalting the beloved to, in effect, become more like the recalled god. Here, however, there is some danger, caused by the twin steeds which drive the soul's chariot. The struggle is between the good steed's obedience and temperance and the evil steed's rashly impulsive act to satisfy mere lust. It is not that the physical act of love is never committed (our notions of "platonic love" seem curiously inhibited), but that the act should never be attempted until mutually desired, after a period of reverence and awe and after the establishment of a love beyond friendship. In this way, the higher elements of mind guide both the lover and his beloved into the ordered rule of the philosophical life. As if the point about philosophy were not already clear enough, Socrates ends his speech by praying to the dear god of love that Lysias will give up his Sophistic habit of matching every argument with a counter-argument and join in the pursuit of true love with the aid of philosophical discourse—which is, obviously, something other than pro-con reasoning and attainable by means of a singular rather than a diverse path.

The speech is superb, colorful and poetic, and earns Phaedrus's admiration. In fact, Phaedrus doubts that Lysias could do better, were he to attempt to write the other side of his first argument. The remark leads to a discussion of speech writing and whether it is an honorable profession. Socrates settles for the point that there is at least nothing shameful simply in writing speeches, that shamefulness lies in speaking and writing badly. Therefore the question would seem to be: What is the nature of good writing and bad? Here now is quite a new question, and it will be resolved not in the Sophistic manner of pro-con reasoning but in the dialectical manner: that is, not only by definition and division but also by interrogating one's own reasoning powers, trustworthy to the extent (v. supra) that they maintain their singular hold on the soul's memory of Truth.

Socrates, accordingly, asks whether a good discourse does not presuppose a knowledge on the composer's part of the truth about his subject.

Phaedrus's answer reflects his Sophistic education. What I have heard, he says, is that the successful persuader needs to give thought to what his audience will *think* is true, and not concern himself about truth in any absolute sense. (The skepticism of the Sophists is patent in Phaedrus's response; Cicero, centuries later, was to turn the teaching into a doctrine for the aspiring lawyer, whose obligation is to *verisimilitude,* to what will seem likely or truthful to the judges.[25])

But by that token, Socrates replies, an orator who is not in possession of the Truth could unknowingly persuade his community of something false or evil. Perhaps, though, we are being too hard on the rhetoricians. Might they not claim that all they're doing is teaching other people who are in possession of the Truth the techniques for making that Truth effective? But if *that* is the case, can rhetoric really be called an art? Can anything be called an art that does not itself have a grasp of the Truth?

A sense of how Socrates's dialectic, his philosophical method, proceeds is evident in this passage:

> SOCRATES: . . . what is it that the contending parties in law courts do? Do they not in fact contend with words, or how else should we put it?
> PHAEDRUS: That is just what they do.
> SOCRATES: About what is just and unjust?
> PHAEDRUS: Yes.
> SOCRATES: And he who possesses the art of doing this can make the same thing appear to the same people now just, now unjust, at will?

---

25. Although Cicero's most explicit discussion of verisimilitude appears in his youthful *De inventione* (see I.vii.9), the doctrine is equally evident in what *De oratore* offers. See Antonius's *inventio* described in my chapter 2. Although the presence of the other, the audience, determines to an extent what one may say or even think, any lapse into mere relativism or solipsism is offset by the doctrine, which we shall later touch on, of *consensus.*

PHAEDRUS: To be sure.

SOCRATES: And in public harrangues, no doubt, he can make the same things seem to the community now good, and now the reverse of good?

PHAEDRUS: Just so. (507)

In the ensuing passages it becomes clear that Socrates, who gets Phaedrus to admit the tremendous power a rhetorician can hold over his audience through words, faults rhetoric for "chasing after beliefs, instead of knowing the truth." Proof of the charge lies in the rhetorician's inability to define and divide his subject—which are, of course, parts of the protocol of dialectic, exactly the protocol Socrates is using, and had used in his sample speeches.

In fact, Socrates goes on to complain, Sophist rhetoricians employ their so-called art most effectively in those situations where the chief terms—like "good," "just," or more to the point "love"—are left undefined, kept vague, allowed to float through the audience's sea of beliefs. Lysias's speech is a good example. His speech lacks an organic wholeness because it does not progress (as Socrates's had done) from a clearly acknowledged (because objectively truthful) foundation in meaning. Any artful discourse should be constructed like a living organism, something which is impossible if the composer does not from the outset have a clear idea about his subject, so clear that he can define and divide it. Composers who do this best are, of course, the dialecticians. (Recall that another practice, which can be part of dialectical protocol, pro-con reasoning, has already been ruled out.)

Well, okay, says Phaedrus, but we still seem to be in the dark about rhetoricians, what it is they're up to.

To begin with, Socrates replies, the rhetoricians do little more than offer manuals telling one the best form to use for any and every speech—exordium, narration, thesis, proof, refutation, and so on (i.e., parts not unlike those to be recommended later by Cicero in *De partitione oratoria* or even later by Erasmus in *De conscribendis epistolis*)—or offering maxims and lessons on style. And this handful of techniques seems to comprise the whole of their "art."

But what about the tremendous power of rhetoric, asks Phaedrus, a power I have seen at work in assemblies?

That power, replies Socrates, is rather like that claimed by someone who, knowing how to make another person vomit or defecate, sets himself up as a physician and gives little regard as to whether the patient's health actually requires vomiting or defecating. The point here is that the rhetorician's power has to be based on knowledge—not only of the truth of what he's talking about but also of the souls on which his admitted power will work. That is, anyone who would offer a "scientific" rhetoric must also know the nature of the soul, what affects it, and which type of discourse operates on what kind of soul (for souls vary from person to person—v. supra, the earlier scale of human beings), and why.

That sounds like a good idea, says Phaedrus. But it certainly makes rhetoric a complicated business.

What's the alternative? asks Socrates. Simply what we're currently offered by the Sophists, that one needs to give most attention to what works in a courtroom. And what works in a courtroom is more often a skillful plausibility than the actual truth. Pursue the probable, they say, and you are equipped with the whole of the art of rhetoric—and the probable is simply that which commends itself to the (ugh!) multitude.

But writing, as opposed to speaking, continues Socrates, seems to stand in a special case. From its inception, the invention of writing was complained about as something which would destroy our ability to store matters in our memory. And in written documents "memory" is destroyed in another sense: you can't question a document the way you can probe another's "memory" in dialectic, for the written document simply goes on saying the same thing over and over. But written words that are the mirror of good speech—the sort of good speech that one might find in dialectic (like the one we are reading)—can, at the hand of a dialectician, be sown like seeds in a fertile and receptive soul.[26] Now that we've got that cleared up, we can return to the other point.

26. Socrates' dialectics is a kind of "erotic dialectics," Ronna Burgh has argued. It is one which, I might add, opens the door to *suasory* writing of the sort I shall try to describe in chapter 5, writing which does not try to say everything, which involves the reader actively, and which does not itself assume the burden of judgment. Burgh states, "Precisely that written work which betrays an awareness of its own lack of clarity and firmness, and thereby demonstrates its knowledge of when to speak and when to remain silent, would reveal the possibility of overcoming the reproach against the shamefulness of writing alienated from Socrates' erotic dialectics," *Plato's Phaedrus: A Defense of a Philosophic Art of Writing* (University, Ala., 1980), 91.

What point is that? asks Phaedrus (memorably).

What might make speech writing an art, replies Socrates. There are these conditions to be fulfilled. First you must know the truth of what you are going to speak or write about, you must be able to define and divide that truth, you must know the nature of the soul and the kinds of souls in your audience, and you must finally address those souls appropriately. (That other desideratum, the organic arrangement, would seem to follow naturally from these conditions, particularly the first two.) Any written discourse, moreover, offers at best only a partial glimpse of the Truth, which itself is always written in the soul of the audience. And because that Truth has for the most part been pre-written in the audience's soul, any written speech is only something of a reminder. Any Sophist or poet or lawgiver who has done his work in knowledge of the Truth, who can defend his statements when challenged, and who takes a certain insouciance toward his own writings—that person should not be called a "Sophist" but a "Philosopher."

With that last move, Socrates has woven all the threads of the discourse into one fabric: the good rhetorician he has described should not be called a "wise person" but a "lover of wisdom." For the philosopher, whose protocol is dialectic (though without any pro-con reasoning), has all the attributes of the lover, who in his selfless devotion and reverence toward the gods, whose vision he maintains, is of all beings the most likely to restore the wings to his soul and to the souls in his audience. The talk with Phaedrus is over, though Socrates does not conclude without confessing that there is one young Sophist who might have an extraordinary future ahead of him—not Lysias, but Isocrates, whose soul seems to have "an innate tincture of philosophy." After a brief prayer to the gods that dwell in that place, Socrates and Phaedrus depart.

Plato's dialogue was a great favorite among Renaissance humanists, partly for some qualities which a paraphrase mutes—its liveliness of speech and eloquence. It also served the syncretistic project of many humanists. There is a heaven in Socrates's philosophy, an ideal, a soul that is immortal, a love that is selfless and reverential. These elements mesh so well with Christianity that humanists could use them to answer charges that their revival of ancient documents amounts to a revival of paganism. On the contrary, humanists replied, documents such as the *Phaedrus* adumbrate the very Truth revealed in Christianity. "An admirable spirit, surely," says Nephalius of Socrates in Erasmus's "The Godly Feast," and he goes on to claim that when he reads Plato he can hardly help exclaiming, "Saint Socrates, pray for us!"

Socrates's opposite number is Lysias, the two representing a clash between "Philosophy" as Socrates defines it and "Sophistry," again as Socrates defines it. The former includes the lover *(philo)*, the latter does not. Lysias is present primarily through his written speech, and written words cannot be examined, not in the way that people speaking can be examined. Nonetheless, let us note, in the simplest terms possible without the pejoratives, some differences between Philosophy and Sophistry. A chief difference, recurred to several times in the dialogue, is one of protocol. The Sophists practice pro-con reasoning, the Philosophers dialectic, which in its Platonic form relies not on pro-con reasoning but on definition and division.[27] But these protocols imply further differences. The Sophists' quest is for plausibility or verisimilitude and is outwardly directed; they seek a truth among people, a possibility that the public would recognize and act upon. The quest could begin in outrage, in entertaining a notion that is at a far remove from common belief, that is in an argumentative excursion or sally. To the Philosopher, such goings on look like a shallow skepticism and a catering to popular whims. For to the Philosopher there is such a thing as absolute Truth, which lies within, a memory the soul carries within it of divine wisdom. (This memory St. Augustine was later in *De magistro* to call our "inner teacher," the Christ within us.) Because the Truth is universal, though known variably by various souls, it can be explored by reason, one soul interrogating another, grasping Truth by matching vision with vision—the Socratic dialogue, as opposed to disputation, which was then within the Sophists' purview.

Cicero knew the *Phaedrus* well, and loved it. And once, at least, for the sake of arguing, he claimed that in Plato's books many things are argued pro and con *(in utramque partem multa disseruntur)*, so much so that nothing is affirmed, nothing is said with certainty *(Academica* I.xii.46). Herein lies the protocol of humanist *inventio*. But in his

27. The other two parts of the dialectical protocol, knitting true arguments and unknitting false, became prominent later when disputation, not Socratic dialogue, was thought to be the end of dialectic; see Cicero's *Orator* iv.16, and chapter 6 below.

masterpiece, *De oratore,* Cicero would carry his vision of that protocol one major step beyond Plato, into an affirmation not simply of pro-con reasoning but of rhetoric itself.

Thus however much *De oratore* echoes the *Phaedrus,* it makes a deeply significant structural change: *De oratore* is a dialogue not between master and neophyte but between mature, professional statesmen. Because the sides are a little more evenly balanced, the protocol becomes more Sophistical than Philosophic—more disputatious than Platonic-dialogical, or, better, more a pingpong battle of wits than a Socratic bullying. Of course, too, Cicero's own skepticism, to say nothing of his life in the court of law, would find the Sophists' protocol more to his liking. Crassus may be *primus inter pares* but he has not been invested by his creator with the moral authority of Socrates. The dialogue is, consequently, more open-ended. The *Phaedrus* is not a debate; *De oratore* is.

2. Invention¹

The following story is Cicero's invention. That is, he made up most of it. And it is mainly about *inventio,* about how one invents or creates discourse.

In 91 B.C., L. Licinius Crassus—statesman, consul, the most illustrious Roman orator before Cicero, and the young Cicero's tutor in rhetoric—withdrew from the crowded festival days at Rome in order to enjoy some peace at his villa in Tusculum. With him was his close friend, Marcus Antonius—the grandfather of Mark Antony, and himself a statesman, consul, and orator. They were accompanied by two of their most distinguished younger followers, and in the course of a leisurely few days at Tusculum were joined by three other colleagues.

Rome was in turmoil—not simply because of the festival days, the *ludi romani.* Its less quotidian turmoil was political. Rome, these men wisely saw, was at the beginning of a series of power struggles over the precise role of the senate, struggles which could (and indeed would) ultimately destroy the republican form of government.

Crassus, Antonius, and the others spent the first day of their Tusculan hiatus discussing the causes and nature of this crisis in gov-

---

1. Some materials in this chapter originally appeared in my "Reinventing *Inventio," College English* 51 (1989): 461–73; the essay is reused with permission of the National Council of Teachers of English.

ernment. But so melancholy had the discussion become that each man welcomed the suggestion of their host, Crassus, that on the following day they turn their attention to oratory—that is, rhetoric, or the art of eloquence—a subject in which they all had expertise. There was some irony in the suggestion, for each man knew that this subject above all others could hardly be divorced from its social and political contexts.

Nonetheless, on the morrow, the men retired to Crassus's garden, gathered under a plane tree, and—in conscious imitation of at least the setting and subject of Plato's *Phaedrus*—held a two-day convocation on what makes a perfect orator. Here Cicero's account, *De oratore,* offered decades later as a second-hand "recollection of an old story," increasingly takes the form of dialogue—appropriately enough, for the *Phaedrus* is in the form of a dialogue. But Cicero's dialogue, as I mentioned in my previous chapter, is hardly Platonic. *De oratore* is a genuine debate, something which Plato abjured: the subject itself does not go unchallenged, and Cicero's personae are intellectual peers, not master and neophyte.

The subject seems Platonic enough: the perfect orator as a kind of overriding ideal. But it is challenged on two issues, practicability and desirability, which eventually center in this question: Just how is *any* effective orator, ideal or otherwise, produced? Although all discussants were politically like-minded there were some sharp differences in their answers to that question. The sharpest differences were represented by the two closest friends: Crassus believed that only extensive learning combined with practical experience could produce the perfect orator. Antonius took the contrary stance, that the quest of the ideal, the *perfectus orator,* could seem terribly beside the point and that for success in speaking all one really needs are some hands-on experience and practice in technique. Thus the practicability issue within the clash amounted to the old, still unresolved battle of "liberal" education *vs* on-the-job training. The other chief issue, desirability, was used to challenge the necessity of having an ideal anyway, whether an ideal is really important as the aim of education.

In spite of these differences, one striking agreement pervades the discussion, and it is this agreement which makes salient the point of "the old story" so far as I am concerned, for the agreement centers on the most fundamental and unquestionably most important pro-

cess of rhetoric. All discussants tacitly agree on the nature of rhetorical *inventio,* on the first step in the creative process, the speaker's
(or writer's) initial review of the available material—fundamental
because it presupposes one's initial conception of the task, and important because it gets at the uniqueness of that task. At its core,
rhetorical invention is pro and con thinking. Indeed, *De oratore* sets
the discussion before us as a veritable demonstration of how *inventio*
itself works: the inventive process in rhetoric is not only dialogic but
controversial, even disputatious in nature. Too, the very structure
of the work is itself a pattern of pro-con argumentation: Crassus
speaks, Antonius answers and then offers his own case, Crassus re-
buts and summarizes. As I shall note later, the similarity in protocol
to a legal dispute (with the prosecution speaking first and last) is not
at all beside the point—particularly so when we consider the humanist impulse to create discourse which enacts its own theory.

Superficially, this debate structure might make the disputants'
conscious imitation of the *Phaedrus* seem to be apt. Vickers, for example, recently described Plato's dialogue as "the first, and still one
of the most brilliant examples" we have of "arguing *in utramque partem,* on both sides of an issue."[2] But the brilliance of Plato's example
lies in a merely contextual and referential matter—whereas Cicero
actually centralizes arguing on both sides of an issue. Cicero, in
short, employs and elevates the very inventive process that Plato has
Socrates dismiss. In this crucial respect, Cicero's dialogue is a reply
to Plato's.

As I have suggested, at least two dissimilarities between the *Phaedrus* and *De oratore* are more emphatic than Cicero's referenced similarities: in the latter dialogue, the central ideas are seriously challenged, and there is no participant who has the moral authority of
Socrates or the naivete of Phaedrus. (Or the disrepute of Lysias. In
fact, no Sophist, we recall, except possibly Isocrates, had any credi-
bility with Socrates or Plato, who so blasted these teachers that we
still use their name as a pejorative.) Whereas Socrates himself argues
in utramque partem (pro Lysias's case, then contra), dazzling Phaedrus
with his rhetorical skills while impugning Sophistic practice, Cicero
actually personifies the two sides of his argument with two highly
successful professionals and, far beyond Plato, shows that both sides

2. Brian Vickers, *In Defence of Rhetoric* (Oxford, 1988), 16.

have merit. Whereas Socrates on the one hand displays his own adeptness at pro-con reasoning on the subject of love and on the other hand in dialogue with Phaedrus counterbalances the Sophistic practice of pro-con reasoning with philosophical seriousness as the true requisite of the ideal orator, Cicero actually employs pro-con reasoning in exploring that very ideal, its practicability and desirability. Arguing *in utramque partem*—one side and then the other—is, thus, the foundation of Ciceronian protocol. As we shall see, however much humanists from Castiglione through Thomas Wilson openly admired the *Phaedrus,* they actually followed the protocol of *De oratore*. What we have in the latter is, I believe, a rich, multifaceted exposition of Ciceronian *inventio:* pro-con reasoning *(logos)* in its complex interconnections with other elements of the traditional rhetorical creative triad, speaker's character *(ethos)* and audience *(pathos)*. The interconnections are explored in a structure that is itself significant.

In *De oratore,* Crassus would seem to be in the favored position structurally. But his position is simply that of the prosecuting attorney, or the affirmative side of any debate. It is he who is proposing a change from the status quo, from the way things are, which is the (negative) position that will be defended by Antonius. It is therefore Crassus who, because he has the burden of proof, also has the time-honored right in disputation to speak first and last. True, the author Cicero, as I shall note later, intervenes to try to tip the balance of the reader's judgment in favor of Crassus. But there is no Socrates-like judge of the differences. Although Crassus makes an effort to bring the differences together, the major burden of judgment rests—maieutically—with the reader. Consequently, there is at work a different, unPlatonic notion of wisdom, *sapientia*. It is a wisdom that, as we shall see, is synthetic and arises from the analytical, pro-con operations of *inventio* and ends in judging a contest between two ideas of seemingly equal merit. (That other structural significance—a discourse which enacts its own theory—is one I shall recur to several times throughout this book as having a peculiarly humanist stamp.)

Let us note too that Cicero himself was only a boy of 15 when the Crassus-Antonius dispute supposedly occurred. He wasn't present. He claimed that he only heard about the debate later, from Gaius Cotta, who had been there. But Cicero returned to this "old story" at a certain, crucial point in his career, at a time when he finally discovered how to talk about pro and con thinking. That is, when he learned to talk about *inventio* in a truly inventive way, he reinvented the Crassus-Antonius dispute to do just that. At the age of 19, he had written a famous and regrettably enduring handbook—*De inventione*—which reflects very little of what Crassus, Antonius, and the others, as well as the mature Cicero, took *inventio* to be. It wasn't until Cicero approached his late forties and early fifties that he acquired a certain handle on the nature of this complex subject and realized that it couldn't be talked about so much as shown in action. *Inventio,* he knew, in the simplest sense is the devising of true or seemingly true arguments for the sake of making one's case appear probable. For that purpose, the *topics* (an exploration of available materials by asking such questions as Who, When, Where, What, and Why) are eminently useful. But, more importantly, he realized— and with this realization *inventio* was moved to the center of his mature efforts to rhetoricize philosophy—*inventio* is dialogic and it must be pursued pro and con, prosecution and defense, affirmative and negative. One must, that is, debate both sides—or, for that matter, all sides—of any case or one's *inventio* will remain not fully invented. The matter inheres in any actional rhetoric, like his, whose conceptual model is forensic argumentation. His youthful book on the subject, *De inventione,* was, he decided, "unfinished and crude." At least that's what he called it when he came to write *De oratore,* his masterpiece on rhetoric, an ostensible imitation of the *Phaedrus* offered as simply an account of that two-day convocation supposedly held at Crassus's villa thirty-five years earlier. In the dialogue, *inventio* is only briefly adverted to, but its action is prominent throughout, as Crassus and Antonius become pro and con spokesmen whose arguments actually structure the discourse. Thereby Cicero's dialogue offers an implicit contrast with, or "literary criticism" of, the Platonic *inventio* of the *Phaedrus.*

The substance and rigor of *De oratore* are such, I believe, that the document serves as a good index to the subsequent history of rhetoric: how seriously Ciceronian *inventio* is taken depends upon how seriously *De oratore* is taken. It disappeared in the Middle Ages, though *De inventione* continued to be read. But with the advent of humanism in the Quattrocento, *De oratore* was revived and achieved considerable popularity. It became the very first book printed in Italy, and later English humanists such as Roger Ascham hailed it as "the best book that ever Tully [Cicero] wrote."[3] Erasmus himself ranked the work with Vergil's *Georgics,* Ovid's *Medea,* Augustine's *City of God,* and Jerome's *Commentaries,* as among the "finished and complete" examples of distinguished writers' art, "by which posterity might be able to evaluate what they would have been able to do, if they had wished to exert their fullest powers."[4] Erasmus had also, moreover, recognized the preeminence of *De oratore* in the Ciceronian *rhetorica:* with his usual precision, he has the wise Bulephorus in his dialogue *Ciceronianus* claim that Cicero "condemned *De Inventione* and substituted *De Oratore.*"[5]

Although it never, even in the minds of many humanists, exactly replaced the earlier work, *De oratore* has remained in print since 1465. I wonder, though, if its *modern* printing history is not more a sign of our respect than of our readership. I would like to propose that the virtual inattention we twentieth-century rhetoricians give the book is itself a partial gauge of our failure fully to understand *inventio*— Ciceronian *inventio* at least, perhaps even humanist *inventio* at most. Part of our problem may lie in understanding how *suasory* discourse works, or even what *via diversa* means, an argument I shall pursue through other examples in Chapter 5. But here, before returning to the dialogue, let me bracket the discussion of it with the report of another curiously similar conference on rhetoric.

There are many conferences I could have chosen for contrast, conferences held both here and in Europe. I recall one in particular, an even more major conference than the one I have selected for contrast, held in Chicago only a few years ago. A large group of scholars met at a distinguished research library to confer on Renaissance rhetoric; but, as several of us rhetoricians began to perceive early, the participants were mainly bibliographers and philologists. "These people," angrily whispered a friend standing with me on the edge of the audience, "aren't rhetoricians. They're Scholastics. They're still talking about how many fucking angels can dance on the head of a pin." Alas, myself, I was waiting to deliver a major paper I had long labored on. So I smiled and complimented him on his Miltonic view

3. Roger Ascham, *The Schoolmaster (1570),* ed. Lawrence V. Ryan (Ithaca, N.Y., 1967), 119.
4. Letter to Carondelet, 5 January 1523. John C. Olin, trans., in his *Christian Humanism and the Reformation* (New York, 1987), 187.
5. Erasmus, *Ciceronianus,* trans. Izora Scott (New York, 1910), 41.

of angels. But he had a point. Therefore, the best conference, it seems to me, to compare with the Ciceronian one has rhetoricians as participants—politicians and lawyers, speakers and writers or teachers of the practical skills of speaking and writing—with as few Scholastics as possible.

In 1970 a group of such people met—this time at a resort outside Chicago. The group included some of the leading rhetoricians of the day—mainly university teachers of composition, writing and speech. The meeting was the second of a two-part conference called The National Development Project on Rhetoric. The first part had featured papers by rhetoricians, plus papers read by two philosophers and a sociologist. The second part reflected on those papers and then broke into three committees (none of which met under a plane tree): on education, on criticism, and on *inventio*. The diffuseness and breadth of the subjects discussed invite a most favorable comparison with the wide-ranging Crassus-Antonius convocation of yore.

There are other similarities. Again, it was feared that the republic was falling apart. The campuses were exploding with violent protests mainly over Vietnam, but also partly over the powerlessness of certain segments of our society. Public discourse had become displaced by actions such as love-ins, be-ins, sit-ins, violence and trashing, and by simple, stunning assertions like "Peace, flowers, freedom, happiness." During the six days the conference lasted (May 10–15), the US invaded Cambodia, and the National Guard killed four protesting students at Kent State University. It seemed clear that things were never going to be quite the same. It certainly seemed so to the conferees, all of whom were from disrupted campuses. Too, each of us was somewhat uncomfortably aware that the conference was sponsored in part by the U.S. government. Nonetheless, the larger battleground, for which the shooting war was a bloody synecdoche, was not politics but education—where the war is still going on.

The place of Crassus and Antonius was taken by two colleagues from the University of Wisconsin, who were the instigators of the conference. Perhaps, though, their more important function was like Cicero's. For they edited and then published the proceedings, with an intention and title not at all dissimilar to the intention and title of *De oratore: The Prospect of Rhetoric* (1971). Lloyd Bitzer had achieved wide recognition for his reasoned argument about the "situations" of rhetoric, unique social locales which require public discourse.[6] His colleague, Edwin Black, had stirred up considerable controversy with his book attacking Neo-Aristotelian rhetorical criticism.[7] Their emphases, if only unconsciously, struck the keynotes of the entire project: rhetoric was to be situated not simply as an educational but also as a research specialty, and rhetoricians were to boldly go where no one, certainly not Aristotle, had gone before.

The printed report of the conference—the so-called "Prospect"— records our revisionary trek. Cicero was casually dropped from the canon, and so was Aristotle but with a little more effort. Cicero's *De oratore* was mentioned only twice, both times in footnotes to a paper ominously entitled "An Autopsy of the Rhetorical Tradition." Richard McKeon made a singular effort to preserve Aristotle, but the mood of the conference—like the growing mood of American universities generally at that time—was to place our phasers on "stun" and aim them toward the past. Antiquarianism was definitely out. We were eager to face a new age, characterized in the report as one in which rhetoricians would study "sloganeering" as critically as their intellectual ancestors had studied verbal eloquence and in which the new buzz words were to become "transaction," "deep structure," "media," "cross-cultural," and "intrapersonal communication." In its report the committee on *inventio* advised that "classical schemes of invention . . . should be re-examined in terms of the dynamic conception of rhetoric" (*Prospect,* 235) which was then emerging. Obviously, however, in our new enterprise we would welcome aboard only those things which were dynamic enough to have survived the treacheries and the irrelevancies of the past.

Once more we see that the subject of rhetoric can seldom be divorced from its social and political contexts. Cicero sought amidst a failing republic to save the best that was available in traditional rhetoric, which for him was its protocol, its mode of thought, and part of his strategy in accomplishing that goal was to write an inventive kind of committee report in the form of a dialogue showing and telling the true nature of rhetorical *inventio*. The National Development Project on Rhetoric, also amidst a shaken republic, sought

6. Lloyd F. Bitzer, "The Rhetorical Situation," *Philosophy and Rhetoric* 1 (1968): 1–14.

7. Edwin Black, *Rhetorical Criticism* (New York, 1965).

if not to bury the past at least to keep it from being a hindrance, and the Project's strategy was to offer a series of papers capped by committee statements hailing a new concept of rhetoric that was, somehow, about to emerge. It's curious—and probably highly significant—that in times of crisis some of us think about rhetoric, as if paying conscious attention to the motives of eloquence will help us strengthen what is best socially, politically, and perhaps above all educationally. The significance of the attention seems to lie in what our crisis-altered states of mind think is worth either saving or changing. Let me explore this significance by leaping backwards to look at three highly relevant pivots in the history of Western rhetoric in education.

Over eighty years ago—more than 50 years prior to the conference I've just described, this time amidst a scholarly rather than a political revolution—teachers of speech walked out of the Modern Language Association, to form their own, more perfect union. A family quarrel had turned into an intellectual crisis. This time, however, the critics and dissidents found their philosophic sanctions by creating new ties with the past. Out of Cornell came a newly translated and refurbished *Rhetoric* by Aristotle. The revival was more than successful. Aristotle began to dominate composition theory not only in speech but eventually in English departments, forming a silent and seldom acknowledged bridge between factions in the old dispute, whose members nowadays hardly recognize their family resemblance. In fact, over-success in reviving Aristotle partly spurred that 1970 conference. But for that matter, every revolt in and revival of rhetoric in the past seventy years has been taken in acknowledgment of Aristotle's dominance.

By contrast, some of the greatest intellectual upheavals of the past have centered not on Aristotle but on Cicero. For example, the movement that we know as humanism, extending from the Quattrocento through the 16th century in England, was to a great extent a revival of Ciceronianism. The centuries between classicism and the Renaissance—centuries we now call the Middle Ages, though humanists like Petrarch spoke of them more darkly—had the use of Aristotle's *Rhetoric* and Cicero's *De inventione* (and, for that matter, the pseudo-Ciceronian *Rhetorica ad Herennium*). These rhetorics were as readily available as any of the classics in that manuscript culture. What those centuries lacked, however, were Cicero's mature writings (and those of Quintilian—the chief educational theorist of antiquity, who virtually grounds his theory in *De oratore*). When these became available, the humanists found in this reborn Ciceronian *inventio* something complex, a new philosophy of practical reasoning.

One of the greatest and most widely read textbooks of the Renaissance, Erasmus's *De copia*—often interpreted today as merely a handbook on style—is actually a book on how to think rhetorically (an argument I shall try to make in my next chapter). That is, how to invent discourse in a public and juridical, pro and con, "now you see it now you don't" Ciceronian manner, not in the straight-forward and asseverating manner of Aristotelian rhetoric—Erasmus was uncharacteristically blunt on this point; philosophy, he asserted, besides having no "literary culture . . . is contaminated with Aristotle."[8] That rediscovery of rhetorical invention made the Renaissance the greatest pivot of all in western education. There is another, earlier, third and final pivot that I wish to touch on.

Centuries prior to the Renaissance, another rhetorician, St. Augustine, had become concerned about quite the reverse of the humanist battles with Aristotle. He was concerned about how philosophy had become contaminated with Cicero. And he believed he found his cure in Plato—albeit a Christianized Plato. In a period of crisis marking the passage from the classical world to the Middle Ages, amidst great social and religious upheaval, St. Augustine penned his *De doctrina christiana,* in which he skillfully designed the first three books to destroy Ciceronian *inventio* and substitute for it a less skeptical and more charitable mode of thought. Cicero's *De oratore* fell directly within Augustine's destructive aim. For the Platonizing saint, one does not conduct an inquiry by means of rhetoric; one does not find a kind of truth through public argument. One searches for signs of *a priori* truth, using the rule of "charity" to resolve whatever inconsistencies one might encounter, and then employs rhetoric to clothe that truth and thereby make it attractive to others. For Augustine, as for his pagan mentor, rhetoric has no intellectually acceptable mode of thought.[9]

8. The statement was offered publicly though in a letter to Martin Dorp; see Clarence H. Miller, trans. *The Praise of Folly* (New Haven, Conn., 1979), 155.

9. See, among other studies, Gerald A. Press, "The Subject and Structure of Augustine's *De Doctrina Christiana,*" *Augustinian Studies* 11 (1980): 99–124; J. A.

St. Augustine would replace Cicero with Plato; Erasmus would replace Aristotle with Cicero. These two pivotal points have been all but overwhelmed by developments which are reflected in the first pivotal point I discussed, that 1970 conference, in which the humanist reform was blunted and, ultimately, discarded. Moreover, the irony in the earlier actions of Augustine and Erasmus is that Cicero apparently thought he himself had preserved what was best in both of his philosophical predecessors, Plato and Aristotle. But in one matter—his doctrine of *inventio*—Cicero's signature is unmistakable, as the humanists seemed to realize.

Let us look a little more closely at Ciceronian inventive procedures. As noted earlier, Cicero's own writings reveal two approaches, *topical* and *controversial*. The *topical* is a way of discovering ideas by processing them through the "topics" (who, when, where, etc., also called "places" in Cicero's Latin, *loci,* or "seats," *sedes*). For example, if your subject is Oliver North—that is, if the *quaestio* is whether North acted against US interest in the "Irangate" affair—think about developing your theme by pursuing such topics as these: exactly what was done, whether what was done may be defined as, say, a conspiracy, whether what was done was illegal. These topics are present in Cicero and in most modern efforts to revive classical *inventio*. But the *controversial* approach is the one more frequently buried, certainly the one St. Augustine sought to bury. For it gets at what is much more Ciceronian, a kind of lawyerly reasoning that when applied philosophically encourages skeptical pragmatism. In the controversial approach, the topics become not simply a list of places to look for ideas but "an armamorium," as Nancy Struever calls them, "an armamorium of flexible, responsive debating tactics, a series of argumentative wrestling holds."[10] In this approach, debate is the process that defines rhetorical thought; pro and con reasoning is the context within which the topics are to be used. You think about Oliver North by imagining arguments in his defense as well as in

---

Mazzeo, "St. Augustine's Rhetoric of Silence: Truth vs. Eloquence and Things vs. Signs," *Renaissance and Seventeenth Century Studies* (New York, 1964), 1–24; and my own *Donne, Milton, and the End of Humanist Rhetoric* (Berkeley, Calif., 1985), 100–111.

10. Nancy Struever, "Lorenzo Valla: Humanist Rhetoric and the Critique of the Classical Languages of Morality," *Renaissance Eloquence,* ed. James J. Murphy (Berkeley, Calif., 1983), 195.

his prosecution, regardless of which side you plan to take ultimately. And you proceed through the topics by playing two roles, or better, three. This is the point on which Crassus, Antonius, and the others agree. Antonius describes the process succinctly:

> It is my own practice to take care that every client personally instructs me on his affairs, and that no one else shall be present, so that he may speak the more freely; and to argue his opponent's case to him, so that he may argue his own and openly declare whatever he has thought of his position. Then, when he has departed, in my own person and with perfect impartiality I play three characters, myself, my opponent and the arbitrator [or judge]. Whatever consideration is likely to prove more helpful than embarrassing I decide to discuss; wherever I find more harm than good I entirely reject and discard the topic concerned. . . . When I have thoroughly mastered the circumstances of a case the issue in doubt [the *stasis*] comes instantly to my mind.[11]

Obviously, this is a lawyerly approach to composition. Both Crassus and Antonius are lawyers, and both agree that every question must be argued on both sides (see I.xxxiv.158) and that once the student has learned forensic rhetoric, which is the most difficult rhetoric, he's learned all of rhetoric (II.xvii.73, III.xxi.80).

This continual practice of debating one side and then the other—*de omnibus rebus in contrarias partes disserendi,* as Cicero puts it in the Tusculan Disputations (II.iii.9), "discussing both sides of every question," or, simply, as throughout *de Oratore, in utramque partem*—is a key to Ciceronian *inventio.* It is as old as the Sophists and is actually present in Aristotle, though muted (as I'll note later). As Cicero (and, for that matter, St. Augustine) knew, it is especially appropriate for skeptical inquiry. True, it was widely employed in medieval dialectics but primarily in formalistic disputations on matters about which the major truths had already been discovered—or, better, revealed—and about which social consensus was largely irrelevant. In our own age, however much Ciceronian *inventio* might seem to be at home in our professed (and dubious) skepticism, its revival would have to confront a curious mixture, composed on the one hand of our outworn insistence that all utterances must somehow be "sin-

---

11. *De oratore* II. xxiv. 102–103, trans. E. W. Sutton and H. Rackham (Cambridge, Mass., 1929), 273–75. Cf. Mill's characterization of this protocol, quoted in my chapter 1.

cere" and, on the other, of our cynical doubts that we really do have a community of values, a consensus, at all—including, one must suppose, sincerity itself. Nonetheless, at whatever peril either to our professions of skepticism or love of sincerity, the present advantages of reviving Ciceronian *inventio* are too great to ignore, as I argue throughout this book—advantageous if not for practical use in the composition classroom, then advantageous for our understanding of certain great documents of the past.

Ciceronian *inventio* is essentially an analytical process, for which Cicero revived a complex lawyerly tactic of the Greeks. At first he called this doctrine *constitutio* and but later he preferred to use the Greek term *stasis*. It simply means, put the subject (whether it's an idea or an accusation) into a debate, as Antonius does, argue it pro and con, and then find the *stasis*—that is, as Antonius says, "the issue in doubt," the precise point on which the dispute seems to turn and on which it is most likely to be judged. Forensic oratory, or better the criminal trial, is paradigmatic; it is, in fact, the conceptual model of Ciceronian theory, from discussions of *inventio* in *De oratore* (as in Antonius's casual advertence to his pretrial preparations) to the most detailed descriptions of style in Quintilian's eighth and ninth books —"an emphasis," Hanns Hohmann states, "shared by most classical rhetorical writings."[12]

Nietzsche, in his extraordinary epitome of ancient rhetoric (extraordinary because it covers much ground in a small space), shows that *stasis* is the starting point as well as the core of *inventio*. Although his explication of rhetoric relies on Cicero and Quintilian, Nietzsche is always the Greekist: Cicero's *De Oratore,* he says, is "crude and distasteful" *(roh und unerspriesslich)* compared to Aristotle's *Rhetoric.*[13] And so it might appear. Certainly Aristotle offers a rather more characteristically philosophical, monologic, and systematic instruction in rhetoric (his treatise on the subject is a single-voiced, ostensibly expository essay), though he speaks of rhetoric as a "faculty," rather than as a system, for sensing and finding all the available means of

12. "The Dynamics of Stasis: Classical Rhetorical Theory and Modern Legal Argumentation," *American Journal of Jurisprudence* 34 (1989): 172.

13. *Friedrich Nietzsche on Rhetoric and Language,* ed. and trans. Sander L. Gilman, Carole Blair, David J. Parent (Oxford, Eng., 1989), 15. Nietzsche goes on to emphasize the obvious importance of the Ciceronian protocol: e.g., *Ein Epilog, in dem nicht die Affekte für und wider aufgeregt werden ist undenkbar* (115).

persuasion. Indeed, the very forcibleness and clarity of his monologue overwhelm any denial of system. Too, although Aristotle insists that one importance of rhetoric lies in its unique usefulness in
constructing arguments on both sides of a question, nowhere does
he offer an actual (and systematically untidy) instance of arguing both
sides at once. For that matter, Aristotle obviously preferred to mar-
ginalize the doctrine of *stasis* and locate the rhetorical "faculty" in less
conflict-centered situations.[14] The humanist preference for Cicero's
dialogue—which not only tells but shows, and does *that* in a lively
if complicated way—should therefore not be slighted by Nietzsche's
remark. It is a preference for a different kind of rhetoric, one that
can simply be better shown than talked about. It is also one that,
contrary to what one might expect in any philosophically serious
work, includes *humor* in its purview—a point Cicero, Erasmus, and
Thomas Wilson deeply grasped, and a point to which we shall recur
several times in this book.

Let us return to the dialogue and, before considering some possible advantages of restoring its doctrine of *inventio,* note again its
structural characteristics.

The progression of the debate is almost labyrinthine, an effect Cicero surely intended as a means of frustrating any seeker after handbooks, like his puerile *De inventione.* The effect still frustrates the
unwary (another point Erasmus deeply grasped) and is a significant
indication of at least one intention: there is no easy and ready way
to learn rhetoric. On that point, all participants would agree, for
even Antonius's teachers (observation and experience) are hard task-
masters. Above all, there is no easy and ready way to learn *inventio*—
to learn, that is, how to fill in or flesh out its pro-con protocol and
apply it usefully. Crassus speaks first in behalf of that difficulty and
advocates a broad education combined with practice and knowledge
of theory.[15] Although on this first day there are some interruptions
and dissent from the other speakers, the major rebuttal is provided
by Antonius, who responds only briefly, for the heat of the day is

---

14. The point has been succinctly made by Yameng Liu, "Aristotle and Stasis
Theory: A Re-examination," *Rhetoric Society Quarterly* 21 (1991): 53–59.

15. In the course of his speech he treats all five "offices" of rhetoric: invention,
arrangement, style, memory, and delivery. See my Figure Two. The Ciceronian
word is *officia,* duties or offices, not "canons," as so casually used today in summarizing classical theory.

almost upon them, a time which requires gentlemen to retire for their health's sake. Nonetheless, in his initially brief attack Antonius articulates his central point, which will become a theme of the next day's debate: practice, not education, is the true avenue to consummate artistry, which itself consists largely of speaking in a way calculated to convince. The argument seems more than a little stunning, coming as it does after the long case Crassus presented in behalf of the moral and intellectual values of a broad education. But Antonius offers an argument which has the weight of the status quo behind it. No one has tried out the sort of education Crassus proposes. Crassus, therefore, has the burden of proof and the right to speak first and last, but presumption ("of innocence" as we yet call it) operates in favor of Antonius's negative or, better, defensive stance.

Antonius's point is developed at length in Book II, a kind of antithesis to the thesis of Book I. Practice, he repeats, is of the essence, and the orator/lawyer's acumen is best revealed in the practical application of his skill at producing effects on an audience. Effectiveness is thus the very end of rhetoric. Art is less significant—all talk of a broadly liberal education notwithstanding—than natural endowment and experience. Who, for example, can actually teach someone how to use that most effective of all techniques, wit or humor? At this point, Antonius defers to C. Julius Caesar Strabo Volpiscus, an acknowledged expert on the subject of wit, who offers a disquisition on the subject, showing that whereas it can be defined, divided, and discussed wit remains less an acquired talent than a natural gift. The point is a simple one: "*est plane oratoris movere risum*"—that is, "plainly, the orator should make people laugh" (II.lviii.236). Caesar's disquisition is a virtual grab-bag of jokes.

This inclusion of wit and humor within rhetoric is highly significant. It is one of the most obvious qualities which forever distinguishes rhetoric from conventionally serious pursuits, like most philosophy or theology. Certainly Erasmus well realized this distinction, when he has Folly praise the rhetoricians and claim to be a member of their party if only because they alone recognize the importance of humor. It is a feature which makes rhetoricians the cousins of Democritus, the famous "laughing philosopher," and even at times purveyors of perversity (Burton, recall, in the Renaissance wrote his at times hilarious but always divagatory *Anatomy of Melancholy* under the nom de plume "Democritus, Jr."). It is a feature which distinguishes the discourse of most Renaissance humanists, receiving practical application and theoretical justification not only in the writings of Erasmus but also in the work of that lesser light, Thomas Wilson. Above all, it is a feature that made Erasmus unique among his contemporary theologians in using humor to inform his theological writing and equally extraordinary among educationists in arguing that a sense of *play* is vital to education ("I'm not sure," he wrote, "anything is learned better than what is learned as a game"[16])—further reasons I would advance to justify my recurrence to Erasmus. But back to *De oratore*.

In the course of Book II, Antonius too covers virtually the whole of rhetorical theory, although he insists that theory itself merely articulates, does not teach, what can only be acquired through practice. Crassus then employs a hoary debating tactic. He insists that Antonius's meticulous discussion of the speaker's stock-in-trade has actually furthered his, Crassus's, own case.

The final book, III, belongs largely to Crassus, who takes as his task the re-uniting of rhetoric and philosophy, by which he means learning generally. He attempts this reunification chiefly by arguing that Antonius separated matters that cannot be separated but that are actually, like style and ideas, dependent upon each other. The orator needs the philosopher's learning, and the philosopher to be effective needs the orator's skill. Otherwise the two disciplines are empty. Have the two ever been united in one person? the reader might wonder. Has there ever been an *orator perfectus?* Crassus himself would seem to fulfill the ideal (and so too would Antonius, as Cicero slyly makes clear). But attention at the very end of the book is centered in hopes for a rising young orator, Hortensius (one of the young Cicero's own role models—recall that Cicero was only 15 at the time of this "old story"). The point is perhaps not so much that hope for the republic is yet alive, for that point had already been mooted by Cicero's introduction to Book III, in which he looks at Roman history beyond this Tusculan hiatus. No, the point of positing a "perfect orator" as the fulfillment of rhetoric—that is, phi-

---

16. On both these points, see Walter M. Gordon, *Humanist Play and Belief: The Seriocomic Art of Desiderius Erasmus* (Toronto, 1990). For Erasmus's quoted statement, see *The Colloquies of Erasmus,* trans. Craig. R. Thompson (Chicago, 1965), 625.

losophy made effective—lies in an educational scheme aimed at preparing one for *statesmanship*. Therein lies the last, best hope for a once and future republic. Therein, too, lies the final rebuttal to the issues of practicability and desirability.

Crassus's rhetoric-centered scheme of liberal education was an indictment, prosecution, and proffered reform of the status quo, of the kind of education available in Rome at the time. Crassus's scheme was to be the means by which the *orator perfectus,* the statesman, was to be produced. Later we shall note that for Erasmus the *orator perfectus* was not a putative statesman but Christ. Too, we shall also note that this ideal of a perfect orator was itself something of a rhetorical strategy, and has been so used by humanists through the centuries, to keep discussions of rhetoric focussed and personalized.[17]

Moreover, Cicero, as I have suggested, has not remained quiet all this while. All three books are in the form of a letter to his brother Quintus, and each one is headed by Cicero's remarks. To introduce Book I he underscores the importance of the subject and sets the scene. To introduce Book II he notes that Antonius in spite of his ostensibly anti-intellectual stance was actually quite as learned as Crassus. (Thus the veil might seem as thin as the one Socrates wears when he redoes Lysias's speech. But Sir Philip Sidney, as we shall see in Chapter 5, grasps the Ciceronian point, about *ethos,* precisely, and it has nothing to do with Platonic sincerity and everything to do with rhetorical efficaciousness: the mask you wear in any one situation is designed to gain credit with your audience.) To introduce Book III Cicero tells Quintus what happened to the men *after* the dialogue and uses the occasion to provide a panegyric of Crassus, who died soon after the dispute, of natural causes. But in spite of these remarks and in spite of the impression a first reading of the dialogue might give, it is not completely accurate to say, as many commentators have, that Crassus is simply Cicero's "spokesman." Antonius's position is sympathetically or at least fairly presented— indeed, if it were not, the dialogue would not work and the doctrine of pro-con reasoning would be a sham. After all, by Crassus's own account "the one and only true and perfect orator" is one who can

17. *Non eum a nobis institui oratorem qui sit aut fuerit,* says Quintilian (I.x.4), *sed imaginem quandam concepisse nos animo perfecti illius et nulla parte cessantis:* We are not instituting an orator who ever was or will be, but we have imagined some perfect one who on no score fails.

"speak on both sides about every subject" and in the manner of the skeptics or Academics "argue against every statement put forward" (III.xxi.80). It is Antonius, moreover, who sets forth the bare *in utramque partem* protocol which Crassus approves and Cicero follows.

That is, there is a second way whereby Cicero also speaks to us, and that is through the structure of the work itself. If Books I and II are, as I have suggested, thesis and antithesis respectively, Book III might be called the synthesis. Indeed, synthesis is the debate tactic Crassus himself employs—with Cicero's sanction. He tries to stick all loose ends onto one ball of wax, his plan for liberal education. Consequently although structured along the lines of a debate, this is not exactly a battle in which one side comes out the victor at the expense of the other. It is rather a dispute in which both sides have equal credentials and almost equally valid points. The tactic which causes Antonius to disappear or keep silent is, finally, the tactic of synthesis—not repudiation but incorporation. The tactic is itself characteristic of Ciceronian *sapientia,* or wisdom, that wholeness of vision whose parts we learn in practice, in theory, by nature, and through study. It might seem to be Platonic. But it is a wholeness which Crassus believes had been shattered in education by Socrates: he it was who, though rhetorically learned and talented, by shrinking from politics and public affairs realigned the educational scheme and segregated rhetoric from philosophy. The Platonic dialogues, in which the genius of Socrates is enshrined, have consequently become

> the source from which has sprung the undoubtedly absurd and unprofitable and reprehensible severance between the tongue and the brain, leading to our having one set of professors to teach us to think and another to teach us to speak. (III.xvi.61)

That initial comparison with the *Phaedrus* is thus put in even sharper perspective. Cicero's impulse, his intention in *De oratore,* is to bring together thinking and speaking as well as knowledge and practice, but not at the expense of elevating philosophy over rhetoric, or broad education at the expense of on-the-job-training, or even finally segregating the two. Crassus's synthesis in Book III lies in his insistence that the larger subject of which both he and Antonius have been speaking is "practical philosophy," and in this he makes an apparently successful effort to resolve the *stasis* of the debate through redefining the question.

As noted, synthesizing is itself the impulse of *sapientia*. And eloquence, in Cicero's famous definition, is wisdom speaking copiously *(copiose loquens sapientia*[18]*)*. The dialogue *De oratore,* like other Ciceronian dialogues, is a practical demonstration of *inventio* under the guidance of *sapientia:* a whole is broken into parts, the parts speak for themselves, the whole is restored at the expense of depriving the parts of their partiality. (Thus wisdom speaks; what is meant by "copiously" will be explored in my next chapter.) Antonius is a part, so too is Crassus. The *stasis* seems to be their disagreement over just how the "perfect orator" is to be produced, and what's meant by that term. With the term defined along the lines of statesmanship and with education realigned to produce the man of public affairs, the dispute begins to dissolve. But underlying all is Cicero's practical demonstration of the elementary protocol of "practical philosophy," argument *in utramque partem.* It is a protocol which will be reborn in Erasmus's *via diversa,* for in both diverse ways are employed in the interests of encompassing the "whole truth."

The roles one must play in this *inventio* are multiplex and judicial—prosecution, defense, and judge, in Antonius's model, though the procedure has significant application outside the courtroom. It has been used in philosophical dialogues, such as *De oratore,* and in monologues. It was obviously taught to Shakespeare, for example, who has Hamlet follow it in his famous Fourth Soliloquy: The *quaestio* is "To be or not to be"; on the one side is suffering (for to live is to suffer), on the other is sleep (for to die is to sleep); but this sleep may include dreaming. Aye, there's the *stasis.* And it becomes literally a *stasis* for Hamlet, who can't move off it, who finds the native hue of his resolution sicklied o'er with the pale cast of dialectical thought. Alas, poor Hamlet. He mistook a philosophical *thesis* for a rhetorical *hypothesis.* Contrary to humanist teaching, he used a general question to answer a specific one; consequently, though he pursued the protocol of *in utramque partem,* he stayed on the abstract level of dialectic, when the practical level of rhetoric was called for.

Let us use Hamlet's confusion to consider briefly the modern paucity in protocol. To help our students find something to say, we teachers of composition revived rhetorical *inventio* in the 1960s. But

---

18. *De partitione oratoria,* xxiii.79.

because we revived a listing of the topics only, cut off from their function as "argumentative wrestling holds," our *inventio* was—and still is—also cut off from its fully analytical functions. The revival of the *topical* mode of invention is certainly classical, sanctioned by Aristotle, but it misses a crucial, Ciceronian feature, its *controversial* use. The latter may be worth reviving today for it might help students form new resolutions and reexamine ones they already hold. Of course, to do that, they must be taught to debate both sides of the question. And that means first of all *finding* the question—as our humanist ancestors advised, linking philosophical *theses* like "To be or not to be" with rhetorical *hypotheses* like "If my stepfather murdered my father, I should seek revenge." Or, better, pursuing such indefinite questions as "Whether covert operations are a legitimate form of American governmental action" through such definite ones as "Resolved that the covert sale of weapons to Iran is a violation of US foreign policy." In both cases, the first question belongs to dialectic, the second to rhetoric. But in Ciceronian *inventio*, the second always encompasses the first, and for extremists in the humanist camp the first seems irrelevant without the second. Once the *quaestio*, the rhetorical hypothesis, has been formulated, the student's task becomes one of putting the matter into debate, voicing the multiplicity of issues until the *stasis*, the point of crucial difference is reached, the point beyond which discussion cannot proceed until synthesis is achieved or some consensus or agreement between people is attempted. It's at that point, the *stasis*, that the student should be ready to begin writing or speaking. It's also at that point that any composer should have accomplished a great deal. Not the least among the accomplishments may be a certain liberalizing of thought.

For pro and con reasoning can be liberalizing. The point was overlooked in that conference near Chicago in 1970. But it was deeply a part of the conference in Crassus's villa two millennia ago, part of rhetoric's overall antidote to political tyranny. As an educational tradition, Ciceronian *inventio* began, so far as we know, with Cicero's intellectual ancestors, the Sophists, the inventers of *in utramque partem* disputation as an educational practice. Indeed, a distinguished modern historian has proposed that—insofar as the purpose of the humanities is not the pursuit of philosophical truth but skill in the liberalizing uses of rhetorical thought—the true founder of the humanities in the Western World is not the philosopher Socrates but the Sophist Protagoras.[19]

Moreover, rhetorical thought is—let us admit it—highly perverse and lawyerly in nature. For it is ready and willing to challenge all perspectives which come within the compass of its initially simple binary division. As such, however, its dialogic invention can be particularly antagonistic to the de-humanizing rhetoric of tyranny, if only because, unlike the dialogic invention of dialectic, rhetoric always pursues another lawyerly impulse, getting down to cases. For those reasons, our humanist ancestors in the sixteenth century—many of whom were lawyers or had been trained in the law—rediscovered in Ciceronian *inventio* a way to challenge authoritarianism and resist coercion.

Shakespeare's age, like ours, was fond of putting down lawyers: the times are becoming overly litigious; lawyers are charging outrageous fees, becoming too numerous, acquiring too much power. These blasts, common in the sixteenth century, sound familiar in our own. Indeed, a put-down often seen in our age, on sweatshirts and bumperstickers, is right out of Shakespeare: "The first thing we do, let's kill all the lawyers." The suggestion comes from the character Dick in 2 Henry VI (IV.ii). But Dick is a rag-tag revolutionary, and his comically diffuse proposal has a serious implication: he seeks to get rid of lawyers as a way of quelling dissent, or of muting critical thought. To think of lawyers, or lawyerly reasoning, as something of a bulwark against tyranny may be more acceptable if delivered indirectly or even bumptiously, as Shakespeare does through Dick. I must try a different approach. "Critical thinking," a good synonym for Ciceronian *inventio,* won't do. It has already been beaten insensible by educationists.

Of all the names for that liberalizing of thought which I believe is potentially the greatest educational advantage of restoring Ciceronian *inventio,* the word *irony* as used by Richard Rorty seems most precise. All ironists, Rorty says, are nominalists and historicists—that is, for ironists, words are conventions only, with more pro-

19. William J. Bouwsma, "Socrates and the Confusion of the Humanities," *The American Future and the Humane Tradition,* ed. Robert E. Hiedemann (Washington, D.C., 1982), 11–22.

pensity for creating reality than naming it, and as conventions they arise from particular situations. Ironists thus have the "realization that anything can be made to look good or bad by being redescribed" but they are at the same time "never quite able to take themselves seriously because [they are] always aware that the terms in which they describe themselves are subject to change . . ."[20] The definition directly recalls Erasmian pedagogy, as we shall note in my subsequent chapters. For some readers it may also recall Hamlet's line: "there is nothing either good or bad, but thinking makes it so" (II.ii), a line he delivers in his dialectical badinage with schoolchums Rosencrantz and Guildenstern. But Hamlet, in thrall to metaphysical circumstance, is no ironist.

For that matter, any metaphysician in Rorty's view is the diametrical, as well as dialectical, opposite of the ironist:

> The metaphysician thinks that there is an overriding intellectual duty to present arguments for one's controversial views—arguments which will start from relatively uncontroversial premises. . . . The ironist's preferred form of argument is dialectical in the sense that she takes the unit of persuasion to be a vocabulary rather than a proposition. . . . An ironist hopes that by the time she has finished using old words in new senses, not to mention introducing brand-new words, people will no longer ask questions phrased in the old words. So the ironist thinks of logic as ancillary to dialectic, whereas the metaphysician thinks of dialectic as a species of rhetoric, which in turn is a shoddy substitute for logic. (78)

A neat distinction. But it does not rule out the role of rhetoric, particularly as I define it in its relation to dialectic, in forming the ironist. Rorty himself forms an ironist in theory by using a dualist rhetoric, in which the controversy is *pro* (irony) and *con* (metaphysical). The ironist may know the techniques and methods of argument, but her preferred way of persuasion is through a kind of vocabulary exploration. "Dialectic" and "rhetoric" are of course the very theories of argumentation. Having allowed "rhetoric" to take over the whole of argumentation, Rorty must find another way to define the "dialectic" which the ironist uses. This he does by calling it "literary criticism." The ironist goes about trying to change people's minds through an examination of texts, preferably literary texts. The tactic

20. Richard Rorty, *Contingency, irony, and solidarity* (Cambridge, Eng., 1989), 73–74.

is not unknown to the humanists, who would frequently imitate an ancient text, like Plato's *Phaedrus*, to invite comparison and contrast.

Though my own thinking has been much influenced by Rorty, his juggling of the terms "dialectic" and "rhetoric" runs afoul of my antiquarianism. For a major theme of my book is contrary to the historicist impulse in this philosophical irony. We have not fully realized and taken advantage of the traditional union of dialectic and rhetoric as coordinate arts of disputation. There is no educational approach—none better than debating both sides of the question—which can so effectively produce the nominalism if not the historicism essential to irony. Nothing, perhaps even absolutely nothing, is good or bad but speaking about it makes it so. The rule fits humanist rhetoric—though I will not claim that humanists themselves held a perfect or unmixed nominalism or historicism.

Having accepted Rorty's definition of *irony* and used it to restate my own stance in this book, let me close this chapter by adverting to his tactical use of *literary criticism* and offering yet another reason to reconsider Erasmus. As has already become apparent, my major mode of argumentation is the close reading of individual texts. In that work I acknowledge the superior skills of Rorty. I acknowledge, too, the skills of Erasmus, one of the great ironists of the Renaissance.

Erasmus shocked the Christian world with his rhetorical, defiantly anti-scholastic literary criticism or hermeneutics (he wouldn't have called it by either term, of course). He paraphrased parts of the New Testament by assuming a position from inside the work, making the speaker's voice his own: *Sum Paulus*, begins his paraphrase of the Apostle's letters, "I am Paul."[21] He transfigured Christ rhetorically, turning him from iconography into action: *in principio erat sermo*, he Latinized the Greek of John I.I, thereby creating a contextual reading that we might put in English as "In the beginning was [not the Word but] the Speech."[22] Other Latinists had used *verbum* for the Greek *logos*, but Erasmus wished to restore the word's place in another ancient trinity, which we now call, with a nod toward Aris-

21. The argument has been well explored by Amy Seltzer's unpublished dissertation, "Erasmus for the Sake of Argument" (Berkeley, 1989).

22. See Marjorie O'Rourke Boyle, *Erasmus on Language and Method in Theology* (Toronto, 1977). Boyle's chapter 3 has an extensive study of Erasmus's *Ratio*, to be mentioned later.

totle, *ethos, pathos,* and *logos*—and in *this* literary criticism he stirred up a hornet's nest indeed. Further, he willingly, at least through his persona Folly, accepted the titles of rhetorician, of skeptic and of nominalist, and his interpretive methods were at times openly historicist and tonally ludic, "seriocomic."[23]

Erasmus's mode of literary criticism (we shall examine his pedagogical approaches later) is succinctly set forth in his *Methodus verae theologiae* (1516), a work in which he too sounds somewhat like Crassus. In effect he argues that the best theologican is the best literary critic. The method of "true" theology, he claims, is best applied by someone who is broadly and deeply learned—someone who knows Latin, Greek, and Hebrew, as well as the trivium, the quadrivium, the study of natural things, geography, and history. He should know of course the schemes and tropes of grammar and rhetoric for purposes of explicating Scripture. But in particular he should know "those parts of rhetoric which are concerned with *stases,* with setting forth cases, with supporting arguments, with means of amplification, and with the passions." Like Crassus, he offers an ideal rhetorical education. But why, one must wonder, should the *theologian* know *rhetorical* means of argumentation? One answer is immediately denied: it is not to make him a contentious wrangler, like a Scholastic. It is, rather, to make him a better student of the various commentaries, able to sort them as arguments—able to understand, for example, what choices Origen made for what audience and occasion in treating the temptation of Abraham by God. Above all, rhetoric equips the budding theologian with the tools necessary for understanding Scripture itself—how some parables, for example, "apply to the disciples and their time, some to everyone; some are given in relation to the passions of their times, not a few smile as though with irony." Any Scriptural passage cannot be interpreted by simply plucking out four or five little words; rather, let the budding theologian "ponder from whence what is said arose, by whom it may be said, to whom it may be said, at what time, upon what occasion, with which words, what preceded, what followed."[24]

In this way, Erasmian literary criticism became the counterpart

23. The word is in the subtitle of Gordon's book, *Humanist Play;* see note 16 above.

24. The quotations are from paragraphs 8 and 9. I am indebted to John McVitty for the translations.

of that lawyerly impulse in rhetoric to descend from the abstract and steep oneself in circumstance, to get down to cases. Obviously, too, the teaching views all utterance as argument and casts even further light on what Erasmus meant by calling Christ "God's speech." By in effect examining choices and considering audience and occasion, Erasmus invites one to re-invent the writer's *inventio.* What is missing from the instruction in the *Methodus,* in spite of its mention of the rhetorical doctrine of *stasis,* is the role of disputation or pro-con reasoning. For that we need to review not the expanded version of the *Methodus* (the *Ratio* of 1518) but the more elementary instruction in the Erasmian textbooks to be examined in my subsequent chapters. In the later *Ratio,* Christ (as *sermo* or *oratio*) is the theologian's active principle of eloquence. One interprets and creates by concentrating on, immersing oneself in, Christ.

In this respect, Christ is the fulfillment of the "perfect orator" posited as the ideal in the *De oratore.* Both Erasmus and Cicero knew that there is no way to make a rhetorical ideal static, or iconographic, or anything unsteeped in circumstance. Nor is there any way to reduce that ideal to "method" or "theory" or "system" (Erasmus's use of those terms are to an extent ironic, as we shall note later). As Michael Cahn has so incisively put it, the notion of an *orator perfectus* actually "functions as a rhetorical strategy. It orients rhetorical knowledge towards the personality of the speaker and removes it from the sphere of a 'pure' knowledge" or, as Cahn also shows, from the sphere of the kind of knowledge reducible to handbooks.[25]

In the present chapter, I have sought to review Ciceronian *inventio* and to claim that its absence marks a gap in our historical understanding and a deficiency in modern rhetoric. Again I speak as an antiquarian, urging at least a new look at if not an actual revival of an important but to modern eyes mystifying office of traditional rhetoric. There may be certain advantages to reviving Ciceronian *inventio* in the modern composition classroom—advantages which go beyond compositional skills and involve acquiring a certain ironical stance toward argument, dogma, language, perhaps even experience, as well as method, theory, and system. But the question remains, How? How do we put the teaching into practice? Answering

25. Michael Cahn, "Reading Rhetoric Rhetorically: Isocrates and the Marketing of Insight," *Rhetorica* 7 (1989): 125.

that question directly is not my major concern, though I accept it as an "end," that is, as the practical point of my argument, and I shall return to it in the final chapter of this book. My continual focus, however, is on the past, on those writers and sometime educators who understood Ciceronian *inventio* far better than we moderns seem to.

My general end is hermeneutical, toward a new understanding of certain documents in the rhetorical tradition. That understanding, as I have indicated, relies in great part upon a revivification of our sense of language as more than words: in meaning it is nominalist, in attitude skeptical, in practical application often ironic. In sum language is gesture. Thus any search for theory in the modern sense, as an explicit setting forth of what one is up to, is likely to be frustrated from the outset. Especially among humanist writers the dividing line between theory and practice was less distinct than we tend to find it today. Why read or write theory, humanists seemed to ask, when textual analysis of successful rhetorical practice teaches all we need to know about how language works while preserving something of the flavor of circumstance? Kees Meerhoff has put "a basic principle of humanist education" precisely, one that "explains why most of the humanists' textbooks are relatively slim, and why they repeat so often *reliqua usus docebit,* 'practice will teach you the rest.'" The principle is, simply, *"[u]sus is not* doing exercises with formal rules, it is, first and foremost, reading texts."[26] In light of that comment we shall now turn to the reading of one of two books in which Erasmus came about as close as he ever did to talking about rhetoric extensively.

26. "The Significance of Melanchthon's Rhetoric," in Peter Mack, ed., *Renaissance Rhetoric* (New York, 1994), 50.

Figure 1: Erasmus of Rotterdam, 1526 (Photograph courtesy of the Henry E. Huntington Library and Art Gallery)

This famous engraving of the great humanist provides its own best caption, appropriately in two languages. Latin: "A representation of Erasmus of Rotterdam by Albrecht Dürer, a portrait drawn from life." Greek: "The better image will his writings show." One of Erasmus's personae has great praise for Dürer: in *De recta Latini Graecique sermonis pronuntiatione* (1528), the Bear says to the Lion that Dürer "could express absolutely anything in monochrome, that is with black lines only . . . Above all, he can draw things that are impossible to draw [such as] feelings, attitudes, the mind revealed by the carriage of the body, almost the voice itself" (Trans. Maurice Pope, *Collected Works of Erasmus*, 26 [Toronto, 1985], 399). In this engraving, Erasmus appears in Churchly habiliments, writing in his study, with his "sources"*(fontes)* nearby. His gaze is inward, perhaps, or on his writing, or on the flowers. But for all the Bear's sanguinity, the portrait drew complaints, then and now. Some of Erasmus's contemporaries did not like it, causing him five years later to comment that if the portrait does not look like him, at least he no longer looks like it. Erwin Panofsky's judgment remains accurate: "Dürer produced merely an excellent portrait of a cultured, learned, and god-fearing humanist; he failed to capture that elusive blend of charm, serenity, ironic wit, complacency and formidable strength that was Erasmus of Rotterdam," and thus the Greek inscription is "truer than it was meant to be" (*Albrecht Dürer* [Princeton, N.J., 1943], I: 239–40). Although the qualities we most prize in Erasmus are available only in his writing, nonetheless the portrait, like most of those drawn from life, shows him deeply involved in that work which was his life. Such at least would seem to be Erasmus's intention, in his careful (and one must say *rhetorical*) attention to the face he presented to the world in the portraits he allowed to be painted or drawn (see Lisa Jardine, *Erasmus, Man of Letters* [Princeton, N.J., 1993]: esp. intro. and chapter 1).

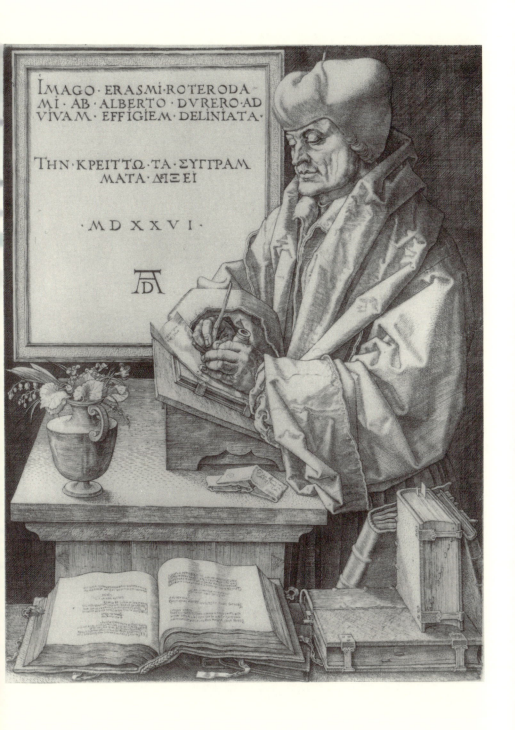

3. Copiousness[1]

Copiousness—Cicero's and Erasmus's *copia*—is not an easily graspable idea. Most modern scholars think of it as having something to do with style. After all, the word seems synonymous with "abundance." In rhetoric *copia* must therefore mean "linguistic abundance." It does, but it refers to another kind of rhetorical abundance as well: abundance of thought. It therefore clearly has something to do with *inventio*.

One good synonym for copiousness was supplied by my old elocution teacher: resourcefulness, "having wherewithal," she said, "at the ready." You may be called upon to act, to say or to do something, so you'd better have resources handy. It's a concept best grasped by someone who sees most uses of language as a kind of performance or gesture. Its necessity will be readily appreciated by anyone who has ever been subjected to the old classroom exercises in "impromptu" speaking or writing or who has ever debated within time restrictions or worked in an old newspaper office with its frantic cries of "copy!"

Of course, the urgency and some of the importance of this resourcefulness can also be demonstrated by the courtroom trial, the

---

1. Some materials in this chapter originally appeared in my "Schoolbooks and Rhetoric: Erasmus's *Copia*," *Rhetorica* 9 (Spring, 1991): 113–29; the essay is reused with permission of the University of California Press.

conceptual model of Ciceronian rhetoric. This Vico well knew when two centuries after Erasmus he described traditional resourcefulness in terms of the lawyerly requirement to give the accused *"immediate assistance."* It is a resourcefulness, Vico believed, unique to rhetoric. When he posited rhetoric's opposite number he used the traditional one, philosophy, wherein when "confronted with some dubious point," the speaker is apt to plead "Give me some time to think it over!" Further, when Vico returned to a problem continuously in his thought, that students were not being taught *inventio,* he offered an equally traditional and equally humanist solution: teach them the topics and "skill in debating on either side of any proposed argument."[2]

Copia, as I have noted, is thus closely akin to the tasks of invention, and, like inventiveness, it could be a difficult, even painful trait to acquire. Formulas are much easier to memorize. Rather than stoking the mind with variety, it's much more convenient to have a thesaurus like Roget's at our elbows, or a list of standard questions to use in a written "theme," or a bunch of stock issues to use in a debate, or a group of formulary reports or letters—or even jokes, like those that yet appear in public speakers' handbooks. Such in short is the history, from a reader-reception point of view, of Erasmus's *De copia,* one of the most important and widely misused textbooks on resourcefulness in the history of rhetoric. In this book Erasmus tried not simply to revive the deepest principles of classical rhetoric but also to make them palatable to schoolboys—a chancy enterprise at best. Although the book failed in its mission,[3] its lessons yet remain available and invaluable, so long as we clearly understand what Erasmus was up to. His aim, like Vico's later one, extended beyond the limited range of a handbook, though the initial and ongoing use of the work fell well within that range.

Published originally in 1512, *De copia* was revised and enlarged at least thrice in Erasmus's lifetime. Commissioned by John Colet, dean of St. Paul's school in London, it apparently filled a pervasive

2. Giambattista Vico, *On the Study Methods of our Time,* trans. Elio Gianturco (Ithaca, N.Y., 1990), 15, 19.
3. I differ with Peter Mack's judgment, that the book "was Erasmus's most successful manual"; *Renaissance Argument* (Leiden, 1993), 305. The book was not successful in serving Erasmus's intention. Nor was it, exactly, a manual, though it was used as if it were.

pedagogical need, not only in England but throughout Northern Europe, and continued to do so long after Erasmus's death.[4] However, as I have suggested, the need it filled is only part of Erasmus's aim. To begin with, resourcefulness, or copiousness of language and thought, is a sign—in this case, an outward and audible sign—not simply of the inventiveness which so mark Renaissance art but also of the richness and variety which distinguish its values. Abundance of both kinds is of course something schoolboys lack. To meet schoolboys' immediate and practical need of linguistic abundance was certainly part of Erasmus's intention, but in fulfilling this need he sought also to provide a protocol useful in pursuing the complexities of *conceptual* abundance. However, a certain rapaciousness deflected Erasmus's ultimate aim then, just as custom deflects it now.

That is, Erasmus aimed at a certain copiousness or facility first in words and then in thought. The latter is dependent on the former but is finally far more complicated and depends upon reading the entire book in a certain way (and perhaps as Jardine has argued, to be noted below, upon fitting the work into a very definite context). However, most of his contemporaries and only few of ours stayed for much more than half the lesson. Erasmus had clearly articulated the principle that in education "[w]ords come first, but subject matter is more important."[5] That is, fluency in Latin words, *verba,* comes first before one can hope to master copiousness in subject matter, *res,* which depends on thinking like such master rhetoricians as Cicero and Quintilian. Fluency, *verba,* comprises the first part of *De copia;* thinking, *res,* the second part—as announced in the title: *De copia verborum ac rerum.* The distinction between the two is functionally vague; they are offered merely as convenient ways of dividing up the indivisible in an effort to approach certain habits of mind,

---

4. For a graphic review of the book's printing history to 1570, see Mack, *Renaissance Argument,* 274–76.

5. The principle is articulated at the first of *De ratione studii: Principio duplex omnino videtur cognitio, rerum ac verborum. Verborum prior, rerum potior* I: 521 (A); unless otherwise noted, all Latin citations of Erasmus's work are to the 1540 *Opera Omnia* ed. Jean Leclerc (Leiden, 1704). Richard Waswo finds in this opening a "fundamental acknowledgment that language is the shaping medium of the whole human world, not a passive tool but an active force" (*Language and Meaning in the Renaissance* [Princeton, N.J., 1987], 219), an implication I accept, though I place the emphasis on a subtly different part of Erasmus's lesson.

though the progression of the two parts is the progression from the specific to the general.[6]

The matter can be put in even more technical terms. Erasmian access to *copia* is through *elocutio*, "style," one of the five "offices" of classical rhetoric, a journey that begins and ultimately culminates in another office, rhetorical thought, or "invention." For this reason, the latter part of the *De copia* moves away from an obsession with words and delves into the most multifarious feature of classical rhetoric, *inventio*. But this latter part, with its concern for *res*, or those arguments and concepts which are to be acquired through "invention," has been largely ignored. Students then wanted a fast and easy way to learn verbal abundance and found the first part, on *verba*, a compendium sufficient to their needs. Compared with other works on invention, Agricola's for instance, which emphasizes "the underlying structures of reason," Erasmus's seems to emphasize "the exuberant verbal surface."[7] Inevitably, appearance and use set a pattern. Historians now, with few exceptions, perhaps stunned by Erasmus's initial presentation of linguistic bountifulness, have proved similarly myopic in sensing his point.

T. W. Baldwin has found evidence that only the first 70 pages or so of Erasmus's book were ever well-thumbed in sixteenth-century England, either by those elementary schoolmasters who were its initial audience or by those advanced students who often carted the book off to Oxbridge.[8] Their usage would seem to justify George Kennedy's remark that "[a]lthough Erasmus knew thoroughly the whole system of classical rhetoric, the only part of the discipline to

6. In this Erasmus was no clearer than Valla, whom he admired. As Mack notes in a discussion of Valla in *Renaissance Argument*, "*res* is more general than the meaning of 'word.' Whereas everything can be called '*res*,' only words can be called 'word'"; 55.

7. The quotations are from Mack, *Renaissance Argument*, 311. My differences with Mack are indicated by my words "seems to emphasize."

8. T. W. Baldwin, *William Shakespere's Small Latine & Lesse Greeke* (Urbana, Ill., 1944; two vols.). Baldwin, as I shall note later, sees the first part, or "book," as being on *elocutio*, the second as being on *inventio* (see 2: 25, e.g.). "But the English-used copies of this work appear to indicate that in the time of Shakespere the schoolmasters drilled the boys only on the first book" (2: 25). Accordingly: "Veltkirchius in 1536 published an elaborately annotated edition of the *Copia*—and thought that systematic drill should cease with Chap. XXXIII, the end of the theory of applied *elocutio*" (2: 179).

which he made a major contribution was style." But there is little justification for Kennedy's subsequent remark—though it is a customary view—that Erasmus "was actively interested in style for its own sake."[9] Erasmus's interest in style should be understood, I propose, in light of what he actually *does* with style.[10] The Toronto translation, which I cite throughout this piece, gives it a title which seems to accord with Elizabethan use and modern neglect: *Foundations of the Abundant Style*.[11] It is easy, perhaps too easy, to read the work as a compendium of schoolroom exercises on simple verbal variety, or linguistic abundance, or even as a kind of work primarily (rather than initially) on rhetorical style. When in the first part of the work Erasmus gives 147 variations of the sentence, "Your letter

9. George A. Kennedy, *Classical Rhetoric and its Christian and Secular Tradition from Ancient to Modern Times* (Chapel Hill, 1980), 205–206. Kennedy is my example of the usual position taken by modern historians of rhetoric. Walter Ong characterizes the *De copia* along with several of Erasmus's works as participating in a general quest for *copia*, which he describes as a "make-up program for fluency" in Latin; see *Rhetoric, Romance, and Technology* (Ithaca, N.Y., 1971), 30–31. Edward P. J. Corbett in his brief survey of history states that Erasmus in the second part of *De copia* offers instruction "in the use of topics *(inventio)*" for the purposes of expressive variation; *Classical Rhetoric for the Modern Student* (New York, 1965), 546. For Sister Joan Marie Lechner, Erasmian *copia* means making themes "ample and verbose"; see *Renaissance Concepts of the Commonplaces* (New York, 1962), 178. One could group with these the historians who slight the work while acknowledging its importance: see the brief mentions by Helmut Schanze, who believes that Erasmus systematized classical rhetoric for students, and by W. Keith Percival, who believes that Erasmus closely associated rhetoric with grammatical form, in *Renaissance Eloquence*, ed. James J. Murphy (Berkeley, Calif., 1983), 118, 329; or Wilbur Samuel Howell's linkage of the work to English books on figures and tropes, in *Logic and Rhetoric in England, 1500–1700* (Princeton, N.J., 1956), 131, 137. There are, of course, exceptions to the usual positions or slights: Ong's comment that Erasmus offers a "rhetorical approach to life" is one, though Ong is not specifically referring to the *De copia* (in *Ramus, Method, and the Decay of Dialogue* [Cambridge, Mass., 1958], 291); Baldwin is an exception; so, too, is Conley, to be discussed and cited in my text. Erasmian scholars and biographers tend to offer readings closer to my own: see Cave (note 18 below); or Richard Schoeck, *Erasmus Grandescens* (Niewkoop, 1988), 99; or Johan Huizinga, *Erasmus and the Age of Reformation* (1924; repr New York, 1957), 114–115.

10. But one could also read what he actually *said* about style, as for example in one of his letters to Budé, in which he takes direct opposition to Quintilian's liking of style for its own sake and states an interest only in that style which is efficacious for recommending its subject. See *The Correspondence of Erasmus*, trans. R. A. B. Mynors and D. F. S. Thomson, annotated James K. McConica, in *Collected Works of Erasmus*, hereafter cited as CWE (Toronto, 1976—), 4: 230–234.

11. Trans. and annotated by Betty I. Knott, in CWE 24: 279–659.

pleased me very much" (348–54) it is not immediately clear that he might have intended either a tour de force or deliberate overkill. Then, too, merely linguistic abundance seems the very point of his own oft-quoted statement of his intentions, to give students the resources to "turn one idea into more shapes than Proteus himself is supposed to have turned into" (302).

Proteus as an emblem of copiousness might seem meaningful. He was, after all, the very god of changeableness and versatility.[12] However, as an emblem of Erasmus's inventive procedure, Proteus is too elusive. Exactly how does one achieve variety, abundance, and versatility? Concentrating on the figure of Proteus, the god who was so adept at changing his shape to elude capture, one might assume that the answer is through saying the same thing in different ways. But there is a deeper wellspring, a procedure at work in *De copia* as in all of Erasmus's writings on rhetorical pedagogy, that has little to do with the simple methods of synonymy, *verba,* and everything to do with *res,* the conceptual product of the multifarious but also heuristic and not infrequently scorned center of classical rhetoric, *inventio,* or how to think in a certain way about what you're doing when you create discourse.

Through exploring that wellspring we shall follow a track brilliantly laid out recently by Jardine, who provides a sound English version of Erasmus's title and full intention, "Reasoning Abundantly." The *De copia,* she has argued, was meant to be part of an Erasmian curricular revision in rhetoric when fitted into a skillfully created context, consisting of Quintilian, Seneca, and above all Agricola. Within that context the *De copia* aimed to detach the study of argumentation "from its formal, technical language-based context in the traditional schools" and open "the way to a training in persuasive and affective discourse more appropriate to the civic and

---

12. A. Bartlett Giamatti in his famous survey of the figure of Proteus in Renaissance thought, finds the figure signifying man's "ability to adapt and to act many roles" enabling him "to assume the burdens of civilization, to create cities on earth and win citizenship among the immortals"; "Proteus Unbound: Some Versions of the Sea-God in the Renaissance," in *The Disciplines of Criticism: Essays in Literary Theory, Interpretation, and History,* ed. George Demetz, Thomas Greene, William Nelson (New Haven, Conn., 1968), 439. Erasmus's own casual and to some eyes shocking reference to Christ as "Proteus" is also not irrelevant (*Ratio verae theologiae* [Basel, 1518], 214), for variety or diversity was fundamental to Erasmus's point.

forensic context of sixteenth-century education."[13] The observation
captures perfectly the shift we shall examine in the following chapter,
from dialectical to rhetorical disputation. In that chapter we shall examine at some length the context Jardine has described. Here let us continue to search Erasmus's intention through the details of *De copia*,
which along with *De conscribendis epistolis*, his book on letter-writing,
constitutes his most explicit and extensive discussion of rhetoric, the
places where we are most apt to find an enunciation of protocol.

In the most general sense, Erasmus's inventive procedure is the
protocol of speech-making. Therein, of course, we grasp the fundamental meaning of "resourcefulness." But the principles of speech-
making are also the principles of targetting one's discourse for a specific audience and occasion, and therein we move toward the conceptual level. For these latter are the principles, noted briefly in my
previous chapter, which underlie Erasmian hermeneutics. There are
many subsidiary procedures inside this general speech-making one;
as a matter of fact, Erasmus lists some eleven subsidiary procedures
(he calls them, with some irony if not contempt, "methods") in the
second, or *res*, part of *De copia*. But of these I shall concentrate on
one in particular, a feature in Erasmus which has been neglected not
only by historians but by modern educators as well: *controversia*, setting ideas into pro and con debate, matching assertion with counter-
assertion, the procedure Cicero called *argumentum in contrarias partes*,
or *in utramque partem*. Like other rhetorical features we have neglected, this one has prior connections with dialectic and disputation, matters we shall discuss in my next chapter. Though it is only
one subsidiary procedure, it is deeply indicative of traditionally rhetorical and Erasmian attitudes toward language and thought.

For this feature the figure of Janus may be a better emblem, the
Roman God of doorways, of entrances and exits, who looks in two
directions at once. Indeed, the Renaissance abounds in references to
Janus as the emblem of a person, usually a skeptic, who can see both
sides of any question.[14] The structure of Erasmus's famous school-

13. Lisa Jardine, *Erasmus, Man of Letters* (Princeton, N.J., 1993), 145.
14. Thomas Browne, for example, writing as a young medical student in *Religio
Medici*, calls "the wisest heads" those who, "almost all Sceptiks[,] stand like *Janus*
in the field of knowledge" (ed. L. C. Martin [Oxford, Eng., 1964], 66). Not only
skepticism but also prudence is connected to the Janus emblem—prudence as a middle position between two extremes, whether of time or of argument: though Victoria

book itself seems Janus-faced. The first part looks toward style *(verba)*, the second toward invention *(res)*; and the book also teaches, in its unfolding, that the two are quite different from each other, and that they require two quite different mental operations. For the first, synonymy is useful; for the second, one must understand the very basis on which synonymy could prove useful in one's creative task. The ultimate lesson of this double-faced work is that true *copia* inheres less in linguistic or even in conceptual abundance and more in the mental agility it takes to cope with that richness or abundance. Thus, one could, at some risk (knowing well that " 'Tis not for every man to go to Corinth"), put the matter in our contemporary terms, and argue that a careful reading of the work shows that Erasmus built into its structure overt means for its deconstruction. For the ostensible simplicity of the first part is challenged—if not undercut—by the principles of the second.

Perhaps the best and least misleading contemporaneity is Erasmus's: one should simply employ his own description and say that the *De copia* is structured in a "clever" way—even, as he rightly feared, too clever to be understood by all.[15] "Clever" is also the best description because, as I shall argue later, it both suggests a possible source of the book's rhetorical failure and invites a new reading of this historically most important document. Erasmus in claiming that his book is "clever" was addressing a frequent needling that he spent too much time in trivial pursuits, like writing elementary schoolbooks. But his claim is more than a rhetorical defense. For the book is "passing strange," a kind of cleverness that, I shall suggest, lies in the book's overt perversity, a perversity that arises on the simplest level from a pervasive *controversia*, wherein one may finally grasp Erasmus's full intention.

Baldwin with his usual acuteness saw the first part of Erasmus's

Kahn does not express prudence in terms of the Janus heads, one of her central images, Titian's Allegory of Prudence, contains the Janus heads; *Rhetoric, Prudence, and Skepticism in the Renaissance* (Ithaca, N.Y., 1985). A discussion of the emblematic role of Janus in rhetorical *inventio* is in my *Donne, Milton, and the End of Humanist Rhetoric* (Berkeley, Calif., 1985), 57–63.

15. Erasmus, in writing to Budé, claimed to agree with the latter's dislike of *De copia*, in spite of the fact that others have found it not only useful but clever. "Even now teachers [*literatores*] in many places complain that the work is too clever [*argutius*] to be understood by readers of moderate attainments." See CWE 4: 106; Leclerc III/I: 214 (A).

book as a work on style, the second as a work on invention. Baldwin, moreover, finds that structural pattern at work in the writings of the German humanist Sturm, who advised that boys should learn "the precepts for copy of words in *elocutio*" and then "learn the precepts for copy of things in *inventio*."[16] Baldwin's view of Erasmus's distribution of material so that the second, the *res,* part becomes a discussion of *inventio* was anticipated by another German humanist, Melanchthon; a few years after *De copia*'s publication, Melanchthon said his own theory of invention "clearly parallels" the second part of Erasmus's book.[17]

My own interpretation differs from Baldwin's, though less radically than from others I cite, in that I see *De copia* as ultimately *centering* on *inventio,* the full range of *inventio,* a centering which accounts for its structure. That centering comes about in this manner: like all of Erasmus's writing this book too continues to conceive of language as speech, as something spoken by someone to someone, and like the *De oratore* it imitates the lesson it offers (though Cicero's imitation is literally more dramatic). And that lesson is not only profoundly oral but "controversial" in nature. Even the most casual reader who stays with the book all the way to its end will note that the kind of discourse in which the book's principles culminate, as shown in its conclusion, is oratory, particularly forensic oratory. But the effects of orality and *controversia* are actually ubiquitous, texturally as well as structurally—for Erasmian theory, as Terence Cave has incisively remarked, tends "to enact (or perform) the very principles it enunciates."[18]

For example, Erasmus's first move in the book is to talk about the "dangers" of studying copiousness—a good advertising move, particularly useful in the classroom by teachers of little boys, but it is also a clear indication of a certain pervasive rhetorical principle: one should offer no brief for any subject without allowing for its possible refutation. *Copia* unless properly used could be dangerous

16. See Baldwin, *Shakespere's Small Latine,* 2: 24–25. Sturm's work is *De literarum ludis recte aperiendis,* 1538.

17. *Corpus Reformatorum,* XVI: 807; quoted in Kees Meerhoff, "The Significance of Melanchthon's Rhetoric," in *Renaissance Rhetoric,* ed. Peter Mack (New York, 1994), 47.

18. Terence Cave, *The Cornucopian Text: Problems of Writing in the French Renaissance* (Oxford, Eng., 1979), xiv.

to your rhetorical health. The point is made by means of *controversia*. Similarly, Erasmus argues, early in the book as well as in its conclusion, the curious position that *copia* is also the way to *brevity*— all one needs to learn are "the principles," for they are the same in both.[19] At least one of those principles, I am trying to argue, is that any assertion—of substance or quality—always suggests the presence of its opposite, a principle that (however much it does, or does not, resemble modern deconstruction) is the controversial heart and soul of Erasmus's understanding of traditional rhetoric and of its complex interconnections with traditional dialectic.[20]

This principle may itself be the motive of Erasmus's widely remarked penchant—in such works as *De contemptu mundi* and the *Praise of Folly*—for irony, for the volteface, or even for a self-consuming structure. In the present case, the penchant is glimpsed first in the joke Erasmus seems to have built into the full title of this book: *De duplici copia verborum ac rerum commentarii duo:* the twofold copia of words *(verborum)* and thought (or arguments, or "matter," *rerum*) in a double commentary. The title is overdone. It is wordy, verbally overabundant. So, too, is the first part, or commentary, on words, which offers instruction in simple verbal varying, through such means as synonyms and figures of speech; and the examples are tiresome, including the 147 variations of the statement "Your letter pleased me very much" and the immediately following 203 variations of "Always, as long as I live, I shall remember you." But there is less playfulness here than purpose. For it is likely that Erasmus consciously overdid the first part, with a nod toward Quintilian's instructions for the young: it is better to work with a boy who has an overly exhuberant expression than one who has an impoverished style (I.4).

19. Herein he echoes Agricola (*De inventione*, III.5), who argues that *brevitas* is produced by reversing the procedures for achieving *copia*. But an overriding principle in both works is one that automatically brings up *brevitas* at the mention of *copia*.

20. Indeed, in the world of contingency, one quality can easily transform into its opposite, as Folly notes when toying with the Silenus of Alcibides or as Erasmus implies, later in the *De copia*, that the same protocol and even the same materials may be used alike for orations of praise and for those of blame. This, too, is part of the very ground of Erasmus's dualistic argumentation, as Wolfgang G. Müller comments, presupposing as it does a world in which appearance *(Schein)* is at times the very opposite of being *(Sein):* "Das Problem von Schein und Sein in Erasmus' *Sileni Alcibiadis* und Shakespeare's *Macbeth,*" *Wolfenbütteler Renaissance Mitteilungen* 15 (April, 1991): 15.

The second part, or commentary, on arguments, is somewhat more methodological (or, rather, *ostensibly* more methodological). It is aimed at what today we might call "critical thinking" if we thought about "critical thinking" critically enough. What the first commentary would offer by way of instruction in simple verbal variety, the second commentary would call into question. Here we move away from a concentration on words and toward an absorption with those matters which are born of an "inventive," controversializing, and in this respect highly resourceful mind.

Here, too, in this second commentary we find, of course, the use of "topics," the traditional "places" of invention (e.g., analyze a statement, such as "he is a total monster" by breaking it into parts: he is a monster in mind as well as in body), features of classical rhetoric which, as I have argued, have received disproportionate attention in historical studies as well as in modern theory. But here, too, in this second commentary we also find the suggested application of *controversia* as an approach to invention, in methods 10 and 11. Actually, however, and above all, Erasmus's controversializing mind begins to be fully revealed in the structure he employs in this second half. Any method *(ratio)* usually overlaps another, as do most divisions and categories throughout the book, but even in their overlapping they show that something more than a topical system of invention is at work. They show that we are in the hands of a writer who would have us be wary of methods, systems, and theory. "This method [*ratio*]," says Erasmus over and over again, maddeningly, "is not too different from the one preceding"—but there is indeed method in such madness, and it's to make a point about the lameness of methodology in treating something as complex as creating or understanding rhetorical discourse.

One of Erasmus's examples in "method" 10 is very much to the point of my argument. For here he shows the rhetorical ease with which one can argue either side of a question. In this example, he goes to some length to explain how the schoolboy might argue *against* learning Greek: it can be an obstacle to attaining Christian happiness, it's so difficult that a lifetime is insufficient for its mastery, and those who study it seem to suffer the unhappy fate of the overthrown and oppressed Greeks. The example concludes by suggesting that the schoolboy might arrange these arguments in climactic style, much as Lucian had done in a declamation which,

Erasmus notes, he had himself recently translated from the Greek into Latin. The final tongue-in-cheek suggestion tips off Erasmus' own position, if it were not already well enough known to his readers (either through his fame or through the point he had just made in Chap. 9 of the first commentary that knowledge of Greek adds greatly to *copia*), just as the example itself tips off *one very clear principle* at work in the *De copia* or for that matter in Erasmus's rhetorical invention: Don't take anything—whether it's the value of studying Greek or the value of learning *copia* or the illusion of systematic exposition—uncritically.

The depth and reach of Erasmus's understanding of this principle can be glimpsed by juxtaposing his textbook with the rhetorical tradition of *inventio* that I have outlined in my preceding chapter. In the Ciceronian tradition, forensic oratory or the criminal trial is the conceptual model. And, as I shall note in my next two chapters, it remained the conceptual model in the schoolroom exercises in declamation and in humanist *suasoria*. Earlier I suggested that the centrality of the practice of requiring students to debate both sides of a question is made abundantly clear by Quintilian, who claims (VI.iv. 1, 3) that there is only one almost exclusively inventive activity, debate, and that the perfect orator is also the perfect debater. Erasmus obviously agrees. In one of his less "clever" and more openly revealing comments he insists that *stasis* is a vital stimulus to the rhetorical imagination (in "method" 10). One might wonder, then, what *stasis,* what controversial issue, is at question in this work. Let us approach that specific matter through the principles on which Erasmian cleverness is based. We must note, first of all, that traditional speech-making principles visualize an ongoing argumentative situation.

Once more, an important way to invent in traditional rhetoric, as Erasmus shows us, is not simply by processing ideas through the topics, but by generating arguments with one eye on the opposition. And, to go even farther in true *via diversa* fashion, by actually developing ideas on both sides of the question. Thus schoolboys in Elizabethan England were advised by their humanist schoolmasters (including Erasmus) to increase their inventive resourcefulness by preparing "copybooks." Indeed, Erasmus laments in "method" 11 that his own youth had been deprived of the practice. Not only were these copybooks full of famous sayings and *sententiae,* like a rudimentary *Bartlett's,* but they also listed arguments pro and con (under such topical questions as Whether a man should marry, and Whether a woman should be taught rhetoric). Several of these books have come down to us, Bacon's and Milton's being perhaps the most notable examples. The tradition of "copy," linked as it is with pro and con argumentation, itself linked in turn with educational disputation (oral debates, not written themes, were the final exams in Elizabethan Oxbridge, as I shall discuss in my next chapter), perhaps preserved *controversia* in *inventio* well beyond Erasmus's efforts to instill it or the Englishman's reluctance to read much more than the first part of *De copia.*

Having lost the full range of "copy," we now might more accurately translate Erasmus's title, as Terence Cave suggests, as simply "Rhetoric" (19). A good title, for Erasmus's implicit claim is that "rhetoric" means not simply finding something to say but also thinking in certain ways. Let us recall, too, that *copia* is Cicero's word for specifically *rhetorical* language: it is a linguistic and conceptual resourcefulness which marks the difference between rhetoric and dialectic (see *Brutus,* lxxii.253). It is also the chief quality wherein Crassus excelled over Antonius, as Cicero suggests in the same dialogue (xxxviii.144). It is a quality which belongs to eloquence *(eloqui)* as opposed to simply but accurately "speaking" *(loqui).* But *without* dialectic, that is without more than fundamental skills in disputation, eloquence itself is impossible (xc.309). And thus copiousness, rightly understood, is also impossible. Copiousness is thus the capstone of rhetorical achievement, and its wellsprings as Erasmus cleverly knew run much more deeply than simple synonymy.

Foundations of the abundant style? The title is acceptable if we place the emphasis upon *foundations* and allow "style" to mean, in the most specific sense, one of the five complex and interrelated offices of rhetoric, and, in the most general Ciceronian and thoroughly Erasmian sense, the inventive and resourceful impress upon a discourse of the person speaking. For Erasmus and his rhetorical progenitors, the point of the schoolroom exercise in *copia* was always more than simply verbal or even argumentative abundance. It was part of the process whereby one was taught, as a means of resourcefulness, skill in *controversia,* with all that that skill implies for inculcating what Richard Lanham has so vividly described as "the rhetorical paideia."[21] Erasmus, who always thought more in ethical than in cultural terms, considered "character" the end and purpose of education—*vir bonus dicendi peritus,* as Quintilian put it, the good man skilled in speaking. The lesson became particularly pointed when Erasmus spoke of the education of theologians, those students most prone to aridity and dogmatism: "Do not believe that you are making progress if you dispute more acutely," he said, "but only when you become aware that you are gradually becoming another person."[22] Once more, as in Cicero, the ideal becomes personalized and aimed ultimately at one's morals and ethics, whether one is speaking of disputation or copiousness. The ultimate aim of the work is a person who has resourcefulness and knows how to handle it.

I shall return to these points, but for the present I wish to center my remarks on this argument: the close connection between rhetoric and education is vital to the historian and to the modern student as well in endeavoring to understand not only what rhetoric was and is but what it yet can be. "The very instability of the 'rhetorical tradition,'" William Covino has recently remarked, "its very indeterminacy, if you will, should alert us to the relationship among versions of history, conceptions of literacy, and teaching."[23] Covino, moreover, insists as I do that the great documents of our history—*Phaedrus,* the *Rhetoric, De oratore*—should be read in terms of what they do as well as what they say. When he so reads, he finds indeterminacy and ambiguity, or a certain inconclusiveness which he believes to be the very point of rhetorical inquiry. "The art of wondering," Covino calls it. But my concern lies in tracking that "wonder" through such strategies as parody, imitation, and "literary criticism" and through such figures as paradox and litotes to the mental habits which produced them, habits which I believe were

21. Richard A. Lanham, "The 'Q' Question," *South Atlantic Quarterly* 87 (1988): 657. Moreover, in light of Bouwsma's argument (cited in my previous chapter), the paideia involved could be called "Sophist Culture." Such, at least, would seem to be Nietzsche's preferred term; see *Twilight of the Idols,* trans. R. I. Hollingdale (London, 1990), 117.

22. In the *Ratio verae theologiae.* The translation is in Cornelis Augustijn, *Erasmus: His Life, Works, and Influence,* trans. J. C. Grayson (Toronto, 1991), 86.

23. William A. Covino, *The Art of Wondering: A Revisionist Return to the History of Rhetoric* (Portsmouth, N.H., 1988), 2.

engendered in part by the educational practice of pro-con argumentation. These habits pervade even the schoolbooks—or at least the best, the most "clever" of them. And all, habits and schoolbooks alike, have as their goal resourcefulness and, beyond that, the shaping of character.

Of the classic rhetorical documents I have adverted to so far in this book, all are either schoolbooks or discussions of rhetorical education, with the arguable exception of Plato. For whom were they written, what is their intention, and what use was made of them? So far as the actual schoolbooks are concerned, these questions may all be, literally, rhetorical. But answers to at least the second of these questions, concerning intention, can suggest some revisionary perspectives on the books themselves while raising the further question as to whether their lessons are yet lost on us.

As noted earlier, if rapaciousness deflected Erasmus's aim in the sixteenth century, custom deflects it now. Undoubtedly there are a host of reasons. Perhaps foremost among these is the ongoing, culminating, and (for rhetoric) far too rigid distinction between the oral and the written, including the so-called decay of our "oratorical culture."[24] Too, the interconnections of rhetoric and pro-con debate, which were deeply a part of the Erasmian, or for that matter humanist, revival of Ciceronianism, have become gradually attenuated through recent centuries: particularly in America, debate has had little role in modern rhetorical theory and virtually no role in the modern composition classroom, to the impoverishment of our theories of *inventio*. Modern pedagogical concerns are somewhat beyond my scope in this chapter, but I bring them up again because they seem related to our historical understanding, to our failure to learn the lesson in at least one great schoolbook by neglecting to read it rhetorically—that is, by neglecting to read it not simply contextually as a kind of occasional piece but also performatively as a kind of enactment of its own meaning, attending not simply to what it says but also to the way in which it says it. Two recent histories, both sensitive to the close connections between rhetoric and education, further illustrate my point.

Thomas M. Conley's *Rhetoric in the European Tradition* (New York,

---

24. Gerald Graff discusses the decay of the "oratorical culture" and the rise of the English profession in *Professing Literature* (Chicago, 1987), chapter 3.

1990) is a comprehensive survey of the subject, extending from the Sophists through McKeon, Toulmin, Perelman, and Habermas. Such comprehensiveness necessarily runs the risks of compression and omission, two risks that the work itself largely escapes, perhaps because of Conley's explicit interest in pedagogy (including the modern rhetoric classroom) as well as his pursuit of certain "thematic principles": he has no singular, overriding concept of "rhetoric" as a stable identity but has looked primarily for concepts of the subject which adhere to "times of strife and crisis, political or intellectual" (viii). His reading of *De oratore* (36–38) is, though brief, a particularly satisfying review of the major ideas in that crisis-borne document. Too, perhaps because of his "thematic principles," Conley gives major importance to *controversia* as a rhetorical genre and to the practice of *in utramque partem* argumentation; and, perhaps because of his concentration on pedagogy, he likewise gives major importance to disputation.

But Conley's treatment of Erasmus is curiously foreshortened. He begins with the observation that "Erasmus was not a professional rhetorician, nor did he ever write a treatise on rhetoric" (120), statements which are only superficially true. He prefers to characterize Erasmus as "[o]ne of the most conspicuous and controversial theologians of his time" (120), using a term that might have caused Erasmus himself to wince. Conley finds the major principles of Erasmian rhetoric in *The Praise of Folly* and in the debate with Martin Luther on the freedom of the will. The former, he says, is a "paradigm of the old humanist cast of mind," and he astutely points out that the work places the final act of judgment on the reader, "a sorting out of competing views" (121; thus, without using the term, Conley places *Folly* in the genre of *via diversa,* which I shall attempt to describe in Chapter 5). The latter, the conflict between Erasmus and Luther, was, Conley states, "a conflict between two quite different mentalities," with Erasmus insisting on "establishing and comparing probabilities" and Luther "playing out the consequences, grim as they may be, of utter certainties" (124). Unquestionably Conley has uncovered certain major principles of Erasmian rhetoric.

But, like the remark with which he begins his discussion of Erasmus, Conley's reading of the *De copia* does not seem based on those principles of Erasmian rhetoric which he has so carefully pointed out in other documents. The work, he says, was

> a treatise designed to inculcate linguistic sensitivity and fluency, which would enable speakers or writers not only to achieve an impressive ability to say the same things in different ways but to have at their disposal a fund of expressions that could be tapped according to the situational demands they might encounter. (120)

The observation is accurate, but only for the length it extends, which is not very far. The foreshortening I have mentioned is in Conley's own view, a view that fails to extend not only his perceptive sense of Erasmus's "humanist mentality" but also his, Conley's, sensitive reading of Cicero. For pedagogically and rhetorically the *De copia* stands close to the *De oratore*. Both share the view that rhetoric is no less complex an undertaking than education itself is. Both agree that rhetoric's inventional process is reducible to little systematizing beyond such fundamental operations as pro-con reasoning or circumstantial analysis and argument. And the difficulty of teaching rhetoric is further compounded, in both *De oratore* and *De copia,* by the necessity to teach the importance of holding debatable truths *provisionally:* thus the *De oratore* by design frustrates the seeker after handbooks; and the *De copia* equally confounds any (late medieval) systematizer with its divisions and categories that are fluid and that are often not subordinate but disparate parts of an apparently indefinable whole. Cicero's dialogue ends with a discussion of style; Erasmus's enterprise begins with style. Both center in *inventio*—and both documents invite an often dispiriting contrast between the authors' intentions and the uses to which the documents have been, and continue to be, put.

Barbara Bauer's stimulating study of developments in rhetoric in the seventeenth century concentrates on curricula and pedagogues. She traces the flowering of the Jesuitical *ars rhetorica* and its transformation of the humanist ideal of eloquence. Her scope is, thus, narrower than Conley's and more focussed, and her reading of *De copia* much more intensive. Illuminating as her argument is, it is nonetheless hampered in its restrictive view of what she has accurately selected as the central document in the construction of the humanist ideal, that is, Erasmus's *De copia*. Erasmus's intention, she finds, is essentially conservative and ornamental, the production of a somewhat expansive copiousness which reconstructed medieval style for the rather more attic eloquence of humanism.

Erasmus's work, she states, "stands on the threshold" between two periods. "Still in familiar medieval raiment, which gives almost exclusive preference to figural and tropical *exornatio* and *amplificatio,* Erasmus compiled exercises in stylistic examples and methodical pieces of advice. These nevertheless served a new humanistic ideal of *elegantia,* speech with an attic clarity which did not depend upon an arrangement swollen with figures of style."[25] In Bauer's view, the narrowness of medieval textbooks is exceeded in the first part of Erasmus's book through his congeries of paraphrases and circumlocutions and in the second through his recommendation, possibly under the influence of Agricola, that examples be collected dialectically by means of commonplaces and through his detailed suggestions for assembling parables, allegories, and antique models of style.[26] Erasmus, states Bauer, had no particular interest in reforming rhetorical theory. His little interest along these lines, as measured by the sort of Roman rhetoric "proposed by Crassus and Antonius in Cicero's *De oratore,* is shown by his readiness to include Geoffrey of Vinsauf alongside Horace and Quintilian in the ranks of rhetorical masters."[27] It was, in sum, less his pedagogy *(Lehrmethode)* which made Erasmus a representative of humanist rhetoric than his service as a conduit of classicism.

Again, Bauer's reading is excellent as far as it goes. But it doesn't go quite far enough, and I believe mislocates the irony at its center: Erasmus, who seems caught up in the medieval love of ornament,

25. Barbara Bauer, *Jesuitische 'ars rhetorica' im Zeitalter der Glaubenskämpfe* (Frankfurt, 1986), 122: "Erasmus' 'Copia' steht an der Schwelle zwischen den mittelalterlichen 'Artes dictaminis' bzw. Poetiken und der neuzeitlichen humanistischen Rhetorik. . . . Noch im vertrauten mittelalterlichen Gewande, das fast ausschlielich die figurale und tropische exornatio und amplificatio berücksichtigte, trug Erasmus stilistische Übungsbeispiele und methodische Ratschläge zusammen, die der Verwirklichung eines gleichwohl neuen humanistischen elegantia-Ideals einer attisch klaren, nicht durch figuralen tumor verunstalteten Rede dienten."
26. Bauer, 124: "Auch das zweite Buch, in dem Erasmus möglicherweise unter dem Einfluß Rudolf Agricolas (1443–1485) mit Hilfe von loci communes eine dialektische Suchmethode zum Sammeln von exempla empfiehlt und anschließend die Parabel, Allegorie und imitatio antiker Stilmuster ausführlich erörtert, geht über den engen elocutio-Rahmen mittelalterlicher Lehrbücher hinaus."
27. Bauer, 122–3: "Wie wenig es Erasmus um Reformen auf dem Gebiet rhetorischer Theorienbildung im Sinne der römischen Redekunst ging, wie sie Crassus und Antonius in Ciceros Dialog 'De oratore' votrugen, zeigt seine Bereitschaft, Geoffroi de Vinsauf neben Horaz und Quintilian in die Reihe der Rhetorik-Autoritäten aufzunehmen."

she claims, all inadvertently prepared the way for the attic clarity of the humanist ideal largely through extending his copiousness to include not simply elements of style but argumentative commonplaces as well, and through giving prominence to ancient models of discourse. On the contrary, a rhetorical reading of Erasmus's book could preserve the irony between its ostensible intention and the uses to which it was put, but the irony would be relocated. For such a reading would take cognizance of the book's primary audience, schoolmasters who themselves were steeped in medieval rhetoric and dialectic and were perhaps more familiar with Geoffrey than with Quintilian. Erasmus's task becomes one of moving that audience from familiar ground to less familiar, as part of his intention of showing them that rhetoric encompasses not merely style but invention as well. The book thus becomes an inventive performance, an oration aimed at reconstructing the true nature of traditional rhetoric by opening up a common ground between the orator (Erasmus) and his audience (schoolmasters) in a shared love of style. Such a reading would also take cognizance—as I have tried to do from the outset of this chapter—of the countermoves Erasmus has built into his work, the initial move to warn of the dangers of *copia,* the lesson that copiousness is also the way to brevity, the structure that demonstrates two-sided argument. The irony would therefore lie in the historical undoing of his intention: whereas the English seemed to have read mainly the first part of the book and seldom wandered off the common ground, the Jesuits concentrated on the second part but transformed the ideal of eloquence therein into something totally ancillary to Erasmus's actual intention.

In many ways, Conley and Bauer, like certain other historians I have cited, demonstrate the *De copia*'s rhetorical failure: if it failed to succeed in fulfilling those intentions I and certain other historians have found in it, it nonetheless captured favorable attention and influence largely through the vocabulary-building or incidental uses to which it could be put. Perhaps it was doomed to failure. For the *De copia,* like much humanism, ultimately collided with a new movement away from the linguistic and philosophical presuppositions on which it was built. Humanist propensity for nominalism and skepticism was not viable either in the *Glaubenskämpfe,* the Reformation and Counter-reformation which ended the period of Erasmus, or in the new scientism which in the eyes of many closed the Renaissance and ended forever its "high humanism." The explanation, of course, does not foreclose the possibility of yet reading the book along the lines I have suggested. Two final questions remain: If my reading of Erasmus is accurate, what uses can it serve?; and, once more, what exactly does it tell us about what Erasmus was up to?

First, my argument might help us interpret other documents of the period. The kind of inventiveness the *De copia* teaches links it with such Erasmian masterpieces as the *Praise of Folly,* with continuing traditions in "debate poetry," and with the controversializing in Tudor drama[28]—or with such curious documents as Anthony Munday's *Defense of Contraries* and the pervasive Elizabethan absorption with paradox and litotes, and with the communicative cleverness scholars have found in Puttenham. Rereading some of these latter documents will be my effort in Chapter 5 below.

Too my argument just might serve pedagogical purposes. It may be significant that no recent book on rhetoric and composition, not one written within the last fifty years, has urged a restoration of debate, of pro and con argumentation. At least, American rhetoric is generally silent on the matter. But this is the very matter which begs for reconsideration, particularly in the composition classroom, not simply because it is an essential feature of the classical tradition but more importantly because it is a possible way, as Erasmus claimed, of enriching students' invention. But could one actually bring debating—above all, oral debating—back as a classroom exercise? Again, the question lies beyond the scope of the task I have assumed in this chapter, though I shall recur to this entire matter in my final chapter. But there is a related classroom exercise whose purpose has bearing on my second question above, concerning Erasmus's intention.

In his textbook on letter-writing, which like the *De copia* was a widely used elementary textbook,[29] Erasmus is far more assertive—uncharacteristically so, and so less "clever"—about his rhetorical pedagogy, and the assertions can be more than a little surprising, if not shocking, to the modern ear: "nothing is so inherently good," he states, "that it cannot be made to seem bad by a gifted speaker."

28. See Thomas L. Reed, Jr. *Medieval English Debate Poetry and the Aesthetics of Irresolution* (Columbia, Mo., 1990). For the controversializing in Tudor drama see Joel B. Altman, *The Tudor Play of Mind* (Berkeley, Calif., 1979).

29. It was, for example, according to Charles J. Lees, the "chief" textbook for letter writing at Eton; see *The Poetry of Walter Haddon* (The Hague, 1967), 13.

(The idea seems to connect with similar sentiments in Rorty and Hamlet; see my preceding chapter). The advice appears in Erasmus's instruction to the teacher to have boys write "recantations" of arguments which they had just handed in. The assignment is itself another kind of debate, of *controversia*.

The point is that "By such practice both fluency and readiness in speaking on any topic will be acquired."[30] Again, copiousness is the point, and it is not simply "fluency," or "the abundant style," but "readiness," resourcefulness, or quickness and fecundity. Too, aside from the practical pedagogy involved, Erasmus's assertions here clarify the function of two-sided argumentation in the *De copia*—including the bald advice in "method" 11 that material can actually be "twisted" *[torqueri possunt]* to serve opposite purposes:

> If you were praising a man for all seasons, endowed with a versatile and dexterous mind, you could dip into your 'inconstancy' cupboard and bring out the polyp which changes colour according to the surface beneath it, and then the Euripus, saying that this sea is not so versatile as this man's mind. You could bring out the flame which cannot stand still, the sky . . . (p. 647)

The word "twist" (*torqueo*—the source of our legal term "tort") is exactly the one Folly uses in complaining that St. Paul tampered with evidence.[31] Folly's complaint centers on the rhetorical distortion of a text, whereas Erasmus's teaching throughout the textbook on letter-writing as well as throughout the *De copia* centers on the rhetorical interpretation of a phenomenon or a characteristic. Tampering with evidence is not allowed, whereas rhetorical interpretation is further evidence of abundance and mental versatility—which may itself be used in controverting and even twisting the praise of those very qualities.

Such is Erasmus's understanding of a thoroughly traditional heuristic. Perhaps the extent to which that heuristic invites the charge that one would thereby teach merely glibness or insincerity measures

---

30. "On the Writing of Letters" *(De conscribendis epistolis),* trans. Charles Fantazzi, CWE 25: 145–46.

31. ". . . *torqueret in argumentum fidei Christianae*"; Leclerc, IV: 492. Folly complains that St. Paul suppressed the full inscription at the base of the statue on Mars Hill in order to quote only that part which served his case: "to the unknown god." See Clarence H. Miller, trans. *The Praise of Folly* (New Haven, Conn, 1979), 124.

not simply the extent to which we have neglected invention and what our ancestors meant by *copia* but, more importantly perhaps, the extent to which we have neglected rhetorical paedaeia itself.

But let me face that possible charge and conclude with a proleptic example, one that will also more directly address my second question, by returning to an early passage in the first part of the *De copia,* on obscene language. Erasmus begins with a general statement, quite appropriately, one might imagine, for a cleric writing for schoolmasters who would instruct little boys in a cathedral school: "Indecent words should be utterly unknown to Christian speech."[32] There follow, however, copious examples of obscenity (e.g., in the English translation, "piss," "shit," "cunt"), sure to provoke the attention of any schoolmaster, with some choice Latin phrases that he might not have heard himself. Reading the passage today, one might wonder about Erasmus's own perversity: if the book is meant to be Christian speech, what is all this obscenity doing in it? But on reflection, Erasmus's purpose becomes clear: it is to make his reader engage in, and then teach, the kind of critical thinking which is at the heart of this "clever" book. Erasmus here makes two points: sometimes obscene words can be used, sometimes they cannot be used—it all depends, as does everything in rhetoric, on audience and occasion. The second point is that one must always beware of flatly dogmatic statements, like the one that insists that indecency should always be utterly avoided by Christians. The one point leads to the other: because context is all, thinking rhetorically deflates the categorical assertion.

Therein one begins to move toward the very heart of Erasmian rhetorical education, the true aim of which was always the development of character. Resourcefulness was not exactly an end in itself. As a protocol, Erasmian copiousness is another way of exploring the *via diversa.* It was meant to educate a versatile mind whose rich resources of language and flexible skill in argument were bulwarks against that narrowness of vision which, in Erasmus's lexicon as well

---

32. The assertion is more forceful in the Latin (*Obscoenas voces oportet ab omni Christianorum sermone procul abesse,* Leclerc, I: 11[D]), partly because *voces* is more comprehensive than "words," partly because *abesse* aims more at avoidance than ignorance, and partly because the assertion comprises an entire thought, i.e., it ends with a period and does not, as in the Toronto translation, comprise the first part of a compound sentence.

as in ours, is called authoritarianism. Here, in sum, is my statement of Erasmus's intention, an intention which differs not at all from his intention in other "clever" works, like *The Praise of Folly.* Erasmus's adversary is the authoritarian. The *stasis* of the dispute centers on protocol, how one is meant to use and respond to language. The work offers a pattern, if such it can be called, in how to think controversially, or critically.

A modern historian has suggested that part of Erasmus's aim may have been even more specific. The attitudinal rigidity and prudishness of the book's financial begetter, John Colet of St. Paul's School, may have been the author's immediate target. Dean Colet had certain authoritarian ideas about proper pedagogical behavior, and so he put limits on the teacher's use of the pagan classics and prohibited from the classroom any mention of sex. It may have been his realization of the very subversiveness of the *De copia* which caused him to delay the payment of Erasmus's commission.[33] If so, the book's intention was initially well grasped, in some quarters at least, and the *De copia* deserves to be hailed as a "textbook" example of a partially successful effort to undermine administrative intransigence. It is gratifying to note that Erasmus finally did get paid, and without suing. And it may be amusing as well as significant to note that, concerning Colet's straight-laced demeanor, Erasmus ultimately offered a purely contrarian justification of it: if the Dean was a prude, he argued, it was only because he recognized in himself such strong tendencies in the other direction.[34]

" 'Tis not for every man to go to Corinth"—the adage is offered in the opening sentences of the *De copia* to illustrate risk; it appears later (I, cap. 50) as an illustration of precision, and yet a third time (cap. 154) as a means of expressing someone's luck. Dredging up pagan antiquity is only part of its function. An affront to readers schooled in the ways of non-Erasmian prudery, the adage could recall the lesson on obscenity: a proverb from Horace's *Epistles,* it literally and primarily refers to the high fees charged by the famous Corinthian whore Lais, who demanded money on the barrel-head regard-

---

33. John B. Gleason, *John Colet* (Berkeley, Calif., 1989), 230–31.

34. See Erasmus's letter to Jodocus Jonas (13 June 1521); in John C. Olin, *Christian Humanism and the Reformation, Selected Writings of Erasmus* (New York, 1987), esp. 171. There is, of course, no reason to assume that Erasmus was here writing an objective life of Colet; the point has been most forcibly made by Gleason, 4–5.

less of how distinguished the prospective client.[35] With or without that knowledge, flexibility is the obvious lesson in Erasmus's repeated use of the adage, a Protean flexibility to be conditioned—that is, determined as well as delimited—by the Janus-like, controversializing, intellectual means of rhetoric.

That means above all others is at work in the *De copia,* however much the book failed to achieve Erasmus's general aim and however much it was put to other uses. If there is irony in my own argument, it lies here: the aim of Erasmus's book is only realized when it is read by that means which so marked his own intellectual approach, at least in this most important schoolbook, by thinking about it rhetorically, as performance. For he sought in this book cleverly, perhaps too cleverly, to teach the very means by which the book itself is meant to be read.

35. Erasmus also uses it, in another work, to refer to the dangerous navigational approach to Corinth; see *Adagia*. I. iv. I (CWE 31: 317–19).

4. Disputatiousness[1]

One of Erasmus's most famous letters was written, he claimed, simply for the amusement of his young pupil and patron, his "Maecenas," he called him,[2] Lord Mountjoy. The letter urges the young Englishman to marry, for all the stock reasons—companionship of a woman, perpetuation of the family name, fulfillment of God's command. But once the letter was made public, as many of Erasmus's letters were, his stated reason for writing it would probably not bear up in court. To begin with, this largely advisory epistle is quite "topical"—not in the sense of using many "topics," though it does that, but in the sense of being aimed at contemporary issues. It is far more topical in that sense than, say, Petrarch's similar though shorter letter to his own Maecenas, Pandolfo Malatesta. Too, Erasmus's letter, however much it might have been designed for a peculiarly scholarly type of amusement, seems highly and often seriously disputatious. Indeed, it was its apparent disputatiousness which

1. Some materials in this chapter originally appeared in "Rhetorical Education and Two-Sided Argument," *Renaissance Rhetoric,* 1993, ed. Heinrich F. Plett, reused with permission of Prof. Dr. Plett and Walter de Gruyter & Co. of Berlin; and in "The Never-Ending Dispute: A Proposal of Marriage," *The Rhetoric Canon,* ed. Brenda Schildgen, 1997, reused with permission of Prof. Schildgen and of Wayne State University Press.

2. See CWE, Vol. 4: *The Correspondence of Erasmus,* trans. R. A. B. Mynors and D. F. S. Thomson, annotated by James K. McConica (Toronto, 1977), 249.

caused the letter to become both famous and notorious. To certain eyes, it told tales out of school, and Erasmus's claim about his intentions seemed all too characteristically disingenuous.

Modern readers of the letter cannot fail to notice Erasmus's frequent use of prolepsis, or anticipatory refutation. Certain of these proleptic arguments seem to indicate that he was perhaps indeed aiming at some larger target than this young man's vow to live a single life. Mountjoy, Erasmus notes at the outset of the letter, had reportedly made the vow either out of grief (his parents had recently died) or for the sake of religion (his sister, apparently out of the same grief, had entered a nunnery). It was of course Erasmus's proleptic attack upon the latter reason which caused the most trouble. When the letter was published in 1518, it outraged a large group of theologians who claimed that Erasmus had virtually mounted a public platform to attack some of their most cherished beliefs. Intellectual amusement, the letter's purported intention, was beside the point. And the author's vaunted ambition, his sought-after role as humanist educator, and his own monkish vows were not enough.[3] Or perhaps they were too much, for they seemed to become the very rationale and center of churchly furor.

A schoolroom exercise in rhetoric or a scholarly disquisition on a current topic? The dividing line between the two, as most humanists realized to their immense satisfaction, could be ephemeral—and in the classroom should be. But the real issue at stake, I shall argue, the *stasis* of the dispute the letter itself generated, lies elsewhere. First, however, let us continue to examine the surfaces of the controversy, for even these give us glimpses into the nature of humanist education.

On the surface, Erasmus's schoolmasterly claims have some substance. As we noted, the epistle is "topical" in the other, more technical sense. It makes explicit use of certain "topics" of invention, e.g. "honest," "profitable," "necessary." In the text of the letter Erasmus actually names these topics and other stock issues, as if showing his student how they may be used in a protracted argument. Then, too, Erasmus's title would seem to place the letter at a far remove

3. For Erasmus's ambition and some of its public recognition at the time, see Lisa Jardine, *Erasmus, Man of Letters* (Princeton, N.J., 1993). In correspondence with Budé (CWE, 4: 103) Erasmus has an amusing remark about his own chastity, confessing to marriage with only one "wife," poverty.

from any hostile intention: *Declamatio in genere suasoria de laude matrimonii*—he called it "a declamation of the suasory kind, affirming matrimony." The *declamatio* was a setpiece in traditional education, designed to teach boys by example the offices of rhetoric (see Figure 2). It had two major forms or genres. Of these the *suasoria* was overtly and literally the less controversial. Unlike the *controversia,* which is adversarial and legalistic, the *suasoria* could be a friendly, advice-giving form of argument—although, like all distinctions in rhetoric, these too are tenuous and depend upon the nature of the audience, actual or ostensible. But at the very least, the title itself and the overt use of topics would seem to affirm Erasmus's stated intentions: the piece was no more than a rhetorical tour-de-force, an almost nugatory essay prepared by a master for the instruction of a neophyte.

However, the superficiality (to say nothing, for the moment, of the historical innocence) of those views could make Erasmus's claim all the more ironic. To begin with, the topics of invention, like the "predicables and predicaments" of logic were in such common currency that their appearance in speech could be more argumentatively emphatic than pedagogically conspicuous.[4] They could serve to flag or signpost points for an audience, most effectively so for one with some learning in rhetoric. Consider too that the conceptual model of Ciceronian/Erasmian rhetoric is forensic oratory, the courtroom trial. And that means that even the gentler *suasoria* (we shall take up these matters later) was based on a lawyerly kind of disputation. In fact, the tradition which the humanists prized not only conflated *controversia* with *suasoria* but also did not posit generic distinctions between argument and other forms of discourse: that is, all discourse argued and was invented by, among other means, pro-con reasoning. Then too, as noted, the humanists insisted that even schoolroom exercises, like declamations, should have bearing on "outside"

---

4. An example from Wilson's *Discourse upon Usury:* "an usurer doth lick with his tongue like a serpent and stingeth like a scorpion, and seeketh ever, like an angry or roaring lion, whom he may devour, being a false deceitful beast throughout all the *predicaments,* that is to say in every part of him, and in every action that he taketh in hand . . ." (R. H. Tawney, ed. [London, 1925], 328; emphasis mine). A groundbreaking study which makes a point similar to mine about the use of logical terms and rhetorical figures for meaning and emphasis is Sister Miriam Joseph, *Shakespeare's Use of the Arts of Language* (Ithaca, N.Y., 1947).

(what our students yet call "real world" as opposed to "academic world") matters.[5] When the humanists used the word "academic," they tended to mean (as did Cicero and even St. Augustine) "skeptical"; they decidedly did not mean "at a remove from current issues." What the humanists seemed to abhor was very much what our own students in the 1960s and 70s claimed they abhorred too, educational irrelevance. In the case of Erasmus's letter, chief among those outside or "real world" matters was celibacy, particularly priestly celibacy.

Little wonder, then, that theologians of the time huffed and puffed when they read the letter. For they found it not at all amusing—like an imitation, or even parody, of educational disputation—but intentionally threatening. And so they censured it heavily. As early as 1519 the vicechancellor of the University of Louvain publicly judged it a weighty attack on the blessedness of celibacy. The letter was to reappear several times nonetheless, usually under its more popular and more pointed title, the *Encomium matrimonii*—a title which makes the discourse an oration offered in explicit praise of marriage and which for some readers surely made it echo Erasmus's earlier and much more notorious oration, *Encomium moriae,* "The Praise of Folly" (1511).

For at least a decade Erasmus's praise of marriage enjoyed not only considerable vogue but also continued, formal condemnation by the Church.[6] Thus, the letter's contemporary reception plus its more pointed title might confirm impressions that its author had indeed a veiled or at least a collateral intention: if the Church was not Erasmus's "true" audience, this troublesome monk had nonetheless seized the opportunity once more to needle ecclesiastical authority. But these conjectures keep us once more on the surface and obscure the central point. We have not located the *stasis* of the dispute because we have not as yet grasped the actual subject of the issue at stake.

Erasmus's response to his critics gives us yet another view of that possible subject—another view, that is, of the debate his letter sought to enter and thus another view of the actual "marriage" his letter may propose. His defense begins ingenuously enough. He tried to

5. One of the best discussions of this point is Marc van der Poel's *De "declamatio" bij de humanisten* (Nieuwkoop, 1987); contains a summary in English.

6. For a brief review of the conflict, see Charles Fantazzi's note to his translation of the epistle: CWE, 26: 528–29.

Figure 2: Rhetoric and Dialectic

RHETORIC: *public speaking (and writing)*

Traditional ends: to teach, to please, to move (i.e., suasion and persuasion)

Traditional offices, or compositional procedures:
 1. *inventio*: reviewing the available material and finding arguments suitable for speaker, audience, and occasion.
      e.g. topics, *stasis*, amplification, pro-con reasoning.
 2. *dispositio*: arranging arguments into a discourse.
      e.g. the parts of an oration.
 3. *elocutio*: giving arguments a style.
      e.g. the figures of speech.
 4. *memoria*: making arguments memorable.
      i.e. for the orator as well as the audience.
 5. *actio*: delivering arguments.
      i.e. through voice and gesture.
      From 1747 to 1940 or so called *elocution*.

(The best review of these is in Cicero's *De oratore*, I.xxxi. 142–143; but see also my Chapter 6 and Appendix A.)

DIALECTIC: dialogical reasoning

Traditional ends: to define, to divide, to construct formally valid arguments, to analyze fallacies.

Traditional offices:
 1. *iudicium* (sometimes called *dispositio*): framing the question for debate.
      e.g. the proposition.
 2. *inventio*: analyzing the question.
      e.g. topics (predicables and predicaments), forms of argument, pro-con reasoning.

(The best review of these is in Wilson: see my Chapter 6 and Appendix A.)

---

appear as a schoolmaster, he claims, doing what most (humanist) schoolmasters of the time did, imparting skills in disputation, especially rhetorical disputation. This was simply an amusing example, he argues, of how one might advance one side of the case. To a narrow theologian who heard only Erasmus the cleric voice the letter to Mountjoy, Erasmus replies, "No. A layman talks to a layman" in that discourse.[7] In that discourse he was speaking not *ex cathedra*

---

7. *Apolicia de laude matrimonii*, ed. Leclerc, IX: 108(A). On this point, see Walter M. Gordon, *Humanist Play and Belief: The Seriocomic Art of Desiderius Erasmus* (Toronto, 1990), 234.

but (literally) out of school—just as, in a sense, his enemies feared he was. And then Erasmus's defense goes yet farther, to seize a certain recurring occasion, wherein he radically departs from his predecessors in humanist apologetics, Petrarch, Jerome, and Augustine, and uncovers what he takes to be the issue at stake.

As always, when his major antagonists were his contemporary theologians, Erasmus eventually takes a singular stance: theologians are notoriously unreliable interpreters of any document, he argues, because they are also notoriously unsympathetic to the classical world and its rhetoric. They refuse to learn what the ancients could teach us not simply about argument but about meaning itself. This defense—which, obviously, thrusts as well as parries—appears in his apologies for *Encomium moriae,* for his Paraphrases of Paul, among other pieces, and in his 1519 *apologia* for his so-called encomium on matrimony.[8]

True, the entire apology is actually premised on the claim that the epistle to Mountjoy was simply a rhetorical exercise. But in the Erasmian view there is nothing simple about a rhetorical exercise. Note that the premise suggests that rhetorical exercise itself may be the subject of the real issues at stake. As if to prove his initial claim, Erasmus argues that, like a good rhetorician, he had also written a counterargument *against* matrimony (which subsequently appeared in his textbook on letterwriting). Apparently, then, he was "simply" training his student in a kind of disputatious "invention," an educational essential. (Further substantiation of his defense, though he does not use it, was that, as we shall note later, one of the most popular schoolroom exercises for boys was to argue pro and con on the subject of marriage.) But his apology would not rest there. He had to connect it to a range of issues, returning to his chief (premised and, for that matter, usual) point, and press it once more against a seemingly impenetrable obtuseness: he advises that any interpreter should always get down to cases and understand arguments in terms of their contexts. Consider, he says, not simply the speech but the speaker, the occasion, the audience, and the examples; consider, in

---

8. Potentially adding to the sharpness of the argument on the other side, the side of the antagonists, though not formally a part of it on either side, is that Erasmus's letter to Mountjoy actually incorporates an earlier encomium on matrimony (c. 1498); see Craig. R. Thompson, *The Colloquies of Erasmus* (Chicago, 1965), 99–100.

short, the *rhetorical context*. This is Erasmus's perpetual lesson.[9] So viewed, he seems to insist, his letter loses the sting certain readers have found in it. Rhetorical exercise or not, all he was trying to claim, the very crux of his published argument, is that marriage may be best for Mountjoy but not necessarily for all people. Thus, in its range of issues, Erasmus's final point concerns not simply the importance of rhetorical exercises but the importance of rhetorical reading as well. Herein lies the *stasis* of the dispute.

Erasmus had turned and returned the argument to his ongoing defense of rhetorical paideia. Of course, like all his apologies, this one too is not simple—and neither are its implications, whether in regard to scriptural hermeneutics (where, as we have seen, Erasmus makes a similar point) or in regard to that profession which so frequently engaged his mind, the education of the young. What Erasmus offers young students is exactly what he usually counterpoises against all his theological attackers, a rhetorical cast of mind. Some of its chief elements we have already noted: an abhorrence of depersonalized argument, an insistence that one always get down to cases, a resourcefulness which draws its strength from a lawyerly willingness to argue both sides of a question, and a contextual view of meaning and intention. The preferred if not habitual discourse of this rhetorical cast of mind is not simply protreptic. Its hortatoriness is often ironic—that is, duplex in tone, in intention, and even in audience—like, in fact, Erasmus's letter to Mountjoy. And irony, he well knew, was beyond the grasp of those who could never acquire a rhetorical cast of mind.

But if Erasmus knew what he was doing, so too did his attackers. Obviously, he tried to take advantage of the dispute to locate its *stasis*, once more, in knowledge of traditional rhetoric. My attackers' difficulty in understanding my letter, he seems to say, is tantamount to the difficulty they have in understanding Scripture: they don't know

9. As I suggested in my previous chapter, our ongoing failure to grasp this key Erasmian doctrine is a source of our misunderstanding of John Colet's character: we mistook as objective biography Erasmus's use of Colet as a argumentative example; see John B. Gleason, *John Colet* (Berkeley, Calif., 1988), 4–5. It is also, as Jardine has argued, a possible source of our misunderstanding of Erasmus's letters; see Erasmus, esp. chapter 6. "Rhetorical context," as Daniel Kinney has argued, comes to be all-important for More's critique of Scholasticism; "More's Letter to Dorp: Remapping the Trivium," *Renaissance Quarterly* 34 (1981): 198.

rhetoric. But those who knew their rhetoric could see that the dispute, like the letter which caused it, was far more complicated. The controversy in this case—again, unlike that surrounding the letters of Petrarch, Jerome, or Augustine—centered in a master-pupil relation, making salient the issue not only of knowledge but of education and protocol. Perhaps, then, knowing the classical world and its rhetoric was not nearly so troublesome as actually using the procedures of Ciceronian *inventio*. Such at least is the very point I would draw from the controversy.

I would further suggest that Erasmus's proposal of marriage is partly aimed, here as elsewhere (for example, the *De copia*), at the union of rhetoric and disputatiousness, a union to be blessed by the birth of the rhetorical cast of mind. Thus, the disputation in which the epistle to Mountjoy is an opening sally is actually a disputation on disputation, on the efficacy and function of rhetorical disputatiousness, on in sum the protocol of traditional rhetoric.[10]

It is significant that when Erasmus himself republished the letter, in his textbook on letterwriting, *De conscribendis epistolis* (1522), he also published his counter-argument immediately following it. Here, however, the design of the refutation is clear: the point of retracting the arguments in favor of marriage is to inculcate in the minds of his pupils the habits of rhetorical debating. Marriage or celibacy is not the point; rhetorical protocol is. At first one might wonder what debating has to do with letterwriting, until we recall that letterwriting was a major argumentative mode in this period; in a sense, the entire debate between Luther and Erasmus was carried on by means of letters. More importantly, we need to recall that debate—in particular, so far as Erasmus was concerned, rhetorical debate—is the traditional way to achieve richness in *inventio*.

Again, however, just as in the Erasmian view the central subject of the dispute over his letter to Mountjoy was not about marriage or celibacy, its ultimate lesson was not simply about achieving inventiveness, or resourcefulness, through pro-con reasoning. Certainly the lesson begins there. In fact, it begins with a lesson dear to the

10. If more cleverly so than the explicit one Bruni wrote a century before. Though both, Erasmus's and Bruni's, deflected attention from their true aims, both ultimately centered in protocol; see Bruni's *Dialogi ad Petrum Histrum*, in *The Humanism of Leonardo Bruni*, trans. and intro. by Gordon Griffiths, James Hankins, and David Thompson (Binghamton, N.Y., 1987), 63–84.

minds of theologians, that, in simplest terms, one matter, one statement, one argument always presupposes its opposite, as in that discipline beloved of theologians, dialectic. However, "dialecticians,"
as he says in *De copia* (cap. L), by which he means theologians, "con-
fuse the different significations of words"—not only because their
Latin is bad but also because they ignore speakers, audiences, and
occasions. They ignore, that is, that meaning is not formalist or pre-
sumptive but context-driven. Otherwise the two arts—dialectic and
rhetoric—are coordinate arts of disputation, of two-sided argument.
But the lesson is not over yet. The inventiveness that needs to be
learned is the inventiveness that relies on the protocol of *rhetorical*
disputation. For theologians do not know rhetoric, its view of language and meaning, its protocol.

Let us pause at this point, in an effort further to understand this
lesson to consider some background material. First we shall explore
some of the conceptual similarities and differences between rhetoric
and dialectic; and second we shall review the nature of educational
disputation in the England of Erasmus's age. Then we shall return
once more to Erasmus's letter and conclude.

1. Background: Rhetoric and Dialectic

Recently Arthur Quinn in reviewing the ancient technique of
"color" (basically, the slant or tendency an arguer places on an argument) insisted that "The color of the Ciceronian rhetorician ought
to be skeptical pragmatism."[11] In a sense, "skeptical pragmatism"
fits the color of the dialectician almost equally well: skepticism provokes inquiry, pragmatism requires an answer. Dialectic begins in
uncertainty and proceeds through inquiry toward more certainty, at
least among experts, those equipped to understand the often esoteric
materials and forms of proof employed in the inquiry. Rhetoric,
however, begins in controversy and proceeds through inquiry to find
the means whereby this or that audience—whether expert or not—
may be attracted to a certain resolution of the controversy.

That is a troublesome feature of rhetoric as inquiry, whether of
Ciceronian or Erasmian stripe. When the humanists revived Cicer-

---

11. Arthur Quinn, "The Color of Rhetoric," *Rhetorik zwischen den Wissenschaften*,
ed. Gert Ueding (Tübingen, 1991), 138.

onianism, they revived a rhetoric whose conceptual model is the criminal trial with its two sides, prosecution and defense, forming a triangle with the third point, the judge or jury.[12] It is this kind of triangulation which best illustrates the use of rhetoric as a means of skeptical inquiry: disputation refined through personality and social context into a multiplex argument, aimed at judgment but predicated less on the immutability of truth than on the possibility of consensus and concord, that possibility Gilmore calls "the essential heritage of Erasmian thought in the sixteenth century."[13]

Cicero and Erasmus, whose philosophies ultimately diverge widely in the matters of skepticism and pragmatism, may echo one another in what each called "consensus," but again they will differ in the philosophical bases of that end. However, while acknowledging these differences and admitting their significance, I must side-step most of them in my effort to explore the commonality of Cicero's and Erasmus's rhetorical heritage. In that quest, other differences become more important, such as those we shall now continue to explore between traditional rhetoric and dialectic.

Dialectic echoes *dialogue,* and the idea of at least two people conversing—or, better, arguing—is inherent in both. Another way of putting what is inherent in both is to say that a "dialogic imagination" is essential—whether for dialectical or for rhetorical creation.

12. That rhetoric *is* a mode of inquiry, not simply a means of persuasion, has been forcefully pointed out by Jack W. Meiland in "Argument as Inquiry and Argument as Persuasion," *Argumentation* 3 (1989): 185–196. See also his *College Thinking* (New York, 1981). My own quest has been for a protocol of inquiry, arising from a profoundly forensic concept of rhetoric. Vico, perhaps the last great humanist, offers an extreme instance. Vico defined "jurisprudence" as "the knowledge of all things human and divine"—and in doing so he believed he was following his master Cicero. See Michael Mooney, *Vico in the Tradition of Rhetoric* (Princeton, N.J., 1985), 159. As Mooney notes, "for Vico, as for Cicero, the forensic is paradigmatic" (71). This process of triangulation which I refer to in my discussion is well explained by Arthur F. Kinney, "Rhetoric as Poetic: Humanist Fiction in the Renaissance," *English Literary History* 43 (1976): 413–43.

13. Myron Gilmore, "Methodus Disputandi: the Apologetic Works of Erasmus," in *Florilegium Historiale* (Toronto, 1971), 82. See also John W. O'Malley, "Erasmus and Luther, Continuity and Discontinuity as Key to Their Conflict," *Sixteenth Century Journal* 5 (Oct, 1974): "Much that on the surface seems contradictory is ultimately reconcilable. Life's great truths, after all, should be more or less accessible to all, and it is the purpose of good literature to convey them. The radically concordistic nature of Erasmus' enterprise derives in large measure from this conviction" (50).

Sometimes the two people or voices are debaters, one taking the pro the other the contra side, as in the Ciceronian and Erasmian dialogues about rhetoric or religion; sometimes the debate is a set-up, as in the medieval dialogues between the body and the soul.[14] Sometimes one of the sides is a teacher, the other a reluctant learner, as in several of St. Augustine's dialogues. Sometimes one of the sides is a philosophical neophyte or ignoramus, as in several of Plato's Socratic dialogues. Sometimes the perspectives are multiplex, the pro as well as the contra distributed across several speakers: *multiplex ratio disputandi,* Cicero called it, meaning that it is not so easy to separate the good guys from the bad guys.

Consider, too, that the art of dialogue is actually more deeply intertwined with rhetoric than with dialectic, not simply in the dialogue's literary dimension, its eloquence, but in its overt efforts to please and move as well as to teach an audience outside the dialogue.[15] Plato's skillful use of dialogue, as in the *Phaedrus,* to dismiss rhetoric thus has an almost Erasmian irony. Too, a certain playfulness inheres in both rhetoric and dialogue: whenever dialogue loses its humanist play of ideas, its humor, or what Bakhtin has called "a carnival sense of the world," the form degenerates into a simple question-answer procedure, like catechism, a procedure difficult to think of as a mode of inquiry or even argument.[16] Thus, though the two echo each other, there is an important sense in which dialectic, however dialogic, does not exactly imply "dialogue." The dialectician's imagination, like the rhetorician's, had to be bifurcated, a pro-

14. Body and soul dialogues represented more of a conflict than those between flesh and spirit, as Rosalie Osmond has shown. Osmond, moreover, also shows that these dialogues continued to be composed through the middle of the seventeenth century. "Body and Soul Dialogues in the Seventeenth Century," *English Literary Renaissance* 4 (1974): 364–403

15. As Snyder's recent study of dialogic art in the late Italian Renaissance has revealed, any methodological distinctions between dialetic and rhetoric were usually confounded in theory: any effort to distinguish the two in terms of content immediately foundered on further attempts to distinguish their ends. Not surprising, perhaps, considering humanist diffidence toward method and theory. Jon R. Snyder, *Writing the Scene of Speaking: Theories of Dialogue in the Late Italian Renaissance* (Stanford, Calif., 1989).

16. Mikhail Bakhtin, *Problems of Dostoyevsky's Poetics,* ed. and trans. Caryl Emerson (Minneapolis, 1984), 110. Bakhtin's work most relevant to the present discussion appears in the four essays gathered under the title *The Dialogic Imagination,* ed. Michael Holquist and trans. Caryl Emerson and Michael Holquist (Austin, 1981).

cess often shown in the resulting discourse. But that discourse was not necessarily a dialogue, for neither is it formally a conversation nor does it stylistically bear the imprint of its speakers' personalities.

Mikhail Bakhtin, in seeking to revivify the full complexities of dialogue in our age, has gone to the very heart of the ultimate difference beween rhetoric and dialectic if in somewhat extreme terms: "Dialogue and dialectics. Take a dialogue and remove the voices (the partitioning of voices), remove the intonations (emotional and individualizing ones), carve out abstract concepts and judgments from living words and responses, then cram everything into one abstract consciousness—and that's how you get dialectics."[17] Four centuries ago Melanchthon put the distinction even more briefly: "What," he asked, "are Cicero's philosophical dialogues but dialectic with the added embellishment of *elocutio?*"[18] For *elocutio,* particularly when combined with rhetoric's other unique office *actio,* covers exactly those qualities Bakhtin enumerates: voices, intonations, living words and responses. For that matter, even when monologic, rhetorical discourse offers no escape from personality.

Let us consider now the dialectic the humanists knew and the rhetoric they sought to revive and enumerate some of the chief differences between the two. Having done that, we shall then briefly review the humanist efforts to reform dialectic in such a way as to blur many of its distinctions with rhetoric.

Refer again to Figure 2. Note that although dialectic is a somewhat truncated art (it has no doctrines of style, memory, or of course delivery), its first two parts, or "offices" (judgment and invention) are inversely parallel to the first two parts of rhetoric. We shall concentrate primarily on a shared intellectual habit regarded from aniquity as common to both dialectic and rhetoric, their primary mode of "inquiry" called in each *inventio,* which proceeds through a given controversy by requiring the arguer to give thought to both sides of the question, pro as well as contra, friends as well as adversaries, expert if not lay.

By the time of Erasmus, dialectic encompassed four basic dry-as-

17. Quoted in *American Scholar* (Spring, 1991): 204.

18. In *De elementis rhetoricis* (1542) in *Opera* XIII, col. 420 (*Corpus Reformatorum,* ed. C. G. Bretschneider et al. [Halle, 1934]); translated and quoted by C. J. R. Armstrong in his "The Dialectical Road to Truth," *French Renaissance Studies, 1540–70,* ed. Peter Sharratt (Edinburgh, 1976), 40.

dust activities, each one of which is present in the resulting discourse: defining a matter, dividing it into its constituent parts, putting together valid arguments, and analyzing the fallacies in false arguments. The first two are absolutely crucial. Erasmus's Folly, who clearly prefers rhetoric, is amused that St. Paul somehow manages to delineate *charity* without either defining or dividing it (1 Corinthians 13: "suffereth long and is kind . . . envieth not . . . is not puffed up"). Erasmus's point has to do with artfulness, above all with *ethos* and audience, and the lack thereof in dialectic and in most "foolosophy."[19] In that move, Folly dismisses Plato's aim in the *Phaedrus,* wherein dialectical thought achieves ascendancy over rhetorical inquiry.

Considering the formalist regimen required of dialectic, it's not surprising that from the high Scholasticism of the Middle Ages through the Renaissance *dialectic* was a synonym for *logic.* When people of Erasmus's time thought of logical procedures, they thought of those four activities. But each of these is involved, like rhetoric, in a dialogical—or, better, bifurcated—process of argumentation, and all rhetoricians, including Erasmus, considered each essential at times.

Whether in dialectic or in rhetoric *inventio* was a quasi-systematic means of "inventing" arguments, in which certain *topics* of argument were shared. The purpose of any topic is simply to suggest a fundamental mode of inquiry, an elementary approach which Crassus (perhaps more wearily than contemptuously) calls the "trite and common precepts of teachers in general."[20] Faced with having to say something about a controversial subject? Consider these topics, whether your task will be dialectical or rhetorical argumentation: the subject's causes, its effects, its attributes, its contraries. Dialectical topics were always far less expansive than rhetorical ones, geared as the latter were toward the circumstances of any one case: e.g., the latter invariably included such questions as what exactly was (or should be) done, or what could be the nature of the deed?

19. See the excellent translation by Clarence Miller, *The Praise of Folly* (New Haven, Conn., 1979), 90, 13.

20. *De oratore* I.xxxi.137. In addition to other works I have mentioned on the subject of topics, I would also refer the reader to these: Marc Cogan's essay on Agricola in *Rhetorica* 2 (1984): 163–194; M. Leff's article in *Rhetorica* 1 (1983): 23–44; Wes Trimpi, *Muses of One Mind* (Princeton, N.J., 1983); Donovan J. Ochs, "Cicero and Philosophic *Inventio,*" *Rhetoric Society Quarterly* 19 (1989): 217–27.

Nonetheless, the close relation of rhetoric and dialectic is nowhere in theory shown more clearly than in their shared use of certain topics. Again, as the medieval master Boethius ingenuously puts it, "The purpose of the Topics [whether in dialectic or in rhetoric] is to reveal *(demonstrare)* a bountiful supply of arguments which have the appearance of truth."[21] The function is not simply resourcefulness but analysis, or resourcefulness through analysis. Or, to put it another way, resourcefulness through finding the holes in an apparently air-tight case—for, given that attitude toward truth mentioned earlier, especially when combined with pro-con reasoning, no case *could* be air-tight. Let us put it yet another way. A key to *inventio*, particularly in rhetoric, as taught by our humanist forebears lay not in a recitation of the topics but in giving thought to the question, Who cares? What is being said by whom on both sides of the controversy? Recalling Antonius's protocol of *inventio* as described in my chapter on the subject, let us recall too that "invention" and "analysis" are virtually synonymous. We would invent through analyzing a question by trying to find the *point at issue* between the opposing sides, the parties who brought the question to the fore to begin with. As noted, *status* or *stasis* or in Latin *constitutio,* was the word for this key, and it unlocks the area where the mind's impulse to argue and take a stand is located. The key was fashioned in Ciceronian rhetoric, but it is almost equally useful in dialectic: for one is simply a full, the other a spare art of disputation.[22] And *that,* finally, is the first and the chief difference to keep in mind.

Second, an old and often repeated distinction between dialectic and rhetoric was that the former disputes by question and answer, the latter by unbroken discourse—as if the chief example of the former were Aquinas's *Summa* or, better, Duns Scotus's *Questiones quodlibetales* and of the latter were Cicero's orations. By the time of

---

21. *De topicis differentiis* I.1181 B; trans. Eleonore Stump (Ithaca, N.Y., 1978), 41.

22. Nicholas Rescher's effort to bring disputational procedures into scientific inquiry neglects, finally, some crucial differences between rhetoric and dialectic and, while not exactly ignoring the analytical function of *stasis* and "triangulation," tends to place the final burden of judgment on formalistic matters. Nonetheless, what he calls "unilateral dialectics" (see esp. chapters 3 and 8) and his schematized discussion of disputational procedure (chapter 1) are quite clarifying in their demonstration of, as his subtitle puts it, "A Controversy-Oriented Approach to the Theory of Knowledge"; *Dialectics* (Albany, N.Y., 1977).

Erasmus—or, for that matter, Peter of Spain—dialectic was not nec-essarily thought of as disputing by challenge and answer, but rather as an increasingly formalistic way of shaping arguments for an au-dience of experts. And rhetoric began to be prominent as an art of composing poems, speeches, and dialogues for lay and expert alike.

Thus, a third difference concerns the audiences for each. The dia-lectician with his "closed fist" prepared discourse for audiences trained in logic; the rhetorician with his "open hand" prepared dis-course for a varied audience.[23] The metaphor applies particularly to the source of sanction, which in rhetoric arises not from forms of proof but from consensus: *consensus gentium,* Cicero called it; *con-sensus ecclesiae,* or *consensus fidelium,* Erasmus called it and it was the container that limited both rhetoric's unruly skepticism and its pro-pensity for indeterminate meaning.[24] In that matter our Romantic and thoroughly undemocratic disgust with the "public" in "public speaking" centers.

It should also center in the "speaking" as well. For deeply inter-twined with this difference in audience is rhetoric's profoundly *oral* orientation toward language, its function and meaning: Thomas Cole has recently defined traditional rhetoric "as the written word attempting to do the work of the spoken word."[25] The Scholastics

23. The "fist" and "hand" comparisons were conventional and widespread; see Wilbur Samuel Howell, *Logic and Rhetoric in England, 1500–1700* (Princeton, N.J., 1956), esp. chapter 1.

24. In this consensus, according to Augustijn, "we have reached the heart of Erasmus' religious conviction." The consensus of which Erasmus was most deeply aware was the community formed by the Holy Spirit, through the *sermo* or con-tinuing speech of God. See Cornelius Augustijn, *Erasmus,* trans. J. C. Grayson (To-ronto, 1991), 152. "Briefly put," J. K. McConica states, "without *consensus* and concord, its social concomitant, no dogmatic certainty could be had about anything, and no problem of faith could be solved. The *consensus,* in Erasmus's thought, is the principle of intelligibility itself"; "Erasmus and the Grammar of Consent," *Scrinium Erasmianum,* ed. Joseph Coppens (Leiden, 1969), 2:89. In a wonderfully Janus-like statement of Erasmus's intentions, Walter M. Gordon captures the point of both consensus and writing or speaking: "Communication follows upon and looks to-ward communion"; *Humanist Play and Belief: The Seriocomic Art of Desiderius Erasmus* (Toronto, 1990), 128.

25. *The Origins of Rhetoric in Ancient Greece* (Baltimore, 1991), 1. Cole's point is the eminently sensible one that rhetoric becomes possible only with consciousness of language, the sort of consciousness that arises from written language, which in turn allows a sense of various means to one's end and the ultimate separation of form from content; see esp. 120–21.

were great speakers and wranglers, as humanists from the time of Petrarch complained; and most of the Scholastics, the humanists also complained, could not write well. Further, the humanists were, besides being great speakers, primarily great writers; but in their writing they more than the Scholastics assumed the profoundly oral, rhetorical orientation toward language. Crucial to this concept of language as speech is the idea of an immediately establishable consensus. What you say, what you can say if you wish to be heard, depends upon the "social matrix." The Erasmian humanist would seem to have little problem with the rule. But that meaning, let alone the nature of argument, should be culturally determined is an idea abhorrent to Scholastics, and other formalists, who prefer to symbolize communication in some non-spoken, non-circumstantially dependent way. In public speaking, by contrast, or in any writing that attempts to do the work of the spoken word, there simply has to be some "social authority" for one's utterance.[26]

A fifth difference is seen theoretically in the forms of proof, a difference which also arises from differences in audience and pertains to the profound orality of rhetoric. Ciceronian rhetoric's forms of proof extend beyond formal validity—and thus beyond the logical, or dialectical—to include character differences and the emotions of the audience. The impress of a speaker's character *(ethos)* and the approval of an audience *(pathos)* are weighty social sanctions for accepting the "validity" of this or that message in rhetoric. For the Erasmian, the latter sanctions are grounded, as noted earlier, in the concept of consensus—or, for that matter, to cite a continuing stance in Erasmus's apologetics, in a contextual view of meaning and intention.

The final, sixth difference is one that readily coheres with the foregoing: the Ciceronian distinction between *thesis* and *hypothesis*. That is, dialectic argued broad, general matters, rhetoric circumstantial

---

26. For an illuminating development of the terms "social matrix" and "social authority," see Martin Elsky, *Authorizing Words: Speech, Writing, and Print in the English Renaissance* (Ithaca, N.Y., 1989). Elsky's view of the humanist concepts of language is drawn mainly from schoolbooks and educational treatises, exactly the places where they are most effectually set forth; see especially chapter 2. "In contrast to the Scholastics," Elsky says (69), "whose ideal was an abstract, transparent articulation of thought in the *oratio* of an isolated mind, humanists generally held that *sermo* (which includes *oratio*) gathers its meaning through its accumulated reverberations in a community of literary texts and moral beings."

matters. Boethius, who revived Cicero's topics and became the leading authority of medieval dialectic, put the difference succinctly:

> The dialectical discipline examines the thesis only; a thesis is a question
> not involved in circumstances. The rhetorical [discipline], on the other
> hand, investigates and discusses hypotheses, that is questions hedged in
> by a multitude of circumstances. Circumstances are who, what, where,
> when, how, by what means.[27]

That is, should a man marry? is a dialectical question; should Lord
Mountjoy marry? is a rhetorical one. Quintilian made a similar point
with a similar example.[28] Dialectical invention endeavored to find
universal premises, widely applicable, at a remove from the individual and the quotidian; rhetoric sought the immediate and specific
application of those premises. In its engagement with specificity, rhetoric necessarily does more to acknowledge that meaning is context-
driven and that the outcome of the dispute is often provisional and
local—a difference that we have seen Erasmus harp on in defending
his letter to Mountjoy before dialecticians.

These chief differences—in flexibility, mode of discourse, audiences, orality, forms of proof, and question—always center in a certain almost uniform inventive procedure whether we are considering
pre-humanist dialectic or Ciceronian rhetoric as an intellectual pursuit or mode of inquiry. Certainly both alike are skeptical, within
certain boundaries—of formal validity on the one hand and, to put
the matter simply, social matrix on the other. Thus dialectic would
begin fashioning its argument, usually a deductive syllogism, by
searching for an ostensibly immutable truth as its major premise:

> Whoever desires to live virtuously, desires to avoid fornication
> (Thesis).

One might then go on to construct a possible argument (borrowing
from Thomas Wilson):

> Whoever desires to avoid fornication desires marriage.
> Ergo, whoever desires to live virtuously desires marriage.

27. *De topicis differentiis*, IV.1205 C-D; trans. Stump, 79. See also Stump's excellent translation of the work on which this one is built, Boethius's *In Ciceronis
Topica* (Ithaca, N.Y., 1988).
28. *Quod ut exemplo pateat, infinita est, an uxor ducenda? finita, an Catoni ducenda?
ideoque esse suasoria potest* (III.v.8).

The acceptability of the conclusion depends largely upon the formal validity of the procedures employed.

By contrast, rhetoric begins fashioning its argument, usually in the loose form of syllogism known as the enthymeme, by searching for what the particular audience believes to be true. The rhetor both identifies with the audience's beliefs and draws a conclusion consonant with those beliefs: e.g., borrowing this time from Erasmus:

> Because marriage was sanctioned by God for the procreation of humankind (Thesis), religion compels us to believe that Lord Mountjoy should marry (Hypothesis).

The acceptability of the argument depends largely upon the audience's assent, just as its form depends upon the orator's confidence that any missing links in the argument will be supplied by the audience itself. In this way, rhetorical argumentation relies less on formal validity to contain its skeptical epistemology than, as mentioned earlier, on social consensus.

But as the humanists knew, Cicero—a great writer of dialogues, the revered master and preceptor of Erasmian humanist rhetoric, and a believer in the *consensus gentium*—said that dialectic and rhetoric belong together. And he made the point, appropriately enough, in several of his dialogues on rhetoric. His masterpiece, *De oratore,* was as we have seen a conscious imitation of Plato's *Phaedrus,* and Cicero's work was as much a restoration of Sophistry—including the educational importance of rhetorical two-sided debating—as Plato's work was a fierce condemnation of the practice. Cicero's philosophical point always rested partly on this premise: it's folly to argue an *hypothesis,* he insisted, without giving some thought to the *thesis,* to argue a specific matter without considering the general belief or value or even fact which encompasses it. To later humanists, such as Erasmus, the reverse was not only equally true but even more compelling: abstract principle becomes important when reduced to cases. For another thing, all theoretical categories and distinctions (about discourse) when viewed from the standpoint of rhetoric tend to be so fluid they threaten to dissolve anyway.[29] At the hands of Cicero's Renaissance followers, other once-firm differences began

---

29. A good and even amusing example is the often bewildering way in which Quintilian juggles the distinctions between *thesis* and *hypothesis* in III.v.

also to fade, but largely in the effort to *incorporate* dialectic *within* rhetoric, their always preferred discipline.

Let us take a brief look at this attempted fusion, for not only does it have bearing on my own case but, more importantly, it helps us understand the protocol I am seeking to uncover. Moreover, the fusion of dialectic and rhetoric is itself a key to the rise of humanism, a gauge of the rise and fall of Ciceronianism.[30]

A commonsensical view, concerning humanism's initial base in

30. Another approach to the intellectual history I am reviewing is possible through the subject of casuistry, or debate involving questions of right and wrong in individual conduct. Ethical or moral choice is the issue at stake, problems of conscience the province, application of *thesis* to *hypothesis* the goal. The debate is not necessarily narrow in scope, for almost all questions—marriage, war, heresy—can veer between politics and conscience. Generally, however, casuistical questions turn inward to involve not so much public policy as one's own (not action but) conduct, and not so much public opinion as the received axioms or maxims on which one's judgment often depends. Nonetheless, the similarities between casuistical and rhetorical debate are impressive. Both had their major philosophical spur in the writings of Cicero: according to Albert R. Jonsen and Stephen Toulmin, *The Abuse of Casuistry: A History of Moral Reasoning* (Berkeley, Calif., 1988), the third book of Cicero's *De officiis* was "the cradle of casuistry" (83) for its instruction that moral and ethical problems must be resolved at the level of individual cases. Both are directly involved in problems meshed with circumstances, "who, what, where, when, how, by what means" (see the quotation from Boethius, above). Both use essentially the same protocol, inventing probable arguments on both sides of the question. Both had major impact on the literature of their periods; see Camille Wells Slights, *The Casuistical Tradition in Shakespeare, Donne, Herbert and Milton* (Princeton, N.J., 1981). The period of "high casuistry" in England (1550–1650) is also the period of "high humanism," when an interest in rhetoric as a mode of thought reached one of its own historical peaks. And both declined for many of the same reasons—the fading in prominence of the militant Protestant emphasis on individual conscience plus a similar fading in the Jesuitical emphasis on "probabilism" or "probabiliorism," to say nothing of the new drive for certainty in reasoning. *Casuistry* became a pejorative, along with *sophistry* and, ultimately, *rhetoric;* a brief history of casuistry is in Jonsen and Toulmin, 47–175; see also Slights, chapters 1 and 2. Jonson and Toulmin have made an effort to revive casuistry in our time, an aim that might seem similar to my own. But their effort is admittedly non-antiquarian. Just as Toulmin has elsewhere proposed a non-syllogistic model for modern argumentative reasoning (*The Uses of Argument* [Cambridge, Eng., 1969]), so Jonsen and Toulmin propose a new model for modern casuistry in which debate centers on whether this or that pre-existent paradigm fits this or that individual problem: e.g., if the usual paradigm for marriage is the union of man and woman, what shall we say about this individual case of a same-sex marriage? (See Jonson and Toulmin, chapter 16.) My own, antiquarian effort is aimed at a much more traditional protocol, itself dependent upon another kind of union—not paradigm with case, but dialectic with rhetoric.

centers of power—that as it spread northward from Italy to Germany, France, and England, it "gained acceptance first in secular courts and bourgeois urban centers, then gradually in the universities"[31]—would seem to pertain mostly to the Kristeller view of humanism, the revival of the *studia humanitatis* (grammar, rhetoric, history, poetry, and moral philosophy).[32] But if one centers humanism in rhetoric as a kind of surrogate philosophy[33] and above all if one links humanism (as we will below) with the rising profession of law, then another kind of gradualism must be taken into account: the attempted liberation of dialectic, for centuries held in thrall to overly formalized procedures and highly speculative, especially theological, questions. A common thread in humanism is not so much the revival of the liberal arts, a thread that gets easily interwoven into that doubtfully humanist fabric known as the Age of Enlightenment, but the abhorrence of Scholastic disputation and its displacement by rhetorical—that is to say, personalized and circumstantial—debate.[34]

Valla struck a keynote of this effort in his early attempt actually to incorporate the "simpler affair" of dialectic into "the more complex province of rhetoric."[35] A correlative movement, aimed at rhetoricizing dialectic—if only to give its *inventio* the primacy it has in rhetorical composition—was carried on by such distinguished pedagogues in humanism's northward sweep as Vives, Sturm, Melanch-

---

31. Bruce A. Kimball, *Orators and Philosophers: A History of the Idea of Liberal Education* (New York, 1986), 85.

32. Paul Oskar Kristeller, *Renaissance Thought: The Classic, Scholastic, and Humanist Strains* (New York, 1961); see esp. "The Humanist Movement," which ends with the argument that Renaissance humanism "in its substance was not philosophical, but had important philosophical implications and consequences" (22).

33. An interesting study of this point is Ernesto Grassi, *Rhetoric as Philosophy* (University Park, Pa., 1980).

34. John F. Tinkler has a succinct discussion of humanist *vs* Scholastic dialogue, with implications for similar distinctions in disputation, in "Humanism and Dialogue," *Parergon*, n.s. 6 (1988): 197–214. The importance of *ethos* in Ciceronian disputation is well discussed by James M. May, *Trials of Character: The Eloquence of Ciceronian Ethos* (Chapel Hill, N.C., 1988).

35. See John Monfasani, "Humanism and Rhetoric," *Renaissance Humanism: Foundations, Forms, and Legacy*, vol. 3, ed. Albert Rabil, Jr. (Philadelphia, 1988), 191. Mack's characterization is perhaps more precise because more specific: "Dialectic is part of a part of rhetoric. It is much easier to learn, but it is also of use to far more people" in Valla's view; Peter Mack, *Renaissance Argument* (Leiden, 1993), 112.

thon, and above all Agricola. In traditional dialectic (review Figure 2), judgment came first and invention came second, because the dialectician's first task was considered to be analysis not genesis, judging a statement not necessarily composing one. (Why this should be so we shall explore later, in my chapter on Thomas Wilson.) But reformers' efforts were centered not only on the primacy of dialectical *inventio* but also on its expansion. Particularly is this true in the case of Agricola.

Agricola, whom the young Erasmus met and admired, became famous for a system of logic that was built on an extended *inventio*. Agricolan dialectic included such traditional matters as the topics, the "predicables" and the "predicaments," the forms of argument, as well as such primarily rhetorical matters as *stasis,* disposition, emotional appeals, and amplification. The work is an historical milestone in drawing together rhetoric and dialectic: Agricola made differences in their inventive processes all but disappear.

His *De inventione dialectica*—the title itself an echo of Cicero's juvenile handbook—became an important document in the characterization of the humanist movement as a "Third Sophistic."[36] He "not only ended the divorce of rhetoric and dialectic," as Marc Cogan puts it, he "actually extended the domain of the instruments and methods of rhetoric to inquiries in all branches of knowledge."[37] Divorce ended, the reunion of rhetoric and dialectic in *inventio* became the humanist *scienta scientarum,* the art of arts and science of sciences—with rhetoric the dominant of the two, if only by virtue of its offering instruction in such other communicative tactics as the parts of an oration, style, delivery, and memory.[38] Peter Mack has recently provided a detailed analysis of the work and in examining various manuals which followed it concludes that an important impact of Agricola's general ideas was the continued close connection

36. See the excellent analysis by James Richard McNally, "*Dux Illa Directrixque Artium:* Rudolph Agricola's Dialectical System," *Quarterly Journal of Speech* 52 (1966): 337–47 and McNally's translation, "Rudolph Agricola's *De inventione dialectical libri tres:* A Translation of Selected Chapters," *Speech Monographs* 34 (1967): 393–422.

37. "Rodolphus Agricola and the Semantic Revolutions of the History of Invention," *Rhetorica* 2 (1984): 181.

38. And thereby the grounds were composed for the Ramist divorce of the two arts in the name of simplicity—or, rather, further simplicity, for both Valla and Agricola offered manuals reducing the complexity of dialectic while expanding it in order to make it more practical.

of rhetoric and dialectic, especially in the period up to 1580[39]—further evidence, if we needed it, of Erasmus's own ongoing sympathy with the reform of *argumentatio*.

Well beyond the position Mack takes, Jardine has suggested that Erasmus and his circle had a major role not simply in the publication but in the actual reconstruction, or perhaps even construction, of Agricola's dialectic. The Erasmian scheme, she argues, was to link Agricola's *De inventione dialectica* with the *De copia* in "a reform (at least in the north) of taught *eloquentia*."[40] The success of the scheme can be measured in several ways; one of those ways, so far as Agricola's work is concerned, is to note that his *De inventione dialectica*

> was the higher education manual of *argumentatio* (argumentation) most widely specified, bought and used in schools and universities throughout Protestant Europe, between the early decades of the sixteenth century and the midseventeenth century (when attitudes towards logic/dialectic in the curriculum altered so as to render it irrelevant). (Jardine, *Erasmus*, 80)

Again, the transformation of dialectic proceeded independently of the *De copia*. The latter work, we have seen, was somewhat misused. But, once more, Erasmus's intentions regarding *inventio* seem recoverable and unmistakable.

Dialectic, Erasmus wrote in his introduction to Seneca's *Declamationes*, should not be expelled from the schools in spite of its seeming irrelevance; but it must be reformed; "all its frivolous niceties" should be "done away with" and "it should be taught for practice and use."[41] It should be taught, that is, for its importance in rhetoric. Thomas More put the connection between the two arts in the plainest of terms: "How can you say that Erasmus doesn't know dialectic?" he asked the theologian Dorp: "After all, you admit that he's especially gifted in rhetoric, and if you admit this then there is no way to deprive him of dialectic."[42] Jardine has argued that the ep-

---

39. *Renaissance Argument:* esp. chapters 12, 13, 14, and 18. "If dialectic governs the ordinary use of reason in language," Mack claims Agricola and the Agricolans believed, "rhetoric adds to it for special purposes and on special occasions" (363). In another sense, Agricolan dialectic became the central organon of rhetorical thought.

40. Jardine, *Erasmus*, 145.

41. Translated by Jardine, Erasmus, 142. Jardine calls the passage "unusually explicit words on the subject of dialectic for Erasmus."

42. Letter to Dorp from Bruges, 21 October 1515. See Leclerc, III.ii.1892.

istolary quarrels involving Erasmus, More, and Dorp were carefully staged, to define issues surrounding the rising centrality of humanist dialectic in education, as well as the role of Erasmus as humanist educator par excellence. Agricolan dialectic as incorporated within the Erasmian process of copiousness, of "reasoning abundantly," were to be integral parts of humanist *inventio*.

In this way the ancient Aristotelian view—that rhetoric and dialectic are counterparts[43] was given a decidedly Ciceronian slant. To consider the function of these counterparts in disputation is our next task. We may approach that task through one of Agricola's premises, which further uncovers the skeptical basis for humanist disputation: "Most matters in human studies are uncertain and require disputation. Only very little of what we learn is certain and established."[44] If uncertainty requires disputation, it was equally true to humanists that disputation in turn invites uncertainty, the holes in any case offered for truth—a practice which forms the very foundation for what I tried earlier to identify as "irony," or what modern educationists could or should mean by "critical thinking."

"In practice," Richard Lanham has recently reminded us, "rhetorical education is education in two-sided argument, argument where the truth is decided by the judge or jury, where truth is a dramatic criticism handed down on the forensic drama which has been played out according to the rules laid down, finally, by a rhetorical education."[45] Lanham's statement is an epitome of the rhetorical cast of

43. *Rhetoric* 1.1. See also Lawrence D. Green, "Aristotelian Rhetoric, Dialectic, and the Traditions of [Antistrophe]," *Rhetorica* 8 (1990): 5–27. For a discussion of the dialectical setting of Aristotelian rhetoric, see "The Academy and Dialectic" and "Dialectic in the Academy" by Gilbert Ryle, *Collected Papers* (London, 1971) 1:89–125. Aristotle, Ryle remarks, "both in his *Topics* and in his *Art of Rhetoric* . . . closely associates the study of rhetoric with the study of dialectic" (116).

44. The translation is by Peter E. Medine and appears in his *Thomas Wilson* (Boston, 1986), 49. Montaigne put the matter poignantly, in his characterization of Cicero as a skeptic: "This method in philosophy of arguing against everything and making no open judgment of anything, started by Socrates, repeated by Arcesilaus, confirmed by Carneades, flourishes still even in our time. We are those who say that some falsehood is mixed with every truth, with so much similarity that there is no criterion in them by which we can judge and assent with certainty." From his "Apology for Raymond Sebond," *Works,* trans. Donald M. Frame (Stanford, Calif., 1967), 376.

45. Richard A. Lanham, "The 'Q' Question," *South Atlantic Quarterly* 87 (1988): 600.

mind, temper and habits inculcated not simply through a humanist marriage of rhetoric and dialectic but also through curricular practices we shall now consider.

2. Rhetorical Education

Given this rhetorical cast of mind, it is little wonder that in the educational tradition descending from Cicero, Quintilian, Seneca, and Aphthonius *controversia* and *suasoria,* the two chief genres of classroom declamation, overlapped—not the result, I would argue, of a conceptual untidiness on the part of these classical rhetoricians but rather a reflection that two-sided argument inheres in both kinds of discourse (just as rhetoric and dialectic inheres in both). We have already examined one of these declamations created centuries later by a famous humanist who sought to revive the principles of a rhetorical education: Erasmus, we have noted, called his letter to Mountjoy a *suasoria,* but we found that its nature as well as its meaning are best grasped when its controversial wellsprings are understood. Certainly battle lines are more neatly drawn in *controversia,* where two sides are targeted, as in a case at law. But even in the advisory *suasoria* when no opponent is manifest the speaker must still refute, proleptically or some other way, unspoken objections in his hearers' minds. One way rhetorical education trained him to do that was by training him to play his own opponent's role, requiring him to give voice to those objections through arguing the other side of the case in a *dissuasoria,*[46] through writing recantations, or for that matter through oral disputation.

Suasoria as an educational *declamatio* was usually a speech written out then delivered orally on an historical theme: e.g. present Cicero debating with himself whether to beg Antony for his life. By contrast, the *controversia* was usually a speech of legal advocacy: e.g., speak in court either for the father or for the rapist who, having won over his victim's father but cannot win over his own, accuses his father of insanity (the trial is based on the supposed law that a rapist shall die unless he wins over his victim's father *and* his own father within thirty days). Both of these examples are from the works of

---

46. On this point, with specific reference to the tradition Erasmus inherited, see Roland H. Bainton, *Erasmus of Christendom* (New York, 1969), 16.

the great preceptor of *suasoria* and *controversia,* the elder Seneca, whom Erasmus at one time prized above Cicero.[47]

That the exercises were fictive mattered not at all. For insofar as "poetics" was a discrete subject in classical humanist education it shared, as Arthur Kinney has argued, the practical goal of other humane arts, to produce statesmen.[48] The field of the classical humanist muses, though free, was neither abstract nor remote. Furthermore, in the case of either a *suasoria* or a *controversia,* much imagination was also required of the composer in giving particular attention to *ethos* and *decorum* (to adopting a style of speaking appropriate to the character assumed, the audience and occasion), as well as to *pathos.* In this respect, both were practical exercises preparatory to composing discourse outside the parameters of the classroom, particularly outside the parameters of classroom disputation, wherein their foundation was laid.

In the next chapter, we shall look closely at some other examples of *suasoria* as a particularly complex type of humanist writing. We need now to examine various other kinds of evidence of the educational practices at its foundation. The foundation of rhetorical *inventio*—and, consequently, the foundation of either *suasoria* or *controversia*—as I have tried to show is arguing *in utramque partem.* That foundation was made abundantly clear by Quintilian, who as we have noted went so far as to claim that there is only one almost *exclusively* inventive activity, debate. Little wonder that he urges students of rhetoric to attend criminal trials and prepare speeches of their own on both sides of actual cases (X. v. 19–20). Erasmus echoes the idea in advocating another kind of disputational exercise:

> The students' skill in invention will be improved if they practise recantations, arguing against what they have just proposed; what you have previously lauded to the skies, you dash down to the depths with violent denunciation; or first advocate something, then urge its avoidance.[49]

---

47. See CWE, 23: xlviii. Erasmus published editions of the elder Seneca, whose writings are available in Loeb editions, the *Controversiae* and *Suasoriae* trans. Michael Winterbottom (Cambridge, Mass., 1974).

48. Arthur F. Kinney, *Humanist Poetics: Thought, Rhetoric, and Fiction in Sixteenth-Century England* (Amherst, Mass., 1986).

49. *De conscribendis epistolis;* CWE, 25: 43.

The point of *both* these humanists was to increase students' inventive skill. In the period which intervened between Quintilian and Erasmus, pro-con reasoning or two-sided argument continued to be practiced in *inventio*. Indeed, disputation was "a way of life" in the Middle Ages.[50] But the capstone of medieval education was theological disputation, which was pre-eminently dialectical, on abstract theses; the grounds were formalist and the questions were theological and, which almost amounts to the same thing, scientific. Disputation was also, as I tried to suggest in the preceding section, perhaps the most important context within which Erasmian humanists revived Ciceronian rhetoric, a revival which would necessarily have an impact on the nature not only of theological disputation but also of educational disputation as well.

Among the many ways of describing the passage of Western culture from the Middle Ages to the Renaissance—such as the philosophical shift from a view of God as the *conditio sine qua non* of epistemology[51] to an obsession with that being who was supposedly created in God's image and likeness,[52]—a crucial one for rhetoric may be the semantic shift described by Waswo, from the "referential," which regarded language as a "transparent vehicle," to the "relational," which regarded language "as a creative agent that constructs its own protean meanings."[53] For that matter, however, both shifts, the philosophical as well as the semantic, seem correlative to the rise in prominence of rhetoric as a mode of thought. The philosophical becomes antagonistic to educational irrelevance, the semantic to argumentative formalism. Rhetoric's emphasis on circumstance thereby answered a new need.

Two professions were directly involved in and affected by the rise of rhetoric in the Renaissance, law and pedagogy. We have only lately begun to understand the impact of the former profession on the latter—or, for that matter, on the nature of the humanist revival.

50. See Thomas L. Reed, Jr. *Medieval English Debate Poetry and the Aesthetics of Irresolution* (Columbia, Mo., 1990), ch. 2.

51. See Marcia L. Colish, *The Mirror of Language: A Study in the Medieval Theory of Knowledge*, rev. ed. (Lincoln, Neb., 1983).

52. See Charles Trinkaus, *In Our Image and Likeness: Humanity and Divinity in Italian Humanist Thought,* 2 vols. (Chicago, 1970).

53. Richard Waswo, *Language and Meaning in the Renaissance* (Princeton, N.J., 1987) , 21–22.

Many humanists, including those most active in educational reform, had received training in civil law. Although the relation between humanists and the universities was at the outset embattled,
the very history of universities is often traced to the founding of the
law curriculum at Bologna in the Trecento. Certainly other phe-
nomena, such as the rise of the bourgeoisie and a new social mobility
are not to be ignored in understanding the intellectual shape of the
Renaissance, but neither is the establishment of law as a major career
pursuit. This *arriviste* became almost the co-equal of the two career
pursuits inherited from the Middle Ages, medicine and theology.

Of course a legal career is and always has been an end of rhetorical
education. This joint venture in rhetoric made the connections between law and humanism deep and complex. Indeed, the legal career
was either a precursor to or fellow traveller of humanism as that
intellectual and educational movement spread from Italy to Germany
to France to England, as William Bouwsma and Richard Schoeck
have shown, and as such it necessarily conditioned the very foundations of humanist curricular revisions.[54] As a new career pursuit,
law began to take its place at the upper reaches of the curriculum
and helped impel the founding of universities, extending rhetorical
interests well beyond "trivial" pursuits.

Though neither may be a philosophy exactly, both law and rhetoric invariably prove philosophically troubling. If the legal career
helped revive rhetoric in the Renaissance, it also helped revive that
ancient charge brought not against dialectic, which has seldom been
liable for its effects on an audience, but against its counterpart in

54. See in particular William J. Bouwsma, "Lawyers and Early Modern Culture," *American Historical Review* 78 (1973): 303–27, and R. J. Schoeck, "The Elizabethan Society of Antiquaries and Men of Law," *Notes & Queries* n.s. I (1954): 417–
21; "Early Anglo-Saxon Studies and Legal Scholarship," *Studies in the Renaissance* 5
(1958): 102–10; "Sir Thomas More, Humanist and Lawyer," *University of Toronto
Quarterly* 26 (1964): 1–14; "Lawyers and Rhetoric," in James J. Murphy, ed. *Renaissance Eloquence* (Berkeley, Calif., 1983), 274–91. Other important studies: F. W. Maitland, *English Law and the Renaissance* (Cambridge, Eng., 1901); Guido Kisch, *Humanismus und Jurisprudenz: Der Kampf zwischen mos italicus und mos gallicus an der
Universität Basel* (Basel, 1955); M. P. Gilmore, *Humanists and Jurists* (Cambridge,
Mass., 1963). That English humanists preferred law over medicine as a career pursuit, has been interpreted by Mark H. Curtis as a preference for man's social over
his physical well-being: *Oxford and Cambridge in Transition 1558–1642* (Oxford, Eng.,
1959), 156.

two-sided argument, rhetoric: that the art makes the "worse" appear the "better" reason and thereby perplexes "Maturest Counsels." Sophistry, in short. (Milton, whom I've just quoted, makes Belial a Sophist in *Paradise Lost* II: 113–4.) Protagoras—"not a true philosopher," said Aulus Gellius, "but the cleverest of Sophists" (*Attic Nights*, I.v.3)—is usually credited with teaching his students of rhetoric how to make the worse appear the better reason. Cicero, however, claimed that the terminology actually came from the Sophists themselves: they, "not without arrogance to be sure," professed "to teach how by the force of eloquence the worse (as they called it) could be made the better cause" (*Brutus*, vii.29).

Let us consider that for the Sophist "worse" could simply mean "weaker" before this or that audience, and if his efforts are to make the "weaker" reason seem "stronger," then those efforts could be aimed at enhancing the marketability of all ideas, of all arguments, on *either* side. The practice has obvious application for anyone seeking to persuade juries or the general public (or to sell one's talents as a rhetorician: "it is the man with the weaker case," Bernard Knox has recently remarked, "who needs the rhetoric."[55] Or a lawyer.) More importantly, it could stabilize if not strengthen the rhetorical cast of mind. Equally important for my own argument, the practice is also the basis on which humanist dialogue/disputation should be judged: Is Antonius, whose arguments Cicero may not prefer, given a fair hearing? If not, then Cicero's own pro-con reasoning is a sham. Herein we may see the very reason that Cicero allows Antonius, not Crassus, to give the most detailed explanation of invention by means of arguing *in utramque partem:* in so doing, he invites an estimation of his, Cicero's, own use of that procedure. "Fair hearing" is a term that applies equally well to the courtroom trial as to the protocol I am trying to describe.

Let us turn more firmly now to pedagogy.

So far as Erasmus's pedagogical efforts are concerned, he did less, I would argue, to revive the *studia humanitatis* than to rhetoricize *inventio* as part of his larger attempt to create a new education—and, beyond that, a new epistemology and hermeneutic. At root, a rhetoricized *inventio* allows a subject to be inquired into and disputed not simply according to the rule of reason (or even, *pace,* Augustine,

---

55. *The Oldest Dead White European Males* (New York, 1993), 91.

the rule of charity) but according to the rule of reason *and* the moving of the will. Thus Erasmus would have schoolboys understand that rhetoric is a kind of logic, too, whose "chief points" are not only rational ones, like "propositions" and "the grounds of proof," but also emotional ones, like "figures of speech" and "amplifications."[56] Moreover, however close Agricolan dialectic came to providing a rhetorical logic—with its incorporation of amplification and emotional appeals into a discussion of the places and forms of argument—rhetoric will have vastly more complex resources for persuasion, not the least of which, as Erasmus knew to his immense gratification, is humor.

"Histories make men wise," Bacon wrote in his essay on the learned arts, but logic and rhetoric together make them "able to contend." By the time of Bacon, the tradition had been reborn and established: rhetoric was not merely ornamented logic but a coordinate art of analysis, inquiry, and above all disputation. It was the co-equal of dialectic and, in the eyes of many humanists, dialectic's superior as a vastly more complex and difficult art. These instruments had come easily to hand for the pedagogues of England, who among all Northern Europeans gave Erasmus his greatest reception.[57] Thus, whether the English student was guided by regulations based on *De ratione studii* or simply by his own desire to enter law, medicine, theology, or the arts, he seldom escaped the explicit commingling of rhetoric and dialectic, and he never escaped trial by disputation.

---

56. In *De ratione studii;* see CWE, 24: 670. Compare, for example, the Ramist Kempe's instructions in *The Education of Children* (London, 1588), G2 v: "Then shall followe the third degree for Logike and Rhetorike, and the more perfect vnderstanding of the Grammar and knowledge of the tongues. First the schooler shal learne the precepts concerning the diuers sorts of arguments in the first part of Logike, (for that without them Rhetorike cannot be well vnderstood) then shall followe the tropes and figures in the first part of Rhetorike . . ." The second part of rhetoric is, of course, delivery—proof again, if we need further proof, that the Ramists in their conceptual tidiness and misunderstanding of rhetoric were decidedly at odds with humanists.

57. "In the treatise *De ratione studii* by Erasmus is the fundamental philosophy of the grammar school in England. On these general principles it was organized and by these methods it was taught. What is more, the strategic textbooks in the system were suggested, prepared, or approved by Erasmus"; T. W. Baldwin, *William Shakespere's Small Latine & Lesse Greeke* (Urbana, Ill., 1944), 1:94. Note, too, Richard J. Schoeck, *Erasmus Grandescens* (Nieuwkoop, 1988): "the teaching of Erasmus is the underpinning of the Tudor public schools" (121).

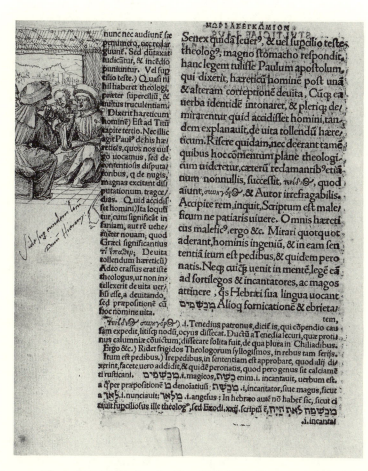

Figure 3: Theological Disputation. By Hans Holbein the Younger, a marginal drawing in a copy of Moriae encomium *(The Praise of Folly) by Erasmus (Basel, 1515).* Photograph courtesy of Oeffentliche Kunstsammlung Basel, Kupferstichkabinett.

Holbein's drawing illustrates this passage: "I myself [Folly says] recently attended a theological disputation, as I often do. When someone there had asked what was the scriptural authority for overcoming heretics by burning them instead of converting them by argumentation, a sour old man, whose supercilious look alone was enough to mark him as a theologian, replied very irritably that Paul himself had laid down this law when he said 'A heretic should be warned once, and then once again; after that, shun him (devita).' And when he went on thundering out these same words and many were wondering what was wrong with the man, he finally explained that a heretic should be removed from life (de vita). Some laughed, but there was no lack of those who thought this explanation thoroughly theological" (trans. Clarence H. Miller [New Haven, Conn., 1979]: 126–27).

How rhetorical that disputation was becoming at the hands of Erasmus and his followers we can only conjecture, but the evidence seems compelling. To look at that evidence, let us turn our attention not simply to the general educational disputatiousness but to disputation itself, that formal, oral means whereby students were tried and tested.

The temper of the age, particularly at Cambridge, was well captured in Master Holdsworth's "directions" for his students at Emmanuel College in the early seventeenth century: controversies (i.e., private, in-house disputations) in the first year centered on logic and in the second year on logic, ethics, and physics; these gradually opened up to allow in the third and fourth years "controversies of all kinds." Meanwhile his students, already grounded in logic, got progressively heavier doses of Cicero's letters and, among other writings, *De oratore, De officiis, De finibus,* and finally the orations. "Logic without oratory is dry and unpleasing," Holdsworth wrote, "and oratory without logic is but empty babbling."[58]

Logic, that is dialectic, continued to be taught but along with rhetoric; together they fulfilled *inventio,* by making it a mode of inquiry actively applied in disputation, an educational practice wherein we begin to glimpse the possibly continuing nature of humanist reform. The marriage of these two disciplines we have earlier touched on in our brief review of Valla and Agricola. It is well known that humanist rhetorical dialectic was at the center of the curriculum at Cambridge.[59] That it would be actively applied in educational disputation at least at that institution seems inescapable. What might be equally inescapable, moreover, is the converse: the contextual importance of disputation in the development of rhetoric, and in our understanding of that development. There can be no question that disputation was the major instrument of Renaissance pedagogy. It

58. Eugene E. White, "Master Holdsworth and 'A Knowledge Very Useful and Necessary,'" *Quarterly Journal of Speech* 53 (1967): 6.

59. In this respect, an especially useful study is Lisa Jardine's "The Place of Dialectic Teaching in Sixteenth-Century Cambridge," *Studies in the Renaissance* 21 (1974): 31–62. Jardine shows that dialectic moved into the center of the curriculum at Cambridge 1560–1590 and that this central dialectic was humanist: it was the study of practical argumentation, drawing widely on literary materials, and it was virtually identical with rhetorical *inventio* with the possible exception that rhetoric seemed to go farther in its insistence upon circumstance.

was a lingering medieval practice and, I believe, the most significant educational context within which Erasmian humanists attempted a revival of Ciceronian rhetoric.[60]

Although humanists based most of their educational theories and practices on Cicero and Quintilian, they often credited Aristotle not only with urging the use of two-sided debate but with pointing out its instructional efficacy. However, in doing so they were partly following Cicero again, who read Aristotle's *Rhetoric* as being far more grounded in disputation than modern commentators tend to. Crassus's ideal orator is someone, he says, who can speak on both sides of every question "in the Aristotelian fashion" and who "by means of knowing Aristotle's rules [can] reel off two speeches on opposite sides on every case" (*De Oratore,* III.xxi.80). The psychological spur of educational disputation was, of course, competition: Walter Ong comments that in this period "the life of the mind was exciting be-

---

60. Among the other works I have consulted, in addition to those cited throughout this study, are such primary sources as Roger Ascham, *The Scholemaster* (1570) and *Toxophilus* (1545); John Brinsley, *Ludus Literarius* (1612); Francis Clement, *The Petie Schole with an English Orthographie* (1587); Thomas Elyot, trans. (Plutarch) *The Education or Bringing Vp of Children* (1533); Gabriel Harvey, *Ciceronianus* (1577) and *Rhetor* (1577); Richard Mulcaster, *The first part of the Elementarie* (1582); Richard Rainolde, *The Foundacion of Rhetorike* (1563), and such secondary sources as Donald Lemen Clark, *John Milton at St. Paul's School* (New York, 1948) and "The Rise and Fall of Progymnasmata in Sixteenth and Seventeenth Century Grammar Schools," *Speech Monographs* 19 (1952): 259–63; William T. Costello, S.J., *The Scholastic Curriculum at Early Seventeenth-Century Cambridge* (Cambridge, Mass., 1958); Harris Fletcher, *The Intellectual Development of John Milton,* 2 vols. (Urbana, Ill., 1961); Joseph S. Freedman, "Cicero in Sixteenth- and Seventeeth-Century Rhetoric Instruction," *Rhetorica* 4 (1986): 227–54; Anthony Grafton and Lisa Jardine, *From Humanism to the Humanities* (Cambridge, Mass., 1986); Paul F. Grendler, *Schooling in Renaissance Italy: Literacy and Learning, 1300–1600* (Baltimore, 1989); M. B. Hackett, *The Original Statutes of Cambridge University* (Cambridge, Eng., 1970); Jo Ann Hoeppner Moran, *The Growth of English Schooling 1340–1548* (Princeton, N.J., 1985); John Mulder, *The Temple of the Mind* (New York, 1969); Ray Nadeau, "The Progymnasmata of Aphthonius," *Speech Monographs* 19 (1952): 264–85; Nicholas Orme, *English Schools in the Middle Ages* (London, 1973), and "An Early-Tudor Oxford Schoolbook," *Renaissance Quarterly* 34 (1981): 11–39; Joan Simon, *Education and Society in Tudor England* (London, 1966); Bromley Smith, "Extracurricular Disputations: 1400–1650," *Quarterly Journal of Speech* 34 (1948): 473–76; Craig R. Thompson, *Schools in Tudor England* (Washington, D. C., 1959); Karl R. Wallace, "Rhetorical Exercises in Tudor Education, *Quarterly Journal of Speech* 22 (1936): 28–51; Foster Watson, *The English Grammar Schools to 1660: their Curriculum and Practice* (Cambridge, Eng., 1908).

cause it was framed in conflict."[61] Here again Aristotle was given
the credit. As the sixteenth century humanist educator Roger Ascham notes, echoing Aristotle's *Rhetoric* (1370b–1371a): "Where is
comparison, there is victory; where is victory, there is pleasure; and
where is pleasure, no man careth what labor of pain he taketh, because of the praise and pleasure that he shall have in doing better
than other men" (*Toxophilus,* to be discussed in my next chapter).
Such readings of Aristotle are less distortive than selective, the views
of antiquarians who knew that their audiences held Aristotle in high
regard (Erasmus's crack about Aristotelian contamination was meant
to be contrarian, if not shocking) and who, like me, find the essence
of rhetoric in debate.

But their views, however partisan and selective, only further substantiate my argument about the ineluctable prominence of educational disputatiousness and its significance as a context within which
the humanists revived Ciceronian rhetoric. It would seem, moreover, that much as the humanists rejected Scholasticism they apparently sought not to banish but to transform its chief intellectual exercise. Disputation was not to be thrown out or ignored but to be
reformed and strengthened, along clearly rhetorical lines. "The practice of our studies," Bruni has Coluccio say, "is conversation, inquiry and the pursuit of those things that are deliberated in our
studies—in word, disputation" (*Dialogi ad Petrum Histrum,* 71). What
better way to serve the humanist goal of helping students write and
speak well, and contrary to their passive attendance at a Scholastic
lectio, to become actively involved in subjects meant to be useful *ad
vitam et mores?*

In an address to Cambridgemen in the middle of the sixteenth
century, the great English humanist educator Walter Haddon responded to an apparent slackening of interest in public disputation
in the schools by vigorously defending it. Sounding very much like
Cicero's *De officiis,* Haddon's *Cantabrigienses, sive exhortatio ad literas*
reverberates with a definition of *humanitas* that places an emphasis
upon public access to knowledge—for that matter, upon the humanist's responsibility to make knowledge public. Debate, more than
the lecture, was the chief medium of public access. Haddon's argument in part chastizes scholars for neglecting their responsibility:

61. Walter J. Ong, S.J., *Rhetoric, Romance and Technology* (Ithaca, N. Y., 1971), 66.

we have given our very selves over too much to lassitude and idleness, we have abandoned the schools to solitude and desolation, schools which, although our ancestors wanted them to be called 'common' because of literature freely travelling to and fro in them, have been so reduced by our idleness and have reverted to such notable paucity, that schools after our time will have to be called the sure seats of certain professors, not common to the community.[62]

In public disputation, as opposed to classroom disputation, the scholars came out of doors, to employ advanced skills in argumentation in a setting that was open to other colleagues and to the interested public. It was a means whereby the universities became "common" in Haddon's sense and unlocked their learning. But the skills themselves were taught early.

At one time, formal disputation was a regular feature of grammar school training. However, as James J. Murphy points out, *disputatio* began to be regarded more and more as an advanced skill, one more proper for the university, particularly when that twelfth-century phenomenon began more and more to stake out its claim on instruction in logic.[63] Nonetheless, oral combat remained an essential feature of grammar school instruction even on the lowest levels, or forms, usually on the subject of grammar. Even in the "meaner schools," as John Brinsley puts it in his argument to reform grammar schools in such "rude countries" as "Ireland, Wales, and Virginia," even in these schools, students must be taught to "write, speak, oppose and answer." And one way of achieving that end is to dispute questions of grammar.[64] Such exercises were preparatory "for witty and pleasant disputations" in the University, "or any like

---

62. I have used the edition of the *Exhortatio* which was published in 1567. The passage cited appears on p. 112: *Languori nimium nos ipsos dedimus, & ignauiae, scholas in solitudine reliquimus, & vastitate, quas cum maiores nostri communes nominari voluissent, propter libere commeates in illis vltro citroque literas, nostra desidia sic contractae sunt, & tam insignem ad paucitatem reciderunt, vt quorundam professorum certae sedes, non vniuersitatis comunes scholae posthac nobis cognominandae sint.* Haddon's definition of *humanitas* appears immediately following. The 1552 edition of the *Exhortatio*, moreover, was edited by Thomas Wilson.

63. "Quintilian's Influence on the Teaching of Speaking and Writing in the Middle Ages and Renaissance," *Oral and Written Communication: Historical Approaches,* ed. Richard Leo Enos (Newbury Park, Calif., 1990), 169.

64. John Brinsley, *A Consolation for our Grammar Schooles* (London, 1622), 7, 55. I have modernized the spelling and punctuation.

opposition, mooting, or pleading in the Inns of Court." They were, moreover, meant to be *fun*, part of the ludic spirit humanists believed essential to education.[65] Erasmus's strictures against schoolmasterly cruelty, his insistence that we learn best what we learn as "games," his seriocomic treatment of theological matters; the ongoing traditions in rhetoric concerning the use of humor; even Ascham's assimilation of education to archery, to be discussed in the following chapter—all these are deeply intertwined. Chances are, these grammar school disputations *would* be fun, especially in a combative age, and in an elementary schoolday that lasted up to twelve hours with only two or three "intermissions."

Formally this grammar-school combat tended to be less like a debate than a catechism, or, better, that type of oral combat once prevalent in American education, the spelling bee. Although grammatical correctness was the point, winning was the supreme point. Hoole, for example, describes the practice in the following way, suggesting each Friday as the best time for the contests:

> Each Form has two "sides," which face one another. Each boy propounds to the boy opposite him points of difficulty in the week's work—"which if the other cannot answer readily before he count six, or ten (in Latin) let him be *captus,* and the question be passed to the next boy on the other side." The lowest boy is to begin the questions. Account to be kept of those who are *'capt,* and how often.[66]

On this verbal combativeness formal disputation was later built, often in the higher forms and regularly in the university.

Some of the questions used in educational disputation in the higher forms are suggested by Erasmus in his textbook on letter-writing:

> for and against learning, wealth, the monastic life, languages, matrimony, and monarchy. . . . Which life is superior, the active life which the Greeks call practical, or the contemplative, which they call theoretical? Is celibacy better, or wedlock? Does art or natural ability contribute more to speaking? Is the modern kind of theology superior to the older one? [Note the casual listing of this explosive question.] Is military ser-

65. John Brinsley, *Ludus Literarius: or, The Grammar Schoole* (London, 1612), 206–207, 281–282. I have modernized the spelling and punctuation.

66. Charles Hoole, *A New Discovery of the Old Art of Teaching School* (1660); quoted in Watson, *English Grammar Schools*, 95.

vice or the study of literature more useful for the acquiring of reputation? Is jurisprudence or the study of medicine more profitable for the securing of wealth? . . . Who was the better general, Hannibal or Scipio? Was Plato a more outstanding philosopher than Aristotle? Which poet was more learned, Virgil or Hesiod? Who was more remarkable for his eloquence, Demosthenes or Cicero? (CWE, 25: 44)

A similar list appears in Richard Rainolde's famous and more elementary textbook, his attempt to English Aphthonius: "Whether are riches chiefly to be sought for in this life as of all things the chief good . . . Whether it is best to marry a wife."[67]

If these lists seem to the modern eye a little pale and abstract, or irrelevant, they bear interesting comparisons with the "Dunsical," or Scholastic list of questions Folly satirizes. Her satire is all the more effective because the questions were actually disputed by Scholastic theologians:

Whether there is any instant in the generation of the divine persons . . . Whether God could have taken on the nature of a woman . . . whether it will be permissible to eat and drink after the resurrection . . .[68]

But Folly is, of course, speaking of disputation in one of its very highest forms, at the thin-air level of theological training. (Note Holbein's drawing and the passage it illustrates, in Figure 3.) Therefore the comparison with lists that were most likely used for grammar-school disputations may not seem fair. But the comparison does give us a glimpse of the kind of conditioning a boy would have had in disputation at the hands of his humanist schoolmasters long before he would have proceeded toward theology, or medicine, or law. If he had debated the questions proposed by either Erasmus or Rainolde—particularly the one Erasmus so casually offers ("Is the modern kind of theology superior to the older one?"), he could hardly approach theological disputation uncritically, whether as disputer or as audience. *That,* of course, was surely the whole humanist point.

Let us return to Rainolde's important textbook. As noted earlier, it was an effort to English Aphthonius, to give boys elementary

67. Richard Rainolde, *The Foundacion of Rhetorike* (London, 1593), see fol. Liii r–v. I have modernized the spelling and punctuation.

68. Clarence H. Miller, trans. *Praise of Folly,* 88–89. Miller substantiates his claim about the accuracy of the list in "Some Medieval Elements and Structural Unity in Erasmus' *The Praise of Folly,*" *Renaissance Quarterly* 17 (1974): 501.

training in composing declamations. Rainolde proposes a certain exercise designed to wean boys away from puerile speech (actually from what we would call exposition and narration) and introduce them to the procedures of argumentation. The exercise seems directly in the Senecan-Aphthonian-Erasmian line: take a statement widely held to be true and subvert it; for example, "It is not likely to be true what is said of the battle of Troy." And in the invention the student was meant to impugn the "vanity" of poets and above all argue the improbability that the Greeks should be so bewitched by one woman, Helen, that they would "cast off the natural love of their wives, their children and country, to bring home again, by slaughter of infinite people, such an one as had left honesty and chaste love of her [own] husband." Then boys were to be taught orations of praise and blame: for example, praise Epaminondas and dispraise Nero. The exercise might seem easy. The difficulty comes in considering the coordinate, traditional lesson: "All things that may be praised, may be dispraised" (fol. xxvii^v and L.iii^v) and vice-versa. Try praising Nero.

In the universities, besides partaking in the frequent "controversies" we noted in our review of Master Holdsworth's "directions," the student beyond his second year became a "sophister" and was required to take part in a stated number of disputations, both in college and in public, as a means of demonstrating not simply mastery of subject matter but also skill in dialectic and rhetoric. Undergraduates in their third or fourth year and for their baccalaureate degrees often treated philosophical questions, not unlike some of those used on the lowest forms.

By the time the student reached the MA level, the questions for dispute could become timely:

> whether a college education will get you ahead in politics . . . whether women should have a liberal education . . . whether there is any certain knowledge of things . . . [whether] the power of the sword is the prince's alone . . . [whether] All change in the commonwealth is dangerous.[69]

---

69. Craig R. Thompson, *Universities in Tudor England* (Washington, D. C., 1959), 27. The very nature of some of the questions is, of course, also a reminder that rhetoric and dialectic were *Latin* subjects and thus primarily the preserve of males in the period under study; see Dilwyn Knox, "Order, Reason and Oratory: Rhetoric in Protestant Latin Schools," in Peter Mack, ed. *Renaissance Rhetoric* (New York, 1994), esp. 66; see also Walter J. Ong's provocative "Latin Language Study as a Renaissance Puberty Rite," *Rhetoric, Romance, and Technology* (Ithaca, N. Y.,

When Elizabeth I visited Cambridge in 1564, she heard public disputations on propositions that were topical, current, indeed quite close to Elizabeth herself: whether the authority of Scripture is better than the authority of the Church, and whether the Civil Magistrate has authority in matters ecclesiastical.[70] A decision for the Affirmative may have been expected; but if the debates were to be anything other than farcical, before a monarch who herself had been schooled by one of her country's leading humanists, opposing arguments had to be rigorous and attended to with respect. Moreover, Elizabeth, as we know, was subjected to all sorts of entertainment as she made her famous "progresses" through the countryside. But that debaters would be trotted out and required to perform for a grave and powerful head of state must strike us as curious indeed. At the very least, it is a reminder that disputation was a prominent educational activity in the year of Shakespeare's birth—and remained so, at least through the age of Milton. Two years later, when she visited Oxford, three days out of her week's visit were devoted to disputations, and one year after *that* Haddon, as we have seen, warned his colleagues about a slackening interest in public disputation.

The form of educational disputation was variable, but it usually included only one proposer and several opposers, thereby complicating the simple binary divisions of pro-con analysis or of the Affirmative-Negative split. Procedures consisted of cross-examinations, refutations and rebuttals. Sometimes the form became overtly triangular and included a Moderator, who resolved the dispute.[71]

1971), 113–41. Bruni's famous letter to Lady Battista Malatesta of Montefeltro (1424) outlines the major tenets of humanist education which are most suitable for women, and explicitly excludes them from the practice of forensic rhetoric and disputation: "Hers is not the task of learning to speak for and against witnesses, for and against torture, for and against reputation; she will not practice the commonplaces, the syllogisms, the sly anticipation of an opponent's arguments. She will, in a word, leave the rough-and-tumble of the forum entirely to men"; in Griffiths, Hankins, and Thompson, *Leonardo Bruni*, 244.

70. See Curtis, *Oxford and Cambridge*, 169.

71. In Cambridge, 1595, the Moderator resolved a disputation on *Nunquam erit magnus, cui Ramus est magnus* (No one will be great to whom [i.e., who thinks] Ramus is great) by boxing a sophister on the ear; an uproar followed. On form, see esp. Thompson, *Universities in Tudor England*, 26, and Curtis, *Oxford and Cambridge*, 88. See, too, Thomas Wilson on the duties of the speakers (*Rule of Reason*, 1551, ed. Richard S. Sprague [Northridge, Calif., 1972], 153–156). See Abraham Fraunce,

Sometimes, too, the form included a "varier" or "prevaricator." Not exactly one of the disputants, the "varier" took the fool's or jester's part in public debates by playing verbally upon the question under dispute.[72] One varier, for example, in a dispute on whether celestial bodies are the causes of human actions averred that all dons present may be called stars: after all, stars are the denser parts of the heavens, and dons are the denser parts of the academic world. As Costello has shown in his study of Cambridge in the early seventeenth century, variers had a field day in disputes on such medieval-sounding questions as whether gold can be produced by chemical art or—the question disputed before James in his 1614 visit—whether dogs can make syllogisms (24–31). This fun-loving "prevaricating" spirit, exercising something of that virtuosity the humanists called "wit," bears interesting and favorable comparisons with certain present day Oxford debates and even with modern American "off-topic" debating. Finally, public debates were usually marked with elaborate ceremony—and occasionally with fights and riots.[73]

Educational disputation, moreover, was *oral.* Earlier I tried to point out that of the two arts of argument, rhetoric was far more oral in orientation and nature than dialectic. The former consistently relied upon personality and circumstance for subject and evidence, and upon consensus for confirmation. Although available evidence suggests that *experts* judged the educational debates, as they would in any dialectical presentation or for that matter in a courtroom trial, nonetheless a mixed audience also served as a kind of jury particu-

---

Lawiers Logike (London, 1588), fol. 101 for an attempt to bring Ramist orderliness to disputation. Note, too, Sidney's question, "Nowe, whom shall wee finde (sith the question standeth for the highest forme in the Schoole of learning) to bee Moderator [between the claims of history on the one hand and philosophy on the other]?";"An Apologie for Poetrie," in *English Literary Criticism: The Renaissance,* ed. O. B. Hardison, Jr. (New York, 1963), 110; Sidney's metaphor will be discussed in my following chapter.

72. The role is not unlike the one Thomas More assigns Folly. As he says in his confutation of Tyndale, the *Moria* "doth indeed but jest upon the abuses of such things [as holy images and saints' relicts] after the manner of a disour's part in a play"; *Complete Works,* ed. Louis A. Schuster et al. (New Haven, Conn., 1973), 8: 178.

73. For a vivid glimpse of the elaborateness of ceremony, see Costello, *Scholastic Curriculum,* 15–17, and for an amusing review of the violence often attendent upon public disputation see Bromley Smith, "Extracurricular Disputations: 1400–1650," *Quarterly Journal of Speech* 34 (1948): 473–76.

larly in public disputation, if only because that audience was ready at times to reveal its judgment through violence.

In sum, the tilt in all these disputations conducted after the arrival of the humanists on the educational scene was surely toward the rhetorical. And at this point we must note a certain irony: it was most likely the humanists in spite of their clear preference for rhetoric who gradually undercut the importance of orality in education—who in placing a new premium on literacy gave us textbooks, term-papers, and in place of disputations, written finals.[74] It was, in short, most likely the humanists who—all inadvertently perhaps—lessened the likelihood that their own revived rhetoric would succeed by weakening its most natural habitat, oral modes of composition and communication, a natural habitat particularly congenial to the insistence that all arguments should be attached to sources and purposes, to speakers and occasions. Writing, like dialectic, moves counter to the humanist view of language. It removes the parameters of speech—convention, consensus, the social matrix—and with them the parameters which kept the profoundest skepticism at bay. (Perhaps the most extreme undoing of humanism lies not simply in the modern disappearance of speech as a discipline but in the modern rise of deconstruction, or of any philosophical system that views written discourse as something other than a reflection of spoken language—as writing, to echo Cole, that attempts to do the work of speech.)

At the outset, however, orality pervaded humanist instruction in writing, with no consideration that writing and speaking may be disparate skills. As Ong remarks of Aphthonius, humanist educators "codified in writing an oral institution."[75] Even on the lowest grammar-school levels humanists following Rainolde-Aphthonius usually required the written declamation to be presented orally in class. They taught letter-writing not in the formulary way of the medieval *ars dictaminis* but in the disputatious mode of Cicero, as if the letter were a kind of conversation, or *sermo,* with, say, one's brother.[76] Again, rules were beside the point; resourcefulness was all.

74. See Ong, *Ramus,* 155; and Curtis, *Oxford and* Cambridge, 110.

75. Walter J. Ong, *Rhetoric, Romance, and Technology,* 39. Moreover, even textual analysis, the influential Bruni had insisted, should have a spoken component: the words on the page should be interpreted orally. See Bruni's letter to Lady Battista Malatesta of Montefeltro; in Griffiths, Hankins, and Thompson, *Leonardo Bruni,* 242.

76. On the point about the oral presentation of written declamation, see van der

Once more, Erasmus is a superb example. Like other humanist theorists of epistolography, he challenged the formalist approaches of the earlier *dictatores* and moved oral disputation to the center of the inventional process. Speaking on both sides of a question, as we have noted, is one thoroughly Erasmian way to perform that pedagogically invaluable function of making the student resourceful. Erasmus is specific in his advice, as well as in his practice, as in this passage from his textbook on letterwriting. Although I alluded to this passage earlier and have several times mentioned the Erasmian practice of requiring students to prepare recantations, note this time not only that Erasmus once more advocates sophistry but that his language also conflates writing with speaking:

> The teacher should . . . criticize [the pupils'] arguments, and then tell them to write a recantation. Sometimes, to sharpen their wits, he should propose disagreeable subjects. One might be asked, for instance, to defend poverty, exile, ingratitude, illness, contempt of study, neglect of language, or tyranny, or to argue that an old man should marry an old woman, or bring home a lewd wife. For nothing is so inherently good that it cannot be made to seem bad by a gifted speaker. By such practice both fluency and readiness in speaking on any topic will be acquired.[77]

Educational exercises of recantations and of composing discourse on disagreeable subjects have been around at least since the time of Quintilian (see XII.34), and formal educational disputation at least since the Middle Ages. A sharpened wit, fluency, and readiness were to become—in both Erasmus and Quintilian—moral instruments, efficacious alike in writing and speaking, though their promptitude is more crucial and more challengeable in the latter mode of discourse. These exercises reappear in such startling documents as (we shall see) Raphael's description of Utopia or Puttenham's consciously

---

Poel's excellent history. On the point about letter writing, see Paul F. Grendler, *Schooling in Renaissance Italy: Literacy and Learning, 1300–1600* (Baltimore, 1989), esp. chapter 8.

77. *Deinde illorum inventa castiget, mox palinodiam scribere jubeat. Nonnunquam etiam acuendi ingenii gratia, infames materias proponat. Veluti si quis suadeat paupertatem, exilium, ingratitudinem, aegrotationem, contemptum studiorum, neglectum linguarum, tyrannidem, ut vetulus vetulam ducat, ut domum ducat uxorem improbam. Nihil enim est ita natura bonum, quin ab ingenioso Oratore depravari possit. Hac exercitatione tum copia, tum promptitudo quaedam, quavis de re dicendi parabitur* (Cap. XLVIII: De Genere Dissuasorio). The excellent translation is by Fantazzi; *CWE* 25: 145–46.

contrarian compliment in calling Elizabeth the "greatest dissembler" of all.

Students who had been through such exercises could be in the morally astute situation of understanding the extent to which anything could be made to seem good or bad by the gifted speaker. Such critical thinking might also invite us to reconsider the importance of these exercises and perhaps even the nature of sophistry as well. From the beginning of this chapter in focussing on Erasmus's letter to Mountjoy I have suggested that letter writing was a slice of disputation, in mode and manner profoundly oral and equally profoundly sophistical—as was the Ciceronian rhetoric the humanists revived, with its lawyerly emphasis on resourcefulness and virtuosity. At this point I wish to suggest that the chief characteristics of humanist writing might best reveal themselves through keeping these points in mind: to listen, that is, for the sounds of contrarianism in the lively flow of conversational writing, and above all to recognize that the discourse bespeaks a rhetorical cast of mind. Let us return to my initial example.

Remarriage

The tradition in which Erasmus composed his letter on marriage, subsequently published as an *encomium,* was a standard *declamatio* in the form of a *suasoria,* i.e., a written speech aimed at giving advice. Suasory discourse could move against the grain, using subjects like those proposed in the Erasmian passage I have just quoted, or it could offer negative advice, in which case it was called *dissuasoria.* We shall explore these matters further in my next chapter. Here, however, where my chief subject is disputation as the contrarian exercise par excellence, we sense again some of its pervasiveness: Erasmus's letter is based on a conventional question offered for schoolboy debate. The subject appears in the lists offered earlier, from Erasmus and Rainolde: *an ducenda sit uxor,* whether a man should marry. So standard was this exercise that one could center an entire history of two-sided argument on it and find a host of examples, extending from the *controversiae et suasoriae* of Seneca and the declamatory exercises of Aphthonius down to dense relics of the tradition, such as Ben Franklin's letter on the advantages of having a mistress rather than a wife (see Appendix B). Perhaps then Erasmus was, as he claimed, merely showing his young pupil how it was to be done.

Certainly Erasmus's rhetorical skill in traditional dispute is observable, perhaps seen best in his adaptation to circumstance: he bends stock arguments, the perpetuation of the family for example, to fit the case at hand, such as the urgency for Lord Mountjoy to marry and not follow his sister into the religious life. On the other side, the argument against marriage, which he published along with this letter in his textbook on epistolography, becomes one of devoting one's life to learning and so finding one's "sons" through teaching, not through procreation. Alas, dogmatics and authoritatians—in this case, the theologians—can apparently take only one argument at a time and imagine only one context, not specific to the intention or purposes of the rhetor. Thus, because their interpretation is dialectical not rhetorical, or formalist and not circumstantial, they cannot fully understand the letter. Nor, of course, are they content to admire Erasmus's skill in argumentation. Any argument against celibacy, once isolated and viewed abstractly, becomes a potential threat.

Such, at least, was the Erasmian defense. On the other hand, Erasmus, like any skillful rhetor, was surely aware of the extratextual confrontation his letter would provoke when first published and there is further evidence that he just as surely enjoyed it. The master's professed love of concord did not prevent him from exploiting controversy and fractiousness—and not always in the interests of curricular reform. Lisa Jardine's recent work pictures Erasmus not simply as an educator sans classroom. He was also a successful self-promoter, the soi-disant leader of a complex educational and intellectual reform, aimed ultimately at changing society's manner of thought. He was, in sum, a thorough-going rhetorician, one whose most meaningful instruction arises not so much from his theories as from his practice. And in that practice perhaps the most notable exemplars are his letters—"rhetorical exercises," indeed, as Jardine has pointed out, "intended to make a particular point of view compelling."[78] His own success in making a point of view compelling in his letter to Mountjoy is patent: he let the chips fall where they might do him

---

78. Jardine, *Erasmus,* argues that with Jerome as his model and mentor Erasmus invites us to read his own letters in the way he himself invites us to read Jerome's, 173.

and his ideas the most good, and the controversy stirred up lasted for at least a decade.

Of those ideas, I have been trying to argue, a significant one in the letter to Mountjoy is not so much the attack on priestly celibacy. It is, rather, the rhetorically effective offense the letter gives the smug protocol of authoritarianism and intellectual stricture, the bête noire of humanist optimism and, for that matter, chief obstacle to Erasmian concord. As I earlier proposed—and, I would argue, as both Erasmus and his attackers knew—the real *stasis* in the dispute was less celibacy than protocol. Those rhetoricians who followed in his wake, with much the same cast of mind, often had similar aims— if slightly askew.

When Thomas Wilson, for example, translated and reprinted Erasmus's letter in his famous *Arte of Rhetorique* in 1553, there could be little doubt that he was aware of its anticlerical thrusts. Although these thrusts suited well Wilson's own brand of dogmatism, he put the letter to a rather different use. In his companion volume on dialectic published two years earlier he had used many of the letter's stock arguments in favor of marriage to poke syllogistic fun at clerical celibacy. But in the rhetoric book, Wilson used Erasmus's letter not so much for purposes of anti-authoritarianism or of his own brand of dogmatic anti-clericalism. He used it, rather, to show his Protestant and newly arrived middle-class audience what a well-written "oration" (declamation) looks like and, implicatively, how such a letter can be used as an important access to the rich and powerful.

Like most humanists, Wilson found rhetoric overlapping dialectic. Although he shows that dialectic always moves toward general application, while rhetoric moves toward specific circumstance, he also shows that what makes an argument effective in dialectic is exactly what makes any "oration"—such as a letter—rhetorically efficacious: one should always keep the opposition in view, including any opposing or unfavorable emotion. "Wariness" Wilson calls it and insists that it is ever thought great wisdom.[79] His traditional appearing book on rhetoric, too easily read today as a schoolbook, is more nearly a demonstration of wary eloquence as an avenue to power—as taught and exemplified by a successful practitioner (I will

---

79. Wilson, *The Rule of Reason*, 153; see also *The Art of Rhetorique* (1553), fol. 35. The referenced editions are cited in my chapter 6.

pursue this argument in Chapter 6), one whose eloquence propelled his rise from the newly mobile middle class through a highly successful political career. In this respect Wilson sheds light on Erasmus, whose own career is a case study in the use of eloquence as an instrument of power and whose retrospective view of his work as an educator was simple: "Erasmus," he said of himself, "taught nothing except eloquence."[80]

It is an eloquence which Erasmus shows and Wilson tells arises from wariness, and in such wariness lies the contrarianism which is the theme of my argument. Therein, too, lies a specific pedagogical principle: rhetorical *inventio* in the humanist tradition I am discussing relies not simply on processing ideas through the topics, but on generating arguments with one eye on the opposition—and, in classroom practice, on actually developing ideas on both sides of the question. Thus schoolboys in Elizabethan England, immersed in disputation, were advised by their humanist schoolmasters to prepare "copybooks" listing arguments pro and con. Erasmus upholds the practice in his *De copia,* and Francis Bacon shows very clearly how it was to be done.

Bacon brings me back to that ancient schoolroom debate on whether a man should marry. Bacon's famous essay "Of Marriage and single life" begins "He that hath *Wife* and *Children,* hath giuen Hostages to Fortune."[81] In the "copy" or "promptuary" book among Bacon's writings,[82] that very statement is listed on the *con* side. The next statement in the essay begins, somewhat grudgingly, to move toward the *pro* side: "For they are Impediments to great Enterprises, either of Vertue, or Mischief." The essay proceeds through a thicket of prolepses, in which pro and con arguments are lifted directly out of the copybook and strung, sometimes violently, together, all leading to a non-conclusion and producing the effect of a preliminary brief that could take the debate in either direction. But even in its ambivalence the essay is an affront to absolutism. As Bacon well shows, rhetorical contention—more than its dialectical coun-

80. In his letter to John Botzheim, 30 Jan 1523. *Opus Epistolarum* (Oxford, Eng., 1906–57), 1:30.1–3.

81. Edward Arber, ed. *A Harmony of the Essays, etc., of Francis Bacon* (London, 1871), 265.

82. *De agumentis scientarum,* in *Works,* ed. James Spedding et al. (London, 1858–75) 4: 472–92.

terpart—always has a propensity for irresolution, if only because its "rules" are more flexible and less dependent upon formal validity.

I have placed this essay, a textbook example of the kind of writing I shall discuss in my next chapter, in Appendix B—there rather than here partly because I am never comfortable with calling Bacon a humanist. There is a certain meanness of spirit and, in many of his writings, a further drive toward indisputable certainty, better suited to inquisitions than to the kind of pursuits most humanists engaged in. Alexander Pope put it best: in a famous couplet he called Bacon the "wisest" and "brightest" and "meanest of mankind." One might join one's voice to the usual complaints about Bacon's dolorous manner of communication. But another, less controversial (and less mean), way of putting my point might be simply to note the thoroughly anti-Erasmian reform of language in which he was engaged (on this point see Waswo, *Language and Meaning,* esp. 50–51). Nonetheless, *structurally* most of Bacon's essays reveal those characteristics I associate with humanism, Erasmian humanism in particular. Irony, duplexity, and ambivalence, I've suggested, are effects coincident with the split-focus of two-sided argument. So too is the effect of keeping two or more audiences in mind. Like triangulation, these effects are born of humanist optimism: readers and hearers have minds capable of entertaining possibilities. The author's purpose is always to engage those minds either, as Bacon does, in a demonstration of rhetoric as a mode of two-sided, skeptical inquiry or, as Erasmus does in his letter to Mountjoy, in a move actually to secure collaboration and assent or at least to make a certain and in some cases highly troublesome point of view compelling.

I am convinced, too, that it was the commingling of *sermo* and *disputatio* which produced certain distinctive characteristics of humanist writing.[83] Sermo, the easy ebb and flow of good conversation, the preferred humanist genre, was both the very motive of the written dialogue and it was also, not surprisingly, the category within which humanists fit their epistolography.[84] As a consequence

83. In *De officiis,* I.xxxvii. 132, Cicero makes *sermo* and *contentio* equally at home in debates. For an excellent discussion of this passage and the place of *sermo* in humanist writing, see John F. Tinkler, "Renaissance Humanism and the *genera eloquentiae,*" *Rhetorica* 5 (1987): 279–309.

84. On dialogue in Erasmus, see R. J. Schoeck, *Erasmus Grandescens* : "In the 1490s to write a dialogue was in itself to take a stand against scholasticism, with its

of its commingling of *sermo* and disputation, some humanist prose appears desultory in its multi-vocal attempt to cast a wide net for truth while at the same time preserving "the integral validity of each point of view."[85] That attempt, the Ciceronian *multiplex ratio disputandi,* may appear to the philosophically serious like an effort to make the worse appear the better reason, as I suggested earlier. Too, like good conversation, the discourse can be irresolute: it does not necessarily move toward closure.[86] It can end in a volteface, or display an ostensible and at times even baffling inconsistency and irony that readers have found in such pieces as *De contemptu mundi* and the *Praise of Folly.*[87] Nonetheless, the practice allows us to grasp a certain ideal: the best communication in this view, though conversational, remains as rhetorically duplex as two-sided debate in which the reader sits in judgment; often it is not *protreptic* but *maieutic.* The point, which will be further pursued in my next chapter, is to capture an audience, or an opponent for that matter, and it is—like the enriched *inventio* on which it is based—a legacy of the marriage of rhetoric and disputation.

---

favorite forms of disputation and *Quodlibets (disputationes quodlibetales,* or 'free' as distinguished from disputations with announced topics)" (95). See, too, Walter Ruegg, *Cicero und der Humanismus* (Zurich, 1946): . . . *im Dialog findet er [Erasmus] seine innere Freiheit, seine Form. Die Komposition ist, wie wir uns gewohnt sind, ganz associativ, unsystematisch, and unproportionert* (121). David Marsh has discussed dialogic precursors in his *Quattrocento Dialogue: Classical Tradition and Humanist Innovation* (Cambridge, Mass., 1980). See, too, Kenneth Wilson (cited in the following footnote). On *sermo* and epistolography, see Judith Rice Henderson, "Erasmus on the Art of Letter-Writing," in James J. Murphy, ed. *Renaissance Eloquence* (Berkeley, Calif., 1983), 331–55.

85. On Ciceronian *multiplex ratio disputandi* see Michael J. Buckley, S.J., *Motion and Motion's God: Thematic Variations in Aristotle, Cicero, Newton, and Hegel* (Princeton, N.J., 1971), esp. 93. The quotation is from Kenneth Wilson, *Incomplete Fictions: The Formation of English Renaissance Dialogue* (Washington, D.C., 1985), 29. Wilson is describing the characteristics of Ciceronian dialogue as used by the humanists, in which "voice" was often dependent upon the "autonomy" of characters in the dialogue.

86. Joel B. Altman in *The Tudor Play of Mind* (Berkeley, Calif., 1978) links this irresoluteness in Tudor drama to *in utramque partem* disputation. Brenda Deen Schildgen finds a similar irresoluteness in Petrarch's defense of secular letters; see "Petrarch's Defense of secular Letters, the Latin Fathers, and Ancient Roman Rhetoric," *Rhetorica* 11 (1993): 119–34.

87. A reading of *De contemptu mundi* in terms of two-sided debate is offered by Bainton in *Erasmus of Christendom,* 14–17. A similar reading of the *Moria* is suggested in the principles I am discussing.

From the first of this book, I have described a view of language and communication that is nominalist, historicist, skeptical, oral, social and consensual. I have consistently indicated that this view is humanist. But now I must add that it is only largely humanist, more humanist than Scholastic. The Renaissance humanists who figure in my antiquarian examples were not perfect nominalists, historicists, skeptics, etc. For them the relation between words and external reality—between *verba* and *res*—was compounded of two radically incompatible influences: a nominalism which insisted that the relation between words and reality lay in usage and convention, and an ongoing realism (or Stoicism, or formalism, or Scholasticism) which said that a word reflected an inner discourse which itself *could* match the nature of outer reality.[88] However, rhetorical-disputatious *inventio,* the chief protocol of Erasmian humanists, always favored the nominalist approach. By its very nature, it had to, predicated as it was on circumstance, on getting down to cases, on the personalities of the people involved. However resistant these humanists might have been to the implications of the disputation they themselves encouraged, the very nature of that disputation always conveyed a certain epistemology, a certain view of language and knowledge of truth. Its proclivity for extreme skepticism, a point invariably raised by its opponents, was potentially held at bay by the parameters of social consensus.[89] Within that proclivity lies the impulse of Erasmus's seriocomic approach to theology and his "cleverness" as a writer.

Given the modern propensity for and appreciation of this kind of irony, it is perhaps remarkable that we have overlooked this humanist protocol. Further, although it is widely acknowledged that of all the elements of rhetoric *inventio* remains the most impoverished in the American revival, no recent book on rhetoric urges a restoration of debate, or even the practice of two-sided argument and the writ-

---

88. On these radical incompatibilities and their combination in humanist thought, see Martin Elsky, *Authorizing Words: Speech, Writing, and Print in the English Renaissance* (Ithaca, N.Y., 1988) and G. A. Padley, *Grammatical Theory in Western Europe, 1500–1700: The Latin Tradition* (Cambridge, Eng., 1976).

89. As Victoria Kahn puts it, "In a move characteristic of the humanists as a whole, the epistemological threat of skepticism is contained by the practice of social consensus"; "Humanism and the Resistance to Theory," *Literary Theory/Renaissance Texts,* eds. Patricia Parker and David Quint (Baltimore, 1986), 377. The point has been around, among some Sophists apparently, since the time of Isocrates.

ing of recantations, let alone the virtuosity of oral composition. Indeed, American rhetoric is notably silent on the matter of disputatiousness, whether oral or written. But this is the very matter we need to consider restoring not simply to our study of the great documents of our past but also to our teaching of composition, for it is both an essential feature of the classical tradition and as Erasmus cleverly proposes, a possible way of enriching *inventio*.[90] We have lost a stimulating innovation of the Renaissance, the use of rhetorical *inventio* in generating arguments pro and con, partly because we no longer honor the marriage of rhetoric and disputation. But partly too perhaps because we no longer honor the equally hallowed union of writing and speaking.

The metaphor I have used—marriage—may seem far-fetched, since the union I propose comprises dispute. The metaphor, however, is the sort Renaissance rhetoricians loved, the sort they called *catachresis,* a joining together of ostensibly disparate elements—itself the difficult pursuit of an age that, like ours, was aware of the fragmentary nature of knowledge and experience and of the perplexing gaps between language and thought, words and things, what the rhetoricians then called *verba* and *res*. Fractiousness as well as irony were virtually unavoidable. That long and complex disquisition Erasmus eventually created in which he argued that marriage is as blessed a choice as celibacy, the *Institutio christiani matrimonii* (1526), was regarded as being suspiciously Lutheran. But it was history, in collusion with the initially innocent author, which gave that work its final

---

90. Recent American efforts to revive stasis theory in the absence of a strong disputational practice in the classroom offer only further evidence of part of my point. Kathryn Rosser Raign provides an excellent review of current work in "Stasis Theory Revisited: An Inventional *Techne* for Empowering Students," *Focuses* 2 (1989): 19–26. My point about the attenuation of debate in modern American rhetoric can be substantiated by comparing the works in Raign's review with those in Antoine Braet's discussion, "The Classical Doctrine of *status* and the Rhetorical Theory of Argumentation," *Philosophy and Rhetoric* 20 (1987): 79–93. For an incisive review of classical stasis theory and an argument that modern rhetoric (assuming an identification of rhetoric with pro and con argument, or conflict) necessitates a privileging of the "fourth" stasis, "Objection" (an interesting translation of *rectene factum sit; De oratore* II.xxvi.113), see David Goodwin, "Controversiae Meta-Asystatae and the New Rhetoric," *Rhetoric Society Quarterly* 19 (1989): 205–16. Stasis can never be a fully operational instrument unless actively applied in two-sided argument.

and thoroughly Erasmian irony: it was dedicated to Catherine of Aragon.

Erasmus's lesson about words—that they are wrapped in their own historicity and circumstance, that (always with a nod toward the *consensus fidelium*) their meaning arises functionally from person, situation, and motive, and inheres not so much in the things they represent as in the story they tell[91]—this is a lesson which, a modern novelist has suggested, is in need of rebirth:

> . . . a perfect *word*, a necessary WORD, is like a dream: once it is said or written, nothing can be added, and what it describes disappears forever: the palace, the desert, the mirror, the library, the compass pass: when they are identical to their word, they disappear forever, they dream forever, they die forever. We must never find the exact identification of words with things—a mystery, a divorce, a dissonance must remain. Then a poem will be written to close the separation, never achieving the re-union. A story will be told.

The passage is from a remarkable encomium, Carlos Fuentes' tribute to Borges upon the death of the Argentinian master.[92] The encomium is in the form of a narrative, a story is told, in which an imaginary Borges encounters an imaginary Erasmus, along with an imaginary Fuentes. The piece is brilliant with insight. It is equally brilliant in its call for a renaissance of, among other qualities, "the desolate Erasmian irony" and a voice insisting that the world is "made of realities, not of shadows."

Thus I begin and end this chapter with encomia. Both center in the uneasy marriage of language to a world of realities, a marriage made a little less uneasy Erasmus believed through copiousness and through an imagination stretched over both sides of almost every argument. The lesson of or in each encomium is utterly humanist and was rearticulated in the Renaissance union of rhetoric and disputation: the very "moment we leave the realm of theory for that of practical experience,"[93] language is first and foremost centered in

---

91. A good review of the doctrine is in Waswo's description of the differences between Erasmian and medieval approaches to scriptural meaning, *Language and Meaning*, 225.

92. Carlos Fuentes, "Borges in Action: A Narrative Homage," *PMLA* 101 (1986): 778–87.

93. Stephen Toulmin, "The Recovery of Practical Philosophy," *American Scholar* (Summer, 1988), 347: "The moment we leave the realm of theory for that of practical

personality and social context, and is instrumental, evanescent, quotidian—that is to say, oral—its meaning the provisional outcome of a never-ending dispute.

Erasmus, George K. Hunter has recently noted, had a most sophisticated understanding of "the gap between the world of contingency in which words are spoken and the world of absolutes to which we are bound by faith and hope." In that observation Hunter has schematized something of the "irony" Rorty describes and most of the "desolate irony" Fuentes mentions. This was a gap, Hunter continues, "that could not be bridged by rhetoric but which rhetoric could delineate by its power of indirection."[94] That power of indirection is the subject of the next chapter, wherein we shall be concerned not with exploring the gap between the two worlds but with the humanists' use of rhetoric to explore living and making moral choices in the world of contingency. As always, we shall be concerned with the protocol of traditional rhetoric, this time through the subtlest devices of its cleverest discourse.

---

experience, the rebuttable presumptions of practical argument replace the formal necessity of theoretical inference."

94. "Rhetoric and Renaissance Drama," in Peter Mack, ed. *Renaissance Rhetoric* (New York, 1994), 111.

5. Suasion

Forty years ago as a freshman composition teacher I gave my students the weary, stale, flat, and dubiously profitable if standard advice: "Write not so that you will be understood but so that you cannot be misunderstood." On the contrary, Erasmus, as noted in my first chapter, would give students, even younger ones than those I taught, this advice (in the *De copia*, CWE, 24: 336): "[O]ne should not write so that everyone can understand everything, but so that people should be compelled to investigate and learn some things themselves." Thus Erasmus voiced a lesson about traditional rhetoric's power of indirection.

The task of this chapter is to show where that heuristic might have led in the past. It might have led, I shall argue, to the composition of a certain diversionary kind of discourse, similar to that described recently by Ronald G. Witt, a kind of composition falling somewhere between speaking and writing and marked by an inferential mode of thought.[1] I shall look for samples outside drama or poetry,

---

1. To George A. Kennedy's now famous division (in *Classical Rhetoric and Its Christian and Secular Traditions from Ancient to Modern Times* [Chapel Hill, N.C., 1980], 4–5) of traditional rhetoric into "primary" (speechmaking) and "secondary" (all written, especially literary genres), Ronald G. Witt has added a third: "a way of thought that seeks conclusions by inference rather than by demonstration, whose weapon is more often the enthymeme than the syllogism" ("Medieval Italian Culture and the Origins of Humanism as a Stylistic Ideal," in *Renaissance Humanism*, Vol. 3,

for in those genres some explorations of this phenomenon have already been accomplished.[2] In light of our previous discussion, we can call the prose we shall examine suasion for it is more like the declamatory exercise *suasoria* than the openly disputational *controversia*. Too, the name will distinguish the discourse from "persuasion," though for some readers that distinction will require a footnote.[3]

Of course, throughout this genre the residue of controversy is always tangible. Early in the seventeenth century John Brinsley described what we would call the "written theme" and what he calls

---

ed. Albert Rabil, Jr. [Philadelphia, 1988], 32). Debate, I am arguing, is an important way whereby this "way of thought" is systematized and learned; see Witt, 31: rhetoricians taught students "to declaim, to debate, and to deliver orations of their own making."

2. The presence of an enriched *inventio* in Tudor drama, that "special child of a rhetorical culture which flourished in England in the sixteenth century," has already been well explored, as I have noted, by Joel B. Altman, *The Tudor Play of Mind: Rhetorical Inquiry and the Development of Elizabethan Drama* (Berkeley, Calif., 1978); the quoted passage is on p. 395. So far as Renaissance poetry is concerned, Thomas J. Reed Jr. in his study of medieval debate poetry has given us the background for a possible examination of the continuing and thoroughly rhetorical "aesthetics of irresolution" in *Medieval English Debate Poetry and the Aesthetics of Irresolution* (Columbia, Mo., 1990).

3. Latin maintained a more precise distinction between the two terms than does English: *suadeo* meant to present something in a pleasing or non-threatening manner, to recommend, whereas *persuadeo* meant to convince, to prevail upon someone. The differences between the two are somewhat elusive and, as the humanists seemed to realize to their advantage, somewhat illusive as well. Erasmus, for example, as we have seen in my preceding chapter, calls his letter to Mountjoy on marriage an *"exemplum epistolae suasoriae."* In doing so, he was positing a difference between exhortative letters and suasory ones, allowing the latter considerably more latitude: see *De conscribendis epistolis* chapters. XXXIII, XLV, and XLVII. It is not quite accurate to Erasmus's intentions to translate (as Fantazzi does in CWE, 25) *exhortatio* as "encouragement" and *suasoria* as "persuasion" even (or especially) in light of their Quintilianesque precedents. True, Erasmus's own use of *suasoria* in chapter X is clearly for persuasive letters of advice. But, again, the point seems to be that *suasoria* allows latitude in one's efforts to be persuasive. As always, however, Erasmus uses generic divisions with some diffidence. Thus, it seems to me that Fantazzi's use of "discussion" to translate *disputatoria* in chapter LXXIV is appropriately slippery. In another place Erasmus offers an even more complex distinction: Christianity, he argues in his treatise on war against the Turks, was spread not by warlike tactics but in a gentler way—"by suasion, not by compulsion, by implanting, not by obtruding" (*De bello turcico* [1530]: *Religio Christiana,* was spread *suadetur non cogitur, & inseritur non obtruditur* [Leclerc, V.355(F)]).

the declamation in a way that exposes the controversy in its compositional as well as interpretive principles:

> The declamation is nothing else but a theme of some matter, which may be controverted, and so handled by parts, when one taketh the Affirmative part, another the Negative, and it may be a third moderateth or determineth between both. We have very good precedents in the Thesis in Aphthonius, as in that question handled both affirmative and negative, viz. *Uxor est ducenda* [a man should marry], *Uxor non est ducenda* [a man should not marry].[4]

Brinsley's description is a condensed summary of the protocol of suasion, particularly when we focus on that third voice, the one that "moderateth or determineth between both." Often the two sides are conflated—or can be—with a judge in the middle somewhere. We shall look at the prose of masters trained in these elementary exercises. Brinsley offers merely a schoolmasterly reassertion that disputation is a conceptual model for all declamation, even that which is aimed indirectly, which capitalizes on doubleness, and which may, maieutic-like, throw the burden not simply of judgment but even of further invention on the audience.

Parody—not in the sense of ridiculing something but in the sense of adapting something, often adapting antiquarian-like something from the past in such a way that the work becomes a "literary criticism" of the text parodied—tends to be a major outer principle of the suasory form I shall discuss, disputation always the inner.[5] The point is not to parodize exactly—certainly not in the modern sense— but to sway others by centering their minds on a collateral matter. Too, such prominently used structural and local figures as *paradox* and *litotes*, we shall find, are suasory echoes of the underlying disputational practice, as was *prolepsis* in Erasmus's letter to Mountjoy. So too is the habit of sallying forth with an outrageous proposal— e.g., all property should be held in common, all wisdom is foolish-

---

4. *Ludus Literarius: or, The Grammar Schoole* (London, 1612), 184; I have modernized the spelling and punctuation of this passage.

5. A related but contrasting study is Sander L. Gilman's *The Parodic Sermon in European Perspective* (Wiesbaden, 1974). Though he gives attention to the writer's intention, Gilman's approach is essentially formalistic: parody results, he argues, when "two unlike approaches to the same form" are juxtaposed (3). The tradition of learned parody, within which he places *The Praise of Folly*, is distinguished not so much by its characteristic modes of thought as by its crystallized forms.

ness, or Lord Mountjoy should break his vow of celibacy. But the real point is often hidden, so that it may be pressed home in a less painfully direct way. We shall approach this genre first through an example offered by someone who is rarely—too rarely—thought of as a humanist rhetorician.

John Donne's preaching, like his poetry, continually dwelt on ambiguities and ironies—a subjective preoccupation he shared with the learned humanists of his time. Like them he was trained in the law, and although he did not pursue law as a career he remained temperamentally attuned to legalistic, and thus humanistic, reasoning. At the center of his concerns were such matters as contracts, promises, terms, and expectations. In any lawyerly quest for available truth, much depends upon definition and explanation of motive, on ambivalences of language and tone, and on such other circumstantial elements of rhetoric as the immediate occasion and the character of the people involved. Ultimately Donne's purpose seemed always to be a thoroughly humanist, thoroughly anti-authoritarian one: things are seldom as simple as they seem, including the discourse we are studying (and even, some critics have argued, including Donne himself).

In one sermon Donne speaks of the doubleness of what one might suppose is the simplest of all forms of discourse, encomia, discourse offered on formal occasions usually to praise some great person. Donne notes that such discourse is not so simple in intention as it seems. The orator in praising his prince for, say, wisdom and generosity is often in fact pointing out the very *absence* of those qualities. Thus, the orator's praise becomes an oblique blame, a rebuke Donne calls, legalistically, a "collateral increpation."[6]

Donne's orator offers flattery, too, of course, and his collateral increpation is therefore most efficacious when used in the presence of easily offended power, a rhetorical situation that Thomas More (in the *Utopia*) believed called for "craft" and "subtlety." But all these are, in turn, elements in a general approach and manner for which

6. *The Sermons of John Donne,* ed. George R. Potter and Evelyn M. Simpson (Berkeley, 1962) 5: 200–201. As O'Malley has shown, Aurelio Brandolini makes much the same point about the doubleness of epideictic oratory: "just as praise was sometimes blame in disguise, reproach was sometimes an integral part of praise"; see John W. O'Malley, *Praise and Blame in Renaissance Rome* (Durham, N.C., 1979), 192.

Erasmus had the most clever term: *via diversa*. Not simply duplexity but complexity is the point of Donne's lesson—and rhetorical complexity may follow many paths in addition to the three elementary ones marked out in disputation.

Suasory discourse born of this complexity could place tremendous demands on readers. It could be Janus-faced in structure. It could proceed, as Puttenham says, "by long ambage." It could be "sinuous, subtle, shifting," as Louis L. Martz characterizes Thomas More's *De tristitia:* More's argument "seems quite Erasmian in its movement," Martz says, "its ironic undertones, its bland assertions of an equable position, while all the time leaning toward one side of the argument."[7] It could seem not only labyrinthine but utterly baffling. Luther, for example, looked up from one of Erasmus's arguments and called its author "Proteus" and an "eel." But Luther surely knew what he was doing. His slander was most likely strategic, aimed at winning support from the truly bewildered members of Erasmus's mixed audience, especially those who were seeking a plainer truth delivered in a less diverse way. Luther, after all, was as unsympathetic toward humanist rhetoric as he was fearful of its success.

Reflecting on these characteristics, we could find that we have already studied some major examples of suasion, several of which make their protocol salient.

De oratore is one. Cicero moves obliquely, allowing us to overhear his letter to Quintus and centering our minds on a collateral matter, "an old story" he calls it which somehow parodies the *Phaedrus*. There is, of course, much duplexity throughout—to-fro, pro-con— so pervasive is the doubleness that the reader is forced to consider its point: not only does this suasion overtly use controversy, but it makes of *controversia* a protocol which is part of the very "inventive" lesson the dialogue teaches. Finally, although Cicero intervenes overtly to prod the reader—that is, Quintus—at the first of each book, he seems to leave the final judgment open, making it difficult to segregate the "good guys" from the "bad guys" or "Cicero's spokesman" from "not Cicero's spokesman."

Erasmus's *De copia* is another example. Its exemplariness is I believe signaled by the word Erasmus used to characterize the book,

---

7. *Thomas More: The Search for the Inner Man* (New Haven, Conn., 1990), 96.

"clever." And the pieces inside the book, like the disquisition on obscenity or the argument against learning Greek, are also clever. That is, in their sallying forth they are so suffused with doubleness that they can catch the unwary reader off guard. In fact "wariness"— as I have noted, again recalling Thomas Wilson, the subject of my next chapter—is part of their point. Indeed, the whole Erasmian corpus is rich with examples of this suasory type, reflecting certain habits of thought, Ciceronian *inventio* at its deepest levels. The letter on marriage—the so-called *Encomium matrimonii*—seems somewhat less complicated. As addressed to Mountjoy, it might be advisory but it also seems to be a sample of advocacy, something which might belong to *controversia*. That it might belong to *controversia* seems part of the point of Erasmus's apology for the letter, a point he further proves first by calling the piece a "declamation" (in which, Brinsely might note, he took only one "part") and then by writing the other side of the argument for inclusion in his textbook. However, as overheard by theologians, or any supposedly unintended audience, the letter moves into the broader realm of suasion. For it was, or became, in the *open* field a "collateral increpation" of celibacy. Faced with categorizing the letter as intrinsically *exhortatio* or *suasoria,* Erasmus in his textbook sensibly and I believe significantly opted for the latter. There were those other, non-theological members of his audience, Mountjoy perhaps among them, who might truly see just what it was the letter sought to rebuke.

The Praise of Folly is probably the cleverest, most complex and difficult, of all; we have touched on this work, and we shall look at a small piece of it shortly. (Elsewhere I have tried to come to terms with this complex and hilarious monologue;[8] only fleeting references will appear in the present book.) The brilliance of the work, an oration given by the woman Folly before an audience of learned theologians, lies in a disputatiousness which ironically denies disputatiousness. In the *Moria* (as Erasmus nicknamed *The Praise of Folly,* the *Moriae encomium*) and throughout much of his "seriocomic" writing, Walter M. Gordon remarks, Erasmus reveals a "pervasive as-

8. See my *Donne, Milton, and the End of Humanist Rhetoric* (Berkeley, Calif., 1985), 67–84. For an illuminating, antiquarian reading of *The Praise of Folly,* one that, controversially, sees Erasmus transcending Academic skepticism, see Patricia Bizzell, "*The Praise of Folly,* The Woman Rhetor, and Post-Modern Skepticism," *Rhetoric Society Quarterly* 22 (1992): 7–17.

pect of his style: his habit of juxtaposing notions in a state of contention and of reducing one idea to its opposite."[9] Folly counters
prevailing opinion in such a self-conscious way that her perversity
forfends rebuttal; she can allow only one kind of response, and only
one is possible: "Applaud my speech, live well, drink your fill, you
worthy initiates into the mysteries of Folly" are her final words.

Moreover, it was in connection with the *Moria,* that Erasmus offered the most compelling explanation of the suasory mode of writing I am trying to describe. He wrote a lengthy reply to Maarten van
Dorp, a theologian with some humanist leanings, who had severely
criticized the work.[10] The *Moria,* Erasmus says, only expounds the
very ideas or matters he had developed in his other "lucubrations"—
such as *The Enchiridion, On the Education of a Christian Prince,* and
The Panegyric of Philip the Duke of Burgundy, works moral, educational, even theological. But in *The Praise of Folly* his means are not
the same. That is, in this difficult, slippery, contradictory work, he
claims, his ideas are presented *via diversa:* with this phrase he sig-
nifies that not only are the means he employed different from those
in the other "lucubrations," the means are themselves diverse.[11] As
always, he calls to his aid antiquarian arguments—Lucianic satire,
the rhetorical efficacy of laughter as advised by Cicero and Quintilian, the sayings of Christ. But the point remains that in the *Moria*
his approach and manner are indirect and oblique. He took a differ-

---

9. *Humanist Play and Belief: The Seriocomic Art of Desiderius Erasmus* (Toronto,
1990), 43.

10. The Latin appears in Leclerc, IX.2(E). An English translation appears in
Clarence H. Miller's edition of *The Praise of Folly* (New Haven, Conn., 1979), 139–
74. Erasmus's famous apology for the work was so well done, Thomas More believed, that we should all be eternally grateful to Dorp for complaining in the first
place. Thereby More offered a further piece of evidence in the case Jardine constructs
for Erasmus as a self-promoter: Dorp may have only been playing a consciously
controversial role, to serve Erasmian purposes. Jardine comments, "the story of the
dispute between Erasmus and Dorp is a performance"; *Erasmus, Man of Letters*
(Princeton, N. J., 1993), 111.

11. *Nec aliud omnino spectavimus in Moria, quam quod in caeteris Lucubrationibus,
tametsi via diversa* (Leclerc, IX.2(E)). The phrase seems to have more the force of a
pun in this location—Erasmus seems to mean not only "a different" but also "a
diverse" path—than his use of the phrase elsewhere: e.g. (in *Institutio principis christiani*), the war against the Turks should not be hastily undertaken when we recall
that Christ began, propagated, and secured his kingdom by different means *(diversa
via);* Leclerc, IV.610(E).

ent path, or rather several different paths for the one he took proved ambiguous.

At first, he says, he was only trying to relieve himself of the discomfort of a kidney ailment by means of an intellectual diversion, so he wrote the *Moria*. But surely this putative compositional situation is meant to be emblematic. For the *Moria* is in effect a diversion for the world's ills; it allows the mind to see them from a startling, new angle. So, just as Socrates veiled his face when he spoke arguments not completely his own, Erasmus says, with a nod toward the *Phaedrus,* he veiled his own face with the persona of Folly, thus setting into motion all the rhetorical considerations of fiction, *ethos* and *decorum*. Dorp had suggested that Erasmus write a "retraction" of the work—a good Erasmian practice in and of itself—as a counterbalance, perhaps a "Praise of Wisdom," to placate theologians particularly. Erasmus responds that it's usually best to let sleeping dogs lie. But Dorp's suggestion is impossible. For for how could one write a retraction of something that is itself already compounded of its own contradictions? Indeed, to consider retracting *The Praise of Folly* uncovers the very movement of the *via diversa.*

In sum, the suasory writing that we are speaking of is somewhere between pompous argument and jeu d'esprit, between fact and fiction, between confrontational invective and titilating comedy, between a straight road and an ambage. The writing takes a "different approach" and pursues a "diverse course." Again, Erasmus's pun is a good one: *via diversa.*[12]

Too, leaving the phrase in Latin may point up a rhetorical problem: suasory writing was primarily for a learned audience, whose members were conversant in Latin. Any discourse that is translated from Latin into English, Thomas More comments in his confutation of Tyndale, always runs the risk of falling into the hands of people incapable of understanding the subtleties in that discourse.[13] The argumentative purpose of More's comment does not diminish a cer-

---

12. He wasn't the only one to use the term, of course. Montaigne makes a famous use of it in an early essay: "By diverse means we arrive at the same end," the first essay in Frame's edition (Stanford, Calif., 1948), an essay which is contradictory in nature and irresolute, offers a fine example of suasory effects. I am indebted to James M. Pearce for calling my attention to Montaigne's love of this kind of diversity.

13. The argument of course fits the point he raises against Tyndale's carelessness. See *Complete Works,* ed. Louis A. Schuster et al. (New Haven, Conn., 1973), 8: 179.

tain wide truth in his observation. English had yet to relinquish its second-class status as the unpolished and frequently singular tongue of the uneducated; it was not until the middle of the sixteenth century, for instance, that logic and rhetoric were made available to readers more at home in English than in Latin. On the other hand, there was no guarantee that *any* segment of the Latin-conversant populace would be either sensitive or sympathetic to suasory tactics. Theologians disputed in Latin. So too did Martin Luther. The preferred audience of suasion was a certain intellectual class, that *consensus eruditorum* (to echo Valla) of humanists knowledgeable in the ways of traditional rhetoric, experienced in *controversia* and *suasoria* and therefore best equipped to appreciate a *via diversa*. Print exacerbated the audience problem, as More seemed to realize in giving readers of his *Utopia* a built-in guide, a tactic seldom favored by Erasmus. Following two Latin examples, the first by More, the second by Erasmus, we shall turn to other authors who while writing in English had variable success in solving the rhetorical problem of readership. But all help us glimpse the nature of this difficult genre.

Utopia by Thomas More (1516)[14]

More, who is both the author of this dialogue and a character in it, offers in this work a further and utterly humanist distinction between two modes of communication, like that between *controversia* and *suasoria*. We have already distributed several qualities between these two, placing with the former advocacy, persuasion, and exhortation, and with the latter indirection, irony, and a not infrequent reader-frustration. But, as noted earlier and as will be reiterated now in the More example, all of these profoundly overlapping qualities come down to a basic distinction between pointed, direct confrontation and latitudinous speech. Like Erasmus with his phrase *via diversa,* More puts the distinction colorfully.

In the conversation in Book One between Thomas More (that is, the character Morus), Peter Giles, and Raphael Hythlodaeus, Morus

14. The English version I cite is the first translation, by Ralph Robynson, 1551, ed. J. Churton Collins (Oxford, Eng., 1904). Again, I have modernized spelling and punctuation. The Latin is the original edition reprinted by the Scholar Press in 1966. An excellent analysis of the *Utopia* as *via diversa* is A. R. Heiserman, "Satire in the *Utopia,*" *PMLA* 78 (1963): 163–74.

has just responded to Raphael's comment that there seems to be little purpose in saying things to people who are quite determined to take the opposite view. And when those people are in power, it seems more than purposeless, it seems risky. Morus agrees and continues,

> I cannot allow that such communication shall be used or such counsel given as you be sure shall never be regarded or received [i.e., attended to or even heard]. For how can so strange informations be profitable, or how can they be beaten into heads whose minds be already prevented [i.e., previously stuffed] with clean contrary persuasions? This school philosophy [*philosophia scholastica*] is not unpleasant among friends in familiar communication. But in the counsels of kings, where great matters be debated and reasoned with great authority, these things have no place. (39)

Although Raphael interrupts (and attempts to use what Morus has just said to confirm his own point, that there is therefore no room at Court for philosophy at all), More/Morus counters that at least there is no room at Court for "school philosophy," the Scholastic mode of communication which uses dialectic, gives no thought to *decorum,* and simply says what it thinks irrespective of circumstances. No, there is another "philosophy more civil" which knows how to behave "herself in the play that she hath in hand."

This "other philosophy," Morus argues, is the one to be used at Court. One shouldn't, after all, abandon ship in a storm simply because one can't control the winds. Decorum, control. One might suppose that Morus is speaking of rhetoric, the discipline humanists habitually used to foil Scholasticism with its narrow, formalist, and abstract dialectic. So he is. But his point in drawing these distinctions goes farther than the usual ones between humanism/rhetoric and Scholasticism/dialectic. What one must have to succeed before the powerful, or before anyone who holds opinions contrary to yours, is a mode of communication that is decorous, subtle, inoffensive, and flexible enough to operate indirectly:

> . . . you must with a crafty wile and a subtle train study and endeavor yourself, as much as in you lieth, to handle the matter wittily and handsomely for the purpose. And that which you cannot turn to good, so to order it that it be not very bad. For it is not possible for all things to be well unless all men were good—which I think will not be [for a] good many years. (40–41)

But, Raphael objects, that could mean that one should lie or dissemble. For if one is to tell the truth always, one just can't be tactful. Consider, too, that at Court you have only one choice: either falsely support deplorable policies or oppose them. If you do the latter, you'll suffer the consequences of being called a spy or a traitor. If you opt for the former, you'll either lose your own integrity or else the "wickedness and foolishness of others" will be laid on your own neck. So much for the practical results of your "crafty wile and subtle train to turn anything to better" (42).

However, Morus/More has the last word, and it arises from the nature of the whole work. *Utopia* hardly impugns this crafty subtlety. After all, any work of fiction is limited in the extent to which it can propose a rejection of lying or dissembling. True, crafty subtlety may be unnecessary in Utopia; but, to raise a perennial question, how seriously is Utopianism itself proposed? The answer lies in the nature of the work, or rather in the very nature of suasion, whose characteristics we are seeking to uncover.

The central speaker, Raphael, the only one who has supposedly seen Utopia, says that he has no intention of actually advocating Utopianism, certainly not with the hope that Europe may be reformed thereby. After all, Utopianism, he well realizes, is based on an idea that European society would utterly reject: the communal ownership of property. Nonetheless, Raphael *does* actually advocate it, with no subtlety and upon minds that he knows are already "prevented with clean contrary persuasions." In his long monologue in Book 2, in which he describes a blissful society, Utopianism is his very point ("the best" commonwealth in the world, he calls it, and the only true republic, 138). But do either More or Morus advocate it, who have already praised wiliness and subtlety? If *that* is the question, then the point of the work becomes resolutely not to resolve it.

However blissful the picture, Utopia is set before us with many of its circumstances intact, and these reveal a disturbingly mechanical and stoical existence. Too, the picture is offered by a man whose name is an equally curious mixture: *Raphael,* the divine messenger, *Hythlodaeus,* Greek for "dispenser of nonsense." If the speaker's name and the disturbing mixture of qualities he pictures in Book 2 were not enough to mark the work as a mind-engaging—not necessarily mind-boggling but truly heuristic—example of suasion, one has yet another guide. We are meant to read Book 2 in the context of the dispute in Book 1 between the fictive Raphael and the "real" More, or Morus, and Giles, with its clear signal about "crafty and subtle" communication. It is illuminating to recall that Book 1 was, most likely, written after Book 2, or so Erasmus claimed: whereas Book Two was written "at leisure," Book 1 was added "at a later opportunity . . . in the heat of the moment."[15] Perhaps More was stimulated by the difficulties readers were having with a similar example of monologic suasion published just five years earlier and dedicated to More, *The Praise of Folly*, or *Mor[e]iae encomium*.[16] So far as "crafty and subtle" communication is concerned, its chief application in More's *Utopia*, I would suggest, is the advocacy of placing an idea on the table for ongoing discussion toward some future agenda. Particularly as filtered through More, Raphael's speech is more like the sally, the opening argument, the retractable and contrarian stance of disputatious classroom exercises—in that respect, not unlike Lysias's oration, though the *entire* work is best read in the context either of Erasmus's *Folly* or of Erasmian rhetorical heuristics.

More the author was no more indirectly advocating Utopianism than Erasmus through Folly was indirectly advocating the overthrow of all conventional wisdom. On the contrary, Raphael's praise of Utopia intentionally "raises rather than allays problems," as John Tinkler observes, for the praise is "a mixture of the acceptably ideal and the culturally unsatisfactory." The entire work is irresolute, like much humanist prose, meant to be "part of an ongoing dialogue . . . a convivial and skeptical conversation."[17] For my purposes, Book 1 offers a rationale for the indirect communicative mode of the entire work, which is itself a particularly complicated example of the suasory techniques that interest me most: now you see it, now you

15. Letter to Ulrich von Hutton, 23 July 1519; CWE, 7:24.

16. Whether this conjecture is true or not, I would nonetheless want to restrict the range of Olin's suggestion, that the dialogue between Raphael and More in Book 1 "seems in many ways a discussion between Erasmus and More, with Hythloday voicing characteristic views of Erasmus, particularly with respect to war." The differences between Raphael and Erasmus are vastly more important, especially in regard to ideas about communication, to say nothing of the differences beween More and Morus. John C. Olin, *Christian Humanism and the Reformation* (New York, 1987), 21.

17. John F. Tinkler, "Praise and Advice: Rhetorical Approaches to More's *Utopia* and Machiavelli's *The Prince*," *Sixteenth Century Journal* 19 (1988): 195.

don't. And what do you suppose you should make of what you think you saw?

Again through comparison and contrast we are led back to the *Phaedrus*. In Book 1 of the *Utopia,* the participants speak in a garden—on a bench, covered with a layer of turf (under their plane tree, Socrates and Phaedrus sat on the ground). By contrast, however, the participants are more *inter pares,* among equals, and therefore more Ciceronian than Platonic. Nonetheless, there is a conceptual similarity: Raphael's long Utopian proposal is more than a little outrageous, as was Lysias's speech (read aloud by young Phaedrus) on the advantages of having sex with a nonlover—as was, for that matter, Crassus's proposal for the *perfectus orator.* The personae, the cast of characters may have changed, but the contrarian impulse which produced the opening sally in a lively discussion remains the same. Too, the discussion was meant to continue at the end of Lysias's oration, Crassus's proposal, and More's *Utopia;* Plato, by contrast, offers closure.

But, as I have suggested, of all the parodies at work in the *Utopia,* surely the greatest is the echo of Erasmus's *Praise of Folly.* The long monologue by Raphael may have comprised the whole of the *Utopia* at first, making its affinities with *Folly* easier to see. If it was partly in response to the difficulties readers were having with the Erasmian work that More composed Book 1, it is significant that the addition invites us to hear echoes of the *Phaedrus* (its setting and discussion of the ideal) and *De oratore* (its protocol and participants). Furthermore, whereas Erasmus's humanism compelled him continually to grapple with theological issues, More's led him continually in the direction of politics. "*Utopia* he published with the purpose of showing the reasons for the shortcomings of a commonwealth," stated Erasmus in his letter to Ulrich von Hutton; but More "represented the English Commonwealth in particular, because he had studied it and knew it best" (CWE, 7: 23–24). A satirical intent is, of course, as Erasmus has already shown us, never outside the bounds of a *via diversa*.

Why did the humanists revert again and again to this risky enterprise? Partly, as Morus has argued (and as we heard Donne advise), because the indirect, "crafty" or "subtle" mode (like a "collateral increpation") is the safest and only sensible communication to use before recalcitrant rulers. And partly, as More and Erasmus

have shown, because the contrarian impulse which suffuses humanist prose is based on a certain optimism about the reading or hearing
public, a sanguine assumption that some audiences have minds of
their own and that because most thinking people abhor coercion or
demagoguery the surest persuasion is self-persuasion. Humanism,
Victoria Kahn has argued, is best defined by the epistemological implications of its own rhetoric.[18] Among those implications I would
list as foremost the optimism involved in this suasory form of humanist discourse: people, at least some people, can judge the evidence as well as, or almost as well as, the author can when it is
unassertively laid before them.

Therein, in that optimism, lies also the basis of humanist failure.
Perhaps *tragedy* is not too strong a word for heroic efforts undone by
their very nature and aim, or for that matter, ironically, by the very
assumptions on which the efforts themselves are predicated. One
recalls More's final days in the Tower of London, refusing either to
swear to the Oath of Supremacy or to condemn it. His political
choice was no choice, a characteristic alternative but alas not within
his prerogative. Equally, the wrong rhetorical choice, such as the
wrong tactic before the wrong audience or at the wrong time, errors
that may simply be a consequence of one's predilection for humanist
rhetoric in the first place—these could also prove disastrous. Some
people might assume, and have assumed, for example, that More
through the *Utopia* advocates communism as a means of achieving
an ideal state. Or, for that matter, even that an ideal state is somehow
within the realm of possibility. The tragedy ultimately lies in the
optimism that at least some people among those in power will know
how to read rhetorically.

There is another, clearer, and more relevant case:

The Erasmus-Luther Debate

Erasmus's Protean, Janus-faced, or in less flattering, Lutheran terms
eel-like treatise on the freedom of the will, *De libero arbitrio* (1524),
was mainly addressed to Luther, in epistolary fashion, with the rest
of us in an overhearing situation. Luther had earlier denied free will,
in a discourse whose subject and for that matter title directly chal-

18. *Rhetoric, Skepticism and Prudence* (Princeton, N.J., 1985).

lenge the characteristics of humanist rhetoric, *Assertio* (1520). Erasmus, the radical concordist who hated confrontation, claimed he had to be urged to respond.

He had earlier decried Luther's methods, in a letter to Jodocus Jonas in 1521. Not only did Erasmus abhor the turbulence and violence of Luther's discourse, he took him to task for ignoring a central rhetorical principle, decorum: one must adapt any truth to the circumstances of its telling (its speaker, audience and occasion). By contrast, Luther has

> poured out everything at the same time in so many pamphlets cast forth headlong, divulging everything and making public even to cobblers what is usually treated among the learned as mysterious and secret; and frequently by some unbridled impulse, in my opinion, at least, he is carried beyond what is just.[19]

Not only is Luther nonrhetorical, he is inaccurate and in his divisiveness nonChristian as well. Erasmus comments later that "no name is more hateful to me than that of conspiracy or schism or faction." What the times require is "a holy artfulness" (154)—a position he refused to abandon when he was finally dragged into confronting Luther. By "holy artfulness" he seems to mean, above all, rhetoric, in particular decorum, a principle outside the purview of dialectic, though the question for debate—whether man's will is free—is indeed a dialectical one. Once Erasmus entered this debate his very ethos contrasted with Luther's. It was, of course, an ethos already well known for adhering to the intellectual principles of rhetoric, with its wariness of assertions, its doctrine of mixed truth, its optimistic faith in the learned (and, again in this case overhearing) audience's powers of judgment and intellection. By those principles, divisiveness, he hoped, might be avoided.

In a long introduction to his own treatise in response to Luther's *Assertio* (the length may reflect his reluctance), Erasmus stakes out his limited territory. In *De libero arbitrio* he claims for himself only a modest role in the debate and discusses whether it is sensible to deal with such a knotty question as the will's freedom and whether it is possible to reach Luther at all. Luther, he notes, has already demonstrated his incapacity to listen to anyone else explicating Scripture.

19. I have used John C. Olin's translation in *Christian Humanism and the Reformation*, 147–48.

Nonetheless, the second part[20] of Erasmus's treatise does just that, explicates Scripture on the subject—first pro, passages which seem to defend the will's freedom, then con, passages which seem to deny it. As we might expect, Erasmus substantiates his interpretation of these passages not simply through his own scholarship but also through the *consensus ecclesiae,* the opinions of the pious and saintly Fathers. (But here Erasmus made one of his tactical errors. He cited uncritically Pelagius, a British monk contemporary with St. Augustine, who questioned the doctrine of original sin. Because Pelagian, and later "semi-Pelagian," doctrine opened the door for a denial of man's burden of sin, because it was in effect too optimistic about the operations of man's own free will in attaining salvation, the Church proscribed it. Humanists were almost invariably tainted with Pelagianism. Luther, as one might suppose, abhorred it. And Erasmus, as one might also suppose, used it whenever he thought it served his purposes.) Any time one encounters contradictions in these opinions, Erasmus insists, they should be regarded as less doctrinal than rhetorical, the result of a statement made by this or that Father for this or that audience and occasion. The Scriptures and the Fathers, in sum, should be read rhetorically and understood in terms of the principle of decorum.

In the third and final part Erasmus examines Luther's arguments pro and con, and even summons additional passages which Luther himself might have used (had he thought of them) *against* the freedom of the will. There are indeed two sides, Erasmus admits, but he concludes almost non-judgmentally by urging "a more moderate opinion," one that standing between the two sides (like a moderator) provisionally resolves the dispute.

The discourse, though it is a far cry from advocacy, may not be the perfect example of suasion. Nonetheless, it employs suasory and maieutic procedures throughout, most notably in its conclusion in which Erasmus claims only to have assembled the evidence and appeals to the reader for judgment. The occasion as well as the subject would seem to call for dialectical disputation, for *controversia* at least. But Erasmus used the less confrontational voice of *suasoria* in hopes of transforming the debate into one in which his tactics

---

20. I have followed Augustijn's divisions of the work, while quoting Winter's translations. Both works are cited in subsequent notes.

would be completely decorous. But his "holy artfulness" proved disastrous.

Erasmus's stance as well as his preference for the tactics of suasion can be grasped in yet another way. Let us compare his voice with Luther's, who subsequently rebutted Erasmus in *De servo arbitrio*, On the Bondage of the Will (1525):

> Erasmus had said in his preface: "I am quite aware that I am a poor match in such a contest; I am less experienced than other men, and I have always had a deep-seated aversion to fighting. Consequently I have always preferred playing in the freer field of the muses, than fighting ironclad in close combat. In addition, so great is my dislike of assertions that I prefer the views of the sceptics wherever the inviolable authority of Scripture and the decision of the Church permit—a Church to which at all times I willingly submit my own views, whether I attain what she prescribes or not."
>
> Luther answers: "To avoid misunderstandings, let me define *assertion*. I mean a constant adhering to and affirming of your position, avowing and defending it, and invincibly perserving in it . . . Far be it from us Christians to be sceptics and academics![21] . . . Why do *you* assert your 'dislike of assertions' and your preferring an open mind? . . . What a Proteus [you are] talking about 'inviolable authority of Scriptures and the decisions of the Church'!—as if you had the greatest respect for the Scriptures and the Church, when in the same breath you explain that you wish you had the liberty to be a sceptic! What Christian could talk like this? . . . A Christian will rather say this: I am so against the sentiments of sceptics that, so far as the weakness of the flesh permits, I shall not only steadfastly adhere to the sacred writings everywhere, and in all parts of them, and assert them, but also I wish to be as positive as possible on nonessentials that lie outside Scriptures, because what is more miserable, than uncertainty."
>
> ★ ★ ★
>
> Erasmus had said in his conclusion: "Hence, I want the reader to consider whether he thinks it is fair to condemn the opinion offered by the Church Fathers, approved for some many centuries by so many people, and to accept some paradoxes which are at present disturbing the Christian world. . . . I have come to the end. It is for others to judge."

21. Then far be it from Christians, in Luther's view, to argue pro and con. Both skeptics and academicians, followers like Cicero of the so-called "New Academy," practiced a philosophical method of arguing pro and con about every proposition; see *De oratore* III.xxxvi.145. Erasmus's Folly confessed adherence only to this school of philosophy.

Luther responds: "That you have failed is quite clear from this: 'you assert nothing, but have made comparisons.' One who is fully acquainted with the matter and understands it, does not write like that. On the contrary, in this book of mine, I have not made comparisons, but have asserted and still do assert. I wish none to become judges, but urge all men to submit!"[22]

Luther's tactics were those of the prosecution, Erasmus's those of the suasory, deliberative orator. The disputants had placed themselves in two different speaking situations, calling for two radically different argumentative tactics. Luther clearly saw what Erasmus was up to: allow him these tactics and the allowance itself grants a large part of Erasmus's case. How could people judge if they did not have freedom of will? The alternative, as Luther realized, is submission. Erasmus's choice of tactics—appropriate to his ethos, but the only ones possible, given his argument—necessarily gave him the disadvantage in combat, a softer voice, an evanescent presence. He was not in the freer field of the muses, but he attempted within the closed field of disputation to be suasory. He almost had to. The debate was aimed at the very assumptions of Erasmian humanist rhetoric and education.

But Luther won the debate, insofar as the debate had a clear winner, through his skillful use of forensic rhetoric including the doctrine of *stasis*. He was helped, too, by Erasmus's overestimation of his overhearing audience's interpretive abilities. Luther stayed within the parameters of *controversia;* Erasmus attempted to go beyond them—characteristically, for as Walter M. Gordon puts it, "the natural movement of Erasmus' mind appears to run more frequently in the direction of synthesis than analysis" (140). But if putting it all together is a difficult task, interpreting the resulting discourse could be no less daunting to the overhearing audience. In this respect, it may have been Erasmus who was forced to "offend decorum," in Folly's words, a risk the "foolish" are sometimes required to take.

Marjorie O'Rourke Boyle, who places the debate in the tradition of disputation, sees Erasmus's discourse as undebaterly, "inductive, not deductive," and "maieutic," and she points out that his tactics, clearly at odds with Luther's, could seem unforceful and even half-

22. The quotations are from the translation and edition by Ernst F. Winter, *Erasmus-Luther Discourse on Free Will* (New York, 1961), 6, 100–102, 94, and 138.

hearted in a debate.[23] But she assigns no fault, finding the approach to flow naturally from Erasmus's mentality. By contrast, Cornelis Augustijn faults Erasmus not simply for displaying little of Luther's passion but for failing to be more confrontational throughout his career. Augustijn misses the point. His final judgment of Erasmus is indicative: "Erasmian piety is marked by optimism and a certain superficiality. It is a piety of the lowlands rather than of the mountains, intimate rather than passionate."[24] There he seems to get the point, only to reject it altogether.

"Not everyone has the strength for martyrdom," Erasmus said in a letter to the English humanist Richard Pace. The letter might seem to confirm Augustijn's opinion of the Erasmian character. Let us admit, following the rhetorical principles of Erasmian hermeneutics, that letters have circumstances, occasions and audience(s). Nonetheless, what Erasmus says in this letter fits the character that we may have grasped in the examples we have reviewed and that we may now be forming as we consider the tactics of suasion. It is a character sure to infuriate radicals and exasperate those who prefer the piety of the mountains.

> I fear that, if strife were to break out, I shall behave like Peter. When popes and emperors make the right decisions I follow, which is godly; if they decide wrongly I tolerate them, which is safe. I believe that even for men of good will this is legitimate, if there is no hope of better things.

(The point about legitimate authority became a tough one to resolve for English Protestant humanists, like Ascham, Haddon, and Wilson, during the Marian years.) At the conclusion of the letter Erasmus returns to a position which is at the very heart of the humanist suasory impulse. I could equally call it the contrarian impulse. He wrote the letter just at the outset of the troubles with Luther, 5 July 1521.

23. The audience took, for example, Erasmus's effort to name maieutically the scope of his discourse as a dialectical attempt to define. See Marjorie O'Rourke Boyle, *Rhetoric and Reform: Erasmus's Civil Dispute with Luther* (Cambridge, Mass., 1983). See also her "Erasmus and the 'Modern' Question: Was He Semi-Pelagian?" *Archiv für Reformationsgeschichte* 75 (1984): 59–77.

24. *Erasmus: His Life, Works, and Influence*, trans. J. C. Grayson (Toronto, 1991), 200.

> . . . let us not be so carried away by our hatred of the falsehood in Luther's writings that we lose the benefit of the good things he has written. (CWE, 8: 259)

Truth is not unmixed; reality is circumstantial. No wonder Erasmus used the tactics he did. There is optimism here, granted. But no superficiality in his choice of tactics: they were, indeed, as I have commented, the only ones his argument on the freedom of the will could sensibly permit and the ones most appropriate to the Erasmian ethos.

What Augustijn fails to recognize and appreciate is that there is another approach to argumentation, exemplified by this suasory genre, with long honorable roots in the rhetorical tradition, and elevated to new prominence by humanist epistemology, as dialogic as disputation but more collateral than confrontational. Boyle locates the source of the tradition (she centers on the *diatribe* without expanding the point, as I have, to encompass humanist *suasoria*) in Cicero's *Tusculan disputations,* which Erasmus had just edited. In this work, Cicero "displayed the virtuosity of arguing on both sides of the question, proposing the most probable opinion, and suspending personal judgment in the Skeptical stance of the New Academy to which its author adhered."[25] Once more we are brought back to the "pro and con of skeptical rhetorical argument"—that is, to the pro and con of traditional rhetorical protocol and the skeptical-appearing movement of suasion. At this point let us attempt a synthesis. In doing so it will be useful to consider a certain terminological nexus.

In many ways, the contrarian movement of Erasmian discourse is, as John Tinkler states, "the to and fro of conversation, which involves the participant in an intimate relationship and a continuing inquiry."[26] Therein Tinkler has, incidentally, expressed the precise intention of Erasmus's *philosophia christi,* to create an intimate relation between Christ and man through the continuing, conversational inquiry of interpreting scriptural passages rhetorically. But Tinkler's observation has brought another term into our purview, "conversation." Once more, although the term seems related to the dialogic movement of the prose I have been describing, at the same

25. "Erasmus and the 'Modern' Question," 60.

26. John F. Tinkler, "Erasmus' Conversation with Luther," *Archiv für Reformationsgeschichte* 82 (1991): 74.

time it seems, again, most contrary to the very idea of debate, disputation, or contentiousness, which I believe are the wellsprings of suasion. Nonetheless, Cicero, who was among the first to address problems of actually "teaching" good conversation, claimed that it is founded on debate (see *De officiis* I.xxxvii.132). *Sermo* is Cicero's word for conversation. *Sermo*, moreover, as Crassus notes, is the best style for irony (*De oratore* III.liii.203). It is, obviously, an informal style of speaking that allows much rhetorical lattitude. Finally, *sermo*, or "conversational," is another way of naming the "plain style" which became a desideratum of humanist rhetoricians. And, as noted in my preceding chapter, it is the motive of written dialogue and the category within which humanists fit their epistolography. Finally, in Erasmian lexicon, the very pattern of *sermo* is the ethos of Christ, the *perfectus orator* whose firm gentleness, mildness and at times maddening patience, would seem more at home in suasion than in disputation, in *suasoria* than in *controversia*, or at least in each of the former as the fulfillment of each of the latter.[27]

More terms could be proliferated *(diatriba, deliberativa, concio)*, but for my purposes all center in a certain humanist approach to communication: proceed "warily," with one eye on the opposition, and argue as unassertively as possible, even by means of a subtle indirection and irony, moving in contrarian fashion not with the intention of saying everything and overwhelming your listener but in the belief that your listener too has a mind capable of grasping your subtlest thought, and your goal is not closure but ongoing conversation. The lesson is an education in readership. When interpreting humanist prose, we should keep that lesson in mind and at the very least look for complex if not in fact purposefully slippery intentions. This we shall do in our examination of the next piece, a tract by one of England's foremost educators, a splendid example of suasion written

27. *Sermo* is the word Erasmus believed should Latinize the Greek *logos* in St. John's statement about Christ ("In the beginning. . . ."). Thereby, we have yet another glimpse into Erasmus's rich meaning: Christ is not God's iconographic "word" but God's rhetorical action, "oration," "speech," "sermon," or, better, "conversation." The best and most detailed discussion of Erasmian *sermo* is Marjorie O'Rourke Boyle's *Erasmus on Language and Method in Theology* (Toronto, 1977). On the linkage of Erasmian preaching with *suasoria*, see John W. O'Malley, S.J., "Erasmus and the History of Sacred Rhetoric: The Ecclesiastes of 1535," *Erasmus of Rotterdam Society Yearbook Five* (1985), 1–29.

originally in English. As noted earlier, this linguistic medium brought its own unique challenge to the communication of the author's intentions.

Toxophilus: The School of Shooting Contained in two books by Roger Ascham, 1545[28]

The epistle dedicatory to King Henry VIII puts the subject, medium, and audience of this book in simple compass: "an English matter in the English tongue for English men." The subject is archery, the material cause of Henry's victory at the head of 30,000 men in France at the seige of Boulogne, 1544. During that time the author, who identifies himself as a "scholar," was writing this book in Cambridge and, he says, chafing at his remove from the action. Then, he further says, he conceived the patriotic desire (equally reflected by his choice of medium and audience) to offer the book to Henry, who subsequently allowed the dedication. In these statements, Ascham has also of course defined his ethos.

By "shooting" Ascham means "shooting in the long bow"—"a most honest pastime in peace" and "a sure weapon in war." Some 30 years earlier, it should be noted, Henry's government had passed a law requiring all male subjects with certain exceptions (e.g., the lame, the clergy, and judges) to learn how to shoot in the long bow. Just three years before publication of *Toxophilus,* another law confirmed the earlier one, set a reasonable price on bows, and at the same time debarred "unlawful games." Ascham's book, therefore, could hardly be controversial. It is, rather, opportunistic. For he makes the subject one more entry into the humanist program. That is to say, "hitting the mark" has more than a literal or even singular aim.

From the outset Ascham not only makes clear that compassed within his larger target are rhetoric and education, but he also offers his solution to a knotty rhetorical problem we discussed earlier. In his preface "To All Gentlemen and Yoemen of England," he adverts to the tasks of writing and composition. There he is talking patriotically, ostensibly about using English—in particular, *plain* English—rather than Latin. However, in all linguistic usage, only one rule ap-

---

28. The edition I have used is Edward Arber's (London, 1868). In all quotations from the work I have modernized the spelling and punctuation.

plies: "He that will write well in any tongue must follow this counsel of Aristotle, to speak as the common people do, to think as wise men do; and so should every man understand him, and the judgment of wise men allow him" (18). The advice appears in other humanist books of the time.[29] But Ascham's particular recurrence to the cliche suggests not only a duality of intention but a duality of audience as well: he writes for the gentlemen and yoemen who will learn, and the learned, who will judge. Surely it was for the sake of the latter that the great (and throughout the writings we shall examine ubiquitous) humanist Walter Haddon wrote his dedicatory poem in Latin (we shall consider in some detail a similar Haddonian strategy in the works of Thomas Wilson). Ascham's solution anticipates one Sir Philip Sidney was to put colorfully four decades later in talking about writing that draws children from play and old men from the chimney corner.

Ascham goes further in his prefacing remarks and links archery itself with rhetoric. The linkage comes about through an argument that expresses an ultimate end of humanist education, an end beyond even the careerist aspirations of statesmanship.

> In our time now, when every man is given to know much rather than to live well, very many do write but after such a fashion as very many do shoot. Some shooters take in hand stronger bows than they be able to maintain. This thing maketh them sometime to outshoot the mark, sometime to shoot far wide . . . (19)

What operates here is something tantamount not simply to the linkage between rhetoric and archery but, as in most humanist suasion, to that between rhetoric and dialectic, or circumstance and general principles. Disputants were taught that every particular subject has a connection with a larger matter, every *hypothesis* links up with a *thesis*. Archery has important linkages with rhetoric, education, and art. Poetry as we shall see later in Puttenham, has linkages with law

---

29. This is how Thomas Wilson, whose *Rhetoric* we will consider in the following chapter, puts it: "Among all other lessons, this should first be learned, [that] we never affect any strange inkhorn [overly learned] terms, but so speak as is commonly received: neither seeking to be over fine, nor yet living over carelessly, using our speech as most men do, and ordering our wits, as the fewest have done" (162). Later historians of rhetoric have considered Wilson's lesson in plain style to be one of his most notable contributions, but it clearly has antiquarian origins and suasory implications.

and dissembling as well as with art. Always available, at times prominent, the linkages smooth the way for what Morus calls the "crafty" and "subtle" mode of communication, suasion as practiced by the humanists we are considering. Here with his explicitly dual audience Ascham has taken the linkage of all his subjects to a humanist desideratum, "to live well."

The goal of living well, particularly the secular goal of living well, because it is coincident with the aims and tactics of humanist suasion and because it is chief among humanist desiderata, will be explored from time to time throughout the remainder of my book. Life, we found Erasmus saying in the *Paraclesis,* means more than debate: the goal of education lies beyond skill in disputation even for students of theology; it lies in the formation of character. As it does for secular humanists, like Ascham. Although we shall continue to explore its equally vital connections with morals, ethics, and character, *ethos,* as well as *sermo,* let it suffice here to note that the goal is achieved, like skill in archery, through discipline and learning.[30]

Ascham continues his prefacing remarks by claiming no excellence in shooting, only an implied and easily proven excellence in writing: "seeing that saying is one step nearer perfection than doing, let every man leave marvelling why my word shall rather express than my deed shall perform perfect shooting" (20). Once more the ideal is present, and once more *De oratore* as well as the *Phaedrus* will be echoed, both in subject but only the former in protocol.

The dialogue itself takes place in the open, with no mention of a plane tree, between Philologus (lover of learning, or "words") and Toxophilus (lover of shooting, or "bows"). Philologus, out for a walk in Cambridge (later mention is made of Erasmus "when he was here in Cambridge," [46]), encountered three or four archers on their way to the range and was surprised to find Toxophilus not among them. Instead he found him reading a book. The book is Plato's *Phaedrus,* and what has entranced Toxophilus is its discussion of the nature of the soul. Pastimes become the immediate topic of conversation between the two men, Philologus ironically chastizing Toxophilus for engaging too earnestly in his, Philologus's, usual pastime and forsaking archery on such a lovely day. Is it possible finally

---

30. And thereby it might be contrasted with ostensibly similar educational efforts in our own age aimed at living "harmoniously."

to speak of an "art" of archery? Or is archery something learned only through practice? The question, of course, echoes the point in dispute about rhetoric in the *Phaedrus* as well as in *De oratore,* though the latter is not directly referred to until toward the end of Ascham's Book 1. Nonetheless, throughout the dialogue Philologus plays something of the Crassus role in quest of the ideal archer—or any ideal, for that matter, as the sine qua non of art. Toxophilus plays something of the practical Antonius's role, with an emphasis not on the ideal but on the "possible." Cicero, "Tully," figures prominently in the discussion, having been brought in early as a sanction for the necessity of "wholesome, honest, and mannerly pastimes."

Obviously, the initial point to be made about archery is its role not in war but in education. The first Ciceronian reference is to *De officiis,* and from that work (as in the last quoted phrase) comes the word *honestum,* which in its various English forms runs like a motif through the dialogue. (Although Ascham's work is in English, not Latin, it is an English that tends to draw its rhetorical and philosophical terms from Cicero.) "Honesty" is the closest we come to it, but we have unfortunately displaced most of its Latin resonances with the Romantic "sincerity." Its Latin resonances are far more important to Ascham's argument: honor, virtue, integrity—qualities which in Cicero mark a certain class and which in *De officiis* are opposed to *utile,* expediency, or the bending of principle to achieve advantage. Archery is an honest pastime, worthy for Princes to be brought up in, for it disciplines the body and "honestly" exercises the mind. Such at least is Toxophilus's chief argument. Philologus resists, however, until the sport has been compared with other pastimes, until its antiquarian basis in the classics and literature has been confirmed, its efficacy in warfare illustrated by history, and finally its artistic ideal posited as a goal of education. When these matters have been accomplished, Book 1 ends.

Book 2 belongs largely to Toxophilus, who instructs Philologus, now a willing student, in the elements of archery—including what to look for in long bows, in shafts, how to stand, how to take the weather into account, why goose feathers are best for the arrow. In this book, too, all fictive distinction between the author Roger Ascham and Toxophilus is dropped. The action is taken when Toxophilus praises Sir Humphry Wingfield, who "brought me up in learning." Wingfield was Ascham's early patron, surrogate parent and provider of his education. But let us not assume that Philologus is therefore the "other." He is, of course, equally a mask for the author, then embarked on a career which made him one of England's best known scholars and educators. This doubleness is a characteristic which makes the dialogue resonate with the *interpares* Crassus-Antonius dispute. At the same time, however, the two halves of one whole make the dialogue resonant with medieval debates between body and soul, giving a certain poignancy to Ascham's larger argument, as I shall explain later in reviewing the work's dialogic style.

The best shooting, both speakers agree, is the "most comely" shooting; in this agreement reference is made to Crassus' argument in *De oratore:* "comeliness" translates Crassus's *venustas* (I.xxviii. 130, III.xlvi.179), a quality which admittedly cannot be taught by art alone but which depends equally upon the other motives of a traditional rhetorical education ("nature, use, and art," Ascham says; *natura, exercitatio, ars,* Quintilian says). The "honest" archer will know his limits of control. These limits must be tested against such uncertainties as the movements of the wind, described in a long and much-praised passage. The work ends with Toxophilus inviting Philologus for a return engagement, at which time Philologus will take center stage to discuss—vide supra—the nature of the soul.

Within this second book is a virtual handbook on archery. But only an impatient reader might wish that the handbook had been allowed to "get out." For the purpose of the discourse—a superb example of humanist suasion—goes well beyond the mechanically informational. Indeed, both *Toxophilus* and *De oratore* are constructed in ways to frustrate seekers after handbooks—especially those that might imagine that handbooks are the prime means of achieving *venustas.* And in the process both manage to treat a great deal more than their announced subjects. In the course of both discussions, much gets said about education, about how people learn, about *natura* and *exercitatio* as well as *ars.* Let us explore the matter further by reviewing the variety of Ascham's intentions.

To begin with, the patriotism of Ascham's effort is patent throughout. With this work, moreover, he won a pension from Henry that, remarkably, continued through the subsequent reigns of Edward, Mary, and Elizabeth. And on this work Ascham founded his own career as an educator, one who fulfilled yet another humanist desideratum by allowing his scholarly world to converge with the political one. He succeeded the famous Cheke as Public Orator of Cambridge, became tutor to Princess Elizabeth and Latin Secretary to Queen Mary, and spent his last years in possession of considerable fame and income, and of Elizabeth's continued favor. It was with him that Elizabeth studied Demosthenes, and it was Ascham who introduced her to what was probably the most influential rhetorical work in her education, Melanchthon's *Commonplaces*. But, patriotism and self-advancement comprise only a part, and perhaps not always a conscious part, of Ascham's educational enterprise. A volume which capped the career that *Toxophilus* began was published posthumously by Ascham's widow, *The Schoolmaster* (1570). This final work continues to advise, incidentally, the comeliness and honesty of archery as a pastime for gentlemen. More importantly, as the culminating work of an entire career, this book also urges, prominently, the constant use of *De oratore* not simply as a textbook of Latinity but as a means of teaching the child "a true judgment both of his own and other men's doings, what tongue soever he doth use." Ciceronian protocol, it would seem, is ever inherent in Ascham's doctrine.

Let us consider, accordingly, that the protocols of judgment may be a theme of this early work. What lessons in judgment does *Toxophilus* offer? I suggest that they are those of most humanist suasion. To begin with—pace, all seekers after handbooks, rules, easy and ready ways—none of the humane arts are to be regarded as ends in themselves. When Philologus notes that Toxophilus rather modestly recurs to Aristotle, he remarks:

> How little you have looked of Aristotle and how much learning you have lost by shooting I cannot tell, but this I would say and if I loved you never so ill, that you have been occupied in somewhat else beside shooting. (98)

The observation, which by its nature echoes Ascham's opening story (as we shall see below, the one Bias tells about Croesus), applies not simply to Toxophilus's previous "occupation" but to his (and Ascham's) business throughout the dialogue itself: archery has complex connections with the humanities. In particular, as we have been made aware of from the outset, it has complex connections with rhetoric. In a culminating passage among many references to rhetoric throughout, Toxophilus says:

> Now, how big, how small, how heavy, how light, how long, how short
> a shaft should be particularly for every man (seeing we must talk of the
> general nature of shooting) cannot be told no more than you Rhetoricians
> can appoint any one kind of words, of sentences, of figures fit for every
> matter, but even as the man and the matter requireth, so the fittest [are]
> to be used. (125)

The very process of learning archery bears important similarities to
learning rhetoric generally, its principles of circumstance and decorum in particular. There are limits to what can be taught, limits to
a handbook's efficacy, limits to the artist's control. The uncertainties
(or contingencies) of the situation—whether one steps before an audience to speak or before a target to shoot—are causes not for complaint but, as Ascham shows in his description of the winds, for
marvel.

Certain modern critics might want to insist that any discourse is
finally about itself. The observation is illuminating when applied
to *Toxophilus,* which begins by making us conscious of the use of
English and of writing. Writing or "saying," moreover, as Ascham-
Toxophilus notes, can actually move closer to the ideal than "doing"
can. If the discourse is about itself, and if discourse is—as rhetoricians of the time believed—a mirror of the mind, *Toxophilus* could con-
ceivably reflect how the mind ideally works. If so, not surprisingly,
the mind works ideally by means of pro-con reasoning. Therein lies
the best answer we get to the question about the kind of judgment
Toxophilus teaches: it is that judgment we touched on earlier, one that
is based on the Ciceronian protocol humanists employed throughout
their writings, perhaps nowhere more subtly than in the composition of suasory prose.

To make that protocol salient may be the purpose of the striking
shifts in Ascham's dialogic style. At least four kinds of dialogue are
employed, in order: disputatiousness, Socratic dialogue, catechism
(or something like it), and a return to a conversational style perhaps best called simply *sermo*. Here again is that parodic use of form
I mentioned earlier, in this case far more literally employed than
Ascham's (or Cicero's) use of the *Phaedrus.* The initial conversation
between Toxophilus and Philologus rapidly gives way to disputatiousness, as Philologus challenges Toxophilus to prove not simply
the benefits of archery but its status as an art. Philologus continually
marks stages in the disputation, often through refutation:

TOX. . . . . Therefore you see that if Apollo and the Muses either were examples indeed or only fained of wise men to be examples of learning, honest shooting may well enough be companion with honest study.

PHI. Well, Toxophile, if you have no stronger defense of shooting than Poets, I fear [that] if your companions which love shooting heard you, they should think you made it but a trifling and fabling matter. . . .

TOX. Even as I am not so fond but I know that these be fables, so I am sure you be not so ignorant but you know what such noble wits as the Poets had meant by such matters, which oftentimes under the covering of a fable do hide and wrap in goodly precepts of philosophy with the true judgment of things. (44–45)

★ ★ ★

PHIL. But now if you can show but half so much profit in war of shooting as you have proved pleasure in peace, then will I surely judge that there be few things that have so manifold commodities and uses joined unto them as it hath. (62)

But then at the end of Book 1, the style shifts from disputation to a different kind of dialogue, in which Philologus plays a Socratic role:

PHIL. And doth every man go about to hit the mark at every shot?

TOX. By my troth I trow so, and as for myself I am sure I do.

PHIL. But all men do not hit it at all times.

TOX. No, truly, for that were a wonder.

PHIL. Can any man hit it at all times?

TOX. No man verily.

PHIL. Then . . . to hit the [mark] always is impossible. For that is called impossible which is in no man's power to do. (101)

Not only the style but the point too is Socratic, to prove to Toxophilus the existence of an ideal which, even though it is beyond the possible or likely, is nonetheless something at which all arts should aim. The point, moreover, in reiterating the function of the ideal in education, is equally Ciceronian, and not surprisingly became a guiding principle of Ascham's educational policy.[31] Point made, but then at the first of Book 2, the dialogic or rather sermonic style shifts once again:

---

31. Edward Grant, who composed a rather verbose Latin oration on the life and death of Roger Ascham in 1576, managed somehow to put the principle succinctly: although Antonius in Cicero's *De oratore* takes away from us all hope of achieving true eloquence, we must nevertheless strive to catch sight of it as nearly as possible and to aspire to it with all zeal and diligence. *(Ad quam quum pervenire non possumus, quia ejus omnis adipiscendae spere omnem adimit nobis ANTONIUS apud CICEROREM,*

PHIL. What is the chief point in shooting that every man laboureth to come to?

TOX. To hit the mark.

PHIL. How many things are required to make a man ever more hit the mark?

TOX. Two.

PHIL. Which two?

TOX. Shooting straight and keeping of a length.

PHIL. How should a man shoot straight, and how should a man keep a length?

Here the point, as in all catechism, is orthodoxy, or instruction in uniform principles. There are elementary lessons to be learned, by rote memorization if necessary. Note that in these shifts, Philologus, the lover of learning, has the "master's" role. It is Toxophilus's knowledge which is being probed.

Book 2 remains in the instructional mode, with Philologus's questions becoming less catechistical and Toxophilus's answers becoming longer and more instructional. The relation between the two is no longer disputatious, for all the major controversial matters have been resolved between both men. Philologus now believes that archery is a significant art among the humane arts. Toxophilus believes that there is an ideal to be pursued. The discourse through most of Book 2 gradually reveals yet a fourth kind of dialogue, more like genuine *sermo*—not disputatious, nor Socratic, nor catechistical—but that easy conversational style made possible when a consensus may be assumed. There is, thus, a progression in this entire work, matched by a progression in dialogic styles, from difference to union. If that progression is a demonstration of how the mind ideally works, it is also a practical demonstration of the protocol whereby judgment is formed.

The work may have furthered Ascham's career. It may have furthered the cause of archery in England. But it also serves yet another, still observable function; it was and still is a means whereby humanist rhetoric, education, and epistemology are advanced. A subtle lesson for the gentlemen and yeomen, but one that was meant to garner the approving judgment of the learned.

---

quam proxime tamen aspicere, et aspirare omni studio et diligentia est elaborandum); see The Whole Works of Roger Ascham, ed. Rev. D. Giles (London, 1864), 3: 347.

Aschamus est author, magnum quem fecit Apollo
Arte sua, magnum Pallas & arte sua.

"Ascham is the author, whom Apollo made great / In his own art, and Pallas also in hers," Haddon says, and he continues: *Docta manus dedit hunc, dedit hunc mens docta libellum* (a learned hand produced this book, so also did a learned mind). The two languages—Haddon writing in Latin, Ascham in English—keep a certain duplexity alive. Of the two audiences, it is the learned humanist, *mens docta,* who will more clearly see that Ascham's interests extend well beyond his announced and generally most explicit subject.

The other audience is brought in by other means. Let us recur, for example, to Ascham's introductory story about Croesus:

> Bias the wise man came to Croesus the rich king [of Lydia in Asia minor at] a time when he was making new ships, purposing to have subdued by water the out isles lying betwixt Greece and Asia minor. "What news now in Greece?" saith the king to Bias. "None other news, but these," saith Bias, "that the isles of Greece have prepared a wonderful company of horsemen, to overrun Lydia withall." "There is nothing under heaven," saith the king, "that I would so soon wish, as that they durst be so bold, to meet us on the land with horse." "And think you," saith Bias, "that there is anything which they would sooner wish, than that you should be so fond as to meet them on the water with ships?" And so Croesus hearing not the true news, but perceiving the wise man's mind and counsel, both gave then over making of his ships and left also behind him a wonderful example for all commonwealths to follow: that is, evermore to regard and set most by that thing whereunto nature hath made them most apt, and use hath made them most fit. (16)

Bias gives advice, and so too through this little collateral story does Ascham, with considerable if unsubtle irony. Note first that the advice approaches the suasive, maieutic kind, only because Bias stops just barely short of coming forth and actually speaking his mind. This story may thus be an opening signal to all readers, learned and otherwise, about the kind of advice and discourse which will follow. If it is such a signal Ascham reveals his deepest intentions through actually controverting the point of this little story.

For the story would seem initially to lead to a singular point: one should evermore "regard and set most by that thing whereunto nature hath made them most apt, and use hath made them most fit." Note that among the speakers in the work Toxophilus seems most fit for shooting, Philologus for book learning. Though distinct in "nature" *(natura)* and "use" *(exercitatio),* the two in centering on a third educational principle "art" *(ars)* become one, a progression we have just found matched by the style of written dialogue. Thus, the introductory story is finally undone in pursuing the humanist pattern whereby it is possible to challenge assertions and systems, marvel at uncertainty, and above all "live well." After all, if that introductory assertion were categorically true, there would be no place for art— or for humanist education either—and who would need rhetoric? It is in the pursuit of that humanist pattern that we find Ascham's deepest intentions, however much they may have been complicated by others, such as the desire for self-advancement.

Let us turn now to a suasory work whose intentions were, most likely, uncomplicated by that desire.

The Art of English Poesy Contrived into three Books: The first of Poets and Poesy, the second of Proportion, the third of Ornament, by George Puttenham (1589)[32]

Of the educational triad discussed in our review of Ascham's work, Puttenham writes on "art," though he has something to say about both "nature" and "practice." In spite of the neat tripartite division announced in his title, the work is one long rambling monologue—rambling and wide-ranging, from the glories of English verse and iambic pentameter to the artfulness of pleading a case of hemorrhoids when one wishes to avoid attending a meeting (who's going to check?). As a handbook on poetry it is sloppy and unfocussed. But as a discourse on the art of dissembling it is a richly ironic work, stylistically as clever as the *De copia*. If a handbook at all, it is one on the *via diversa*.

In advancing an *English* art of poetry, Puttenham's work is no less patriotic than others of the time. It is, though, as I have suggested, less self-advancing than the *Toxophilus*. Perhaps it didn't need to be. George Puttenham, who received a humanist and lawyerly education—having enrolled at Cambridge the year following publication

32. The edition I have used is the one edited by Gladys Doidge Willcock and Alice Walker (Cambridge, Eng., 1936). Again, I have modernized spelling and punctuation.

of Ascham's work and then ten years later enrolled at the Middle Temple—moved in the very highest circles of government. His status near the "slipper top" was partly the result of family connections, including his marriage to Lady Elizabeth Windsor circa 1560.

Although written in English, the *Art* was explicitly intended for an exclusive audience, with apparently little thought of publication, at least initially. It was addressed to the Queen and intended to be overheard by courtiers, who circulated the manuscript. However, some two decades after its early parts were composed, it was published and sent out before a larger, far less exclusive and potentially far more resistant audience. It continues to be read in our own age, primarily as an example of early modern literary criticism, although scholars have recently begun to explore its efforts to set forth a kind of courtly "code" or manual for preferment.[33] My argument, by contrast, will center on Puttenham's suasoriness. I shall propose that Puttenham, making no subtle or clever effort to control his meaning in the presence of the overhearing courtiers or the larger reading public, used the tactics of suasion simply because they are inherent in his subject. In this regard, the book is an almost comic version of the choices Erasmus had to make because of the nature of the question to be debated with Luther. We must therefore be very clear about just what Puttenham's subject is.

Dissembling would seem to be one definite answer to that question. The work is premissed on the praiseworthiness of all sorts of dissembling. In his initial address to Queen Elizabeth, Puttenham calls her "the most excellent poet of our time" because she is "a most cunning counterfeitor." His reasoning may be shocking and somewhat ironic but it is hardly convoluted: a poet, after all, is a maker,

33. For the former, see for example O. B. Hardison, Jr., *English Literary Criticism: The Renaissance* (New York, 1963), 147–181. For the latter, see Daniel Javitch, *Poetry and Courtliness in Renaissance England* (Princeton, 1978). See, too, Javitch's "Poetry and Preferment at Elizabeth's Court: Some Preliminary Observations" in *Europäische Hofkultur im 16. und 17. Jahrhundert* (Hamburg, 1981): 163–69, and in the same volume Heinrich F. Plett, "Elisabethanische Hofpoetik Gesellschaftlicher Code und ästhetische Norm in Puttenhams 'Arte of English Poesie,'" 41–50. Plett's argument is especially illuminating, that Puttenham sought to assimilate poetry to courtliness and vice-versa (*Die Poetik wird höfisiert, der Hof poetisiert,* 47); Javitch's essay goes beyond his earlier book to conjecture that, with Puttenham's ideas as sanction, "verbally gifted Elizbethans seeking entry at court were strongly motivated to write poetry" (163).

that is to say an artificer or imitator of precedents and patterns laid before him. Elizabeth is a great poet by virtue of her skill in representing "*Venus* in countenance, in life *Diana, Pallas* for government, and *Juno* in all honor and regal magnificence" (4–5). She is a good "imitator," to use a troublesome term from rhetorical education. The terms of the praise, moreover, and most of the argument within which it is set could be more than a little troublesome outside their aristocratic confines. An in-group with a shared community of values give such sallies a stability that they risk before other groups.[34] Erasmus, whose *Praise of Folly* was addressed to Sir Thomas More but ultimately went before "theologians" with their more serious and less irony-tolerant minds, suffered because of just such instability; similar to Puttenham's argument on dissembling, Folly's argument on the necessity of illusion (it relieves the *taedium vitae*) was not so well received outside the in-group. Such sallies, however, are exactly those which give Puttenham's curious book its coherence— and, for that matter, its tone. And such sallies, as I have noted— Lysias's speech, Crassus's stance, Folly's and Raphael's monologues —however unstable they became before certain audiences, have a kind of traditional, debaterly, contrarian, intentional vulnerability inside the in-group. They provoke.

Book 1 continues by directly controverting Cicero, who claimed that orators were the first civilizers of man. Puttenham argues that *poets* were, because "their eloquence was the first rhetoric of the world" (8). But, Puttenham argues, poetry has fallen into disrepute in our age among those who are unable "to contrive, or in manner to conceive any matter of subtlety" or who fail to recognize the value of the imagination to "all good poets, notable captains stratagematic, all cunning artificers and engineers, all legislators, politicians, and counsellors of state" (18–19). Invariably Puttenham presses his argument to its limits. But throughout we begin to see something of the centrality of poetry and literary criticism in humanist education: poetry and literary criticism make salient the values of imagination, cunning, craftiness, and subtlety. To put his subject in the terms I have employed, Puttenham's overriding argument is that po-

34. "Ironists," Wayne Booth notes, "have often been accused of elitism" (*A Rhetoric of Irony* [Chicago, 1974], 29). But, as he argues, irony is often a way of forming a community of readers who grasp and mutually appreciate the norms at work.

etry itself is an outgrowth of the assumptions of humanist suasion. Book 1 is largely devoted to the praise of poetry, with attention to its types, to its pleasures, and to its English craftsmen.

Book 2 Puttenham employs to discuss verse forms, meter, and rhyme. Rhyme was a not uncontroversial subject at the time, especially among those antiquarians who could not agree on its classical sanctions or, with Puttenham, on its musical necessity. Nonetheless, Book 2 is closest to a handbook, though Puttenham seldom ignores the Queen's imagined presence or misses an opportunity to note that courtly poets are the principal artificers he has in mind.

Book 3, the final book, is lengthy. It is in fact as long as the first two books combined. Here Puttenham moves directly onto his larger subject, for his argument is centered not simply on "ornament" but on *decorum* in the use of ornament: the lesson, a thoroughly rhetorical one, is that any style should suit not the subject alone but the speaker, audience, and occasion, whether the artistic effort is aimed at producing poetry, oratory, or courtly behavior. The best art is always that which conceals art—rather, the best art is that which dissembles skillfully. Nor is there any decorous reason to abandon good Englishness in discourse in order to pursue "inkhorn" terms (145)—the same phrase and argument had been used by the humanist rhetorician Thomas Wilson twenty years earlier.

It is in this book too that we find the clearest indication of Puttenham's own rhetorical situation and ostensible intentions:

> . . . our chief purpose herein is for the learning of ladies and young gentlewomen or idle courtiers, desirous to become skillful in their own mother tongue and for their private recreation to make now and then ditties of pleasure, thinking for our part none other science so fit for them and [their] place as that which teacheth *beau* semblant, the chief profession as well of courting as of poesie. (158)

Few books of the time were written in open acknowledgment of a female audience. This one is, and it delights in the double meaning of "courting." Poems and poesy are useful to both kinds. However, an earlier passage only underscores the hazards of Puttenham's approach and mode of address should his argument become abstracted from its Courtly rhetorical situation. Having earlier praised the importance of poetry as the civilizer of mankind, he comes perilously close to trivializing it when he argues for the importance of figurative language, using the standard model of the courtroom trial:

> . . . our maker or Poet is appointed not for a judge but rather for a pleader, and that of pleasant and lovely causes and nothing perilous, such as be those for the trial of life, limb, or livelihood, and before judges neither sour nor severe but in the ear of princely dames, young ladies, gentlewomen and courtiers, being all for the most part either meek of nature or of pleasant humor . . . (154–155)

The contrast is with oratory, especially legal pleading. And it involves Puttenham in an *hyperbole,* whose extremes are to be moderated by the reader. The moderating task, however, is easier to achieve when it is recalled that the artificers in question are themselves in positions of power. We shall return to this comparison later, after a consideration of Sidney's essay. But let us simply note for the present that all comparisons in humanist suasion, as Luther has already warned us, are to be treated warily—for they are a deplorable substitute for Lutheran assertion. Recall, too, that outrageousness is at home in humanist suasion and serves a function.

The larger subject, dissembling, is reasserted in Book 3, most notably in the following passage, which is itself an overstated if not outrageous description of the techniques of suasion:

> And ye shall know that we may dissemble, I mean speak otherwise than we think, in earnest as well as in sport, under covert and dark terms, and in learned and apparent speeches, in short sentences, and by long ambage and circumstance of words, and finally as well when we lie as when we tell truth. To be short every speech wrested from his own natural signification to another not altogether so natural is a kind of dissimulation, because the words bear contrary countenance to the intent. (186)

Not directly contrary in every case, for Puttenham is leading up to a discussion of *allegory*—a subject which, as we have seen in our reading of Erasmus, is always close at hand when the subject is modes of communication. (Erasmus's advice to young writers, which I quote at the opening of this chapter, appears in his discussion of allegory.)

But Puttenham's prime example of dissembling comes later, in talking about a highly polished ornament, a poem attired "with copious and pleasant amplifications and much variety of sentences all running upon one point and to one intent" (247). The example is a poem written by Elizabeth—a rather plodding piece of doggerel, baffling out of context. As Puttenham explains, the poem was written to courtiers, particularly to those courtiers who were supporting Mary Queen of Scots. Elizabeth, long aware of the potential for subversion in her own court but skillfully dissembling that knowledge, wrote the "ditty" as a warning. It reads in part:

> No foreign banished wight shall anchor in this port,
> Our realm it brooks no strangers' force, let them elsewhere resort.
> Our rusty sword with rest shall first his edge employ
> To poll their tops that seek such change and gape for joy.

Clearly any subtlety or cunning in this effort has been overpraised. Nonetheless, Puttenham's point remains: Elizabeth dissembled her knowledge at first, then revealed it through the agency of artifice, another form of dissembling. The value of the poem as a poem is thus beside the point. To dissemble well—whether in art or in behavior, in revealing one's previously concealed knowledge or, as he goes on to advise courtiers, in artfully pleading a not easily detected false excuse (like migraine headaches, lethargy, or "a fistule *in ano*," 300) to escape unwanted duties—that's the point. But outside a closed circle, the point—like irony—risks becoming unstable.

The *Art* as we have it is apparently a stratified work, layer upon layer having been added by Puttenham over a couple of decades. If it is true, as the work's modern editors argue, that the volume was a product mainly of the 1560s (li–lii), it coincides with the suasory prose of such other Cambridge humanists as Ascham and Wilson. Some layers clearly reflect times closer to publication in the late 1580s (see 146). Nonetheless, for all its stratification, the argument reveals a consistent focussing on a theme, one that assimilates poetry to its larger art, dissembling, with the argument worked out in a most decorous labyrinthine or ambagious fashion that is perfectly consonant with the tactics of suasion. Civilized behavior—"living well," in Ascham's phrase—itself depends upon a "decorum," or "decency," the result of skillful and often learned dissembling acquired so deeply and displayed so artfully, Puttenham argues, that it seems "natural" (261–98).

But when the *Art* was published in 1589 and wrenched from one audience to be set before another, there was a rhetorical shift in how its intentions were understood. To use modern terminology, the work now stood before a new "hermeneutical community," which included Puritans, Lutherans, and other dogmatics and authoritarians, readers who preferred assertiveness to irony and for whom moral choices were simpler and man's lot far more serious. "I cannot deny but these conceits of mine be trifles," comments Puttenham in what may be a late layer, "[but] no less in very deed be all the most serious studies of man, if we shall measure [the] gravity and lightness" of Ecclesiastes, who after considering these studies cried out, "Vanity of vanities, all is vanity" (112). But this sally was surely no more efficacious when Puttenham's work was sent before a larger audience than it was when Erasmus had employed something like it three quarters of a century earlier.

For *The Praise of Folly* is replete with similar riskiness. That work too, like Puttenham's, attempted to vindicate imagination and pleasure, and turn "living well" into a kind of game, of artful illusion. But it is a game not everyone is willing to play or to understand. Consider this story which Folly tells:

> Nor was there anything wrong with the judgment of the Greek who was so mad that he sat alone in the theatre for whole days on end, laughing, applauding, enjoying himself, because he thought that wonderful tragedies were being acted there, whereas nothing at all was being performed. But in the other duties of life he conducted himself very well: he was cheerful with his friends, agreeable with his wife; he could overlook the faults of his servants and not fly into a mad rage when he found a winejar had been secretly tapped. Through the efforts of his friends he took some medicine which cured him of his disease, but when he was completely himself again, he took issue with his friends in this fashion: "Damn it all!" he said, "you have killed me, my friends, not cured me, by thus wresting my enjoyment from me and forcibly depriving me of a most pleasant delusion." And rightly enough. For they were the ones who were deluded, and they had more need of hellebore than he did, since they thought such a felicitous and gratifying madness was some kind of evil that needed to be expelled by means of potions. (Trans. Miller, 58–59)

We don't approve the madness of the man in the theatre. Nor do we approve of the well-meaning act of the family. We see the rightness and wrongness in each. We don't endorse either. We are required to judge. And when we do I think we arrive at the speaker's position: The behavior of the man in the theatre is indeed madness. But there's nothing wrong with a little illusion or even delusion. In fact, pursuit of either for its own sake is often necessary to living well. Something of that judgment is offered in the opening assertion of this example—but the entire example, in which that assertion is somewhat validated, is spoken by someone who calls herself a fool—who is being consciously contrarian.

As I suggested earlier, the difficulty with reading *The Praise of Folly* is partly the difficulty of all humanist suasion: the reader continually has to figure out where the author, Erasmus in this case, stands—and how the author differs from his spokesperson, who in this case is a fool but not altogether foolish (i.e., her foolishness is not unmixed). But it's in that very process—that difficult process of trying to figure out where the author stands—that Erasmus makes humanist rhetoric reveal its most complex techniques and power of indirection. Erasmus's work, like Puttenham's, is especially baffling to any readers, among their contemporaries or ours, who have little sympathy for irony or who are locked into the dusty preaching that all utterances must somehow be either clear or "sincere."

To put the matter another way: any discussion which seems to prize playfulness will acquire a kind of urgency when it flies in the face of a deadly and threatening seriousness. Puttenham's work, like Erasmus's, acquired that urgency when it was published. I base the conjecture not simply upon what is known about readership and society in Elizabethan England (I recur to this matter in my next chapter) but also upon the apparently multi-layered nature of Puttenham's writing. The later layers reflect the riskiness of sending the work before a mixed audience, of removing its exclusivity. Those layers show Puttenham adopting an apologetic tone—without, however, altering the work's essentially suasory character.

Let us consider now another work prepared, as Puttenham's was not, to meet an urgency created by readerly seriousness. Then we shall return to at least one point which our discussion of Puttenham's apology has left hanging.

An Apology for Poetry by Sir Philip Sidney (1583)[35]

Like Puttenham's book, Sidney's essay was written primarily for an exclusive though somewhat broad audience. He speaks primarily

35. The edition I have used is Olney's of 1595, as reprinted by O. B. Hardison, Jr. in *English Literary Criticism: The Renaissance* (New York, 1963), 99–146. I have modernized the spelling and punctuation.

to other gentlemen, as shown in the *exordium* where he addresses the equine concerns of knighthood. Like Ascham, he is openly patriotic in his use of English. Unlike Puttenham he commits no outrage in speaking for his art. Unlike Ascham he uses a structure that is only conceptually dialogic.

Unlike both Puttenham and Ascham, Sidney does not dedicate his work to anyone. It was, indeed, the dedication of another man's work to him which apparently provoked his efforts. Too, that other man's work forced Sidney, unlike Puttenham, to keep the Puritan threat much more central to his concerns. It was, in fact, the increasing strength of that threat which led others to publish Sidney's discourse, well over a decade after it had been composed, and send it out before the widest possible audience. But on either count it is a mistake to read the work simply as a disputatious action. Like other humanists, Sidney too has a larger subject, one with this time direct bearing on humanist protocol and one which is developed in the suasory fashion I have tried to describe—with a fleeting but nonetheless highly significant guide for his intended audience.

Dedications of works in this period were always rhetorical. They were strategies used on the dedicatee to appeal for support (financial or otherwise) or on the readers to impress them with the author's allegiances and character. Unauthorized dedications, however, could prove troublesome. Gosson's unauthorized dedication of his Puritanical attack on poetry, *The School of Abuse* (1579), to Sidney was unintentionally provocative and counter-productive. It was flat, assertive, and no sally. But although Sidney's discourse controverts Gosson's arguments, it is—and in this respect it fits well into the suasory kind—not exactly a reply. Sidney addresses Gosson's arguments, but never names their author ("he," he says, once, at 121), preferring to speak in a general, and I believe significantly more courtly, way than Erasmus did in the consciously glancing blow he aimed at Luther.

Sixty years ago, at the very beginning of a resurgence of interest in rhetoric, an American scholar observed that Sidney appears to use a form of judicial oratory—appropriately, since "the art of poetry is on trial."[36] Or so this scholar believed. But to literalize the argumentative situation which Sidney only suggests is to distort his tone

36. Kenneth Myrick, *Sir Philip Sidney as a Literary Craftsman* (Cambridge, Mass., 1935), 58.

and restrict his aim. A more accurate characterization of Sidney's rhetoric is offered by Arthur F. Kinney, who sees the essay not simply as part of a disputation but as a *parody* of Gosson's case for the prosecution. Sidney's defense burlesques the tactics of Gosson's attack.[37] I shall argue that Sidney's burlesque apology for poetry is equally a defense of something else, a certain manner that is itself the embodiment of humanist suasion particularly when viewed in light of the Brinsley passage with which I opened this chapter.

To an extent this aim has already been acknowledged by several modern scholars. Most recently it was described by John Hunt in his intensive examination of a protean passage in Sidney's apology. Hunt imagines Sidney saying, "the reader may obtain some of my meaning by a casual perusal . . . but if he wants it all he must work as hard to achieve it as I have."[38] I wish to put the aim in terms of the disputatiousness which underlies Sidney's discourse.

To begin with, Sidney's manner throughout the discourse is less accusatory or defensive than protean and suasive, and it is that manner which is I believe not only one of the most significant features of his "craftsmanship" but also his larger subject itself. Of the two titles the essay was given when published twice in 1595, "An Apology for Poetry" and "The Defence of Poesy," the former seems tonally more appropriate because it is less confrontational. Sidney's own sensitivity to indirection (in spite of his curiously flat reading of the *Utopia*) is patent throughout, so much so that I believe it becomes his very point. He notes that the Vergilian pastoral, for example, written during times of "hard Lords or ravening Soldiers," told "pretty tales of wolves and sheep" but actually offered "whole considerations of wrong doing and patience" (120). And Erasmus's *Praise of Folly*, Sidney says, "had another foundation than the superficial part would promise" (125).[39] But it is not simply Sidney's *stated* ap-

37. "Parody and Its Implications in Sydney's Defense of Poesie," *Studies in English Literature* 12 (1972): 1–20.

38. "Allusive Coherence in Sidney's *Apology for Poetry*," *Studies in English Literature* 27 (1987): 13.

39. In this respect, eloquence, as Arthur Kinney has incisively noted, could be "a two-edged sword. Just as Erasmus's Folly could talk wisdom or foolishness—and who would distinguish?—so might More's Hythlodaye" (17). The observation makes all the more surprising Sidney's rather flat reading of More's *Utopia* (see 112). Kinney's own reading of the *Utopia* is actually much more in accord with Sidney's

preciation of indirection which makes the discourse a complicated example of suasion, whether suasion masked as advocacy or vice-versa.

Sidney, the Renaissance man par excellence—poet, courtier, scholar, critic—never saw this work in print. His death on the battlefield occurred several years after he wrote the essay, in English, and a decade before it was published. Obviously written to be transmitted in manuscript to a select and powerful audience, it is a fine example, as many readers have noted, of what Castiglione would call *sprezzatura*—off-hand excellence: as a case of pleading it makes its points firmly and conclusively but in a gentlemanly way, without shouting or without even giving much offense.

But the very function of *sprezzatura* (to be discussed further below) is both strategic and suasory. To begin with, it is a quality designed largely to create an effective *ethos,* which to any humanist is always the most efficacious persuader: it is the speaker's character *(ethos)* more than the speech *(logos)* or our own emotions *(pathos)* which persuades us. Sidney himself makes the point (in a perfect example of the figure *gradatio*) when he notes that Cicero in *De oratore* sees through the masks of Antonius and Crassus:

> [of] the great forefathers of *Cicero* in eloquence, the one (as *Cicero* testifieth of them) pretended not to know art, the other not to set by it, because with a plain sensibleness they might win credit of popular ears, which credit is the nearest step to persuasion, which persuasion is the chief mark of oratory. (143)

"Dissembling," Puttenham would call these masks. Sidney himself shows a most sensitive appreciation of the artful use of dissembling, both in what he says and above all in what he does. For his larger suasory aim moves on the oblique, away from the purposes and uses of poetry, to reveal an effective ethos, one designed to cope with adversity (in this case, intellectual adversity). As he says in the quoted passage, if you credit the orator, you will credit the orator's case. Therein lies his larger subject and the rationale of his rhetorical manner, his suasoriness.

---

observations on Vergil and Erasmus; see *Rhetoric and Poetic in Thomas More's Utopia* (Malibu, Calif., 1979), Vol. 5 in UCLA *Humanita Civilitas* series. I am tempted by the thought that Sidney's own youthful Calvinist leanings may have ironically made him more receptive to Erasmus, just as his firm royalist tendencies may have made him resistant to More.

Indeed, the proposition Sidney argues ultimately centers on ethos: although the sciences have ends in themselves, yet all are

> directed to the highest end of the mistress Knowledge, by the Greeks called *Architectonic,* which stands (as I think) in the knowledge of a man's self, in the ethical and political consideration, with the end of well doing and not of well knowing only. (108)

Thus poetry, like all knowledge properly understood, increases our sense of self and enhances our effective action in the state. Too, if as M. J. Doherty has argued Sidney's "mistress Knowledge" is an appropriation of feminine power, he has made a move not at all extraordinary for a humanist. After all, Folly's marginalization as a woman was a stimulus to her power of inventiveness: she could and indeed would say almost anything. But this feminine *copia* becomes in Sidney also a recognition of both kinds of courtliness; the mistress is romantic as well as political, the latter perhaps in deference to Elizabeth.[40] More to my point, the Ciceronian ethos of a learned, engaged citizen (someone who knows well and does well) is the explicit aim of Sidney's argument, and any "defence" of poetry is constructed on its efficacy in producing that ideal.

But because Sidney shows as well as tells, let us take a closer look at how that ethos which we are meant to credit thinks.[41]

First, a precis. Sidney, addressing other gentlemen, identifies himself as a fairly young (he was 29) poet, "my unelected vocation" (100), and argues that those who look deeply into the art will find that it deserves "not to be scourged out of the church of God" (103). Looking deeply into the art involves Sidney in searching myth, history, philosophy, religion—all the learned sources of the humanist inquirer. Throughout the discourse, he is patriotic, if only inciden-

---

40. The "mistress Knowledge" metaphor becomes, M. J. Doherty has argued, a "centering" one in Sidney's essay: see Doherty's *The Mistress-Knowledge, Sir Philip Sidney's Defence of Poesie and Literary Architectonics in the English Renaissance* (Nashville, 1991). Conversely, to a lover of Plato, like Augustine, the view of *rhetoric* from the standpoint of *dialectic* is vulgar and (literally) material: rhetoric is fornication, carnal, in gender female; see Marjorie O'Rourke Boyle, "Augustine in the Garden of Zeus: Lust, Love, and Language," *Harvard Theological Review* 83 (1990): 117–139. Appropriately enough, Erasmus's most rhetorical persona is a woman, Folly, whose praise both she and Erasmus deliver.

41. Another, not at all disparate example is offered by Hunt in the essay mentioned earlier.

tally, insisting on the glories of "our mother tongue" (101). And he is even more pointed than Ascham in insisting that "virtuous action," or "well doing" and not "well knowing only," is "the ending end of all earthly learning" (108). Having praised poetry as the source of wisdom, Sidney reduces his scope to aim the conclusion of his discourse directly at his gentlemanly audience: poetry is not only suited for cases of courtship (no pun) but it is also—here striking the "eternizing" theme popular with his and his preferred audience's class—a means of commemorating one's life. Such, in sum, is his argument. But, as many readers acknowledge, certain details take on a significance beyond that of the argument itself.

One of these details is a virtual illustration of my case. At one point in his apology, Sidney makes patent the disputatious techniques I have pursued in the various examples I have used and offers a significant if fleeting guide for his intended audience. Throughout his discourse, he obliquely refers to courtroom trials and disputes. Thereby, although he rarely confronts Gosson or any of his putative antagonists, he clearly reveals the conceptual model at the core of his own protocol. At one point the actual procedure of disputation is made explicit, when Sidney endeavors to place poetry among the humane arts.

The terms of the question in this dispute about poetry's place are taken from the Puritan attacks (from those who *would* scourge poetry "out of the church of God"): who or what is the best teacher of virtue? The premier position—that is, *primus inter pares*—can be vied for by two arts in particular, each having claims on imparting wisdom: moral philosophy, which teaches us what virtue is, and history, which gives us examples of virtuous action. Sidney resolves the contest in the following way.

> Now, whom shall we find (sith the question standeth for the highest form in the school of learning) to be Moderator? Truly, as me seemeth, the Poet. . . . Therefore compare we the Poet with the Historian, and with the Moral Philosopher, and if he go beyond them both, no other human skill can match him. For as for the Divine, with all reverence it is ever to be excepted, not only for having his scope as far beyond any of these as eternity exceedeth a moment, but even for passing each of these in themselves. And for the Lawyer, though *Ius* be the Daughter of Justice, and Justice the chief of Vertues, yet because he seeketh to make men good rather *Formidine poenae* than *Virtutis amore* ["by fear of pun-

ishment" rather than "by love of virtue"], or, to say righter, dooth not endeavor to make men good but that their evil hurt not others (having no care how bad a man is so long as he is a good Citizen)—therefore, as our wickedness maketh him necessary, and necessity maketh him honorable, so is he not in the deepest truth to stand in rank with these who all endeavor to take naughtiness away, and plant goodness even in the secretest cabinet of our soules. And these four are all that any way deal in that consideration of men's manners, which being the supreme knowledge, they that best breed it deserve the best commendation.

The Philosopher therefore and the Historian are they which would win the goal, the one by precept, the other by example. But both not having both, do both halt. For the Philosopher, setting down with thorny argument the bare rule, is so hard of utterance, and so misty to be conceived, that one that hath no other guide but him shall wade in him till he be old before he shall find sufficient cause to be honest: for his knowledge standeth so upon the abstract and general, that happy is that man who may understand him, and more happy that can apply what he doth understand. On the other side, the Historian, wanting the precept, is so tied, not to what should be but to what is, to the particular truth of things and not to the general reason of things, that his example draweth no necessary consequence, and therefore a less fruitful doctrine.

Now doth the peerless Poet perform both . . . (110–111)

To the stylist, Sidney's rhetorical figure is the *expeditio*.[42] More to my purposes, it is important to note that Sidney's model, which frames his argument, is educational disputation, of an advanced kind ("the question standeth for the highest form in the school of learning"—an American would say "level" instead of "form"). The question he is pursuing devolves first into a dispute between the Historian and the Moral Philosopher. Sidney asks, Who shall be Moderator? In the university disputation described in my previous chapter, the Moderator was the judge of the dispute, the one who determined which side won. In Sidney's case, neither side wins. For Sidney is *also* playing on the other, closely related meaning of the term, as someone who stands in the middle ground between two extremes.

---

42. Defined by Richard Sherry as "when many reasons [are] rehearsed up, whereby a thing might be done or not, the other[s] are taken away, and one left that we intend"; *A Treatise of Schemes and Tropes* (1550), Dii^v. I have modernized the spelling and punctuation. A half century later, Hoskins (see the following note) defined *expeditio* simply as a "reckoning upon divers parts" which "destroys all but that one which you mean to rest upon" (45).

The Poet performs that function but then, in Sidney's argument, actually surpasses the Moderator's role by combining the very best in the two extremes, the two claimants, but with none of their limitations. Thus, it is, finally, Sidney himself who performs the Moderator's role as judge of an imagined dispute. But the dispute that he would have us imagine places poetry on the one side and such other humane arts as moral philosophy and history on the other. Sidney moderates the dispute by arguing that only poetry has virtues which themselves moderate the extremes in question. It is a role not only that Sidney has adopted but that he would impose upon his audience—or, better, invite other gentlemen to adopt.

It is illuminating to take this doubleness (Sidney's compound, ironic application of the term *moderator*—meaning both a middle point and a resolver of disputation) and use it as a basis for interpreting that word in this period. Puttenham, for example, defines *litotes* in the following way:

> [By *emphasis* we] enforce our sense, so by another [figure] we temper our sense with words of such moderation as in appearance it abateth it but not in deed, and is by the figure *litotes,* which therefore I call the *Moderator,* and [it] becomes us many times better to speak in that sort qualified, than if we spoke it by more forcible terms, and nevertheless is equivalent in sense, thus. *I know you hate me not, nor wish me any ill.*
> Meaning indeed that he loved him very well and dearly, and yet the words do not express so much, though they purport so much. Or if you would say, "I am not ignorant," for "I know well enough." "Such a man is no fool," meaning indeed that he is a very wise man. (184)

Around the end of the century, partly in admiration of Sidney's *Arcadia,* John Hoskins—an Oxonian, lawyer, and schoolmaster—wrote a readable study of the figures of speech (in which the definitions themselves are not, as in Puttenham, labyrinthine). He describes the effects of *litotes* under the figure "diminution":

> by denying the contrary, as, if you should [mean] *reasonable pleasant,* [in saying] Arcadian speech is *not unpleasant; hardly liked—not misliked; not unfit, not altogether modest, not deny.* But why should I give examples of the most usual phrases in the English tongue? As, we say *not the wisest man that ever I saw,* for *a man of small wisdom.*[43]

43. *Directions for Speech and Style* (1599) ed. Hoyt H. Hudson (Princeton, N.J., 1935), 35.

The conceptual relation of the figure to pro-con reasoning should seem obvious. To create a *litotes* one must imagine two contraries and then apparently affirm one by denying the other, to say "he is no fool" when you wish to affirm something of the opposite, "he is a very wise man." (Or, "truth is not unmixed.") To what effect? To interpret a *litotes* one must imagine *both* alternatives, just as one must study both contraries in a disputation, a kind of "paradoxical and double vision" as Elizabeth McCutcheon puts it in her analysis of this most prevalent figure in More's *Utopia* (a vision that discovers "the best state of the commonwealth in an island called Noplace"). That the figure is, as Hoskins says, among "the most usual phrases in the English tongue" indicates some of the pervasiveness of the Renaissance habit of mind I am trying to describe, "a tendency to see more than one side to a question." McCutcheon continues: "Intellectual, judicial, and persuasive," the figure asks us "to weigh and consider alternatives which the writer himself has considered."[44] The effect, in sum, is to involve the audience, in the way a suasive rhetor might, by making it ostensibly part of the creative process. The habit of mind may be the point Quintilian was making when, in the statement I have used to preface this book and cited several times throughout, he uses a litotes to stress the inventive purposes of debating: "Nor is the perfect orator without this skill" *(neque perfectus orator sine hac virtute [altercatione] dici potest).* (Nor should the prominence of the figure in Cicero, e.g. *Brutus,* go unnoticed.)

The litotic mode of speech is "becoming," Puttenham notes. It can be ironic, used to say what one more or less does not mean. But it is always, more or less, indirect. If I mean that truth is mixed, why say it is not unmixed? Always the function is to engage the mind, to compel it to "moderate," to affirm one contrary by means of the other, as if both were present. Too, often one must at the same time find a position that is more or less midway, as "reasonable pleasant" is more or less midway between "unpleasant" and "pleasant." Or one must often, like Sidney, resolve the dispute by drawing qualities from both extremes, as in Hoskins' final example: he is not the wisest man that ever I saw, nor is he the stupidest, but he combines the two as "a man of small wisdom."

---

44. "Denying the Contrary: More's Use of Litotes in the *Utopia,*" *Moreana* 31–32 (1971): 109–10, 119–20.

The logic involved is not unlike the "fuzzy logic" described by Berkeley scientist Lofti Zadeh. An alternative to either-or thinking, "fuzzy logic" has been applied in modification of the simple binary operations of computers, and lately of other kinds of electronic appliances. Its ancient forebear, the sort of thinking which impels the use of the litotes, is best grasped when seen in light of the categorical distinctions of academic disputation: it is neither con nor discretely pro. The distinctions involved are if not actually fuzzy, less than starkly clear. Indeed, the litotic rejection of the either-or mode of thought, besides serving as a tactic to engage the mind, seems to reflect the Erasmian doctrine of mixed, circumstantial truth, apprehensible best by a *via diversa*.

Some trials of judgment are also present in yet another figure which belongs under a rubric quite the opposite of diminution, *hyperbole,* or exaggeration. Puttenham, who sees *hyperbole* as an active dissembler, calls it "the loud liar"—and his warning about its use centers, as we might suppose, not in its lying but in its rudeness, its propensity for loudness. The figure, which may be too easily dismissed by modern readers as simple exaggeration, was another one of the most popular figures in the period. Its true function, along with that of most figures and tropes, may also be clouded for modern readers because most Renaissance theorists classified figures and tropes as "ornamentation." About *hyperbole* the rhetorician Hoskins says,

> Sometimes it expresseth a thing in the highest degree of possibility, beyond the truth, that it [i.e., the mind] descending thence may find the truth; sometimes in flat impossibility, that rather you may conceive the unspeakableness than the untruth of the relation. (29)

There is a general precept here, one that fits the tenor of humanist rhetoric and makes the function of figures like litotes and hyperbole serve more than decorativeness or even expressiveness. They serve the writer's purposes by requiring the reader not simply to judge the truth but often to invent it, in either case acting like a moderator within the parameters of disputation. They are suasive figures, engaging a reader by further challenging that reader to determine where the writer stands. The writer has apparently only made the subject speakable.

There is yet another form which fits well into this suasory mode, the *paradox*. The classic example is the self-contradictory statement. Epimenides the Cretan said, "All Cretans are liars." Was he lying then or telling the truth? A simpler scriptural example is Jesus' apparent equivocation, "You must lose your life in order to find it." Puttenham calls the paradox "the Wonderer." Moreover, the paradox form could also expand to include that contrarian adventuresomeness I have called the "sally." But for that matter it could encompass any entire discourse that took a stance contrary to popular opinion, like Vergil's praise of a gnat or, again, Erasmus's vastly more complicated *Praise of Folly*. Cicero's *Paradoxa Stoicorum* was an almost equally complicated example: he used theses about which there could apparently be little dispute ("only what is morally noble is good"), but he used them as a kind of collateral increpation of the very oddity of these positions in his contemporary society.

The Elizabethans had a great love of paradox, as Rosalie L. Colie has shown, one that reached epidemic proportions in the sixteenth century.[45] Nor does Colie overlook the presence of *textbooks* on paradox-writing in this period, though perhaps she gives too little attention to the deep and complex relations between paradox and the disputatiousness of humanist rhetoric. One of the more popular textbooks on paradoxes in the period was Ortenso Lando's *Paradossi,* translated into English by Anthony Munday and entitled *The Defense of Contraries* (1593). Munday's prologue is itself a fair example of protean prose, not unlike suasion, full of contrarian spirit.[46] In his book

45. *Paradoxia Epidemica: The Renaissance Tradition of Paradox* (Princeton, N.J., 1966).

46. Gentle Reader, euen as contrarie thinges compared one with another, do giue the better euidence of their value and vertue: so the truth of any matter whatsoeuer, appeareth most cleerely, when the different reasons against the same, is equalled or neighboured therewith. Beside, whosoeuer would prepare a Knight to the field, must first exercise himselfe, in the most common and vulgare actes of Armes, that cunning strategems may seeme the lesse laboursome to him. In like manner, for him that woulde be a good Lawyer, after he hath long listened at the barre; he must aduenture to defend such a cause, as they that are most imployed, refuse to maintaine: therby to make himselfe more apt and ready, against common pleaders in ordinarie causes of processe. For this intent, I haue undertaken (in this booke) to debate on certain matters, which our Elders were wont to cal Paradoxes: that is to say, things contrary to most mens present opinions: to the end, that by such discourse as is helde in them, opposed truth might appeare more cleere and apparant. Likewise, to exercise thy witte in proofe of such occasions, as shall enforce thee to seeke diligentlie and laboriously, for sound reasons, proofes, authorities, histories, and very darke or

Lando/Munday offers disquisitions on several elementary and unorthodox propositions: e.g. that ignorance is better than knowledge, that drunkenness is better than sobriety, that the barren woman is more happy than the child-bearing woman; that it is better to weep often than to laugh at any time; that scarcity is better than abundance. As I noted earlier, the educational principle is at least as old as Quintilian, and may in fact go back to the Sophists. Lando/Munday's list should be compared with the one Erasmus offers in his textbook on letterwriting (see my preceding chapter); the rationale is identical, if more flatly and simply explained by Munday: increased love of diversity and increased abundance of one's inventive powers. We shall explore the paradox further in the next chapter, on Thomas Wilson. As in all suasory forms, a challenge is offered to the reader's resourcefulness.

Perhaps we are now ready to return to an argument left incomplete in our review of Puttenham: how could one possibly invent a moderator for *his* description of the poet? Recall that he described the poet as a "pleader . . . of pleasant and lovely causes and nothing perilous, such as be those for the trial of life, limb, or livelihood, and before judges neither sour nor severe." The poet's opposite number is the trial attorney, the barrister. There is no middle position. Both alike are rhetoricians, practitioners of eloquence, and it would seem that the poet is by comparison involved in a far more trivial pursuit. But, however wide open Puttenham may have left the matter when his book went before the larger audience, the question is not about who is the more trivial. The question is whether both the poet and the lawyer must be skilled "counterfeitors." We are asked to be a moderator of the other kind, to resolve the dispute. This we can do through deference to the major premise of Puttenham's argument: the true importance of poetry lies in its artistic skill at dissembling, for that skill is necessary to all important civil, legal, and political endeavors. Puttenham must have believed that at least for his preferred audience this major premise was itself sufficient to

---

hidden memories. Notwithstanding, in these conceits, I would not haue thee so much deceiued, as that eyther my sayings or conclusions, should make thee credit otherwise, then common and sensible iudgement requireth: and yet withall remember, that diuersitie of things, doth more comfort mens spirites, then daily and continually to behold, whatsoeuer is common and frequent to our iudgements.

control all the litotes, hyperbole, paradoxes and sallies in his argument.

It is finally Sidney who *shows* us how to be a moderator. An antiquarian's virtue not unknown to Plato and Aristotle, with their abhorrence of excess, moderation is yet another key to humanist protocol, to suasion. And to my final subject in this chapter

A Renaissance Frame of Mind

In analyzing these discourses and referring to figures of speech I have tended to slight their authors' use of personification. Thereby I have ignored their central figure and blunted one of their main points. Ascham, for example, does not talk about archery but lets us hear a master archer. Puttenham and Sidney, in spite of their titles and announced subjects, purposefully speak not so much of poetry in the abstract as of poets. Whether through their authors' surrogate or through the author's ethos itself, these three discourses converge to arrive at a similar ideal, the ease and grace of "hitting the mark," qualities born of discipline and learning and suited for any artist—courtier, archer, theologian, poet, knight, controversialist—whether the qualities are called *honestum* (Cicero), *urbanitas* (Horace), or *sprezzatura* (Castiglione), "moderator," "art," or "honesty." "The hitting of the mark," Toxophilus says, is "the end both of shooting and also of this our communication." Puttenham's work leaves us with a scattered picture of poetry but with a fairly integrated picture of the rhetorical mind. Sidney's work is often regarded as an example of humanist poetics, one that conflates Aristotle, Plato, Cicero, and Horace. But in that conflation he manages to give us an example of something else as well, the rhetorical mind in operation. The end of communication, "hitting of the mark," does not end with the end of the communication. The rhetorical mind once formed is ready to continue the conversation, on a related topic possibly, "to meet here again," in Philologus's final words.

There are similar ends, to return to the first of our examples, in the writings of Erasmus and More. Erasmus, having earlier given us an embodiment of folly, shows us clearly—perhaps all too clearly—the nature of the humanist suasory ethos in confrontation with Luther. Among his contemporaries and through the centuries, critical commentary has centered not so much on the character of Folly herself as on the values and morals of her author. *That* character, Erasmus's public role, stands unmasked in the debate with Luther, so much so that a distribution of rhetorical principles may be attempted. In *The Praise of Folly* we find the protocol of humanist rhetoric at work; in the debate with Luther we find the non-assertive, combat-hating, "radical concordist" who, forced to reveal his private values and morals by the very subject of the debate, can be no match for his fierce opponent, can only yearn for the "freer field of the muses," the field of Folly, or for rhetoric's power of indirection, and hope for the audience's ongoing conversation in an act of judgment.

It may be that when More completed the *Utopia* for publication he sought to avoid a certain artistic flaw in *The Praise of Folly*, a growing readerly confusion about where the author himself stood. So he added other speakers to his *Utopia,* changed the work from its original monologic structure and, to Erasmus's mind (in the letter to von Hutton [CWE, 7:24]) made the entire discourse "uneven in style." Of course, in such a complex work there yet remains some question as to the clarity More achieved, at least for certain readers. Nonetheless, the narrator's voice, which at times blends with the voice of the character Morus, is our surest guide. More's narrator sets the tone of the discourse initially with his reference to a certain political difference of opinion which took him, Morus, to Flanders. Insofar as the work itself is something of a continuing difference of political opinion if not an actual dispute, it is Raphael who promulgates his ideas with a Lutheran assertiveness and it is Morus/narrator who responds with a pondering, reluctant deliberateness, not unlike that which was later to mark Erasmus's character as a public debater. *Utopia* ends significantly, with Morus promising to think over all that Raphael has said about Utopia in hopes of further discussion and with the narrator commenting:

> I cannot agree and consent to all things that he said [although he is] without doubt a man singularly well learned and also in all worldly matters exactly and profoundly experienced. So I must needs confess and grant that many things be in the Utopian [republic] which in our cities I may rather wish for than hope after. (143–44)

Discussion—conversation or even disputation—about ways and means the political economy of England, if not of all Europe, is the aim of the work. Raphael has offered an opening sally, and Morus/

narrator responds in a manner echoed by Erasmus a decade later in defending Folly: not everything this contrarian voice has said should simply be dismissed. The author's tactics of indirection in *Utopia* are aimed at making the ideas if not palatable then (to echo Hoskins) not unspeakable. He admits that not all the ideas are appropriate. But there are many features which he likes. Thus his very conclusion is, tonally at least litotic and conceptually deeply ironic—and in effect no conclusion.

The primary handbook of the rhetorical frame of mind, both character and action, in the Renaissance was penned by Baldassare Castiglione. It is a handbook to the same extent and in the same way that *De oratore* is a handbook. Its rules cannot be set forth either simply or systematically. A brief glance at that work may help us further understand humanist suasion, the frame of mind that produced it and the frame of mind it sought to conduce, the hitting of the mark which is the end of "this our communication."

Over a dozen aristocrats participate in Castiglione's dialogue, first published in 1528, then translated into English and published as *The Book of the Courtier* in 1561. Although the setting is indoors, the dialogue, offered as a kind of epistle from Castiglione to Ariosto, owes much to Cicero and through Cicero to Plato. Thomas Hoby, Castiglione's translator in 1561, summarizes the author's Ciceronian precedent; as we might suppose, it derives from *De oratore:*

> Cicero an excellent Orator, in three books of an Orator unto his brother fashioneth such a one as never was, nor yet is like to be. Castiglione an excellent Courtier, in three books of a Courtier unto his dear friend [Ariosto], fashioneth such a one as is hard to find, and perhaps impossible.[47]

Not only are both epistolary in form, both posit ideals as the all but unattainable goal of their principles. *De oratore* is, in sum, "the major subtext" of Castiglione's work.[48] But it is a work that also clearly recalls the *Phaedrus*.

---

47. But even Hoby's translation has four books. He may have excepted the third, on the subject of women. All my quotations are from Hoby, as edited by Ernest Rhys and printed in London and New York in 1937. I have modernized the spelling and punctuation.

48. Wayne A. Rebhorn, "Baldesar Castiglione, Thomas Wilson, and the Courtly Body of Renaissance Rhetoric," *Rhetorica* 11 (1993): 251.

These similarities notwithstanding, it is important to note that in Castiglione several of the participants are women—one of whom, the Duchess of Urbino (in whose palace the dialogue takes place), invites the discussion, and another of whom somewhat actively joins in the disputes. Most of the talking is done by men, even when the subjects are women, beauty, and love—appropriately enough, perhaps, in respect either of echoing the *Phaedrus* itself or of reflecting the Platonic ur-model for dialogues.[49] Of course, it was mainly men who were trained in the niceties of dialectic and rhetoric anyway. Furthermore, in this case, one can almost see the awkwardness that occurs when an antique, platonizing, male-centered philosophical dialogue displaces a perceptibly changing social order. Our purpose, however, is to examine what the dialogue offers by way of instruction in humanist ethos.

The talk becomes wide-ranging, as in Cicero, although the ideal courtier is the center of discussion. The subject of rhetoric is never far away. Most of one book is given to "jests" and "merry pranks," parts of rhetoric's time-honored purview. In disputes the questions are various: whether the courtier must be of noble birth, whether it is ever efficacious to use inkhorn terms, whether painting or sculpture is the more admirable art, whether women are the equals of men, whether monarchy or republicanism is the better form of government. Again, these lists obscure the thoroughly traditional point: abstract ideas, or (as Milton would put it a century later) "untried virtues," are less important than getting down to cases and knowing actually how to conduct oneself, not simply in order to advance but primarily to achieve that other humanist desideratum, "living well."

These desiderata ultimately find their center in one kind of behavior, *sprezzatura*—off-hand excellence, or "an air of perfect naturalness acquired through discipline,"[50] Because the management of the body is an essential part of this discipline,[51] *sprezzatura* becomes another area in which the view of language as speech—and the profound rhetoricizing of humanism—is prominent. "Behavior" is an

49. Kenneth Burke argues that Platonic dialectic between men, freed of biological love, was also a move toward "either a *transcendence* of homosexuality or a transcendence of *homosexuality*"; see *A Grammar of Motives* (Berkeley, Calif., 1969), 427.

50. Friench Simpson, intro. to his translation of *The Courtier* (New York, 1980), iv.

51. See Rebhorn, "Baldesar Castiglione," esp. 241–59.

operative word in the definition, action whose impression involves an artful concealment of art through a studious avoidance of all appearance of affectation or even much effort. An art, one might say, of skillful dissembling. Count Ludovico expresses the matter concisely:

> Therefore that may be said to be a very art that appeareth not to be art. Neither ought a man to put more diligence in anything than in covering it. For in case it be open, it looseth credit clean and maketh a man little set by. (46)

Later Federico adds:

> And in every thing that he hath to do or to speak, if it be possible, let him come always provided and think on it beforehand, showing notwithstanding the whole to be done *ex tempore* and at the first sight. (130)

In that observation lies one point of resourcefulness, part of what Erasmus calls *copia*. Throughout Castiglione's book, most of the disputations are left unresolved by the participants, the conversation is meant to continue; but as always in humanist suasion certain norms are unmistakable. Although ideal courtliness, whether in male or in female, may be all but unattainable, yet the very pattern of the ideal should remain a more or less indisputable goal of education. Of that pattern is born the ideal we have just touched on, *sprezzatura*. The ideal is further sanctioned, if only in a minor way, by Castiglione himself, who claims to have written *The Courtier* "in a few days"— a claim of effortlessness and lack of studiousness which itself set a pattern for countless authorial prefaces in the period. But, of course, that claim is unmasked in the dialogue, as we have just seen, by Count Ludovico and Federico.

The vice is to mind this virtue so much that you "make a show not to mind it" (47), for "too much diligence is hurtful" (48). The virtue of *sprezzatura* is born of discipline, a certain consciousness of choice and reflection on one's own actions; again, Federico:

> Afterward let him consider well what the thing is he doth or speaketh, the place where it is done, in presence of whom, in what time, the cause why he doth it, his age, his profession, the end whereto it tendeth, and the means that may bring him to it. And so let him apply himself discreetly with these advertisements to whatsoever he mindeth to do or speak. (95)

The analysis is rhetorical and centered in decorum—and the point was restated by, among a host of others, Morus. One's speech like one's actions must have "decency" or "decorum" in consideration of their rhetorical situation, and they must be unnoticeably artful through skillful "dissembling" (the quoted words are Puttenham's). By such means one creates a certain ethos and, again to echo Ascham, lives well.

But (pace, Raphael) the fulfillment of this greatest of all desiderata could indeed require some painful compromises. How does one finally maintain one's integrity—without which, as Crassus argued, eloquence is a powerful weapon in the hands of madmen (III.xiv. 55)—while fully engaged in the frustrations of education and theology or in the intrigues and compromises of law cases, courtly life, statesmanship? Cicero's ethos in his legal pleading, particularly as evidenced in his surviving orations, is an artful fulfillment of his own theory about constructing an effective character when speaking to this or that segment of the public. That the character was partial is suggested by the ethos of the *Tusculan disputations,* which in turn suggests that perhaps this latter work was an effort at artful re-integration. Thomas Wyatt's moving poem "Stand whoso list" is a dirge on the theme of the emptiness of having only a public self. That the poem is in part a translation of Seneca (the Younger) is antiquarian evidence that the problem of what happens, often disastrously, to the private self when one achieves an effective public persona was not unknown to the ancients.[52] In this respect, "living well" was an especially poignant struggle for any man of integrity who "goes public"—a struggle of reconciliation.

Another form of this tension was that between the *vita activa* and the *vita contemplativa,* or between civic humanism and philology, or for that matter between rhetoric and philosophy. In each humanist case rhetoric became the approach or protocol of the latter. Rhetoric, for example, was Erasmus's habitual protocol, whether he wrote as preceptor or as propounder of the *philosophia christi.* In both of those pursuits, however, Erasmus—no statesman, no civic humanist—brilliantly revealed the nature of humanist rhetoric. But the full ap-

---

52. See Thomas A. Hannen, "The Humanism of Sir Thomas Wyatt," in *The Rhetoric of Renaissance Poetry,* ed. Thomas O. Sloan and Raymond Waddington (Berkeley, Calif., 1974), 37–56.

plication of that rhetoric, nonetheless, lay in the success of one of its ultimate quests, the effective public persona of the man engaged not necessarily in education or even in theology but above all in politics—in "well doing," Sidney would say, and "not well knowing only." Thereby, the full application of humanist rhetoric lay in a life where "dissembling," even *sprezzatura,* the effort to be effortless could be most compelling and could most take its toll. Terry Eagleton's radical characterization of the subject is much to the point: after the classical period and the Middle Ages,

> rhetoric remained a textual training of the ruling class in the techniques of political hegemony . . . The textbooks of rhetoric were the densely codified manuals of such politico-discursive education; they were handbooks of ruling-class power.[53]

Therefore, to complete our study we need to examine the career of a civic humanist, as we shall in the following chapter.

Here, however, we can begin to end on this note: the ethos of humanist suasion is compounded of voices. Just as the discourse it produced is conversational in manner and end, so the Renaissance frame of mind is itself dialogic in nature—at least, the Renaissance humanist frame of mind as pictured in the discourse reviewed in this chapter. Although a dialogue between "body" and "[compromised] soul" may be implicit, the split usually involves two ostensible or actual opposites. We have overheard an eyewitness account of utopianism, while we listened to a believer talking with a skeptic. We have heard Erasmus's moderated tones in response to Luther's stentorian righteousness. We have listened to a lover of bows and a lover of words, as they embark on a dialogic quest, in which the two sides are moderated by a certain ideal—a paradoxical ideal, for perfection is admittedly easier to achieve in words than in deeds, but is obviously efficacious in both. A pleader at the bar and a pleader at love are similarly distinguished by Puttenham, who finally poses the latter as the artful exemplar of a skill necessary to the former. We have heard, too, a case for poetry as a capstone of all the courtly and humane arts, as offered by a gentleman who so compounds the voices involved that he skillfully dissembles his pleading and transforms the dispute.

---

53. *Walter Benjamin: Towards a Revolutionary Criticism* (London, 1981), 101.

But one of Sidney's earliest readers disagreed with Sidney's point, took issue with his manner, and said so at length. Let us take a brief look at his argument. For it reflects a radically different, unhumanistic idea about the ends and aims of art, and thus a radically different frame of mind. The humanist would create an ethos suited for the action of skeptical, ongoing, convivial conversation *(sermo),* often on public matters. The opposition sought the impersonal means of assertion, persuasion, and closure, on all matters.

The Ramist William Temple, about ten years before the "Apology" was published (and given its titles), calls Sidney's essay a "treatise" (*"De Poesie tractatio"*).[54] The appelation is neutral enough. But Temple's reading is highly controversial, often breaking Sidney's statements down into syllogistic form in order to prove, Ramist fashion, that, contrary to Sidney, not poetry but logic (i.e., Ramist dialectic) is the most effective teacher and the art of arts. Temple's character has nothing of *sprezzatura* about it, although he speaks respectfully and deferentially—and Sidney responded in kind; in fact, Temple later became Sidney's private secretary. Temple reveals himself totally unsympathetic to the kind of rhetoric on which the "Apology" is based; like all Ramists, he hates fuzzy logic. Toward his conclusion, Temple shows Sidney how he, Sidney, could have better made his case (unwarranted though it be) for the superiority of poetry: what he should have done, Temple suggests, is offer a methodical unfolding of a syllogistic argument from a major premise ("Poetry is an art of fiction-making for teaching and delighting" [173]). Like any narrow, Scholastic dialectician, Temple would have Sidney's argument proceed with no attention to audience, nor any thought of an opposition. He suggests, in short, that Sidney practice an art of discourse like his own, assertion upon assertion with no pro-con reasoning. No rhetoric, in short. As noted, no *sprezzatura* either.

Again, form and intention tend to coalesce. Indeed, our view of one almost invariably reflects our view of the other. Those who assume Sidney's intention is to argue the other side of Gosson's case are content to see the form of his essay as a Ciceronian oration. Tem-

---

54. John Webster, ed. and trans., *William Temple's Analysis of Sir Philip Sidney's Apology for Poetry* (Binghamton, N.Y., 1984), 64. All my quotations are from this Latin-English edition.

ple, however, assumes that the essay's purpose is to teach, and therefore he looks at the essay for its Ramist-Methodical form (and its
shortcomings therein).[55] By contrast, I find an important inner principle of form, and therefore intention, in the passage I have examined
at length. Sidney uses disputation to assume the role of *moderator.* He
does not confront Gosson. He stands apart from the dispute to moderate it. In so doing he emphasizes protocol and reveals its end, in
the rhetorical manner appropriate to a certain kind of character.

Like Martin Luther, William Temple may have realized all too
well the rhetorical complexity of the opposition's procedures and
just how to make points by counter-balancing them. Part of the great
appeal of Ramists lay in the argumentative barrenness they practiced
and preached. At root was a doctrine unlike anything in the humanists' canon: the mind will accede to truth once it is revealed in
its stark simplicity. And truth, these philosophers believed, could be
so revealed. Thus there were extant two profoundly differing epis-
temologies and two equally profoundly differing ideas about the nature of truth itself. "Simplicity?" one might hear Erasmus on the
contrary remark. "Christ is simple. In fact, nothing could be simpler," he actually says when he calls Christ of all things a "Proteus."[56]

But in our time an effort simply to grasp those *other* procedures,
the protean ones, the *via diversa,* eludes us. I am speaking, of course,
not simply of the binary pro-con reasoning but of that other mul-
tivocal reasoning which often ended in suasion and which was predicated on pro-con reasoning but took a step just beyond it. George K.
Hunter's description of humanist dialogues applies equally well to
the suasion we have examined: "The flow of to-and-fro discussion
. . . is not intended to end in unison but to raise, turn around, and
speculate on alternative versions of the possible truth, which may
well be incompatible but are not pressed to reach that point" (111).

55. See John Webster, "Oration and Method in Sidney's *Apology:* A Contemporary's Account," *Modern Philology* 79 (1981–1982): 1–15, for an excellent review
of these intentional-formal matters, contrasting Myrick's Ciceronian view with
Temple's. Webster, however, tends too easily to assume that the Ramists meant by
"teaching" what we mean by "expository." Our meaning is a late-Romantic, "scientific" one. The Ramists were talking about "natural" persuasion.

56. *Adeo cum nostro Christo nihil sit simplicius, tamen arcano quodam consilio Pro-
teum quemdam representat varietate vitae atque doctrinae; Ratio verae theologiae* (Basel,
1518), 214.

Our failure to grasp this protocol, I have tried to argue, is one reason why our theories of *inventio* are so impoverished. And the failure is equally evident, I have tried also to suggest, in our histories of rhetoric. It shows up to stunning effect, it seems to me, in a recent important history from which I have drawn the subtitle of this section.

Brian Vickers' *In Defense of Rhetoric* has been well praised for its complex summary of classical origins.[57] It is perhaps most significant that in this summary he centralizes educational problems. That centralization is, of course, no guarantee of accuracy: his complaint, for example (36), that Cicero botched *De oratore* by failing to accede to the impulse (which Vickers finds evident in the work) to produce a handbook, is clearly contradicted not only by Cicero's own prefacing complaint about the insufficiency of his earlier handbook, *De inventione,* but also by his equally evident impulse to educate the real as well as the ideal orator through means that lie well beyond the limits of any mere handbook. Handbook implies system, and Cicero's point is not unlike the jabs Erasmus takes at "method" in his handbook-appearing *De copia:* the complexity of rhetoric will not, and should not be made to, yield to system. The point seems to lie beyond Vickers' grasp. Most notably Vickers finds Cicero failing in an area which he, Vickers, regards as the sine-qua-non of rhetoric: Cicero neglected to give the tropes and figures "the detail they deserve" (38).

It is little wonder, then, that in continuing his history through "medieval fragmentation" to "Renaissance reintegration," Vickers locates an achievement of the latter period in its realization that the tropes and figures are not simply ornaments but effective movers of the passions, suitable for an active role in rhetoric's renewed function, persuasion. Thus, the Renaissance "pursued *elocutio* with enormous zest" (283). "Medieval fragmentation" apparently does not signify, for Vickers, the virtual disappearance of rhetoric as a mode of thought, nor does "Renaissance reintegration" signify the return of a full Ciceronian rhetoric, let alone a re-centralizing of *inventio* at the heart of rhetorical operations. The key to the two periods, for Vickers, seems to lie in a functional view of figurative language.

57. Oxford, Eng., 1988. See the review by Arthur J. Quinn in *Rhetorica* 7 (1989): 291–94.

Thus, though he discusses at considerable length the characteristics of Renaissance schooling, it is not surprising that Erasmus's *De copia* is only lightly treated, a "seminal work" on "amplification," he calls it, from which students "would graduate to the list of figures in Susenbrotus's popular collection *Epitome Troporum ac Schematum* . . . or in *Ad Herennium,* Book 4" (258).

Vicker's "defense of rhetoric" is an argument in behalf of figures and tropes: "It is true that rhetoric as a whole network of relationships and procedures is now available only to those who reconstruct it by study, but the expressive function of the figures remains, whether or not as part of a larger system" (433). What the *De copia* offers, then, is available without much study but hardly worth the whistling. Though Vickers obviously sees, to a greater extent than many previous historians, the importance of the history of education in writing a history of rhetoric, his pursuit of a singular thesis may account for his faulting Cicero and slighting Erasmus. The thesis reveals itself again in Vicker's comments concerning the matter which provides the subtitle of this section:

> If you cannot pick up a list of the figures and read it through avidly, thinking of all the instances of their application and re-creation in Petrarch or Racine, Shakespeare or Milton, then you have not yet thought yourself back into a Renaissance frame of mind. (283)

Vickers in this book has pursued a conventional notion of rhetoric as style and, as noted, become an apologist for the figures as "expressive" ornaments of thought.[58] Once more the "Renaissance frame of mind" proves elusive. But because actions of that mind usually culminated in style, as Cicero reveals in *De oratore* or Erasmus in *De copia,* Vickers' interest is not misplaced, only incomplete.

Let me conclude with an example of a prose piece which like Vickers' history is, prima facie, an exception to my argument. This is an example of Renaissance prose which is far more exhortative than suasory. Nor was it composed for an exclusive audience. It is from another of Donne's sermons. One critic in studying the piece located its beauty and craftsmanship in rhythm. I would suggest that they may be located as well in the dialogic impulses of a resourceful

---

58. Some of his best and most sustained analyses are to be found outside this book. See, for example, "The *Songs and Sonnets* and the Rhetoric of Hyperbole," in *John Donne: Essays in Celebration,* ed. A. J. Smith (London, 1972), 132–74.

and disputatious *inventio,* the wellsprings alike of suasion and advocacy—however far apart those two may appear to be and however
disparate the manner required in each—and a key to the Renaissance
frame of mind.

One of our greatest critics and historians of style, George Saintsbury, singled out a certain passage in Donne (see *Sermons,* 6: 172)
for high praise. Saintsbury claimed there was no more "exquisitely
rhythmed" passage in English prose—it was "never . . . surpassed,"
probably never "equalled."[59] I repeat the passage below, with Saintsbury's scansion, and invite the reader to supply from materials I have
tried to offer in this chapter perhaps equally compelling causes of
the exquisite rhythm.

If some king | of the earth | have so large | an extent | of
dominion | in north and south | as that he hath | winter and summer |
together | in his dominions; | so large | an extent | east and west |
as that he hath | day and night | together | in his dominions, | much
more | hath God | mercy | and justice | together. | He | brought
light| out of darkness, | not | out of a lesser | light; | He can
bring | thy summer | out of winter | though | thou have no | spring; |
though in the ways | of fortune, | or understanding, | or conscience, |
thou have been | benighted | till now, | wintered | and frozen, |
clouded | and eclipsed, | damped | and benumbed, | smothered | and
stupefied | till now, | now God | comes to thee, | not as in the
dawning | of the day, | not as in the bud | of the spring, | but as
the sun | at noon | to illustrate | all | shadows, | as the sheaves | in
harvest | to fill | all | penuries. | All | occasions | invite His |
mercies, | and all times | are His | seasons.

By the way, some of the figures and tropes involved (to cite only
those in Vickers' glossary) are *anadiplosis, antanaclasis, antithesis, asyn-
deton, chiasmus, epanodos, epiphonema, hypotyposis, isocolon, metaphor,
metonymy, parison, pariphrasis,* and at least the suggestion of a *zeugma.*

59. *A History of English Prose Rhythm* (London, 1912), 162.

6. A Case Study: Thomas Wilson

Civic humanism, as Hans Baron called it,[1] the practical application of humanist—in this case Erasmian—rhetoric to the world of politics, is the larger subject of this chapter. In it we will approach from another angle our observations and conjectures about rhetorical education through studying someone who was so definitely a product of it and who succeeded in times when "living well" could be a deadly game indeed. If the statesman whose career we shall examine was a lesser light than either Cicero or Erasmus, let me suggest that a lesser light can offer its own special illumination. For one thing, a lesser light can concentrate our attention by limiting our vision. For another, it can often surprise us with the subtlety of the brilliance it does afford—as we shall find at the end of this chapter, in our recovery of a minor rhetorical masterpiece.

Thomas Wilson (1523/24–1581) was not simply a statesman. He was also a dialectical and rhetorical theorist, educator, controversialist, lawyer, able Latinist, and (not always typical of humanists) Greekist. He was also a militant Protestant, an initially complicating flaw in the picture. (One might wish to find another flaw in his evident opportunism, or his careerist ambition; but this flaw, if it is one, is not uncharacteristic of humanists, most of whom had to find some

1. *The Crisis of the Early Italian Renaissance: Civic Humanism and Republican Liberty in an Age of Classicism and Tyranny.* 2 vols. (Princeton, N.J., 1955).

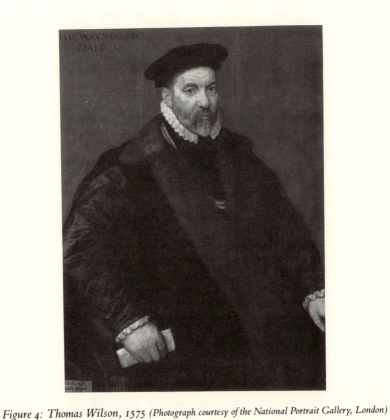

Figure 4: Thomas Wilson, 1575 (Photograph courtesy of the National Portrait Gallery, London)

This portrait, like the Erasmian likeness in Figure 1, is also drawn from life, this time by an unknown Flemish artist. It shows Wilson the ambassador at the age of 52. Peter E. Medine notes that the signet ring on Wilson's index finger contains a coat of arms representing the marriage of Wilson's father and mother, of Strubby in the county of Lincoln (*Thomas Wilson* [New York, 1986] 167). Wilson never turned his back on his Lincolnshire origins, but he seemed also never to have missed an opportunity to show the distance he had come. The portrait, misidentified since the seventeenth century as a portrait of another highly placed member of Elizabeth's government, Nicholas Bacon (as evidenced by the inscription in the bottom left-hand corner), bears interesting comparisons with Erasmus's portrait. Wilson's portrait reveals wealth, power, and the marks of high office and responsibility. He confronts the viewer. But his gaze has little of the arrogance or awesomeness of the politically powerful of the time. His face may even show some of the inward reflectiveness of the Erasmian humanist. However, the portrait shows none of the subject's irony, wit, humor, or—for that matter—any of the other qualities Panofsky faults in the portrait of Erasmus. Thus it shares an important characteristic with the Dürer engraving: Wilson's most significant likeness too is to be found in his writings.

means of using their literate or lawyerly skills profitably. Very few humanists—not excluding Erasmus[2]—had the means or for that matter the inclination to pursue knowledge for its own sake.) Protestantism itself is not necessarily at odds with humanism, as Erasmus's foes were all too quick to point out. But militancy is, particularly when it leads to an uncompromising, relentless pursuit of a set of convictions that brooks no skepticism or seeks no "moderator," no middle way even in the play of ideas, no open debate of contrarian values[3]—when it becomes, as perhaps Protestantism had to become in the sixteenth century, an intellectual sobriety and authoritarianism even concerning manners and morals, the secular arena of "living well." Its Catholic counterpart, we recall, had earlier forced a halt to Erasmus's "radical concordism."

Militants too in this age, many of them at least, had been brought up in the kind of disputatious educational environment I have been attempting to describe. They too had been subjected to the chief instruments of rhetorical education—such as debating one side and then the other—instruments which not only can be at odds with militancy but, more than that, were meant to be so. But there is no built-in guarantee that dogmatic adherence to a set of beliefs will not slip its bounds and overthrow the rules of the game or turn them into a rhetoric-stifling "political correctness." If Wilson shows us humanist protocol at work, he also shows us its limits as well—and, as I have suggested, he at times reaches those limits sooner than a brighter light might have done.

As a graduate student, tutor, and perhaps general hanger-on at Cambridge, he completed the first work we shall examine, which was the first English logic (that is, dialectic). Then as a scholar enjoying a summer's holiday at an upperclass country home in Lincolnshire, Wilson wrote the first complete and still one of the best

2. Lisa Jardine's work, *Erasmus, Man of Letters* (Princeton, N.J., 1993), which I have referred to throughout this book, finds in Erasmus's opportunism a search for fame. But Erasmus's arena differed from Wilson's more secular one.

3. Montaigne, for example, in adverting to a lesson from antiquity suggests the extent to which humanist protocol can be at odds with righteousness and sobriety of either the Catholic or the Protestant variety: "When Agesilaus invites Xenophon to send his children to be brought up in Sparta, it is not to learn rhetoric or dialectic there, but to learn, as he says, the finest science there is, namely, the science of obeying and commanding"; see *Works*, trans. Donald M. Frame (Stanford, Calif., 1967), 105.

English humanist rhetorics. These two books were popular in their own age and deserve to be read in ours, not simply as intellectual antiquities but as lively embodiments (if somewhat slanted) of what we have earlier referred to as "rhetorical paideia," or a certain Renaissance frame of mind. Like the *De copia* but in a far less clever way, these theoretical works enact their own principles.

Then, toward the end of his career as a member of Parliament, distinguished jurist, and author Wilson wrote his final book, a dialogue on usury. When this third mentioned work is read in the context of the first two, it illuminates the writer's mature humanism. The work must also of course be read in the context of its own age, and its age was one that both set political limits on religious as well as rhetorical ideals and began to deflate humanist optimism. If Wilson's life culminated in the fulfillment of his careerist ambitions, it also culminated in the maturing of his humanism. But that maturing came, ironically, in a period that began to mark the very demise of that intellectual movement, the passing of what later ages have termed Erasmian "high humanism." All strands of Wilson's thought culminate in this final book, a misread masterpiece of rhetorical disputation, one that Wilson subtly at first and then not so subtly gave a clearly suasory aim. Like the other two books, it is a work that deserves rereading in our own age, not so much for its ideas as for its protocol. And for its literary qualities as well. It is a notable remnant of its time.

A brief review of Wilson's career will give us an initial glimpse of his development as a writer.[4]

---

4. Though some recent research has been done into Wilson's life since Pollard's excellent DNB essay, no one has been able to pinpoint his birthdate. Peter E. Medine's *Thomas Wilson* (Boston, 1986) will be cited several times in this chapter. In constructing an overview of Wilson's biography, I have used other secondary sources, but I've taken issue with interpretations of fact that do not seem to square with the ethos or "implied author" of the Wilson I have come to know in my study of his books. Modern editions of those three books offer fairly complete biographies: see Richard S. Sprague, ed. *The Rule of Reason conteinying the Arte of Logike* (Northridge, Calif., 1972), xi–xxv; G. H. Mair, ed. *Wilson's "Arte of Rhetorique"* (Oxford, 1909), v–xv; Thomas J. Derrick, ed. *"Arte of Rhetorique" by Thomas Wilson* (New York, 1982), vii–lxi; and R. H. Tawney, ed. *A Discourse Upon Usury* (London, 1925), 1–172. In addition, I have also consulted these essays by Albert J. Schmidt: "A Treatise on England's Perils, 1578," *Archiv für Reformationsgeschichte* 46 (1955): 243–49; "Thomas Wilson, Tudor Scholar-Statesman," *Huntington Library Quarterly* 10 (1957):

Wilson was born sometime between August 1523 and January 1524. He was the eldest of five sons of a solid, prospering middle class family (an economic distinction that is itself something of a Renaissance phenomenon) in Strubby, Lincolnshire. A gifted student, he was sent off to prestigious Eton, where he became friends with the master, Nicholas Udall, whose *Ralph Roister Doister* was to provide Wilson with an amusing example of "ambiguity" in his first book, on logic. Eton, moreover, was one of the first schools after St. Paul's to adopt the Erasmian curriculum, including *De copia*. The provost of Eton, Robert Aldrich, had studied with Erasmus, and Udall himself translated several of Erasmus's works.

From Eton Wilson went to Cambridge (King's College) in 1542, where (as Toxophilus tells us) stories were yet told about Erasmus's stay and where curricular records give us much insight into the nature and prominence of educational disputation. There Wilson took a BA, then MA, and thereafter remained in residence four years, through 1553. At Cambridge he worked and studied in close association with Roger Ascham as well as with some of the other leading humanists of his day: John Cheke, Thomas Smith, and the revered Walter Haddon.

A brief note should be entered at this point concerning Walter Haddon (1517–1572), whose Latin poem, we recall, prefaces Ascham's *Toxophilus*. We shall encounter Haddon several times throughout this chapter (and in Appendix B). Walter Haddon was "born of a knightly family, [and was a] lawyer, orator, celebrated poet, easily the prince of Greek and Latin eloquence in his own time"—so read the inscription on his tombstone.[5] He was also one of the most influential educators in the English period of high humanism and a lifelong friend of Thomas Wilson. A son of Eton, Haddon too had proceeded to Cambridge, where he took baccalaureate and advanced

205–18; "Thomas Wilson and the Tudor Commonwealth: An Essay in Civic Humanism," *Huntington Library Quarterly* 23 (1959): 49–60; "Some Notes on Dr. Wilson and his Lincolnshire Connections," *Lincolnshire Historian* 2 (1961): 14–24; and "A Household Inventory, 1581," *Proceedings of the American Philosophical Society* (Philadelphia, 1957) 101 (1957): 459–80. A. W. Reed has an interesting piece on Wilson: "Nicholas Udall and Thomas Wilson," *Review of English Studies*, 1 (1925): 275–83. Russell H. Wagner, who has done some of the most important work on Wilson's rhetoric, has a brief review of Wilson's life in "Thomas Wilson's *Arte of Rhetorique*," *Speech Monographs* 27 (1960): 1–32.

5. Charles J. Lees, ed. *The Poetry of Walter Haddon* (The Hague, 1967), 34.

degrees and ultimately became regius professor of civil law and vice-chancellor of the university. Though long associated with Cambridge, he also spent a year as president of Magdalen College, Oxford. Moreover, he was Master of the Court of Requests and a member of Parliament. His life, as we shall see, bears certain interesting parallels with Wilson's, particularly in its mix of the academic, legal, and political worlds. But there are at least a couple of notable exceptions. Unlike Wilson, he never went into exile, for he practiced a kind of Protestantism not so militant that it could not bend to what he considered the legitimate authority of the Marian regime. In fact, he wrote a stunning poem to the young Elizabeth *(Carmen consolatorium in rebus afflictis serenissimae Principis Elisabethae)*, advising her to obey her sister not because Mary is just but simply because she is by right Queen of England. A similar stance could be found in Erasmus, and in Ascham. But not in Wilson. Too, Haddon's Protestantism was developed earlier than Wilson's, at Eton. Wilson did not acquire "the new religion" until he reached Cambridge.

During Wilson's Cambridge years, the great Protestant patroness, the Duchess of Suffolk, chose him to tutor her two young sons. When these two sons, Henry and Charles, died of "the sweating sickness," Wilson collaborated with Walter Haddon in composing a commemorative epistle, *Vita et Obitus duorum fratrem Suffolciensium*. The commemoration was published in 1551 by William Grafton, the learned London publisher who was also the King's printer, perhaps the foremost English publisher of his time (issuer of the first Book of Common Prayer). This was but the first of Wilson's publications with Grafton and but the first of his published associations with the senior scholar Haddon. Further mention of Wilson's association with the Duchess of Suffolk appears in his book on rhetoric.

In the same year, 1551, Grafton published Wilson's first major work, *The Rule of Reason*—"a pioneering book," a modern editor calls it, "the first manual of logic for Englishmen in the vernacular" (Sprague, ed. *The Rule of Reason,* xi), and another coup for the humanist-controlled press. An immediately successful work, the book underwent six editions in the sixteenth century and was recognized as the first of its author's major achievements. Wilson identifies himself simply as a "poor student." Nonetheless, he was one whose work carried the (figurative) imprimatur of the famous Dr. Haddon and an untimorous dedication to young King Edward VI, only fourteen years old at the time and in the fourth year of his reign. The book is as emphatically patriotic as it is Protestant. Wilson, all commentators agree, had clearly chosen his party and cast his lot.

His second major treatise, *The Art of Rhetoric,* also published by Grafton, appeared in January, 1553, bearing earmarks of support from some of the most powerful Protestant families of the time: the book is dedicated to John Dudley,[6] son of the John Dudley who was Lord Protector and the real power behind Edward's throne; it was written, Wilson claims, during a quiet vacation at the estate of Sir Edward Dymoke, the King's champion and sheriff of Lincoln. Appearing only two years after the *Logic,* the *Rhetoric* bears the signs of Wilson's increasing success, not necessarily as a scholar but as a humanist preparing for the *vita activa,* or "civic humanism," his more or less secular aspiration in a period not known for any easy division between the secular and the religious. The book, if not exactly the first English rhetoric, was certainly the first full Ciceronian theory of public discourse, treating all five offices from invention to delivery. It is, in fact, largely a pastiche of translated passages from Cicero's major works,[7] suffused with Wilson's own personality and intentions. The book was the most reprinted English rhetoric in the sixteenth century, and underwent at least eight editions before the century drew to a close.

But six months after the rhetoric book appeared, Edward VI died and was succeeded by Mary Tudor. These political events may be among those which produced significant hiatuses in the publication history of Wilson's first two books.

Logic: 1551, 1552, 1553—1563, 1567 (twice)—1580.
Rhetoric: 1553—1560, 1562, 1563, 1567—1580, 1584, 1585.

In each instance the first hiatus was probably the result of Catholic suppression of overtly Protestant books (Mary's reign lasted from

6. The younger Dudley, also known as Lord Lisle and the Earl of Warwick, had been cited by Walter Haddon in his *Exhortatio ad literas* (1552) as an example of the "noble enthusiasm of the aristocracy" *(generoso nobilitatis ardore)* and an "outstanding" *(pr[a]estantem)* model of industriousness for all Cambridgemen. The praise is offered in the form of a *gradatio* that peaks with the praise of the scholarly young Edward VI.

7. See my *Donne, Milton, and the End of Humanist Rhetoric* (Berkeley, Calif., 1985), 130 n 71.

1553–1558). Too, the violent accession of Catholics (who beheaded the elder John Dudley for his attempt to secure the throne for Lady Jane Grey) may have proved too fearsome or too enraging for any Haddon-like proclivities on Wilson's part. He fled from the centers of power. He went first into retirement in Lincolnshire and then into exile on the Continent. In Italy he went to Padua, to join other Marian exiles in the study of civil law at that venerable university, and then he went on to Rome, a center of power where his efforts to reenter the active life ran into a dead end. He was denounced by Mary as a heretic and arraigned before the Inquisition. The basis for Mary's charge, Wilson was to claim in his 1560 edition of the *Rhetoric,* was "this book of Rhetoric and the Logic also." Perhaps the claim heightened the appeal of the two books in the 1560s. But, however wide of the mark it may have been,[8] the claim at least shows the extent to which Wilson himself acknowledges the political values and religious perspectives which pervade these two works. We must not, therefore, assume that either work is merely the product of objective scholarship (there was none such in the period) or that either is simply a "manual" of logic and rhetoric, something designed only for the aid of students of these subjects.

The other hiatus, the one between 1567 and 1580, is somewhat more difficult to explain. It may have been due to Wilson's expressed desire to have nothing further to do with these troublesome books. It may have been due to Wilson's increasing involvement with politics, now that Protestantism had become the official dogma in England. The hiatus may have also been due to England's increasing obsession with Ramism. Ramism had achieved notable successes in the 1570s, partly as humanist-seeming renewals of ancient wisdom and partly as radically Protestant reformations of the arts of logic and rhetoric; as such, they could have overshadowed Wilson's popularity. Finally, the hiatus could simply be due to the fact that Wilson was also at work on two other books, one of which we shall consider at length. Let us return to chronology.

Clapped into prison at Rome in 1558, Wilson was freed the following year by the Roman mob—or, in his own words, "by God's

---

8. Derrick, ed. *"Arte of Rhetorique,"* xxxii–xxxiii places the claim in a wider context, one that includes Wilson's own possible misrepresentation of his credentials to the Pope. Medine, *Thomas Wilson,* 18–28 has an interesting account of Wilson's exile, though it relies a little too much on a flat reading of Wilson's own statements.

grace I was wonderfully delivered, through plain force of the worthy Romans (an enterprise heretofore in that sort never attempted) being then without hope of life, and much less of liberty" (Prologue to the second edition of the *Rhetoric*). But the Roman revolt may have only incidentally freed Wilson, who escaped when his prison was torched—one of his successful "trials by fire" he was dramatically to insist. The revolt, an uprising against the Inquisition, was occasioned by the death of Pope Paul IV in August 1558.

It was still not safe to return to England. So Wilson fled to Ferarra, where he obtained a degree in civil law—perhaps completing the degree he had been pursuing at Cambridge after the MA.[9] By December, 1560, now in his middle thirties, he was home. On the seventh of that month he penned "a Prologue to the Reader" for the second edition of the *Rhetoric*. This Prologue, which was quoted above, contains this interesting story and disavowal:

> And now that I am come home, this book is showed to me, and I [asked] to look upon it, to amend it where I thought meet. "Amend it?," quoth I. "Nay, let the book first amend itself and make me amends." For surely I have no cause to acknowledge it for my book, because I have so smarted for it. For where I have been evil handled, I have much ado to show myself friendly. If the son were the occasion of the father's imprisonment, would not the father be offended with him, think you? Or at the least, would he not take heed, how hereafter he had to do with him? If others never get more by books than I have done, it were better [to] be a carter than a scholar for worldly profit. Now therefore, I will none of this book from henceforth, I will none of him I say: take him that list, and wear him that will. And by that time they have paid for him so dearly as I have done, they will be as weary of him as I have been. Who that toucheth pitch shall be defiled with it, and he that goeth in the sun shall be sunburnt, although he think not of it. So they that will read this or such like books shall in the end be as the books are. . . . I would be loath that any man should hurt himself for my doings. And therefore to avoid the worst for all parts, the best were never once to look on it, for then I am assured no man shall take harm by it. But I think some shall read it, before whom I do wash my hands if any harm should come to them hereafter—and let them not say but that they are warned. (Av^{r-v})

One cannot but marvel at Wilson's salesmanship.

9. See Russell H. Wagner, "Wilson and his Sources," *Quarterly Journal of Speech* 15 (1929): 525.

My mind is not to discourage any man but only to show how I have been tried for this book's sake, *tanquam per ignem* [even by fire]. For indeed the Prison was on fire when I came out of it, and whereas I feared fire most (as who is he that doth not fear it?) I was delivered by fire and sword together. And yet now thus fearful am I that, having been thus [punished] and restrained of liberty, I would first rather hazard my life presently . . . than to abide again without hope of liberty such painful imprisonment forever. (Av^v)

Before us is an apparently dangerous book, one of two which put the author's life in peril. Indeed, even reading the books could implicate us should Fortune's wheel turn again. The stance, or ploy, continued to preface all other editions of the *Rhetoric* and might have affected—that is, heightened—the popularity of the *Logic* as well.

The decade of the 1560s saw the steady advancement of Wilson's political career, aided by the intervention of Robert Dudley (later Earl of Leicester—whose older brother John had died without issue in 1554, the year after his father's beheading) as well as, on the other side of the political spectrum, William Cecil (later Lord Burghley). In fact, from 1560 for the remainder of his life Wilson was employed in state business: master of the Court of Requests, twice member of Parliament, representative of the Crown on a number of missions, including an ambassadorship to the Netherlands and official roles in such famous events as the trial of Norfolk and the interrogation of Mary Queen of Scots. In his public career, probably his most important work was in diplomacy. Ultimately, in 1577, he succeeded Thomas Smith as secretary of state under Burghley—perhaps the result, or so thought the Spanish Ambassador, of Leicester's moving his friends into positions of power to further his, Leicester's, own project of marrying the Queen.

Before he reached the pinnacle of his career, however, Wilson authored two more important books, the second of which we shall study in some detail. The first, appearing in June 1570 and dedicated to Cecil, was a translation from the Greek of orations by Demosthenes—another first. Again, the work is a characteristic blend of scholarship and advocacy, as the full title suggests: *Three Orations of Demosthenes, chief orator of the Grecians in favour of the Olynthians . . . with those his four Orations against King Philip of Macedon; most needful to be read in these dangerous days of all them that love their country's liberty and desire to take warning for their better avail.* In English Protestant syncretism, Philip of Macedon became identified with Philip of Spain. If the equivalence should be missed by the reader it is reinforced in Wilson's preface, where he compares Athens and England, and it is doubly reinforced in marginal glosses throughout.[10] In this way Wilson sought, like many humanists and antiquarians, to bridge the gap between ancient times and his own, and to find past solutions for present problems.

The second work, though completed earlier, in 1569, was not published until 1572: *A Discourse upon Usury, by way of Dialogue and Orations,* a book Wilson dedicated to Leicester. In this work the ever uneasy balance between scholarship and advocacy is clearly tipped in favor of the latter; most modern readers regard the work as a diatribe against lending money at interest. I regard it as something of a rhetorical *tour de force.* No real diatribe, it is actually more like the suasion discussed in my preceding chapter: it is aimed at showing how to "live well" in the face of intellectual and moral adversity, an argument offered by a writer who had learned to accept the painful costs of that adversity.

Twice married, Wilson was a widower when he died on May 20, 1581—a man of clearly marked influence and accumulated wealth. Only one year before his death, he was appointed Dean of Durham. This was another first, Wilson's last: he was a layman, had been all his life, and remained so, but a deanship was a high clerical office. The appointment was most likely his final political reward. It marked a triumph over his antagonist Ralph Lever, a contemporary of Wilson's at Cambridge, who was then canon of Durham cathedral. Lever, who had published his own English logic in 1573 (preferring the more purely English "witcraft" to the Greek "logic" and hoping eventually to publish his own rhetoric, or "speechcraft"), had objected to Wilson's appointment, arguing that the deanship should

10. For example, among prefacing materials is this statement: "my meaning was, that every good subject according to the level of his wit should compare the time past with the time present, and ever when he heareth Athens, or the Athenians, to remember England and Englishmen, and so all other things in like manner incident thereunto, that we may learn by the doings of our elders how we may deal in our own affairs, and so through wisdom by our neighbor's example avoid all harm that else unawares might happen unto us" (B1v). I have modernized the spelling and punctuation of all quotations from Wilson. I would call the reader's attention to an association, which I shall discuss later, of "wisdom" and "wariness."

have gone to a professional churchman. A modern biographer seconds some of Lever's argument when he comments that Wilson "was less concerned, it is to be feared, with the cure of souls than with supplementing the exiguous income allowed by Elizabeth to her secretaries of state" (Tawney, *Discourse,* 2). During his tenure he never so much as set foot in Durham, and was even installed by proxy.

What is most salient in this life? Certainly it shows that Wilson had come a long way from Lincolnshire, a distance in which he took some pride:

> The Shire or Town helpeth somewhat towards the increase of honor, as it is much better to be born in Paris than in Picardy, in London than in Lincoln. (*Rhetoric,* biii^v)

Fashionable Elizabethan society was ever contemptuous of rusticity or in fact of almost any place outside London. And it was Wilson's nature never to miss an opportunity for self aggrandizement. Perhaps the pride was deserved, though he managed the distance with more than a little help from his Lincolnshire friends, such as the Duchess of Suffolk, the Cecils, and Sir Edward Dymoke.

Mair, who prepared a famous (1909) edition of Wilson's *Rhetoric* calls him not an Elizabethan but an Henrician, for temperamentally he belonged to that "elder and graver age" (xxvii). But the comment slights Wilson's sense of humor, his risibility, as well as his liveliness of voice and keenness of wit, all of which are accessible in his books. It comes down too heavily on Wilson's recurrent sobriety. It overlooks the propensity for *irony* (again, in the Rortian sense) even in so apparently doctrinaire a man. And without humor, risibility, voice, wit, and irony, one is that much less an Erasmian humanist in the view I am attempting to develop. Mair, oddly, emphasizes the limits of this lesser light, too little of its genuine brilliance.

As did Tawney almost seventy years ago. In characterizing Wilson as a "distinguished" man of "tough" prejudices in his discourse on usury, Tawney seconds Mair's opinion of Wilson's dourness: "The economic outlook, the pre-occupation with morality which he inherited, was that of the middle ages, and his target was the individualism which was destroying it" (14). But, as Tawney goes on to note, what he had just said about Wilson is also true of the very age in which Wilson lived, which transported a messy baggage of older ideas and sentiments into a new order of things. On the contrary, I would suggest that Wilson, in taking advantage of the circumstances afforded within that new order, shrewdly made use of the instruments at hand. His lawyerly training and spirit equipped him well to find and use workable instruments, or arguments—as Tawney himself shows. (Derrick, too, offers a clear instance of a action wherein Wilson's lawyerly instincts actually superceded his standards of public morality, xxxix–xl.) Perhaps Wilson's fatal flaw —the flaw which kept him just this side of achieving greatness—is not his mournful nostalgia but another characteristic that is itself best named by Tawney when he says, "Even in that age of versatility, he was perhaps too versatile to be supreme" (10). If this versatility is, as I think, an almost uniquely humanist virtue, its disparagement may finally refer to the resourcefulness and lawyerliness of a mind that simply lacked the range and depth of a More, a Cheke, or, better, an Erasmus. But in that convivial company gravity and dourness are out of place.

Let me return to my initial comment. Wilson came a long way from Lincolnshire. He was, to say the least, a self-made man in a great age of self-fashioning, and Wilson found his chief instruments —in more ways than one—through logic and rhetoric. A new social mobility made such self-fashioning possible, as Stephen Greenblatt has argued.[11] True, this was also a mobility whose boundaries began to look ominously expansive to several men of the time. But not to Wilson. By contrast his near-contemporary Elyot in *The Governor* (1531), for example, argues that the full range of humanist education should be preserved only for the sons of the nobility. Even Erasmus expressed some similar concerns from time to time, as in the debate with Luther when he opined that debate itself or educational disputation was really not an instrument for the common people. Certain humanists feared that the old order was passing. Nonetheless, no astute "new" man of the middle class, humanist or otherwise, was going to miss the opportunity mobility afforded. Wilson was just such an astute man, a middle class opportunist, who used his humanist knowledge to expand his connections and reach for the top. How?

An initial answer is suggested in Terry Eagleton's perceptive view

11. *Renaissance Self-Fashioning* (Chicago, 1980).

of rhetoric manuals as "handbooks of ruling-class power,"[12] but we must of course continue to record the evident humanist doubt that not much of importance can be reduced to "handbooks" exactly. We might therefore conjecture that humanist manuals of rhetoric as well as dialectic could be efforts not simply to codify tactics of ruling-class power but also to achieve something else in a collateral way, as we have seen in our examination of Agricola and Erasmus. Wilson's interest in ruling-class power is patent throughout his career, but there are other interests as well, some not so patent: I mean not simply his self-aggrandizement but also his very deep interest in humanism and its protocol. As I shall argue, in Wilson's books we have good examples of "literary criticism," allowing that term to mean what it has meant from the outset of my study—attempting to persuade others by centering their minds on collateral analyses of texts. As we shall see, his *Logic* asks us to reconsider the dry-as-dust teachings of Scholasticism, his *Rhetoric* reexamines Cicero, his translation of Demosthenes looks at his London through an Athenian lens. In each of these works the "literary criticism" offers us something more than instruction in the announced subject: in each the announced subject is imbricated with the tactics of ruling-class power and not infrequently with the career opportunities of Wilson himself; but in the process a light is shed on the salient features of Erasmian humanism and its chief protocol. That light becomes clearest in Wilson's last, most mature work, his dialogue on usury.

Thus my approach to this writer rests on that ancient observation which Dürer too echoed, *si monumentum requiris, circumspice:* if you seek Wilson the humanist, look not simply at the portrait of the wealthy man which prefaces this discussion; rather, look around in the very monuments most leading humanists erected to their memories, public discourse.

In studying Wilson we have, discounting the Demosthenes in which his own voice is marginal, three lively publications for our use. To these we shall now turn, in chronological order. A complete review of the contents of the *Logic* and *Rhetoric* may be found in Appendix A.

---

12. *Walter Benjamin: Towards a Revolutionary Criticism* (London, 1981), 101.

The Rule of Reason, Containing the Art of Logic[13]

Reason did not mean to Wilson quite what it means to us. We tend to think of the word as having such cognates as "sensible," "thinking," "unemotional." But for Wilson the word stood closer to the Latin *ratio*, which is best translated with such words as "calculation," "scheme," "method." We have seen Erasmus use *ratio* (as "method") in a clever, even contrarian or perverse way: e.g., in his "handbook" on copiousness, *Nec admodum discrepat ab his quarta locupletandi ratio*, he says (Leclerc, I:78[D]), "This fourth method of enrichment is not all that different" from those preceding, an observation that uses *ratio* almost oxymoronically—especially when we consider that Erasmus had called the second method "like the first" and the third "not so different" from the second.

In Latin, Wilson's work could be entitled *De ratione rationis*, "on calculating calculations." Even in English the titular point would seem to be that this subject (unlike rhetoric) can apparently be reduced to calculations, to rules. Reasoning would seem to be a process that can be systematized. And for the humanist it could, but only within certain, highly significant limits. For Wilson does not overlook the ambiguity of the English word *rule*, meaning also a reign or realm with boundaries.

An Aristotelian observation, commonplace in the sixteenth century, claimed that man differs from other creatures by virtue of his "reason," a ratiocinative quality which Wilson associates with "the power given him of nature to speak" (17). Reason therefore is *discursive*,[14] and a prime difference betweeen logic and rhetoric is, as we have seen, a difference in modes of address (an audience of experts *vs* a mixed audience). A difference between logic and rhetoric

---

13. The edition cited in this study is that of 1972 (see note 4 above). Not only, as I have mentioned, have I modernized the language and punctuation, I have also enclosed in brackets words I have substituted or added to make the meaning clearer for modern readers.

14. Milton's famous pronouncement in *Areopagitica* (1644) seems much to the point: "when God gave [man] reason, he gave him freedom to choose, for reason is but choosing." Man's immortal part would seem to be a calculating faculty. But Milton's idea is not so closely connected with discourse as is Wilson's, for Milton was entranced, like the Ramists of his day, with another idea, that there can be thinking without speaking, language, or discourse. That idea would be alien to Wilson.

is essentially a difference between two ideas about arguing well, each dependent upon the nature of the audience.

Thus, when Wilson calls logic "the rule of reason," he means the discursive calculations, schemes, and methods by which we arrive at probable conclusions for an audience of experts. Too, he's not thinking of reasoning about matters of certainty (like mathematical quantities) but about those matters concerning which there is an active and arguable difference of opinion. In short, he is thinking—as his age usually did when the word "reason" or "logic" appeared—of dialectic generally, and of dialectical disputation specifically. Logic is the almost bare art of arguing *in utramque partem:* "an art to reason probably on both parts [i.e., pro as well as con] of all matters that be put forth, so far as the nature of every thing can bear" (8). In his discussion of *inventio,* he defines *disputation* itself as, simply, "reasoning of matters" (153) and by that he means, on both sides of the question. Not surprisingly, Wilson makes disputation the end of logical *inventio,* the veritable destination, exercise, and test of its argumentative principles. Most importantly, Wilson's *inventio* in its complex structural relations with rhetoric becomes a humanist demonstration of the limits placed on *ratio,* an emphasis on the boundaries of its "rule." For that matter, the observation applies equally well to the nature of the book itself. As we shall see, the limits of reason and the way they are set forth make the book a prime example of the humanist protocol I have sought to uncover.

Logic is the "almost bare art," as I have termed it, because logic attempts to rely on a singular form of proof, *logos,* the argumentative calculations in the speech itself. Rhetoric, recall, adds two other forms of proof, *ethos* and *pathos.* Logic has only two offices, invention and disposition or judgment, to which rhetoric adds three more. Logic, moreover, tends to stay on the abstract level, the level of the *thesis:* should a man marry? whereas rhetoric adds the circumstantial *hypothesis:* should Lord Mountjoy marry? Nonetheless, as Wilson says,

> Both these arts are much alike, saving that logic is occupied about all matters and doth plainly and nakedly set forth with apt words the *sum* of things by the way of argumentation. . . . Rhetoric uses gay painted sentences, and setteth forth those matters with fresh colors and goodly ornaments, and that at large [i.e., before a mixed audience]. In so much that Zeno being asked the difference between logic and rhetoric made

answer by demonstration of his hand, declaring that when his hand was closed it resembled logic, when it was open and stretched out it was like rhetoric. (11)

Note that the two arts are in effect the same hand in two gestures—the same instrument, here constricted, there expanded—or the same protocol, here closed, there open.

Considering the limitations of logic, one might expect that a book on the subject would be dry as dust. Most were. In Wilson's case, however, the dullness is more than a little relieved by the author's irrepressible but purposive sense of humor. Take this passage, for example:

> A Proposition is a perfect sentence spoken by the *indicative mode*, signifying either a true thing or a false without all ambiguity or doubtfulness, as thus: Every man is a liar. (46)

And even Wilson's desk-pounding dogmatism as a militant Protestant at least helps him avoid that most cardinal of all rhetorical sins, dessication: e.g.,

> Thus many hundred years have men used to pray to saints departed.
> Ergo they do not amiss that pray to the dead still.
> I answer, whoredom hath been used these many hundred years; ergo it is lawful both to have stews and to go to the stews still. (199)

Both of these qualities—humor and dogmatism, often fused—arise as naturally from Wilson's character as they do from his speaking situation in this book, a situation which in turn clarifies his intention. Mair calls the book "one long Protestant tract" (xv), which is partly true. Wilson never misses an opportunity to further the Protestant cause at the expense of Catholics (a word which, he says under the guise of discussing philology, is a Greek word which "signifieth nothing in English but 'universal' or 'common,'" which casts grave doubt then on what could possibly be meant when one calls a woman "catholic," 8). Nor does he miss any opportunity to impress on his readers the use of the rule of reason in sorting out religious questions for oneself—i.e., without the aid of clergy or Church. But let us examine his intentions a bit further.

In the dedicatory epistle to young King Edward VI, Wilson attempts to define his own speaking situation. He is a "poor student," he says, who was encouraged by the learned printer Grafton to put the art of logic into English; this Wilson has done in hopes that by making this knowledge available to his fellow countrymen he might turn them into scholars like their sovereign lord. The availability of knowledge, unmediated, is of course a Protestant theme. But perhaps of equal if not overriding importance—a matter which makes Mair's interpretation only partial—is the deep patriotism and, closely connected with that, ambition which pervade Wilson's effort. Particularly when we consider the book's appearance and popularity in the early 1550s and its reappearance, after the Bloody Mary hiatus, in the late 60s, we begin to see a Wilson who having chosen his party also actively pursued the means of his own advancement. "Actively" is the operative word. For Wilson's efforts at self-advertisement both give function to his dogmatism (making the book indeed *appear* to be a long Protestant tract) and at the same time explain the absence of any strategic subtleties, of any of those risky virtues that Erasmus might call "cleverness." At least for one of his two audiences.

True to his *stated* intention, Wilson writes simply, with little pretension of learning. He translates all the Latin, with two notable exceptions, and explains most arcane and classical references. His elementary explanations of the forms of syllogism are models of careful pedagogy for the intelligent if unlearned reader, surely one of his audiences.

But if Wilson addresses the unlearned—that is un-university-learned—reader most directly, with the young king at some remove, he goes forth with the blessing not simply of an important and learned printer but also of the Cambridge humanists. Among the latter, one of the leading intellectual lights, Walter Haddon, placed his imprimatur on the book in a form of a dedicatory poem, in which "our Thomas Wilson" by bringing the knowledge of logic "to our ears" is praised for being of great use to his countrymen: *Attulit hanc, nostras Thomas Wilsonus ad aures / Vtilis & patriae sic fuit ille suae.* Haddon's poem, moreover, like Wilson's which immediately follows (and which rather modestly promises to teach what is already known to us by usage), is not translated from the Latin. These are the two notable exceptions mentioned earlier, and they suggest that Wilson may have had two audiences in mind. For by their very language, both poems are addressed not to Wilson's unlearned reader but to his other audience, those university-educated observers of this innovative project—who are also those who may fully realize the work as a kind of "literary criticism." Like his humanist contemporaries, Wilson was ever deeply aware of Latin as an exclusionary mode of communication; indeed, its linguistic exclusiveness was itself the quality that—ostensibly—stimulated this project in the first place.

Two audiences, two intentions—for one, teaching; for the other, that subtle mode of advocacy called "literary criticism." Within the latter mode we may find the operations of suasion. Within both we shall find that humanist-rhetorical protocol which defines and delimits the "rule of reason." We shall keep both intentions in mind as we explore this book. Let us note simply at the outset that it is highly unlikely that the very innovativeness of this project, this first attempt to create an English logic, was missed by any of the parties involved—least of all Wilson himself.

What's in the book? Because of the strangeness of "Logic, otherwise called Dialectic (for they are both one)" (10) to modern students and because Wilson's book is in some ways typical and in other ways unique, readers may wish to supplement my discussion with references to Appendix A. The point of my discussion is that Wilson's effort places a humanist twist on Scholastic logic, a characteristic which in turn only enhances the point I wish to make about Wilson's opportunism. Logic and rhetoric, once more, are in the service of causes. For Erasmus, the cause was the humanizing of Christianity. For Wilson, the causes were Protestantism, patriotism, rhetoric, and Wilson himself.

Structurally there is an understandable progression in Wilson's *Logic:* he takes the reader from examining "words" in a "question" (concepts in a problem for disputation), to "knitting several words in order" (framing a statement), to the procedures of disputation, and finally to a review of logical fallacies and argumentative tactics. The reader is obviously involved from the beginning in a debaterly process, a matter which Wilson makes quite explicit. But if the structural progression is understandable, it is hardly orderly or methodical in the Scholastic sense. For one must note in all this material that Wilson's own divisions are compounded of an Erasmus-recalling overlapping and ambiguity. Indeed, his work offers that typically humanist, unmethodical kind of theorizing which the Ramists will make much of later in the century, when they will seize on the traditional lesson about division (that the best has two contrary parts) and about *methodus* (always proceed from the general to the specific) to reorganize theoretical discussions and restore them to an orderly state of clarity, brevity—and dessication. The Ramists, of course, were far more worried than Wilson, or almost any humanist, about the operations of irony and ambiguity in any writer's effort to offer a handbook for reason. Wilson's theory is suffused with both qualities—his patent instructions to the contrary definitely not withstanding.

To return to an initial example, Wilson could not repress his own predilections when he set forth a key definition:

> A Proposition is a perfect sentence spoken by the *indicative mode,* signifying either a true thing, or a false without all ambiguity or doubtfulness, as thus: Every man is a liar. (46)

Wilson may not be worried about overlapping divisions or about being un-methodical. Most humanists knew that in treating above all the art of discourse it is foolhearty to be overly systematic. But isn't Wilson concerned about contradictions? His unmethodical approach has already widened the gap between contract and performance, between his promise to offer rules and then what he actually does with those rules. Here his example would seem directly to contradict the dangers of ambiguity about which he had warned us so extensively earlier (23–25). Or does it? Let us consider here the very last example in Wilson's book (216), where he speaks of fallacious reasoning:

> *Pseudomenos* / This is called a lying argument, for whatsoever ye shall say [in response], ye must needs say amiss. Epimenides, a man born in Crete, said that the people born in Crete were liars. Said he true, or no?

All you have to do to make "Every man is a liar" an example of a proposition that has no "ambiguity or doubtfulness" is simply remove the context, simply ignore for the nonce that the statement was spoken by someone to someone in a debate—and the virtual impossibility or pointlessness of doing *that* proves to be a kind of humanist joke on the unwary reader who too easily swallows this traditional, Scholastic theory. That is, take away speakers and audiences, take away specific circumstance or context—take away the very things which make rhetoric differ from logic—and you end up with an absurdity like calling "Every man is a liar" a clear example of a proposition devoid of all ambiguity or doubtfulness. As noted in my preceding chapter, the example is an ancient one—in fact, it had been around for a long time before St. Paul used it in his letter to Titus—meant to show the nature of paradox. That logicians loved to play with this paradox in a way that seemed removed from all human significance and import is part of the point of Wilson's joke, just as it was part of the point of Erasmus's long excursus into epistemology when he made a *fool* speak in praise of *folly*. I've pursued the matter at some length, at the risk of flattening out the humor in Wilson's provocative example to reveal some of the humanist impulses in this work, best seen not in an isolated example but in the accumulated context within which the example appears. I shall recur specifically to this matter of humanist impulses in this work later.

In Wilson's book, as in all traditional dialectics, "judgment" is discussed first, then "invention." This curious inversion needed no explanation for his contemporary readers. For modern readers the key to the explanation lies in Wilson's definition of *disputation* (see my Appendix A), which he offers in his discussion of "invention," the second part of logic.

In that passage, Wilson clarifies both the function of logic itself and the purpose of its two parts. Judgment is for the Negative side, invention for the Affirmative. One might assume that since the Affirmative speaks first (like the prosecution), theoretical consideration of that side's task should have precedence. However, the placing of judgment first only reconfirms an inner principle of arguing *in utramque partem:* whoever would affirm, or declare, something in dispute must give primary attention to the other side as part of the assumption of the burden of proof. What I would point out above all, however, is that here in this major structural principle as throughout the work, Wilson makes very clear that the function of logic—its aim as well as its conceptual model—is disputation. Disputation is what logic is all about. And "reasoning of matters" is pro-con analysis. Wilson thus offers further antiquarian evidence of the point I tried to make in my second and third chapters, that traditional *inventio*—whether in logic where it comes second or in rhetoric where it comes first—draws its riches from disputation.

In that same passage, he also clarifies in a bare-bones way the role of disputation in suasion, the kind of writing we explored in my preceding chapter. Wilson tells us that disputation can end either resolved, that is with the "truth" revealed, or unresolved. In the latter, when the "truth" doesn't appear, at least the "hearers" have been made aware of both sides of the issues involved. The final moderating is theirs to do.

The first piece of advice Wilson gives the Affirmative expresses an assumption underlying traditional *inventio:* "In all debating of causes, wariness is ever thought great wisdom" (153). That is, keep an eye on the opposition. This is a debater's tactic, and it partly explains the precedence of judgment in logic. It is also linked in Wilson's mind with "wisdom," a both-sides encompassing Ciceronian *sapientia.* (The linkage appears in all his major writing.) Wilson goes on to declare that the Negative must also be wary, as of course must anyone who attempts to reason or think in an adversarial situation. Accordingly, "the whole matter of answering [negating] any argument" (156) with the coordinate skill of "fencing" oneself when one must affirm his own cause (157) is best learned by giving thought to the tactics of the adversary. (As we have seen, this is Antonius/Cicero's point, and John Stuart Mill's as well.)

The third and final part of the book (the first is on judgment, the second on invention) is on "false conclusions or deceitful reasons," consisting not only of a discussion of the logical fallacies but also a review of certain debaterly tactics, like setting traps for an opponent. This section is on a par with the first two—its equivalence marked by that peculiar Elizabethan device used to mark equivalent parts: the final words of each of the book's three parts proceed funnel-like down the page. In the long tradition Wilson inherited, the two parts of logical theory (judgment and invention) comprised the whole, with lingering doubtfulness about the appropriateness of discussing "sophistical reasoning" at all. Indeed, when he makes this third section equal in importance to the first two he places it in something of a "moderator's" position: these matters pertain alike to judgment and invention, and by correlative matching to Negative and Affirmative in the debate. He thereby only underscores his basic teaching about what logic is.

To rephrase that basic teaching: Logic, or dialectic, is the art wherein one finds how to reason on matters about which there are differences of opinion among experts. Reasoning consists of following those procedures which are most at home in that form of "dialogue" known as debate, in which one voice affirms, the other negates. One must therefore know how to define the terms in the question, how to divide it into its parts, how to construct valid arguments about it, and how to protect oneself against false arguments, fallacies, and traps—as Wilson states in his opening discussion of the art (12). These are usually cited as the four basic ends of logic (see Figure 2). But Wilson also makes it equally clear that the function of logic depends upon knowing how to argue both sides of the question. Doing so is essential to invention. It is also essential to judgment, either as the debater's first operation in entering the fray or as the audience's final operation on a debate left unresolved. With that summary, let us return to the humanist impulses in Wilson's theory.

Two leading historians of Renaissance rhetoric and logic seem to have diametrically opposed views of Wilson's book. Howell calls it a "translation of scholastic logic into native English speech." Walter Ong, however, finds that the book, particularly in its treatment of invention, "has very little in common with the central scholastic tradition feeding through Peter of Spain and a great deal in common with the antischolastic humanist logic of Rudolph Agricola."[15] Scholastic or humanist? Wilson does more than simply translate Scholastic logic. He imports it and makes it at home in a new age, by putting it to the service of something other than Christian (or even Protestant) apologetics. In the process he gives Scholastic logic a humanist twist. He does not go so far, for example, as Agricola and actually conflate rhetorical invention with dialectical invention. Nor does he go so far as the later Ramists and abolish rhetorical invention altogether in favor of logical invention. In Wilson the two inventive processes are theoretically separate but at times conjoined, for reasons which his irony, ambiguity, and frequent examples make clear.

"Truth" for Wilson is not simply logical validity, nor (in spite of his patent militance) is it simply the apparent righteousness of the Protestant "cause." Like a humanist, he is fascinated by what works, what holds sway over peoples' minds—or, better, their will—as shown in an example which uses an argument that he could in his anti-papist stance find abhorrent:

> As where nature telleth us that the whole is greater than the parts, we cannot otherwise know it but by showing it to be true in this substance

15. Howell, *Logic and Rhetoric,* esp. 15–17. Walter J. Ong, *Ramus, Method and the Decay of Dialogue* (Cambridge, Mass., 1958), 120.

and that substance and so in all other. Whereupon we conclude that this general saying is truth. Aristotle saith this argument serveth well to persuade the multitude, when we gather many like things and at last after such heaping conclude that our argument is generally true. As I heard once a doctor of divinity, [who] was not so great in knowledge as he was in title, a little before the banishment of the Mass earnestly defending his cause with examples of such and such worshipful as dwelt there in the country. "Does not such a man," quoth he, "devoutly hear Mass?" Does not such a Knight, such a Lord, such a Lady, and such a Gentleman, full reverently come to the blessed Mass? "Then, neighbors," quoth he, "if all these do so, and none but Heretics follow the contrary, why should not you follow the best, and forsake the worst?" With that, the people hearing such a patched reason were wonderfully persuaded to say as he said, and if need had been, ready to have died (but not with him, for he would none of that himself, being come home since gaily well) but alone, and together themselves if such extremity had been offered. Again, this kind of argumentation profiteth much to dilate a matter at large, that thereby the truth may the rather be allowed when it is found true in every singular thing. (80–81)

This bandwagon argument—so we would call it today ("everybody's doing it")—is listed among the fallacies in Wilson's book (see 199). Nonetheless, what's inescapably "true" for the *rhetorician* is that such fallacies work, hold sway over people's minds, and should therefore either be defended against or used warily. So far as the latter is concerned, one of its common uses is in "dilating a matter." The point is that once more with Wilson we have moved beyond formal validity, even beyond considerations of simple fallaciousness, and toward rhetoric.

Of all the humanist impulses in Wilson's work, perhaps the most pervasive is the one we have just touched on: reason alone does not move people, does not even suffice to teach them. For one thing, the matter has to be "dilated," a procedure that activates one's resourcefulness. Thus Wilson's treatment of logic is not altogether "logical" —and in this regard what he means by "reason" continually bucks against its own boundaries. Thus, I agree with Medine's characterization, that Wilson's *Logic* is "one that combines original Aristotelian and scholastic elements with a definition of logic and a theory of logical invention that are fundamentally humanistic" (31). We see a shift from the certain to the contigent, from the formalist to the relevant or practical or even topical (logic thus becomes a preparation for civic humanism). *Inventio* is important in this shift, says Medine, and I agree. So too is something Medine seldom remarks on, Wilson's sense of humor. But hardly anyone else comments on it either. "The book is of course a mere work of popularization," proclaimed C. S. Lewis, "and aims at no originality. A modern reader, heir to many improvements in the art of making textbooks, will find it dark and crabbed."[16] Not quite. The characterization better fits a thoroughly Scholastic textbook such as the Latin *Dialectica* by John Seton, which appeared in England six years before Wilson's, in 1545. Wilson invites a self-reflexive view of Scholastic logic from the standpoint of humanism, that is from the standpoint of rhetoric, a stance that as we have seen necessarily provokes questions of resourcefulness and *copia,* as well as contingent truth, irony, ambiguity, and humor.

His humor, his voice, his use of topical examples, including his anti-Catholic thrusts throughout, all these give us a discussion sparpled[17] with liveliness, and offer consequently a veritable demonstration that "reasonableness" has limits and that the efficaciousness of its "truth" has finally to be rather expansively considered. The point will become increasingly obvious as we turn to his next work.

Returning to the present work, let us note finally that Wilson's humanism is also revealed in his unsystematic approach to the discursive arts, a matter which I touched on earlier and which deserves some re-examination as the concluding note in this discussion of the *Logic.*

System, whether thinking or writing systematically, was an important and increasingly controversial matter. It was, in fact, the cause of a revolution in theories of the discursive arts, the aforementioned conflict between the Ramists and the humanists. (The

16. C. S. Lewis, *English Literature in the Sixteenth Century Excluding Drama* (Oxford, Eng., 1954), 290.

17. This wonderful word is almost invariably adopted by readers of Wilson. It might seem to be one of Lewis Carroll's portmanteau words, a combination of "sprinkled" and "sparkled" with "purple" thrown in. but it was an actual word, signifying "dispersed" or "scattered," a word whose use according to the OED peaked in the sixteenth and seventeenth centuries. The OED exemplifies it not with Wilson (who uses it frequently) but with a passage from Wilson's schoolmaster, Udall, who used it in Englishing a passage from Erasmus's paraphrase of St. John.

Baconian revolution was something else, less centered on discourse than on concepts, though Bacon instituted the first serious critique of language through his famous "idols.") Within two decades after the appearance of Wilson's books on logic and rhetoric, the Ramists began their long and destructive ascent, shoving aside the humanists in the name of system. The Ramists won partly by using a debating tactic Wilson himself advocates: "to make such answer that the opposer may take little advantage thereby" (155). Humanists, like Wilson, had proposed that when one desires to teach he should arrange his material *methodically,* proceeding from general to specific, and use a division of two contrary members. And since according to the Ramists any speaker or writer can have only one of two intentions, either to teach or to deceive (a dilemma that the later sixteenth century did not seem to find false), one should therefore teach by a methodical application of method, dividing all the arts and sciences into two discrete, not overlapping parts and placing first things first. Ramist logic, therefore, had only two parts: *invention,* which "naturally" comes first, and judgment, or *disposition;* Ramist logic was thus not simply or even primarily for disputation. Ramist rhetoric also had only two parts: *style* and *delivery.* So set out, there was little overlapping. In Ramist invention you only invented, in judgment only arranged and judged, and if you needed to learn how to invent you went to logic only, regardless of whether you were inventing an oration or a lecture or a disputation or a poem. Simplicity and clarity made the Ramist system stunning, so much so that no one lamented the loss of *memory* as one of the discursive arts. After all, with simplicity and clarity—"plainness" was the Ramist word—things became easy to memorize. By contrast, the humanist "system" looked like no system. It looked haphazard and disorganized.

But was it? Doesn't the dispute falter on the very point Wilson warns us about, definition? Between the Ramists and the humanists there are widely divergent views of reality and language, of *res* and *verba,* of "system" for that matter. A modern rhetorician, Richard Lanham, argues that the rhetorical view (the view deeply characteristic of humanists) is profoundly "nonlinear":

> dynamic rather than static, studied as a constantly changing emergence rather than a fixed entity; global rather than specialized into disciplines

and constituent parts; a system which seeks to describe the confusion of everyday experience rather than narrowing it into a delimited, predictable field of study.[18]

The argument in effect makes the Ramists, or any theorists who offer a linear systematizing of the discursive arts, non-rhetorical. Wilson, though the word "non-linear" would be alien to him, sounds much like Lanham and much like Ascham in *Toxophilus* when he argues, in the book we shall next consider:

> Now a wiseman that hath good experience in these affairs, and is able to make himself a Rhetoric for every matter, will not be bound to any precise rules, nor keep any one order, but such only as by reason he shall think best to use, being master over art, rather than art should be master over him, rather making art by wit, than confounding wit by art. (x4ᵛ)

Though Wilson and his age may not have had the modern terms to reject rigid, linear systematizing and theorizing, his ostensible lack of organization, overlapping or fuzzy theoretical divisions, and ostensibly divagatory talk could very well have been undertaken in full consciousness of their implications. (In the above quotation from Wilson, using our knowledge of his *Logic,* we could substitute "wary" for "wise," "calculation" for "reason.") We examined the lack of linearity in Erasmus's writings on rhetoric in my Chapter 3. Marjorie O'Rourke Boyle has pursued the idea even farther, into Erasmus's *Praise of Folly.*[19] Just as Erasmus called his praise of Folly "not altogether foolish," so Wilson's logic is not altogether logical, as suggested earlier—or "rational" for that matter, whether in the Scholastic or the Ramist sense or even partly in his own.

Insofar as the movement of Scholastic logic, or dialectic, is toward linear systematizing, Wilson's own treatise on logic emerges as Scholasticism with a heavy (or rather light-hearted) humanist overlay. His next book, the best and most complete humanist theory of rhetoric ever written in English, has little Scholasticism within it and is, as I have already attempted to suggest, purposefully nonlinear—purposefully and overtly, in a sense, unsystematic. Too, just as Wil-

18. "Twenty Years After: Digital Decorum and Bistable Allusions," *Texte* 9 (1990): 71.
19. "Folly Plus: Moria and More," *Journal of Religious History* 15 (1989): 436–47. See also her "Fools and Schools: Scholastic Dialectic, Humanist Rhetoric; from Anselm to Erasmus," *Medievalia et Humanistica* 13 (1985): 173–95.

son's logic leans on rhetoric, his rhetoric presupposes a thorough grounding in logic. Or, to echo my previous statement, the movement of his logic is toward rhetoric. Therefore, that was an astute as well as an enterprising scholar who sometime after 1585 bound Wilson's *Logic* and his *Rhetoric* together, and in that order, in one volume.[20]

The Art of Rhetoric, for the use of all such as are studious of Eloquence[21]

Power is the name of the game in rhetoric so far as Wilson is concerned, a point he virtually announces at the outset. We have seen that Erasmus thought of himself as a teacher of "eloquence," and we must acknowledge that he too was not uninterested in power. But more than Erasmus Wilson brings into sharp focus and then

20. This volume, which I examined at the Huntington Library, contains the 1567 *Logic* and the 1585 *Rhetoric*.

21. Derrick's argument for the accuracy of his 1982 edition in representing Wilson's textual intentions is a good one. He chose the first edition (1553) as the "copytext for the present edition, with the new material from the 1560 edition incorporated into it" (cxix). The argument becomes especially compelling when one reflects on Wilson's own vow to disengage himself from this book; the 1560 is the last edition which we can imagine Wilson had some direct involvement in preparing. The most famous modern edition, Mair's, is based on the final one, that of 1580. However, while I second Derrick's editorial efforts if not all of his interpretations, there are no startling revelations in his work, and the fussiness involved in trying to supercede Mair's edition seems beside the point, particularly for my own purposes because I have modernized the language and punctuation in all my quotations from the work. Moreover, one finally becomes impatient with Derrick's edition. By casting the book into a photocopy of typewritten pages, Derrick's publisher has trashed Wilson's own use of typography, like the funnelling effect to mark sections. Derrick's work, though valuable in its tracking of sources, has itself been poorly edited: e.d., Commentary 321.8 invites us to "See Commentary, 29.16" but there is no Commentary 29.16; and there are some curious "scapes" in Derrick's work: e.g., "sikilnesse" (46.7) is clearly meant to be "fikilnesse." Peter E. Medine has published a most attractive modernized version of the 1560 edition. Medine's edition contains a brief summary of Wilson's life and career as well as an argument that usefully places Wilson's rhetorical theory in a context of developments from Trapezuntius and Melanchthon. Though well and carefully edited, this work too ignores Wilson's significant use of typography. I have therefore used Mair's work, which is yet widely available in libraries. All page numbers refer to that 1909 edition. I refer to all four of the original (1553) dedicatory poems, though only two of these—Haddon's and Wilson's—appear in Mair's edition.

exploits the virtual equivalence between eloquence (the subject of rhetoric) and a certain kind of power.

To begin with, power is implied by and in the four Latin dedicatory poems which preface the first edition. Of course, dedicatory poems were conventionally in Latin, but the use of that language is here again one that takes on added significance. The poems were written by Walter Haddon ("There is no better Latin man within England," Wilson says in this book, 123, "except Walter Haddon the Lawyer"); Nicholas Udall (identified in our discussion of the *Logic,* who was also a translator of Erasmus's *Apophthegms,* a source Wilson uses in the *Rhetoric*); Robert Hilermy, whose identity remains unknown; and Wilson himself—all trumpeting, in Latin, the effort at long last to English (and in more ways than one) this important knowledge. Let me offer a prose translation of Haddon's curious poem:

> Sister Logic spoke to her sister Rhetoric: what she learned recently, she said, was English speech *(sermo Britannos).* Rhetoric was silent, struck with great sorrow, for she had not yet learned to speak in our tongue. Wilson heard these things by chance, who had been Logic's schoolmaster *(magister)* and had given her our language. He called aside mute Rhetoric, comforting her with friendly words, and asked whether she wished to be English. Casting down her eyes, she answered that she did, very much, but that she could not find a way by which she would be able. 'I myself,' Wilson says, 'will relate the ways and the laws of speaking, how you may speak English words perfectly.' He gains her trust, Rhetoric is polished by our speech, and now both sisters are made ours. England, if the speech of the noble sisters is estimable to you, so also will be the author of the speech.[22]

22. *Retoricem Logice soror, est affata sororem:*
    Quem didicit nuper, sermo Britannos erat.
Retorice tacuit, magno perculsae dolore:
    Nam nondum nostro nouerat ore loqui.
Audiit haec, Logices, Wilsonus forte, magister:
    Qui fuerat, nostros addideratque sonos.
Retoricem mutam, verbis solatus amicis:
    Seuocat, & rogitat num esse Britannia velit?
Deijciens oculos respondit velle libenter:
    Sed se, qua possit, non reperire, via.
Ipse vias (inquit) tradam, legesque loquendi:
    Quomodo perfecte verba Britanna loces.
Liberat ille fidem, nostro sermone politur:

The curiosity of the poem lies in its reversals—a mute rhetoric that becomes polished by English *(nostro sermone politur)*—patriotic ploys that lead to the final climactic marriage: the sisters Logic and Rhetoric are now at last *ours*. But the real irony of the poem is that, like the other dedicatory poems appearing in this book whose celebrated purpose is to bring Latin learning to the English reader, it speaks solely in Latin. This linguistic controversion underscores the poem's function, it seems to me. As in the *Logic,* a double or split audience and intention are created—each having something to do, I shall argue, with power, in this case above all with political power.

Rhetoric is a requisite of political, or ruling class, power, argues Wilson in his dedicatory epistle to John Dudley, Earl of Warwick. The letter begins with a story of how oratory managed a victory that otherwise would have been hard won "by the sword." Wilson argues that "no man ought to be without [knowledge of rhetoric who] either shall bear rule over many or must have to do with matters of a Realm"; and he goes on to claim that this scion of a powerful ruling family had himself requested that Wilson set forth "the precepts of Rhetoric . . . in English, as I had erst done the rules of Logic." Then, immediately following, Wilson in his Prologue to the Reader only further advertises the puissance of his subject by vividly recounting his troubles in Italy.

By these associations, eloquence itself becomes more than simply effectiveness or clarity or even what today we might call vaguely "rhetoric" or "communication." It is an instrument of and access to power—a larger subject that is, as I shall argue, also in a less than subtle way the author's personal aim. Something of the point of his linking eloquence with power, a point which becomes increasingly clear as the book proceeds, begins to be revealed in Wilson's opening essay, entitled "Eloquence first given by God, after lost by man, and last repaired by God again." Recall that "reason" is the "calculating" part of man's mentality. Recall, too, that in a Christian view, like Wilson's, reason also "fell" and now must depend upon "eloquence" to prevail. Keeping these matters in mind, let us compare

---

Retorice, nostra est vtraque facta soror.
Anglia nobilium si charus sermo sororem.
Est tibi, sermonis charus & author [sic] erit.

parts of Wilson's discussion with the Ciceronian passage on which it is based. First Cicero:

> For there was a time when men wandered at large in the fields like animals and lived on wild fare; they did nothing by the guidance of reason *[ratione animi]*, but relied chiefly on physical strength; there was as yet no ordered system of religious worship nor of social duties; no one had seen legitimate marriage nor had anyone looked upon children whom he knew to be his own; nor had they learned the advantages of an equitable code of law. And so through their ignorance and error blind and unreasoning passion satisfied itself by misuse of bodily strength, which is a very dangerous servant.
>
> At this juncture a man—great and wise I am sure—became aware of the power latent in man and the wide field offered by his mind for great achievements if one could develop this power and improve it by instruction. Men were scattered in the fields and hidden in sylvan retreats when he assembled and gathered them in accordance with a plan; he introduced them to every useful and honourable occupation, though they cried out against it at first because of its novelty, and then when through reason and eloquence [or as the young Cicero puts it eloquently, *rationem atque orationem*] they had listened with greater attention, he transformed them from wild savages into a kind and gentle folk. (*De inventione.* I.ii.2–3; Loeb, 5–7).

Now Wilson:

> Man (in whom is poured the breath of life) was made at his first being an everliving creature, unto the likeness of God, endued with reason, and appointed lord over all other things living. But after the fall of our first father, sin so crept in that our knowledge was much darkened, and by corruption of this our flesh, man's reason and [will] were both overwhelmed. . . . Long it was ere that man knew himself, being destitute of God's grace, so that all things waxed savage, the earth untilled, society neglected, God's will not known, man against man, one against another, and all against order. . . . Therefore even now when man was thus past all hope of amendment, God still tendering his own workmanship, stirred up his faithful and elect, to persuade with all reason all men to society . . . after a certain space, they became through nurture and good advisement, of wild, sober; of cruel, gentle; of fools, wise; and of beasts, men. Such force hath the tongue and such is the power of eloquence and reason that most men are forced even to yield in that which most standeth against their will.

So far this, part of the "Preface" in the edition I used, sounds like a Christianizing of Cicero: God is the source of eloquence, not some wise man. In both, eloquence is a powerful, civilizing instrument. But Wilson has uniquely center-staged power itself, most forcefully in the concluding statement. Equally significant, whereas Cicero speaks of maintaining society through maintaining justice, Wilson goes on to speak of maintaining class structure:

> For what man I pray you, being better able to maintain himself by valiant courage than by living in base subjection would not rather look to rule like a lord than to live like an underling if by reason he were not persuaded that it behooveth every man to live in his own vocation and not to seek any higher room than [that] whereunto he was at the first appointed?

The gloss Wilson has placed on the Ciceronian argument, an argument already familiar to those readers among his contemporaries for whom the Latin poems do not need to be translated and for whom Wilson's gloss would operate as "literary criticism," is more than a simple Christianizing. Having dedicated the book to the son of the power behind the throne, Wilson in the passsage we have just examined characterizes rhetoric/eloquence not simply as itself an impressive power but also as a power especially useful in maintaining social control, order, the status quo. Yet the passage was written, I shall argue, by a man who seemed to have every intention of using rhetoric's power in order to do just the opposite, to take advantage of a newly functioning social mobility. That is, a strong and I believe unmistakable dimension of Wilson's theoretical work is his own self-aggrandizement. Nonetheless he advances this intention among others in a way that once more, as in the *Logic,* makes salient certain features of the Erasmian humanism that was and is his legacy. Before we continue, we need to have in mind the structure of this book.

This time the division into three "books" is somewhat more than typographically marked. But, again, the distribution of material into three books is more than a little problematic because of the humanist approach to the material discussed: even more than the rule of reason the realm of rhetoric is a field of activities. And even though these activities may be traditionally divided into five offices, from "invention" to "delivery," all five as Wilson says "go together." Too, for the humanist, rhetoric is ultimately more of a general attitude toward the world—a cast of mind, evident at times in Wilson's *Logic*—than a subject which can be arranged and explicated systematically. Not surprisingly, the first book of Wilson's *Rhetoric* only generally pertains to invention, as does the second, which also includes disposition, and the third discusses the remaining three offices. Neither is Wilson concerned, as the Ramists later became concerned, about the overlapping of the offices of rhetoric, nor is he at all constrained by the evident overlapping of rhetoric and logic.

It is significant too, it seems to me, that the discussion in the second book of the *Rhetoric* on "delighting the hearers, and stirring them to laughter" is Wilson's *longest instructional section*, comprising twenty-two pages in Mair's edition. Of course, the quantitative emphasis thus given the subject will come as no surpise to any student of the *De oratore,* wherein a large section of the second book is devoted to a discussion of humor or "wit" as a crucial strategy in moving an audience. Nonetheless, the profound relation between rhetoric and making people laugh has perhaps never been given the attention it deserves. *There is no other subject, other than rhetoric—except perhaps comedy—to which laughter and its uses belong.* Its uses in forensic oratory were particularly well demonstrated by Cicero. Its uses in another rhetorical division, preaching, were demonstrated by Erasmus and are insisted upon by Wilson himself, who says in a statement that might have been uttered by Folly in justifying humor: "Yea, the Preachers of God mind so much edifying of souls that they often forget we have any bodies" (136). Once more, throughout the rhetorical, and later speech, tradition, the physicality of language has primacy.

Perhaps, therefore, a certain unruliness is unavoidable. Rules might be easily constructed in the imagination if one were to make lists of the places or formulas about the parts of an oration, so long as one sets aside delivery, decorum, circumstance, or any of the other qualities which distinguish rhetoric from logic. Rules *can* be set down, to a certain extent, for logic, as Wilson has demonstrated in *The Rule of Reason.* But the art of rhetoric can offer no more than a few guidelines based on experience that will help aspiring practitioners to, as Wilson puts it, shape a rhetoric for any situation in which they find themselves. The principle, we recall, is one Toxophilus uses, to compare the task of writing "rules" for rhetoric with that of writing "rules" for archery. Finally, it is not insignificant that Wilson locates the "rules" of rhetoric in that faculty whose name is synonymous with humor, *wit,* echoing *De oratore* I.xxxii. 146: "I cannot deny but that a right wise man unlearned shall do more good by his natural wit than twenty of these common wits that want nature to help art. And I know that rules were made first by wise men, and not wise men made by rules" (159). In this important respect, the almost defiantly unsystematic Wilson shows that he read his classical sources and Erasmus very well indeed.

Thus, for example, it should come as no surprise to discover that you cannot enter Wilson's *Rhetoric* and expect to find a definitive answer to such a question as, What is a proposition? The invariable answer is, "It depends"—in this case, it depends upon the kind of discourse *or* the perspective you're using. There are propositions in logic, as we've seen, and in rhetoric as well. The differences between the two would seem to be "circumstantial," the rhetorical proposition being compounded of circumstances (who, when, where, what). But a proposition, as Wilson goes on to show in Book 3, can also be a figure of speech, "a short rehearsal of that whereof we mind to speak" (182), a figure because it's out of the ordinary. We don't ordinarily use propositions in our daily talk. What *is* a proposition in rhetoric, then? The only answer is, "What it is depends on what you're going to use it for." To uncover the answer further, you must use your own wit.

Wilson's wit as well as his ideas about art are nowhere better demonstrated than in the third book of the *Rhetoric,* wherein he urges the use of "plainness." Indeed, he has been credited with virtually having invented the term "inkhorn" (we've noted its presence in Puttenham):

> Among all other lessons this should first be learned, that we never affect any strange inkhorn terms but to speak as is commonly received . . . Some seek so far for outlandish English that they forget altogether their mother's language. And I dare swear this: if some of their mothers were alive they were not able to tell what they say. (162)

Wilson gives a brilliant example. Before we examine it, let us note his reference to English as our "mother's language"—or, as we still put it, our "mother tongue." The metaphor is significant. Latin was a language among *men,* learned men, and as such it was the language of the very power to which Wilson was making English aspire. Walter Ong has an interesting essay on Latin as a kind of male puberty rite for the privileged class in the Renaissance.[23] It was an exclusionary language, a means not simply of keeping women marginalized (there were notable exceptions: Elizabeth's Latin was apparently extraordinarily good, as was the Latin of such exceptional females as Thomas More's daughter Margaret) but of keeping certain classes of men marginalized, too.[24] Wilson may have been at the forefront of those who would break Latin's hegemony, but he also knew when to use it to his advantage—as in the dedicatory poems.

Back to Wilson's example. He claims the following was a letter written by a Lincolnshire man—i.e., someone in the boondocks— to a gentleman close to the lord chancellor. The writer, recalling that he and the gentleman were old school chums, appeals for a "void benefice"—appeals, that is, for his own appointment as rector or vicar in a certain parish.

> Pondering, expending, and revoluting with myself your ingent affability and ingenious capacity for mundane affairs, I cannot but celebrate and extol your magnifical dexterity above all other. For how could you have adepted such illustrate prerogative and dominical superiority if the fecundity of your ingenie had not been so fertile and wonderful pregnant. Now therefore being accersited to such splendent renown and dignity splendidious, I doubt not but you will adiuvate such poor adnichilate orphans as whilom were condisciples with you, and of antique familiarity in Lincolnshire. Among whom I being a scholastical panion obtestate your sublimity, to extol mine infirmity. There is a Sacerdotal dignity in my native country contiguate to me where I now contemplate, which your worshipful benignity could soon impetrate for me, if it would like you to extend your sedules, and collaude me in them to the right honorable Lord Chancellor, or rather Archgrammacian of England. You know my literature, you know the pastoral promotion, I obteste your clemency, to invigilate thus much for me, according to my confidence, and as you know my condign merits for such a compendious living. But

23. Walter J. Ong, "Latin Language Study as a Renaissance Puberty Rite," *Rhetoric, Romance & Technology* (Ithaca, N.Y., 1971), 113–41. A subsidiary, and often overlooked, point made by the essay is that "[b]ecause their sex was so committed to the vernacular, women could become . . . both a major audience for English literature and some of its chief patrons" (120).

24. As I noted in my preceding chapter. Besides being primarily for certain men, Latin, as Thomas More comments in his confutation of Tyndale, also marks out a certain intellectual class; see *Complete Works,* ed. Louis A. Schuster et al. (New Haven, Conn., 1973), 8: 179.

now I relinquish to fatigate your intelligence with any more frivolous verbosity, and therefore he that rules the climates be evermore your beautreur, your fortress, and your bulwark. Amen.

> Dated at my Dome, or rather Mansion place in Lincolnshire, the penult of the month sixtile.
> *Anno millimo, quillimo, trillimo. Per me Ioannes Octo.* (163)

Whether this "John Eight" was a "real" person or the letter a "real" letter, hardly matters. The point is made, perhaps more vividly for Wilson's readers than for us: Latin was the language of the learned, and obviously Latinate English the language of the learning-pretenders. E.g., "ingent" is a variant of *ingens,* vast or enormous; "accersited" of *accersitum,* called or summoned; "adiuvate" of *adjuvo,* to help or assist. Wilson continues:

> What wise man reading this letter will not take him for a very calf that made it in good earnest, and thought by his inkpot terms to get a good parsonage? (163)

Later Wilson argues the Erasmian point that anyone who "mindeth to persuade must needs be well stored with examples" (190), and the more humorous the better. Obviously he practices well the lesson that he preaches. But this particular example goes beyond simple humor into satire—and is at least double-edged. Not only does the letter satirize overblown language, it also satirizes the letter used crudely to curry favor. Thus in the latter regard, it satirizes what I take to be one of Wilson's purposes in using letters as examples or, for that matter, in writing the book itself, as I shall argue further at the end of this discussion.

Of course we must acknowledge the simple truth: this first English rhetoric was a conduit for classical learning about the subject. Good humanist that he was, Wilson used as his chief sources Cicero, the *Rhetorica ad Herennium,* Quintilian, and Erasmus with a little Sherry (a wording Erasmus would have appreciated), and a little Udall, too,[25] but with very little Aristotle (another quality Erasmus

---

25. Sherry has been properly credited with providing the source for much of Wilson's discussion of style, though it must be remembered that one of Sherry's own sources is the *De copia* and that the *fons* of both is the Ciceronian corpus. However, at one point, Wilson makes an overlooked reference to a recent work by Udall. In discussing the figure *circumlocution,* Wilson declines—as Sherry does—to offer an example of the third type, paraphrase, suggesting that "the large Commentaries

might have applauded[26]). It is, of course, the Erasmian influence that I would call renewed attention to. "The influence of Erasmus on English rhetoric has thus far scarcely been suspected," stated Wagner over sixty years ago. We may now suspect a little more than we did then,[27] but we have yet to go to the heart of the matter. Certainly we acknowledge Erasmus's influence on English rhetoric in the areas of style and amplification, including the teaching (which Wilson adopted) on the use of examples. But we have yet to understand that his most influential teaching, like Cicero's, as I have tried to argue in the opening chapters of this book, is in the area of *inventio*. Certainly Wilson emphasizes invention; indeed, he devotes more than half his entire work to it. More than that, however, his very approach to rhetoric—a vaguely structured discussion that demonstrates not simply a *modus dicendi* but a *modus vivendi*—is a mixture of Erasmianism and Ciceronianism, the Erasmus of the *De copia* and the Cicero of the *De oratore*. But Wilson is uniquely Wilson in the ends or uses of rhetoric, including those he employs himself.

I am thinking of Wilson's evident, non-Erasmian, and uniquely personal interest in power, above all political power, a keynote of his rhetoric from the opening of his book to its conclusion:

---

written and the Paraphrasis of Erasmus Englished are sufficient to show the use thereof." Wilson's reference to "Erasmus Englished" points to a work which appeared only a year after Sherry's and a year before his own: Nicholas Udall, et al., *The paraphrases of Erasmus upon the newe testament eftsones conferred with the Latine and throughly corrected . . . with a perfect concordaunce diligently gathered by Nicolas Udall* (London, 1551–1552), 2 vols. See my earlier mention of Udall in discussing the dedicatory Latin poems. Wilson's point is that a way to help his non-Latin-reading countrymen learn rhetoric is through studying what Erasmus they have available: here Erasmus's work on the New Testament offers good instruction in what a rhetorical figure is and can be.

26. Wagner finds only one use of Aristotle's *Rhetoric,* in Wilson's discussion of contraries; see "Wilson and his Sources," 529. Erasmus's own feelings about Aristotle were surely complex, though anti-Scholasticism as Folly herself well realizes was also anti-Aristotelianism. Medine, in his introduction to his edition of Wilson's *Rhetoric,* finds Wilson Aristotelian in at least one respect: his "theory provides that persuasion is not the immediate end of a single part of an oration but the ultimate end of its entire substance" (16).

27. Wagner's observation is in his "Wilson and his Sources," 531. A more recent observation: "Erasmus's influence on renaissance discourse can hardly be overestimated," states David Norbrook in "Rhetoric, Ideology and the Elizabethan World Picture," *Renaissance Rhetoric* ed. Peter Mack (New York, 1994), 143.

> But here an end. And now as my will hath been earnest, to
> do my best, so I wish that my pains may be taken
> thereafter. And yet what needs wishing, seeing
> the good will not speak evil, and the
> wicked cannot speak well? Therefore
> assured of their gentle bearing
> with me, I fear none,
> because I stand
> upon a safe
> ground.

At first the assurance seems a little too pious and naive, like the old Quintilianesque moral side-step that defines an *orator* simply as a "good man skilled in speaking."[28] God knows, Wilson seems to say, rhetoric must not be used to empower evil, and he goes on to suggest that it's possible to define "speaking well" in such a way that the "wicked" are excluded (only the good speak truly well). But for some readers this curiously fumbling conclusion will only underscore the powerfulness of the subject. These might be the readers who upon reading this conclusion recall Wilson's subsequent "travails" in Italy, as recounted in the Prologue to the editions published after 1560, when he claims that his tampering with this subject put him not on "safe" but perilous ground politically. Prior to Wilson the subject of rhetoric had been insulated by Latin and was therefore arcane. But once Englished the subject's potential for dangerous misuse politically must be acknowledged, if not addressed—and Wilson makes a parting gesture in that direction. Nonetheless, for readers of all editions after the first, after Wilson's incarceration and torture, as retold in prefaces from the second edition onward, the book's still-standing, unrevised, original conclusion becomes poignant and loaded with irony. But my point is not that *any* interest in or suggestion of power is non-Erasmian.

On the contrary, one could argue that Erasmus may have even provided something of a model of a skillful use of rhetoric as an access to power: after all, it was his excellence as a Latinist and as a letter-writer which got the young Erasmus out of the monastery and into the service of the Bishop of Cambray, and thus eventually into

---

28. This dodge and how it continues to plague humanist education have been brilliantly discussed by Richard A. Lanham, "The 'Q' Question," *South Atlantic Quarterly* 87 (1988): 653–700.

the greater, secular world of learning. Wilson, too, uses his skill as a writer for a similar sort of mobility, to move out of his graduate student days and the world of scholarship and into the world of politics, diplomacy, and power-brokering. Skill and success in self-promotion seem equally evident in the careers of both men.[29]

But if these similarities with the influential Erasmus are important, so too are the contrasts: Wilson was simply more narrowly patriotic as an Englishman (Erasmus Roterodamus was foremost a citizen of the larger Christian world of humane knowledge and wisdom) and finally more personally ambitious for specifically political power. For that matter, nowhere in Erasmus do I find such capitalizing on the subject as Wilson's explicit, approving, and mainly Ciceronian equation of eloquence with political power. Indeed, among the themes which Erasmus suggests in *De ratione studii* (CWE, 24: 676) that a teacher might discuss with his class is that "the unrestrained eloquence of Demosthenes and Cicero was their undoing." A classroom pro-con analysis of the theme could limit an uncritical acceptance of the Ciceronian equation. At the very least, by centering on the qualifier "unrestrained," the debate could lead the disputants into the realm of morals, the always preferred area of Erasmian humanism.

Although I agree with the central argument of Hanna Gray's often cited essay, her observation that "[t]he bond which united humanists, no matter how far separated in outlook or in time, was a conception of eloquence and its uses,"[30] needs some modification. Or rather, dialectical analysis: it needs *definition* and *division*. For differences in Erasmus's and Wilson's conceptions hint at other differences that might caution the ready and easy application of Gray's observation. Erasmian eloquence is perhaps nowhere better described than by Bulephorus, the chief if long-winded speaker in *Ciceronianus*: eloquence is language that breathes, persuades, convinces (by virtue of its appropriateness), and fully expresses the speaker's self. And the Erasmian end of eloquence is perhaps nowhere better set forth than in Bulephorus's statement that the purpose of eloquence is "not only to speak with greater polish but to live better"—i.e., through know-

---

29. On this point, so far as Erasmus is concerned, see Lisa Jardine, *Erasmus, Man of Letters* .

30. "Renaissance Humanism: The Pursuit of Eloquence," *Journal of the History of Ideas* 24 (1963): 498.

ing Christ.[31] If Ascham would have us "live well" through honesty and discipline, Erasmus would have us achieve the same end through following Christ.

Wilson would surely subscribe to all these sentiments. But, in addition to the twist he gives "eloquence," he also suffuses his theory with something of the blind Ciceronianism that Erasmus wrote the *Ciceronianus* to caution us about. In that work, Erasmus ridicules all slavish devotees to Cicero—either those Latinists who insist upon using only words found in the Ciceronian corpus or those students who continue to read that corpus uncritically—by pointing to (a thoroughly rhetorical lesson) the disparity between Cicero's world and the Christianized European world of the early sixteenth century. Wilson, however, seems simply to transport into his world blindly and uncritically bits and pieces of the Ciceronian corpus. His opening discussion, for example, of the "matter" of rhetoric and of the four "causes" is a literal translation from *Rhetorica ad Herennium,* which Bulephorus rightly dismisses as not being by Cicero at all and ridicules as not even belonging to the same class as Cicero's *rhetorica*.[32]

31. Izora Scott, *Controversies over the Imitation of Cicero* (New York, 1910), part 2, 116. Other parts of the argument cited may be found on 41, 48, 58, 123, 129.

32. Bulephorus's putdown is on 48. Note the similarities between Wilson's translation and the one to be found in the Loeb edition of the *Rhetorica ad Herennium:* First, what Wilson calls the "matter whereupon an Orator must speak": "An orator must be able to speak fully of all those questions which by law and man's ordinance are enacted and appointed for the use and profit of man, such as are thought apt for the tongue to set forward" (Wilson, 1) And now here is the modern translation of the passage in *ad Herennium,* I.ii.2: "The task of the public speaker is to discuss capably those matters which law and custom have fixed for the uses of citizenship, and to secure as far as possible the agreement of his hearers" (Loeb edition, 5).

Or compare the two in teaching the kinds of "causes" from *ad Herennium,* I.iii. 5: "That is called an honest matter when either we take in hand such a cause that all men would maintain, or else gainsay such a cause that no man can well like./ Then do we hold and defend a filthy matter when either we speak against our own conscience in an evil matter or else withstand an upright truth./ The cause then is doubtful when the matter is half honest and half unhonest./ Such are trifling causes when there is no weight in them . . ." (Wilson, 8). "A cause is regarded as of the honourable kind when we either defend what seems to deserve defence by all men, or attack what all men seem in duty bound to attack . . . A cause is understood to be of the discreditable kind when something honourable is under attack or when something discreditable is being defended. A cause is of the doubtful kind when it is partly honourable and partly discreditable. A cause is of the petty kind when the matter brought up is considered unimportant" (Loeb, 11).

But Wilson does not hesitate. More than that, he provides an almost comic inversion of Erasmus's lesson about Ciceronianism when he Christianizes Cicero's discussion of the origins of eloquence, which we reviewed earlier. Furthermore, in that inversion, however Christian its patina, Wilson offers an admiring look at Hercules, who:

> being a man of great wisdom had all men linked together by the ears in a chain, to draw them and lead them even as he lusted. For his wit was so great, his tongue so eloquent, and his experience such, that no one man was able to withstand his reason . . . (Preface, sig. Avii)

This well-known image does not appear in the Ciceronian passage Wilson adapts, though it adds poignancy to what each has to say about the power of rhetoric. Wilson, moreover, was adapting Book I, section 3 of the *De inventione,* a work Bulephorus also dismisses as one Cicero wished dropped from his corpus. Putting aside its own rhetorical ends (as well as its self-reflexively satirical jabs at Erasmus himself[33]), Erasmus's *Ciceronianus* makes Wilson's theory—for all its author's Protestantism—look as if it is aimed several notches below an ideal, spiritualized, or even complex use of the rhetorical tradition. Obviously more for political than for moral ends, Wilson's rhetoric seems to grab indiscriminately for the pragmatic, the efficacious. Is this what we find, then, when we look at traditional rhetoric by means of a lesser light? Perhaps, but the contrasts are nonetheless instructive.

Let us explore an end Wilson's *Rhetoric* shares with Erasmianism, the use of language to fully express the speaker's self. "Conduit," which I earlier called Wilson's work, tells metaphorically only one side of the story, the scholarly side, about Wilson's sources. As an interpretive metaphor for Wilson's *Rhetoric,* "conduit" is far too impersonal. The book is suffused with his personality, his "voice," far more so than is his *Logic.* In fact, the *Rhetoric* is so suffused with Wilson's personality that it virtually exemplifies a traditional tactic about which it is curiously silent: *ethos,* or character.

The verbal means of proof *(logos)* are mentioned explicitly in Wil-

---

33. Erasmus "degrades and hurries everything; he does not give natural birth to his creations . . . [he does not even try] for Ciceronian style but uses theological words and sometimes even vulgarisms" (105). But the criticism is offered not by Bulephorus, the "physician," but by Nosoponus, who needs to be cured of his slavish and mistaken Ciceronianism.

son's discussion, particularly when he treats the "places" and the forms of reasoning. Of course, any lengthy discussion of *logos* has been made unnecessary by the prior appearance of *The Rule of Reason*. "Why did Wilson publish the *Logike* first, and the *Rhetorique* later," asks Wagner, "if rhetoric was so important in the work of Cambridge reformers?" He then provides two answers: logic had long been important, more important than rhetoric, and it preceded rhetoric in the trivium (students studied grammar, logic, and rhetoric in that order).[34] But I think there is yet another, complementary answer: humanists recognized that rhetoric is incomplete without logic, which as a simpler art takes precedence. Wilson himself says: "I would wish that every man should desire and seek to have his *logic* perfect before he look to profit in *rhetoric*" (113). Both, after all, are arts of argument, and any skillful arguer—particularly any skillful disputer—must know how to "confirm his causes" with the "places of logic." I would also add that Wilson was thinking of a reformed dialectic—a logic reformed not along Agricolan lines but along the lines Wilson pursued in the preceding book, which made logic a limited art, restricted in application to a closed communication among experts, those rare souls whose understanding (if not their will) may not need the added confirmation of emotional and ethical forms of proof. It is simpler, more limited and, in the practical world of affairs, less significant, certainly less politically significant, than rhetoric.

Emotional proof, *pathos,* is likewise a major subject of Wilson's *Rhetoric,* as a passing review of the book's contents would indicate, even more than *logos* is. The continual insistence upon getting and keeping the audience's attention, the author's frequently expressed worry about wearying his own readers and so providing them with examples and "merry tales," and the long discussion of humor (the explicit incorporation of humor as yet another supra-logical way of establishing your case)—all these are evidence of the importance of the subject of *pathos.*

But Wilson says virtually nothing about *ethos,* a strange neglectfulness considering not only his sources[35] but the very "ethos" of hu-

---

34. "Thomas Wilson's *Arte of Rhetorique*," 8.

35. For example, see Cicero, *De oratore,* II.xliii.182–84. Erasmus, like most humanists, saw the development of character as the end of (rhetorical) education. In

manism itself with its emphasis on individuality and self-fashioning, to say nothing for the moment of the Erasmian insistence on the expression of character as an end or aim of eloquence. Wagner commented that Wilson's apparent "omission of ethical proof, whether influential or not, is probably to be deplored."[36] But if ethical proof is not discussed, the related subject of ethics, or moral character, is certainly evident in all of Wilson's examples and doctrines. And another ethos is certainly *shown*: Wilson's own emerges clearly from a reading of the book, the "implied author" we would call it today, and it is a compound of lawyerliness, Protestant piety, wit, and ambition.

Moreover, the demonstration of ethos in general, and Wilson's in particular is, to return to my argument, part of what I take to be the point of the book. Let us pursue this matter by considering Wilson's audiences, then his intentions.

An audience is of course indicated in his title: *for the use of all such as are studious of eloquence*. And, as I have also suggested, and will explore further below, the title indicates an intention, for Wilson immediately associates "Eloquence" with power. With that association, an audience has become defined (the "preferred audience" in modern rhetorical theory) as those interested in using rhetoric as a means of gaining power over others. Two kinds of speakers mentioned most frequently, as we've noted, are lawyers and preachers. But Wilson's chief examples of eloquence—e.g., the example of "comfort" or Erasmus's letter to Mountjoy on marriage—have nothing to do with lawyers or preachers and everything to do with the wealthy and powerful. The dedicatory poems praise Wilson for his patriotism in making a knowledge of classical rhetoric available to the English reading public. Haddon, we found, calls Rhetoric the "sister" of Logic; Udall seems to follow through on the metaphor and claims "*Utraque nempe soror, patrem cognoscit eundem / Anglia iam natis mater, utramque fovet*" (Of course each sister knows the same father [Wilson] / And England, now mother to the children, nourishes them both).

view of my argument in my chapter on *inventio*, it is significant that as indicated by the 1523–1524 catalogue Erasmus made of his own writings, he placed *De copia* and *De conscribendis epistolis* among his educational and literary works and among those works aimed at the building of character, or *ethos*, he listed *The Praise of Folly*.

36. "Thomas Wilson's Contributions to Rhetoric," in *Historical Studies of Rhetoric and Rhetoricians*, ed. Raymond F. Howes (Ithaca, N.Y., 1961), 111.

As I suggested earlier, since the poems themselves are in Latin and left untranslated, they seem to controvert the very point they make, unless we are clear about the actual point of this Latinizing.

Let's attempt another question: who could have been in this primary audience? Not, who actually were in Wilson's audience, or who constituted his "preferred audience," or even what use was actually made of his book. As I tried to argue in Chapter 3, books are often innocent of the uses actually made of them. My purpose in a close reading of Wilson's book, like my close reading of Erasmus's *De copia*, is to find the author's apparent intention, or intentions.

On the simplest level, the question I have now posed could be one of literacy: who could read? It is not surprising that for this period the answer has to be structured along class lines. In *De republica anglorum* (1583) Sir Thomas Smith claimed that "we in England divide our men commonly into four sorts, gentlemen, citizens and yeomen, artificers, and labourers" (20). David Cressy, in his study of reading and writing in Tudor and Stuart England, comments that Smith's division "corresponds quite well, at least in outline, with the order of literacy."[37] Most gentry and other gentlemen, including those members of the rising middle class who had already risen, knew their Latin as well as their Cicero and might consequently center their interest in Wilson's efforts to put something familiar into their "mother tongue" (true, almost 90 percent of their mothers remained illiterate, but Wilson's book is clearly not intended for women). Clergy, members of other professions (lawyers, physicians), freeholders, tradesmen, and artificers—as we begin to move down the class structure toward laborers (the vast majority of whom were illiterate) we move through a burgeoning middle class whose members had only a little Latin and even less Greek, but who also had a clear drive to ape their betters and set their sons up as gentlemen. "Who would be more 'studious of eloquence,'" Wagner asks, "for example, than this generation of self-made men who, in Protestant England, entered the Parliaments of Elizabeth?"[38]

Therefore, Wilson, to repeat, has at least two audiences in mind (as in the *Logic*). These we might try to specify: first, the learned

37. *Literacy & the Social Order: Reading and Writing in Tudor and Stuart England* (Cambridge, Eng., 1980), 122.

38. Russell Wagner, "Wilson's Speech Against Usury," in *Historical Studies of Rhetoric and Rhetoricians,* ed. Raymond F. Howes (Ithaca, N.Y., 1961), 233.

Latin-reading-and-speaking lawyers ("Civilians" particularly), preachers, courtiers, and humanists among his countrymen, who knew his subject already and could judge his efforts to translate it into a wider arena (i.e., those who might read the book as a kind of "literary criticism" and so find its author, as Haddon claimed they would find him, "estimable" [*charus*]); and secondly those literate countrymen, even those with little or no Latin, who comprised the English versions of the *bourgeois gentilhomme*. The brilliance of Wilson's satire on "John Eight's" letter is made all the more apparent when the double audience is considered. The first, the Latinists, will have a refined sense of John's butchery of two languages, Latin and English. The second, like most modern readers, having little or no Latin, will find the satire amusing primarily for its apparent buffoonery, the pretentiousness of John's polysyllabic absurdities in so crudely appealing for a benefice. But for that matter, the more either group acknowledges its own clumsy efforts to satisfy rising aspirations, the closer the letter hits home—and strikes a glancing, satirical blow at one of Wilson's own intentions.

For Wilson's intentions in writing the book are I believe also at least two fold. He demonstrates for one audience (the middle class) what he hopes to achieve with the other: access to political power. The first end, demonstration, makes the book share an intention with the *De copia*: an effort to transform the reader through giving him a new mode of thinking. It is Erasmian in its enactment of its own theory. But, just as Wilson shows his first audience how to use the very "eloquence" he would teach, so he uses the book itself as a means of self-advertisement before those who can assist him to further his own ambitions. That is, Wilson's own aspirations to rise are intertwined with the nature of the book, its view of eloquence and power, and its use of examples.[39] In one respect, the book falls

39. Medine's view is thus close to my own when in his book-length study of Wilson he cites the *Logic* and the *Rhetoric* as "intended in part to establish his reputation outside the university" (12). Medine, however, does not argue the point through an examination of details such as I have tried to provide. Moreover, in a careful examination of certain details Wayne A. Rebhorn finds in Wilson an inconsistency that I would attribute more to Wilson's rhetorical stance than to his social position ("Baldesar Castiglione, Thomas Wilson, and the Courtly Body of Renaissance Rhetoric," *Rhetorica* [1993]: 241–74). According to Rebhorn, Wilson's own social marginality (escaping the lower classes by virtue of his education and aiming

outside the humanist textbook tradition in not being "slim" nor does it end with the traditional advice "practice will teach you the rest"[40]; for its discursive ambage was designed to teach something other than classroom rhetoric while fostering its author's particular ambitions.

Let me admit that in researching commentary on this book, I find that views of it usually coincide with whatever hermeneutic is prominent at the time. An eighteenth century reader, in that great age of criticism, called the work "the first book or system of criticism in our language."[41] In the 1950s, when the establishment of "speech" as an academic discipline was beginning to peak, the work was regarded as having "greatly influenced the theories of public address we hold today."[42] Now in the 1990s, influenced by Derrida and Foucault, to say nothing of Marx, our view would seem to be swerving toward the ideological.

But at least the ideological restores our attention to context, the requisite (as Erasmus knew) of rhetorical reading. Ideologically Wilson was a patriot and a Protestant (the two were virtually correlatives when the book was in favor). He was also, in an important passage, an upholder of the status quo and insists—in an argument sure to attract the ears of the powerful—that rhetoric is a means of social control, a means of insuring that it "behooveth every man to live in his own vocation and not to seek any higher room than [that] whereunto he was at the first appointed." What better person to move into positions of power and responsibility, even though doing so might place him in a higher room than the one whereunto *he* was at the first appointed? Advancement in the world of politics, it seems

---

toward an upper class from which he was excluded by virtue of his birth) caused him to be "ambivalent" or "conflicted" in his use of humorous examples and in his teaching on delivery: Wilson, argues Rebhorn, preferred the decorous and orderly "body" of the courtier while acknowleding the rhetorical efficacy of the kind of grotesquery associated with the lower classes. Although I accept Rebhorn's argument that this inconsistency appears in Wilson, I would shift the view somewhat: through this inconsistency, Wilson "credentials" himself with both of his audiences, displaying an authoritative knowledge of both ends of the social spectrum while arguing, for the sake of both, that rhetoric is a powerful means of social mobility.

40. The quoted phrases are from Kees Meerhoff's general observations about humanist textbooks, in "The Significance of Melanchthon's Rhetoric," in *Renaissance Rhetoric* ed. Peter Mack (New York, 1994), 50.

41. Thomas Warton, *The History of English Poetry* (1778 reprint London: 1870), 841.

42. Wagner, "Thomas Wilson's Contributions to Rhetoric," 113.

to me, is a crucial intention served by the contextual values Wilson activates. But, as Wilson sees here, and as he was to see more clearly and more urgently at the time of writing the third book we shall consider, if rhetoric is indeed a powerful means of social control, it must be placed in trustworthy hands. The book's final words—"I stand/ upon a safe/ ground"—only served to underscore the point, particularly in subsequent editions in which Wilson's new "Prologue to the Reader" told of his troubles in Italy and so raised the book's final words to the level of dramatic irony.

One scholar finds Wilson's intention overridingly Erasmian. But I shall insist, once more, while acknowledging Erasmus's strong influence, that a certain contrast between the two is equally instructive: Wilson's interests were far more secular. Mark E. Wildermuth, who interprets the *Rhetoric* in the context of the Erasmus-Luther debate on free will, sees Wilson as mainly fulfilling the Erasmian project of redeeming pagan rhetoric for the use of preachers.[43] Luther had impugned eloquence and charged Erasmus with using it to cover up his own lack of knowledge. Erasmus, by contrast, recognized the importance of using eloquence to move the will—toward salvation, however, toward peace, toward the fulfillment of the *philosophia christi;* again, not once does he equate eloquence with power in general, or political power in particular to the extent Wilson does. In Wildermuth's view, Wilson by frequently pointing out and exemplifying the uses of pagan rhetoric in Christian preaching "offers a brilliant rebuttal to Luther's way of dealing with eloquence" (51), and thus Wilson's book "represents a brilliant attempt to demonstrate that post-Aristotelian rhetoric is admirably suited to spread the Word of God in eloquent, persuasive language" (56). Thereby Wilson has ideologically extended the lesson which Erasmus left incomplete. But Wildermuth's interpretation is partial at best.

The book hardly centers on the Christian preacher. Consider the chief examples, the longest of which are letters:

Commending the late Duke of Suffolk and his brother,
Commending King David,
Commending justice,
Advising a young man to study the laws of England,

---

43. "The Rhetoric of Wilson's *Arte:* Reclaiming the Classical Heritage for English Protestants," *Philosophy and Rhetoric* 22 (1989): 43–58.

(by Erasmus) Persuading a wealthy gentleman (Lord Mountjoy) to marry,

Comforting the bereaved Duchess of Suffolk,

Prosecuting a soldier who murdered a wealthy farmer.

To these we could also add the dedicatory epistle to John Dudley, particularly since the letter continued to appear in editions of the book long after Dudley's death and long after the beheading of his notable (and notorious) father at the hands of Catholics. The examples allow Wilson as tactician to step into a role he played most effectively, as champion and advocate—if not priest—for the wealthy and powerful. In his dedicatory poem, the great Haddon (whom Elizabeth too had praised, calling him "second to none" among men of learning[44]) aimed his commendation of Wilson at only one of the two audiences, the Latin-reading learned one in power who will surely esteem the author for allowing England now to posses this eloquent Rhetoric as well as her sister Logic.

Ambition fulfilled, Wilson at the peak of his political career produced a book which in retrospect makes some of these values and intentions ever more salient, if by contrast, for the work is actually Wilson's most Erasmian and his literary masterpiece. That book we shall consider next.

A Discourse upon Usury
By way of dialogue and orations, for the better variety and more delight of all those that shall read this treatise.[45]

Wilson wrote this book while in a position of power, basking in some of the favor and reputation that his earlier books as well as his career in law and government had helped him to achieve. If it could be argued that the earlier books actually played little part in currying favor and achieving reputation, I would counter that at the very least (and still to my point) they reveal a writer sensitive to power and its

44. Her reply was clever. When asked whether she preferred George Buchanan or Walter Haddon among men of learning, she said, "*Buchannum omnibus antepono, Haddonem nemini postpono*" (I put Buchanan before all, I place Haddon second to none). See Haddon entry, *Dictionary of National Biography*.

45. The edition I have used is the one edited by R. H. Tawney and published in 1925. See note 4 above.

social centers. Wilson was unmistakably a political animal. And a moral one, too.

Wilson's last book, on usury, centers on a new, rising, and powerful class in England: the capitalists. Power is still the name of the game. But the rules of this new game were, Wilson and others were quick to see, making a change in the way people lived and thought. Ambition aside, this new game may have activated Wilson's religious or moral impulses somewhat more than it appealed to his political opportunism. Although the two, morals and politics, were never exactly divorced in Wilson, it is their conflict and the apparent impossibility of their harmonious marriage which provide the drama in this work. And it is the stunning if only momentary victory of the former over the latter which gives the work its uneasy and fleeting resolution. At first glance one might find Wilson in this last book more thoroughly Erasmian in subject and intention, for not only does he put aside his personal ambition but he grapples directly with the difficult task of giving moral behavior primacy. But a deeper analysis will show that Wilson's truly Erasmian qualities lie elsewhere. They lie in the nature of the discourse itself, in qualities signalled by his subtitle, "variety" and "delight," curious qualities to be found in a morally and at the same time politically troubling subject but qualities that seem to arise as naturally from Wilson's character as they do from from his continued use of traditional rhetoric's disputatious protocol. To preview my conclusion, the Erasmian qualities of this book lie in Wilson's transformation of *disputatio* into *sermo*; they lie, that is, in the author's affirmation of the *via diversa*.

In his *Logic* (60), Wilson had proposed this question for dispute: "*Nullus Christianus est foenerator,*" which he promptly translates: "No Christian is an Usurer." However, in this particular dispute moralists had known that the question could not be resolved by simple definition of either of its major terms, especially the latter. What is usury? Indeed, from the eleventh century this vexatious question had actually "exercised the finest theological and canonical minds."[46] Wilson was deeply aware of that long casuistical tradition, which he briefly reviews in *A Discourse Upon Usury.* At the same time he was also more directly in touch with the troublesomeness of the prop-

---

46. Albert R. Jonsen and Stephen Toulmin, *The Abuse of Casuistry: A History of Moral Reasoning* (Berkeley, Calif., 1988), 181.

osition "No Christian is an Usurer" in 1569 when he was employed in state business and at work on this book than he was in 1551 when the *Logic* was published and he was but a "poor student." In fact, so politically troublesome had the proposition become in the late 1560s that (I shall conjecture) certain powers moved to limit the scope and the vexatiousness of the debate—and, most likely, prevented Wilson from publishing this book until its political implications had become virtually moot.

What power-sensitive or self-advancing purposes then could publishing the book have served? Few if any, it seems to me. Nonetheless, there are those readers who believe that in this work Wilson was no less ambitious than he ever was. On the other hand, is the book, perhaps, mainly casuistical, as some other interpreters believe, one that seeks to relocate the battleground from public policy to individual conscience? The latter conjecture seems particularly relevant in view of the book's curious conclusion and its total publishing history. But the conjecture, as we shall see, does not quite get at the quality that drew highest praise when the unpublished book was read in manuscript by a learned and morally sympathetic reader in the sixteenth century. We shall, finally, take that reader's lead. In doing so we shall find that the point of the book is actually the protocol it follows, not its preferred arguments nor its problematic conclusion.

There were three editions: 1572, 1583, and 1925. We shall begin by concentrating on the book's first appearance, taking particular note of the curious gap between the completion of the manuscript in 1569 and its publication three years later. In order to interpret Wilson's argument as well as this publishing history we shall need, first, to review some of the moral and political issues the book addresses. Then, after a discursive examination of the book itself, we shall explore its re-appearance in 1925.

To understand the context of Wilson's book we must imagine a brave old world, in which there were no banks as we know them, certainly no savings and loans, and no institutionalized lending. The first banks of the kind that we would recognize were established later, during the next century's Civil War. Institutionalized lending, however, was just about to receive its first major impetus, from a bill Wilson strongly opposed in Parliament. In short, we must imagine a "precapitalist society"; the wording is that of R. H. Tawney

(30), the distinguished British economic historian who republished Wilson's book in 1925.

In imagining that brave old world, we must not suppose that banks and lending agents did not exist. On the contrary, they were there, but they were for the most part informal and often concealed by other kinds of economic transactions. Goldsmiths, whose occupation required considerable security, were known to accept, even from members of royalty, deposits of money for safekeeping, deposits that were then available to the goldsmiths themselves to use for temporary loans. Too, neighbors would lend what surplus money might be on hand to help out the less fortunate. Credit had always been essential to the farmer and frequently important to the landed gentry as well, to tide them through hard times.

By the Renaissance, though, credit was becoming increasingly necessary to the rising commercial middle class, the very class of which we spoke in discussing Wilson's *Rhetoric*. The rise of the commerical middle class also saw the rise of lenders as a kind of profession. In fact, at the time Wilson wrote his book, Tawney says, agriculture, industry, and foreign trade were all "largely dependent on credit" (86). The country, too, was becoming a debtor, raising loans not only from its own upper-classes but from foreign sources as well, where of course transactions are complicated by foreign exchange. Given that dependency and given the loosely regulated and for the most part informal nature of such financial dealings, opportunities for quick and often unscrupulously acquired profits abounded. One form of rapaciousness that was particularly abhorrent in the eyes of English moralists was the kind known as "dry exchanges," in which one profitted not from any exchange of goods for money but parasitically from fluctuations in the relative values of different currencies. One might pay Peter Woolexporter in pounds sterling in order to collect a bill due him later in Antwerp in French currency, gambling that when the bill comes due French currency will be worth more pounds sterling than one has actually paid; in fact, if Peter is eager to have his money now, he might possibly take a discount on the due bill, thus increasing the dry-exchanger's potential profit. The morally troubling if not horrifying aspect of the situation is that the dry exchangers, the lenders, or even what we now call the "middle men" (such as those who buy raw materials and sell them to industry)—all these were in effect feeding on the honest, productive labor of others. A contemporary, whom Tawney quotes (89), intoned that "he who liveth upon his usury as the husbandman doth upon husbandry ought to be thrust out of the society of man."

Usury—that is the issue upon which the outrage and the legislation centered. Again, as any reader trained in the "rule of reason" would know, no resolution of any dispute can be attempted without prior definition of the terms, plus some careful division as well. But here, as we noted, most vexatiousness arose. Does *usury* mean excessive (whatever *that* is) interest or simply all interest whatsoever? In Wilson's time the meaning fluctuated between those two poles as wildly as the interest rates themselves fluctuated. Moralists believed that usurers were castigated in the Bible (Psalm 15.5 was a favorite source[47]). But if we imagine that *usury* means all interest, moderate as well as excessive, we shall have to admit that the supposedly highly unsecular Middle Ages practiced and apparently sanctioned it. The difference seemed to be that both medieval parties, the lender and the borrower, stood to profit by the productivity of the latter. (Officially, at least. Furtive and destructive borrowing and lending could not have been unknown in those ages.) Medieval lending, even at what *we* might consider usurious rates, was more like a business investment, in which if the deal fell through no one profitted and the lender stood to lose all. But by the sixteenth century a certain morally upsetting codicil was added to loans insisting that principal and interest *had* to be repaid, so that the lender was protected, whether the deal succeeded or not. When the bill comes due, the pound of flesh—Shylock's character seems constructed to satisfy certain middle class perspectives—had to be forfeited.

The situation thus seems to be one in which moral concerns were on the one side and the absolute necessity for credit was on the other. But, again, the sides were not so neatly divided. Indeed, in the ongoing casuistry over questions of usury, so many individual exceptions proliferated that "there arose a theory of interest."[48] Little

47. Wilson refers to it in a marginal note in the 1572 edition as "Psall. 15." Tawney mistakenly prints "115" (178). The Psalm begins, in the King James version, "Lord, who shall abide in thy tabernacle? who shall dwell in thy holy hill?" And verse 5 answers, "He that putteth not out his money to usury, nor taketh reward against the innocent."

48. John Noonan, *The Scholastic Analysis of Usury* (Cambridge, Mass., 1957): 100; quoted by Jonsen and Toulmin, *The Abuse of Casuistry*, 188.

wonder, then, that *usury* was defined by Christians themselves in two incompatible ways. Calvinists allowed the lending of money at interest but disallowed extortion (another term that was variably defined). By contrast, the Church of England, as it was later called, took a stance against the lending of money at any interest whatsoever, a stance the church maintained—but with variable vigor—until the end of the seventeenth century. Wilson, though I have earlier called him a radical and militant Protestant, was of course a staunch Anglican—a favorite son, even, smiled on by Bishops and the ruling class when it was mutually advantageous to smile.

But the latter, the ruling class, apparently did not find it advantageous to have Wilson's book published upon its completion in 1569. The outcome of a crucial piece of legislation, which Elizabeth's government needed, could have been complicated by the book's appearance, and consequently the government in an effort to manage the press (under its ostensibly religious prerogative but in this case for clearly political reasons) probably blocked its publication until such time as its appearance would be harmless. Such at least is my conjecture about the gap between the completion of the manuscript in 1569 and its publication unchanged three years later, in 1572.

At the time Wilson wrote his manuscript, political concern was centering in the possible repeal of the Act of 1552. That Act had defined *usury* as the taking of *any* interest and had required that any apprehended usurer must forfeit principal as well as interest and suffer fine and imprisonment. (For "no Christian is an Usurer," as Wilson's book had put it only the year before.) However, a long time coming, a law was finally passed in 1571 which did in fact repeal the Act of 1552 and sanction a rate of interest at ten percent. Elizabeth's government, eager to regulate an increasingly complex fiduciary scene and sorely in need of money itself, threw its weight behind the new measure. But Wilson in the first of his two terms in Parliament rose in "the nether House" to speak against it. He had plenty of material ready at hand, thanks to the book whose publication had been frustrated, and he used it in his speech.[49] But the new measure became law and the question of usury seemed resolved

49. See Tawney, *A Discourse Upon* Usury, 159–60; and Wagner, "Wilson's Speech on Usury."

for Wilson's lifetime. Soon thereafter his *Discourse upon Usury* appeared.

But let us pause and note what can actually be said about the nature of Wilson's political opposition to the bill. We have only four paragraphs paraphrasing his speech in the nether House against the Act of 1571—a slender remnant of an oration that may have lasted an hour or more. The paragraphs themselves were penned not by Wilson but by an anonymous reporter, and were later included in Sir Simonds D'Ewes *Journals* of Elizabeth's Parliaments (1682). The first paragraph reports Wilson apologizing for having to speak at length on this matter of so great weight, and the third paragraph consists of one long joke which Wilson told to make the length of his speech more acceptable. Wagner, using this slender evidence, conjectures that Wilson possibly used the arguments of the two principal speakers in his already composed book.[50] If so, then Wilson's speech could have pursued two divergent points of view, as we shall see. It is clear that Wilson opposed the proposed Act, but the nature of his opposition and the complexity of his feelings can be grasped more from the *Discourse* than from these few reported paragraphs. After all it should be equally clear, from what has been seen of humanist prose, that only an entire discourse is sufficient evidence of intention. Let us return to the book.

The title page identifies the author as "Doctor of the Civil Laws, one of the Masters of Her Majesty's honorable Court of Requests," indicating Wilson's high standing at the time (his standing was to become even higher later). He was a "Civilian," a professional in the area of civil laws. He was also a Master of Requests, an adviser to the lord chancellor.[51] Too, those who read Latin will be reminded in the following "Commendatory Verses" of Wilson's achievements in Englishing logic and rhetoric. And those who are knowledgeable of governmental matters might also know that Wilson had recently returned from a successful mission to Portugal, largely concerned with commercial matters (his surrogate in the book, the Civilian, uses Portuguese examples several times; see, e.g, 309).

50. Wagner, "Wilson's Speech Against Usury," 227, 235.
51. In the sixteenth century the duties of a Master of Requests "were to receive petitions from subjects and to remind the Lord Chancellor of affairs of state, pending business and petitions, that they might be put before the King for consideration"; see David M. Walker, *The Oxford Companion to Law* (Oxford, Eng., 1980), 817.

Among these prefacing displays there is a perhaps clinching piece of evidence for my hypothesis concerning the publication delay. The title page also carries another notice which did not appear on the previous two books we have examined: "Seen and allowed, according to the Queen's Majesty's injunctions." When the *Logic* and the *Rhetoric* first appeared, there was no Licensing Law or effort to require the Court of High Commission (which was not established until 1559) to censor books. (In fact, the only "imprimatur" given each is a figurative and scholarly one through the agency of the Latin verses written by the highly esteemed Haddon.) But by the 1560s the licensing of books for religious purposes seemed necessary, given the flood of Papist tracts. And, however agreeable licensing might have seemed to the turbulent society of that decade, the worst fears of those who oppose censorship of any sort—the fears John Milton was brilliantly to articulate in the next century—were realized when the function of licensing spread beyond its original bounds. The delay in placing an imprimatur on Wilson's book would seem to be a good example. It may not be coincidence that in the same year as the passage of the "usury" Act of 1571, the queen awarded Wilson an annuity of one hundred pounds for life. Something of a consolation prize perhaps.

Astute politician that he was, Wilson in speaking against the "usury" bill eventually passed in 1571 as well as in seeking to publish his book whether before or after its passage—this Wilson must have known which way the wind was blowing. He may have sought somehow in both actions, as Wagner conjectures, "to advance his own political fortunes: rather than trying the impossible task of turning the tide of rampant mercantilism."[52] Perhaps. But this Wilson was not the tide-bucking Marian exile of his youth. He was now a learned Civilian already moving with some of the most powerful currents of his time—and his ambitiousness was surely now less youthful and flamboyant and far more discreet.

Modern readers I have quoted assume that the Preacher wins the debate we are about to hear. However, a careful review of the disputation will make it clear that the debate has no real winner—and, for that matter, that the book offers no categorical rejection of usury. Too, it is the Preacher who is the "stern moralist" that twentieth-

52. "Wilson's Speech Against Usury," 237–38.

century commentators often take Wilson himself to be—wrongly, I believe. A more sensible view, evidenced by structure and confirmed by at least one sixteenth century reader, is that Wilson's true surrogate is not the Preacher at all but the Civilian. Nonetheless, he is "in" both speakers. And both speakers and the views they represent—one completely moral, the other mainly political—are united in their only viable medium, disputation. To put this point in another way: the Civilian's support of usury but final, extempore acquiescence to the Preacher's violent opposition hardly amount to unqualified support of the Act Elizabeth's government sought. That is, the book complicates the discussion—and complication of issues is hardly to be prized by politicians seeking action on a piece of legislation. Once more, the major hazard of this, as of the discourse reviewed in my previous chapter, is the risk it runs outside its preferred audience.

To understand further some of the purposes the publication of Wilson's book seems designed to serve, whether in 1569 or 1572— or for that matter 1925—we shall need a slow review of its contents, form and strategies. We shall need to understand this "dialogue" for what it is, a rhetorical disputation. As we track the "dialectical" movement of its argument among unequal experts, we shall find that its final effects are, most likely, suasory. We might find, too, that its final resolution, as conjected earlier, is left up to the reader, maieutically. But at least one feature—the protocol of traditional rhetoric— is strongly affirmed.

Preface: Dedicatory Epistle to Robert Dudley, Earl of Leicester.

Wilson, writing from St. Catherine's Hospital (where he was master) in the Tower, professes familiarity with the Dudley family (185, a familiarity which has grown since the publication of the *Rhetoric* in the last decade and which surely redounded to his favor). His intention, he says, is so to disclose the plaguey mischief of usury that it may be "somewhat reformed if not altogether amended or taken away" by His Lordship (177).

Perhaps, then, in light of the passage of the Act of 1571 between the penning of this epistle and the appearance of the book, Wilson's purpose is simply to make us all "wary" of the issues involved in the subject, so that we might separate the corn from the chaff, for— he echoes a point made in the other two books we have examined—

"wariness in all things is evermore very wisdom"(176). Perhaps he seeks to remove the question from the world of politics to the world of casuistry. But anyone who stops with this conjecture has not heard the disputatious resonances of what Wilson means by "wariness" or what he subsequently does by way of defining terms.

Much of the epistle is devoted to an argument in behalf of a strict enforcement of the law—an argument Wilson advances vociferously: if the current law (the Act of 1552) against lending for money were enforced, or if usurers were hunted down like wolves, or if their goods were confiscated upon their demise, as in olden days—at least then there might be "fewer usurers" (184). Not "none," but "fewer." The argument of the epistle might seem like the shocking or stunning opening move in many debates we have read, the sally, or an attention-getting position which becomes negated, altered, or moderated in the subsequent talk. The foundations of the debate are initially constructed *in extremis,* or *on the contrary,* a radical and often impractical stance toward the status quo—e.g., "usury only is the chiefest cause of the greatest misery in this land" (180). None of the terms are defined, and the whole epistle is delivered in a stern, moralistic tone: e.g., so evil is the spread of usury that "I do verily believe, the end of this world is nigh at hand" (177). There is very little variety in this speech, and no delight at all. But though the position becomes moderated in the subsequent discourse, it does not exactly become negated. It genuinely expresses part of Wilson's own mind.

Christian Prologue to the Christian Reader

The most interesting move Wilson makes in this little essay is to co-opt the "usury" metaphor, to transform it from materialistic to spiritual ends. The shift begins with a contrarian stance: "And let them not say that I am such an enemy to usury that I will have none at all to be used. For I am an usurer myself so far forth as I am able . . . and I will teach others to be greater usurers than I am myself" (189). Lend to your neighbors, this metaphor says, only in anticipation of great reward from God and not in expectation of interest. This Wilson calls "spiritual usury." Apparently, then, not all usury is to be categorically condemned, even though the distinction—at this point—seems fairly simple, the shift having been prepared for by a few comments in the epistle to Leicester (see 185).

The four speakers in the dialogue are also listed: each is given first a Greek name, then an English name and a brief description. All are referred to in the disputation by their English names or descriptive titles. The Greek names, which do not appear again, are probably offered largely to antiquate the issues involved as well as to "credential" the learned Civilian who authored this discourse, though they also make clear a certain moral-political distinction:

Misotókos (hater of interest)—*Ockerfoe,* the Preacher or enemy to usury. (*Ocker,* according to the OED, is Middle English for "usury." The Civilian later tracks the etymology of "usury," 241, with no mention of *ocker.*)

Kakémporos (evil merchant or trader)—*Gromelgainer,* the wrongful Merchant or evil occupier. (*Occupier* is an old term for businessman, as in something of the present use of the word "occupation." *Gromelgainer* in the period, according to the OED, is a common term for "skinflint" or "miser.")

Politikós (adj., of or relating to citizens)—*Advocate* or *Civilian.*

Kerdaléos (adj., cunning, shrewd)—*Lawyer,* or rather pettyscholar in law. (The narrator also refers to him as a "pettifogger.")

Let us consider the differences in occupation and status between the Lawyer and the Civilian. Although both are called "Lawyers," the Civilian is only infrequently referred to as such. A professional difference between the two in this period is not unlike the modern English one between solicitors, who may advise and draw up contracts but not appear at the bar in the higher courts, and barristers, who are employed by solicitors to argue cases in the higher courts. The most functional difference, however, for the dialogue we are examining is one of *learning.* The Lawyer later admits, "I know neither Hebrew nor Greek, nor Latin neither very well, but only do smatter of broken Latin, as the most of us lawyers do, seeking not for any deep skill or sound knowledge therein" (241). Later, too, the Preacher comments that the "Master Doctor" has knowledge "in both laws, as well canon as civil," and is a "professor in them both" (273). The Civilian, to say the least, is a learned lawyer. In this dialogue he is frequently referred to as "Doctor"—just as Wilson himself was.

Commendatory Verses

There are three, all in Latin. These were written by William Wickham, identified as Elizabeth's chaplain; John Garbrand, "of Oxford"—later identified, in a headnote to the following letter as Prebendary of Salisbury and literary executor of the Bishop of Salisbury's estate; and John Cox, possibly the writer of a dedicatory poem for Wilson's Demosthenes book, there identified as Director of St. Paul's School.[53] But, that these voices, because they all speak in Latin posit two audiences seems less likely in this book than in the *Logic* or the *Rhetoric,* simply because the point of this book is not explicitly to English traditional, or Latin, learning. Nonetheless the use of Latin here, besides being simply the conventional language of commendatory verses, serves, again, to credential the book's author as a learned man. The praise, however, though learned and religious, is actually climaxed by the following, accessible to all readers.

A Letter from John, Bishop of Salisbury

A headnote explains that after the Bishop's death this letter was found in his study by John Garbrand.

The letter—in English—commends Wilson for his Discourse, a copy of which had been sent the Bishop in 1569. "But of all other things this liketh me best," the Bishop says. "Of the three parties you make each one to speak naturally like himself, as if you had been in each of them, or they in you" (196).

---

53. *Guilielmus Wickham, capellanus serenissimae Reginae nostrae Elizabethae* (this is perhaps the William Wickham who later became Bishop of Lincoln) praises Wilson for learning and for Englishing Logic and Rhetoric and for, through his rare devotion *(per rara pietate)* undertaking the condemnation of usury. Garbrand simply blasts the taking of profit through interest-bearing loans and prays that Wilson's extraordinary sword will advance his cause *(Prodeat egregius tuus ensis).* John Cox (here the poet's name is spelled "Ioannis Coci"; in the Demosthenes book, his name and identification are given as *"Ioannis Cooci [sic], scholae Paulinae moderatoris"*; possibly, too, he is the John Coxe, or Cockis, whom the *Dictionary of National Biography* identifies as a "translator," fl. 1572) begins and ends by praising Wilson for his learning and above all for his patriotism in condemning usury, than which there is no worse evil. Sounding very much as if he had just read the dedicatory epistle, Cox wrote the longest verse, more than twice as long as the other two combined, and in it he claims that Wilson, having in his judicial role found nothing worse than greedy usury *(Nil avido reperit faenore deteruis)* will labor endlessly for his country's advantage *(Acris et Herculeos exantlet mille labores, / Ut pariat patriae commoda mille suae).*

This is high praise, but it seems to be based on a miscount. A modern reader conditioned to a Boothian rhetorical analysis of fiction might find that there are at least five or possibly six speakers in the dialogue: the four listed above, plus an "apprentice" who speaks only once and briefly, and a narrator. Allowing that the apprentice could have been reasonably omitted from a list, if not overlooked, why does the Bishop mention only "three"? The reason, I believe, is that Wilson himself is both the Civilian and the narrator. The title page is a sufficient clue, and no pretence is made of fiction (which had little aesthetic insularity in this period anyway). The transparencies of these two masks are emphasized at a significant point in the dialogue, as we shall see when we review the Civilian's oration. The two masks are the "you" whom the Bishop finds in the other "three parties."

The praise becomes poignant when we recall the nature and purposes of humanist dialogue, discussed in the preceding chapter. Dialogue can be the very process of "reasoning" discussed in the *Logic* as "disputation" fleshed out with the "circumstances" so essential to the argumentative procedures described in the *Rhetoric*. Humanist conversation can be a mode of inquiry, a *multiplex ratio disputandi*, a multiperspectival method of reasoning. And the honesty of the process must be preserved even when the author's position is known— or even starkly set out—as it seems to be here, from the beginning. Thus, the Bishop has in effect touched on the very essence of *in utramque partem* disputation: all parties must be given an honest hearing. (This final point, the most important of all, is the basis not only of Salisbury's commendation but of C. S. Lewis's praise of the work: Lewis insists that "Wilson's literary fame ought not to rest upon his *Rhetoric*" but upon the *Discourse upon Usury*, whose "great merit is that, unlike most literary dialogues, it gives fair play to both sides."[54] I would bracket my own interpretation with the responses of these two readers, almost four hundred years apart, and stress the similarity in what they have chosen most to praise. We shall recur to this matter following our review of the discourse.)

But let us keep in mind that the Bishop's remark presupposes that the Preacher (or the Merchant or the temporal Lawyer) is not exactly Wilson's mouthpiece. Wilson's only surrogates are the narrator and

54. C. S. Lewis, *English Literature in the Sixteenth Century*, 291.

the Civilian. Let us keep in mind also the order of the Bishop's praise: what he liked best was Wilson's skill in arguing *in utramque partem*. Then he strikes a note very much like the one Wilson will sound when he penned his afterword: what the outcome of this debate (the Preacher's ostensible victory) will amount to, "what it shall work in other I cannot tell." He goes on to conclude, switching to Latin, that he did not presume to speak at length condemning this horrible sin *(horrendum peccatum)*, leaving that instead to Wilson. "Let this book live, that usury may perish" *(Ut vivat liber, usury pereat)*. But the actual imprimatur by more politically powerful ecclesiastics—the clergy who composed the Court of High Commission—was withheld.

> A Communication or Speech between the rich worldly Merchant, the godly and zealous Preacher, the temporal and civil Lawyers, touching usury, or the loan of money for gain.

The narrator begins by recalling an episode from two years earlier (1567, supposedly), when a "jolly merchant" invited several friends to dine with him following a sermon against usury in his parish church. The Preacher was there, as was the Lawyer; during the repast, the Lawyer "had most talk . . . for as he had a good ready wit, so wanted he neither boldness nor utterance to set it forth, as commonly lawyers have plenty of both" (199–200). Following the meal, and the departure of some of the guests, the Merchant, Lawyer, and Preacher retire to the garden to continue their conversation (once again, the *locus classicus* of humanist dialogue).

The Preacher offers his premise: "It is very certain, as I take it, the world is almost at an end"—primarily because of the lack of charity, he goes on to argue, as best seen in the evil practice of usury. The premise directly echoes Wilson's dedicatory epistle, and the more the Preacher speaks the more he sounds like Wilson's Prologue as well. The characteristic roles of the Preacher, Lawyer, and Merchant are shown in the following passage:

> PREACHER: . . . But touching lending of money, I think men rather seek their own gain than anything [to] the benefit of their Christian neighbor.
> LAWYER: Nay, both, and who I pray you would lend but to have some benefit of his money? And is that any harm when both do gain?
> MERCHANT: God's blessing of your heart for so saying, for I did

never lend money in my life but for gain, and whether my neighbor gained or no I know not. I wish well unto him, but by Saint Mary I would be sure first to do well myself, whatsoever came of him. (202)

The modern reader must recall that these participants are all Christians, all churchgoers, all members of a certain moral community. The Lawyer seeks to probe and define, the Merchant is in quest of his own advantage, and the Preacher advocates a strict Christian morality. Perhaps it is most important to note that the conceptual combatants are morality on the one hand, personal gain on the other—an adversarial division not unlike *honestum* and *utile,* moral character and expediency, in Cicero's *De officiis,* e.g.:

> PREACHER: . . . Therefore I say still [that] charitable dealing is the most assured and best wealth that a man can purchase upon earth, for where all other worldly substance faileth and consumeth away, this continueth forever, and is a token of perfect Christianity, when men show their faith and belief by their good living and well doing.
>
> MERCHANT: When I am dead I may perhaps do good, but so long as I live I will save one and be sure not to want. Lay it up in Heaven, quod he? a merry jest indeed! So long as I live, I will keep it in a chest, and have the key about me.
>
> LAWYER: Indeed I must needs say that willful poverty is the greatest folly in the world, and for a man to want himself by giving to other is the eighth deadly sin, the which I call extreme folly or madness.

Considering the intellectual imbalance of these opponents, we are likely to be baffled when we recall the Bishop's praise—at least thus far in the discourse. The Lawyer's point throughout is that the Preacher doesn't really know what usury is, having had little direct knowledge of it. It is better, therefore, that the Preacher "profess divinity" only and leave the operation of the world to those who know it best. His point is reinforced by the appearance of an apprentice, who echoes the Lawyer's sentiments but is dismissed because of his youth. Before his appearance, however, the Preacher has called himself "Ockerfoe" and the Merchant "Gromelgainer," names which the narrator then appropriates.

Then the Civilian appears, apologizing for his lateness. He is acknowledged by all as an expert on usury, having written "books" on the subject and argued on the subject in court. (If these are fictive clues to Wilson's actual career, the leads have yet to be followed.)

Obviously, the purpose of this initial dialogue is primarily to set up the debate, presently to be carried forward by means of orations. A chief issue is—at long last—definition. All interest-taking is usury, the Preacher not surprisingly says. No, says the Lawyer, only that lending which involves "extreme and unmerciful gain" (208), a transparently legalistic point. The Preacher indicates a willingness to learn from his opponents, the Merchant to listen to both. So far the Civilian too is content to listen. Like the Affirmative speaker or the prosecutor, the Preacher speaks first. The placing of this oration as a contrarian one, with the burden of proof and so privileged to come first, may be further indication of Wilson's sense of which way the political winds were blowing in 1569.

Ockerfoe, or the Preacher's Oration

"Love God above all things, and thy neighbor as thyself. This is the law and the prophets, sayeth our Saviour Christ." The Preacher has thereby set forth the scriptural premise of his forensic argument. He follows through on his earlier definition of *usury* as "a fraudulent and crafty stealing of another man's goods" (216) and "whatsoever is taken above the principal" (219). Too, he shows himself a master of amplification: "So that to gather all these together, and to lap them up round in one bundle, you shall hear that a covetous man is hell unsatiable, the sea raging, a cur dog, a blind mole, a venomous spider, and a bottomless sack, whereby you may be well assured that the devil dwelleth tabernacled in such a monster" (220), or "the usurer is deaf as a door nail, as blind as a beetle, and as hard hearted as a flint stone, whose mind God for his great mercy soften" (224).

That the Preacher is skilled in other techniques of rhetoric is further shown by his extensive use of examples, a technique Wilson recommended in the *Rhetoric* for persuasion (as had Erasmus). The examples are drawn mainly from the Bible, with a few from classical history, and with a few more from contemporary England. The final examples provide good credentialling of the Preacher's knowledge of practical affairs (as, for example, what he says about the practice of mortgaging, 227). Such credentialling is called for, in the face of the Lawyer's disparagement of the Preacher tampering with matters outside his "divine" bounds. Among his contemporary examples, the Preacher makes a move his contemporaries might find more persuasive than we would: the Jews are universally so hated partly because they are usurers (232). Nonetheless, they at least lend at a lower rate than most Christians. Jews lend, the Preacher notes, at usually under ten percent. (The dramatic irony of the example is that this rate, ten percent, is exactly the rate sanctioned by the Act of 1571.)

When the oration ends, the Lawyer reiterates his point: "I tell you plain, it is not in you preachers to judge precisely what usury is" (233). Gromelgainer, however, is "almost persuaded never to lend money or wares again for interest." Then (in a move which every humanist would—will, I hope—applaud) the Civilian advises everyone to keep from affirming any truth until "every man have said his mind at large" (234). From this point on, the brief conversations following each oration will typically raise points for clarification but will mainly keep from either affirming or denying.

The Lawyer's Oration

The keynote of the Lawyer's speech is "reason." The word appears like a motif throughout. But, lawyerlike, he combines the "reason" of logic with the "circumstances" of rhetoric: e.g., one should give to the poor, he agrees, but why should one not lend to the wealthy in hope of gain? As he seems shewdly to see, not only is the definition of *usury* in question, so too is the definition of *charity*: "For whatever you say of love towards our neighbour, me thinketh no man should love his neighbour better than himself, which they seem to do that lend to others freely and want themselves" (235). Therefore, he reasons, just as he is under no obligation to lend to any and every man who asks him, so a consideration of circumstances may reveal that this or that borrower is well capable of paying a moderate interest. Why should he not take it?

The chief complaint which the lawyer has against his society is *unregulated* borrowing and lending. (Here he begins to sound like the forces behind the Act of 1571.) There are too many men of "such niceness . . . that they had rather one gained a thousand pounds without law than get one hundred pounds with law" (244). Therefore he regrets the present law—i.e., the law in effect in 1569, which forbids all lending for gain—a law dating from 1552, which annulled a (to the Lawyer) much more sensible law (under the reign of Henry VIII) that set a reasonable rate for lending (10 per cent, not unlike the law in effect when the *Discourse* was finally published).

That this "reasonable" speech is persuasive and attractive (the earlier naming of the lawyer as a "pettifogger" notwithstanding) is the first real evidence we've seen that the bishop of Salisbury's praise is well justified. It is an effective counter to the Preacher's oration.

Gromelgainer's, or the Merchant's, Oration

This is the shortest opening speech, and the plainest. The Merchant speaks simply and briefly out of his own thirty years' experience. He makes no pretence of learning, and offers an attractive argument based on the practical world of business affairs: "For I pray you, what trade or bargaining can there be among merchants, or what lending or borrowing among all men, if you take away the assurance and the hope of gain?" (249)

Merchants, he says, who are often called upon in time of need by the prince and other "gentlemen of service . . . lend not for usury but for interest"; and they also earn their money through currency exchange (from this point "the exchange" becomes a chief subject in the dispute). Above all, merchants should not be "overthwarted" by preachers and others who have had little experience of the business world (250). Finally, "a man may take as much for his own wares as he can get" (251).

This final point perhaps undercuts the possibilities of morality in his argument. The Lawyer at least moved toward a kind of "situation ethics," but the merchant seems to hang much upon caveat emptor.

The Preacher's Replication [Response]

At first the Preacher makes a long speech directly to the Lawyer, answering him point by point and example by example, either by granting—e.g, allowing that damages collected for money not returned on time is not usury—or by refuting. His refutation consists largely of arguing that, circumstances be damned, usury is usury: e.g., "in God's presence and before His Majesty there is no respect of persons that are of one faith, and as well do you commit usury in lending to a king for gain as you do in lending to a poor wretched man" (260). He therefore upholds the wisdom of the present law (i.e., the Act of 1552) and condemns the Henrician law which it repealed (and which unbeknownst to the Preacher is about to make a comeback in the Act of 1571) "because it is against God's word to have any such toleration in any Christian commonweal, no more than theft, adultery, or murder are to be winked at" (261).

The second part of his speech is directed to the Merchant. Though, again, he goes point by point, he does less arguing and more advising—more "preaching"—appropriately, perhaps, considering the Merchant's admitted and revealed limitations: e.g., "I pray you heartily, remember God in the midst of your occupying, and deal not willingly against His will" (265). Too, the Preacher directly calls the Merchant an "usurer" and chastizes him for poor citizenship: "cursed be that lending that maketh the borrower go abegging, that undoeth the state, that destroyeth nobility and gentlemen, that driveth the prince to seek aid of his subjects by Parliament to pay her debts" (268). The "exchange" has become a cloak for usury and is unlike "buying and selling" because gain in the practice is certain (a keynote of the Preacher and other Ockerfoes since the Middle Ages: the usurer does not take the same risk as the buyer and seller of goods). But the Preacher admittedly begins to run out of his arguments, and so he gladly defers to the Civilian.

The Civilian's, or Doctor's, Oration

This is the longest and most complicated speech in the book. It is over seventy pages long in the edition I am using, and impressive in its fulfillment of the promise to reveal a store of learning. After a brief entrance—in which he employs a little self-effacement to remind them of his status: "we professors of learning do love oftentimes to hear ourselves speak"—the Civilian provides a *divisio* of "five or six" points. The sixth, he says, may appear later (and it does) after his conclusion, "upon farther conference and private debating." Here he echoes a promise he made in his exordium: You shall hear, he says there, "what I have read and gathered of others than know mine opinion directly" and then "upon further speech and private conference amongst us you shall know the very bottom of my mind and the reasons that move me to affirm (274)." This will be the sixth point, which the Civilian delivers later. His affirmation of usury is actually a negation of the Preacher's oration (which was itself, technically if ironically, the First Affirmative in this debate).

He follows through beautifully, impressively, if somewhat tediously. He gives many examples, but they are for the most part dry and textbook-like, with a couple of exceptions—as I shall note under the Civilian's third point. In spite of his prefacing and concluding coyness, it is difficult to find his approach suasory. More accurately, it is best characterized as *casuistical,* a search primarily through canonical and theological authorities for sanction and belief.

1. He begins with a definition of *usury.* The Civilian ranges widely through learning, like a humanist, from the classics and the Bible to the history of western Europe, and then turns to Melanchthon for a definition of the term in question. (This may be a politically astute citation.[55]) His definition is put quite simply: "usury . . . is a gain demanded above the principal only for the benefit or pleasure showed in lending" (276). Again, the parasitical nature of usury is emphasized, as is the motive of the lender—but the motive is put in such a way that, the Civilian claims, "every receiving above principal is not usury."

2. However, usury so defined is evil, as shown by a simple syllogism: "Where no charity is, there is no virtue. But in the usurer's heart there is no charity; therefore the usurer is void of virtue" (278). The syllogism is immediately followed by more enthymematic reasoning, complementing the Preacher's points by reference to canon law, the decretals, and the Clementine canon. Even the Popes, the Civilian declares, can make laws that "be right Godly, say others what they list" (281).

3. There are several contracts and bargains that are made which are designed to avoid the imputation or appearance of usury. The Civilian gives special attention to "merchantly dealings," but also to "political dealings" (as when one lends money in hope of getting an office) and others. Within this third point, the Civilian includes a long disquisition on "The Exchange"—i.e., the *cambium,* the exchanging of one country's currency for another's. This dealing is not usury, he argues, if it is done by governmentally regulated authority. He is, of course, much more concerned with the exchange which, unregulated and driven by the motive in Melanchthon's def-

55. Not only was the German humanist Philip (Schwarzerd) Melanchthon, 1497–1560, famed as a dialectician and Lutheran apologist, his 1555 *Loci communes* (argumentative "commonplaces") were said to be a favorite of Elizabeth herself. They were most likely introduced to her by her tutor Ascham. Elizabeth was said to have had the *loci* virtually memorized; see Baldwin, *Shakespere's Small Latine,* 1: 259, and Clyde Leonard Manschreck, *Melanchthon the Quiet Reformer* (New York, 1958). Manschreck has provided a translation of the 1555 *loci* in his *Melanchthon on Christian Doctrine* (1965). Medine in his introduction to his edition of Wilson's *Rhetoric* discusses the possible relation between Wilson's theory and Melanchthon's (9–15).

inition, simply takes advantage of temporal fluctuations in rates of exchange—whether that exchange is "rechange" or "dry exchange." But the argument does not lead to an appeal for extending governmental regulation. It leads, rather, to an appeal which rests ultimately on the Preacher's opening premise, the Golden Rule:

> And surely merchants should not live by gain of money [rechange] but by gain of wares, and yet not selling time therein neither [dry exchange], but following a known lawful trade, for the maintenance of common society, doing as they would be done unto, and helping one another charitably as need shall justly require and time give opportunity. (309)

The most egregious example of the contrary—one which controverts plain dealing and charitable lending—is the consortium of businessmen (occupiers) in the money capitals of Europe (London, Antwerp, Lisbon, Paris) who conspire to control the value of any country's money: "Now, Lord God, what mean princes to be thus abused, to suffer private men to set price of their public coin," driving its value up or down unnaturally?

4. There are instances of contracts and dealings in which not usury but proper interest-taking is involved. An example is the taking of "portage money" for one's pains when he carries a considerable sum for someone else. That is not usury but a "reward" for one's "travails" (316). Again, however, any *merchandizing* in money is, of course, usury itself.

5. The last part of the division concerns the punishment of usurers, a veritable catalogue of penalties provided under canon and civil law. But to the modern reader the most interesting feature of this part may arise from certain structural moves which lift a veil that was gossamer to begin with.

For example, the Civilian has just announced his fifth and final point, when he says (and here I shall reproduce the original):

> But suche a plentyfull fielde, howe maye it be lightly ranged over?
> Wyth that they all said, they weare rather refreshed then wearyed, savinge that the griselye merchant was put to hys noddes now and then; wherfore, sayde hee, it is good to cutte shorte. And hereupon I wished bothe hym and all other not to geeve occasion, and then men woulde speake the less against usurie. . . . (320)

Who is speaking when? Even if the answer is clarified somewhat through the use of modern punctuation ("Wherefore," said he, "it is good to cut short"), the line which follows makes the Civilian's mask transparent: he is not only Wilson, he is also the narrator, both of whom find the merchant a grisly usurer. The remainder of the paragraph continues the Civilian's oration, with no further narrative travails.

A second structural move is made in one of the few non-textbook-like and therefore interesting examples the Civilian offers. It is a move similar to moves in modern metafiction, an acknowledgement that the entire work is a consciously contrived illusion. The first move made us aware that Wilson is both the narrator and the Civilian; this second move, a story within the story, heightens our awareness of certain thematic arguments.

The Civilian tells a tale of a Preacher, "zealous in religion and therewith so vehement against sin" (the narrator had already called Ockerfoe "a godly and zealous Preacher"), who after having delivered a fiery sermon against usury was invited to dine with several parties, including a merchant. (Since none of the present parties comment, the similarities in the two situations are perhaps meant to be noticeable mainly to the reader.) In the tale, the Merchant complimented the Preacher on his sermon. Whereupon one of the Merchant's friends asked him why he gave such great thanks for a sermon against usury: "I do not know him in London that gaineth more by his money than you do, and therefore, me thinks, you speak either hollowly or not advisedly." "Tush," quod the Merchant, "you are a fool. I do thank him and thank him again, for wot you what? The fewer usurers that he can make, the more shall be my gain, for then men shall chiefly seek me out." The Merchant, moreover, in the Civilian's story is perfectly willing to pray that "graceless people, abject persons, and reprobate heathens" will have a change of heart and learn to live by the Golden Rule. Of course (326).

But the Civilian's own solution, which comes several paragraphs later, in his peroration, seems to ring equally hollow: "I would have everybody live in order, follow his vocation, be not wasteful, spend nothing vainly, look twice upon their money before they lay it out, and that their expenses do not exceed their revenues, but rather to live under than above their degree, remembering always that in sparing is great getting" (338). The Civilian is speaking only of those who are likely to borrow: if they followed his avuncular advice there would be no need for usurers. The former are apparently more salvageable than the latter.

The three other parties respond favorably. Ockerfoe emphasizes the difference between him and the Civilian: it is one not of value or beliefs (at least at this point in the dispute) but of rhetorical skill, of "sifting causes" (341). It would appear that the Civilian's oration has not simply refuted the Preacher's. The Lawyer, however, seconded by Gromelgainer, provokes the Civilian into further speech, and finally into taking a stand: the two ask for further explication of the Justinian law, mentioned by the Civilian, which enacted moderate interest.

The Civilian responds by explaining that the Justinian law set the interest rates by class or occupation: e.g., nobles could charge only 4 percent, but merchants could charge 12 percent. Two contemporary writers are cited, one in canon law and the other in civil law, in favor of the action. The Lawyer, not surprisingly, responds that the Civilian in this exposition has confirmed his, the Lawyer's, opinion. Before revealing his own opinion, however, the Civilian first defers to the other two—who simply repeat their earlier stances, Gromelgainer preferring either no limitations on interest or an appointed rate, Ockerfoe insisting that any loan made "for the very act of lending" is usury. The Civilian responds that, alas, people cannot live such perfect lives as those who expound Scripture would have them live—and here he sounds, significantly, I believe, not so much like the Lawyer as like Antonius.

Nonetheless, an opening has been created for the Lawyer, who sees his chance and pounces. He disputes with the Preacher over the Englishing of certain anti-usury passages in the Scripture. But his understanding of the text is in turn refuted by the Civilian, who thereby finds himself pressed to reveal the "bottom" of his mind, as he had said at the outset that he might. His sixth point, as it were. It is one with which the Civilian directly challenges the Preacher: "The best of this age, [such] as Bucer, Brentius, Calvin, and Beza, with others, are not against moderate usury, but do rather think it needful to be permitted, and say also that temperate taking, according as it is rated by the civil law, is not against God nor His Laws because it is not against charity" (351–52). The Civilian, induced to reveal the bottom of his mind, would therefore seem to support regulated lending at interest, a stance not unlike the one which became the law of the land two years later, in the year before the book's publication, though it falls short of supporting the uniformly high rate the Act of 1571 allows. It is, nonetheless, a curiously prescient defense of most of what became the status quo, and so technically it is in its proper place in the debate. It is quite at odds with the Preacher's position—*and* the position that we might have assumed, from reading the dedicatory epistle and the prologue, is Wilson's.

The Preacher rises to the challenge, insisting that his only foundation is "the word of God" as confirmed by "the old catholic general counsels and learned fathers," and therefore he is not bound to modern opinion. Calvin and Beza, he later says (Erasmus-like), enlarged scriptural interpretations for temporal reasons, "to help the needy banished men then dwelling amongst them" (360). The response leads to the next part.

The Preacher's Rejoinder, and last Oration

Again the Preacher recurs to Christ's commandment that we love one another. This charity provides the premise of the Preacher's argument and the basis on which all lending for profit is once more condemned. Again, the Preacher's style is elevated, as in this passage with its jab at the Lawyer: usurers, the Preacher argues, sell something which they do not own, time, the time involved in the loan, whereas Christians must

> have special regard above all things to God above, who seeth all our follies and forbiddeth so expressly these merchants of time, and these sellers of sun and moon, as he forbiddeth nothing more, willing all men to deal freely in their lending as He doth freely suffer the sun shining, the moon and stars to have their course, and the world to continue with seasonable weather and time. (355)

The Preacher rebukes the Lawyer's argument for offering only what men seeking profit wish to hear. And he disallows the Civilian's argument in behalf of regulated moderate interest-taking as being contrary to God's own commandment. But he urges the Merchant—the point is amplified and occupies the remainder of the oration—to "live in his vocation truly and justly" (365), that vocation being merchant, not usurer. The Preacher's conclusion pulls out all the stops:

> Wherefore, considering God, nature, reason, all scripture, all law, all authors, all doctors, yea all counsels besides, are utterly against usury, if you love God and His Kingdom, my masters, if your natural country

be dear unto you, if you think to have merry days in this world and to live in joy and your children after you both now and ever, yea, if you have care of your own souls, for Christ's sake abhor this ugly usury and loathe with all your hearts this cursed limn of the Devil, and lend in deed freely as God hath commanded you, and depart with your goods or wares as freely for time as you would bargain to be paid for them out of hand, or at sight, or for ready money, having always a charitable intention with you to help your poor neighbors with part of your plenty, and make no merchandizes hereafter by the sun shining and moon shining, by years, by months, by days and by hours, lest God take his light from you and shorten all your days and all your hours. . . . (373)

All parties acquiesce. The Civilian is persuaded by the arguments from the "Old and New Testament," which he wishes he had studied as deeply as he had studied canon and civil law. The Lawyer confesses having been swayed by "natural reason and man's policy" (375), by which man simply replaces God's revealed wisdom. Nonetheless, he goes on to praise that law and precedent whereby usury—now broadly defined—was condemned. The Gromelgainer determines to reject worldly wealth and pursue wealth in the world to come. Right.

> . . . with that, they all tooke
> theire leaues, & departed in cha =
> ritye one with an other, like
> ioyfull and spirituall bre =
> thren in Christ. God
> Graunte all others
> to doe the like.
> Amen.
> Finis

Here endeth the 1569 version.

A Conclusion to the Loving Reader (added for publication
in 1572)

The Civilian/narrator drops his masks and speaks as author. Echoing the bishop of Salisbury's final estimation of the outcome, he confesses more than a little uncertainty as to how long the acquiescence, the confessed conversions, will last: "whether it will fall out so or no hereafter, God knoweth, and not I. Therefore," Wilson says, "I shall tell you a short merry tale" (383). The tale, meant to be "somewhat to the purpose of this last speech and compounded agreement," actually puts an even finer point on the inconclusiveness of the *Discourse*. The tale concerns an incident which took place sixteen years earlier in Rome ("where I was forth coming afterwards against my will, God knoweth," Wilson reminds his readers). A certain priest had been required by the pope, then at war with the Emperor Charles, to get his parishioners to pray for peace, the very peace the pope might have had if only he would stop the war he himself had instigated. "But I know he will not," the priest says, "and therefore your prayers will be in vain. And yet pray, sirs, for manner's sake" (384).

Wilson, then, commenting that "betwixt doing and saying there is great odds," concludes by lapsing into prayer himself, calling for the hasty appearance of the ideal life at last and "perfect ending of all things." Unlike most books of the time, and unlike the ending of the 1569 version, the words do not funnel down the page to a close.

This curious, inconclusive conclusion was penned at the house of the publisher Richard Totell in 1572, in the year of—perhaps on the very eve of—publication, but three years after the completion of the manuscript and within a year after the passage of the new law setting the rate of interest at ten percent. The conclusion seems to do two things: it allows the reasonableness of the law, given the uncertainty that men will abide scriptural lessons; at the same time it does not abandon the truth that even regulated lending is usury. It seems, in short, to acknowledge the force of expediency while not exactly giving up on the ideal—which apparently can only come to pass when there are no longer such great odds betwixt doing and saying.

Form is the best gauge of intention, and the form of this discourse is disputation. But the disputation offers no resolution, particularly as we have it now. The original ending would seem to be undercut by the afterword, in which Wilson questions the conversion of the opposers, including that opposer who was so transparently a mask for himself. Too, it is possible to argue, as I have suggested, that even the original version, without Wilson's afterword, is irresolute. Recall that the bishop of Salisbury, who read the original version only, questioned the conversion of the opposition, and his dubiousness was only further underscored by Wilson's afterword, which was penned three years later. Recall, too, that the Preacher is in the contrarian position, the Affirmative who opposes a status quo that Wilson must have realized, by virtue of his placement of the Preacher's orations, was rapidly becoming law. In either view, all Wilson's afterword does is make the irresoluteness salient, and we are left to wonder what purposes that quality serves.

Let us summarize by using as our model a form of disputation discussed in Chapter 4: one apposer (Affirmative or pro-speaker), two opposers (Negative or con-speakers), and a Moderator. Obviously the Preacher affirms, the Lawyer and the Gromelgainer negate. The third role would seem initially at least to be fulfilled by the Civilian, to whom all parties defer as the most learned in the subject under question. As Moderator, the Civilian at first seems to come down on the side of the Preacher. But then, when pressed—in the conversation which he had earlier predicted might force him to reveal the "bottom" of his heart—he seems to confirm the Lawyer's opinion and calls for regulated lending. The Preacher then has the last word (the traditional prerogative of the Affirmative), and his speech echoes the fieriness of his preaching, as he condemns all interest-taking lending in such a way that he wins the hearts and minds of his three auditors, each of whom confesses his error, including the Civilian, who thereby abandons the Moderator's role we have imposed upon him. Then the Preacher's word is undercut by the conclusion Wilson himself penned three years later. Condemning all interest-taking lending would seem to be an ideal, toward which men should strive but under which they cannot live. Therefore, let us pray.

Thus various sides of an argument are offered, with the final moderating to be provided by the readers, not unlike the readers' role in suasion. The Preacher's victory over the minds and hearts of the opposers, as well as of the readers, is allowed to be only temporary—as fleeting, perhaps, as the victory of any sermon. That Wilson—whether as author, Civilian, or narrator—yearns for the Preacher's position is unmistakable. But the continual argument thrown against that position by the other speakers, that it is impractical, is also inescapable. Of course, were these opposing voices not so accurately or vividly presented, the force of *in utramque partem* disputation would be lost. But it is surely not simply Wilson's skill in arguing all sides of the question which makes him despair of the Preacher's victory (and so undercut the conclusion of the debate) and give compelling arguments to the opposition (including the opposer who represents Wilson himself in the debate). He was, after all, a practical man of affairs, knowledgeable in the ways of the world, ways compounded of honesty and expediency.

Certainly the Preacher represents a part of Wilson, but only a part, a matter the afterword perhaps more fully reveals than does either the dedicatory epistle or the prologue to the Christian reader. The placement of the Preacher in the debate shows that Wilson knew that he, this Ockerfoe, had the real burden of proof. And Wilson's real-life experience as a learned civilian and successful politician, to say nothing of his scholarly knowledge of logic and rhetoric, must have given him a sophisticated familiarity with the limits of the Preacher's argumentative effectiveness. If Wilson's afterword undercuts the Preacher's stance, it hardly undercuts Wilson's own.

Consider too that Wilson had seen the forced delay in the publication of this work and during the delay the passage of the Act of 1571, which he had in some way opposed in Parliament. Nonetheless, he proceeded to publish this work and to write an afterword for it. *Some* cause, he must have believed, is not lost. Perhaps through the scholarly balance of this publication he sought to save his own hide or further his own ambitions, a conclusion one might be led to by Derrick's observation: it was this work, Derrick says, along with Wilson's translation of Demosthenes which "helped advance the author from membership in Parliament to a position in the Privy Council" (xliii). Wilson, as we recall, was yet moving toward the top, which for him was finally attained when he became secretary of state and, later, the nominal but beneficiary holder of the deanship of Durham Cathedral. Perhaps he was headed ultimately and inevitably for a nominal but beneficiary title appropriate for a fighter of lost causes—one who having suffered defeat politically sought to remove his cause to the world of casuistry. There is some truth in this conjecture. Nonetheless, it seems difficult to accept Medine's final judgment, that Wilson "maintains his absolute position against usury in the light of reality" (126).

I have praised the discourse on usury as a fine example of arguing *in utramque partem*. Actually, however, as I noted earlier, the praise was first voiced by the bishop of Salisbury, who read only the first version and never saw Wilson's afterword. What drew the bishop's praise is not the moral victory of a fellow cleric but Wilson's honest and fair dealing with the opposition. Recall that he wrote Wilson that "of all other things this liketh me best": you make the parties speak "as if you had been in each of them or they in you." But then, he continues, "What it shall work in others I cannot tell." If he were an usurer, he would think himself "most unhappy if such persuasions could not move me" (196–97). But of course he is not an usurer, and the textual implication that the Preacher has won too easy a victory was evidently more apparent to the bishop than it was to Wilson's 1925 editor, who ended his reading where the Bishop did. Although he reprinted Wilson's 1572 afterword, he largely ignored it and obviously failed to read it carefully. What might have stimulated that editor's interest? The question is worth posing at this point, for it shifts our view to a position contrary to the one I am attempting to develop.

To begin with, Wilson's *Discourse* might stimulate any reader's interest simply because it provides a dramatic overview of lending and exchange at the time. For some readers, it might provoke the question (not unlike the one that often arises in considering civic humanism), Where in the world of practical affairs is the center of morality? That question became particularly urgent at the time of Wilson's writing, given not only the sundering of the Church but also the rise of secularism, or of what Tawney calls "the doctrineless individualism" of the commercial class (170). It was perhaps for both of these latter two reasons—its overview of economic practices at the time and the question of morality—that Tawney republished the discourse in 1925.

But Tawney's opening comments might make one wonder whether the discourse itself should be read at all. He says it is neither "original" nor "profound" but (erroneously) "typical of one side in the discussion of credit and money-lending" (vii). After these prefacing remarks, Tawney provides a long introduction, only twenty-seven pages shorter than Wilson's work itself. As noted, it is an introduction that fails to take into account Wilson's appended conclusion: "Dr. Wilson's book ends with the triumph of the Preacher and the conversion of the Common Lawyer and the Merchant. We will not follow them into an age in which the rôles were reversed" (172). Tawney's despair outdoes Wilson's, just as his prefacing comment undoes the bishop's praise. As Tawney sees it, the sixteenth-century struggle to control usury "was transferred from the plane of morality to that of expediency" (133). Wilson's apparent one-sidedness is therefore nostalgic.

Tawney offers an even more despairing point in a passage which seems to reveal more of his own motives in republishing Wilson's discourse: Intervention in economic affairs was characteristic of Tudor governments, he says.

> But, like the rest of their social policy, it was capricious and irregular, and, at most, did no more than impose an occasional brake on the economic forces which were widening the small instalment of freedom granted to the capitalist in 1571. But it seems clear that, in its effect both on practice and on opinion, the Act was a turning point. The process by which a measure intended to concede little and restrict much was made in practice to concede much and restrict little was partly due to the difficulties inherent in all legislation which seeks to protect the economically weak against the consequences of their own frailty. (165)

Tawney would seem to share some of the nostalgia he finds in Wilson for a public policy based on a clear morality. Because Wilson's discourse reveals the pivotal nature of its period, it bolsters Tawney's argument, or rather discovery, for which he had achieved some fame among economic historians, that capitalism arrived in our culture long before the industrial revolution. Equally important for Tawney, Wilson's discourse shows that the arrival of capitalism, and doctrineless individualism, coincided with the stultifying of most interference by church and state into commercial dealings.

We need to probe the 1925 editor's intentions a bit farther, to try to understand the exact points where they seem to converge with or diverge from Wilson's. Doing so may help us further understand Tawney's one-sided reading—and, perhaps, reflexively, that one-sided reading which blocked the initial publication of the *Discourse.*

Tawney (1880–1962) is noted for his democractic socialism, set in a context of religious morality. Indeed, he has even been called, by an Anglican dean, "the saint of English Christian Socialism."[56] Industry, he had argued in a book which appeared a few years before his edition of Wilson, should be the servant, not the master of society, whose parts must be arranged to carry on the work of man

---

56. David L. Edwards, "Introduction," *The Idea of a Christian Society, and Other Writings, by T. S. Eliot* (London, 1982) ,16.

(quoting Bacon) "for the glory of God and the relief of men's estate."[57] In a book published just a year after his edition of Wilson, *Religion and the Rise of Capitalism,* he shows only further affinity with an argument he seems to find in Wilson, that religious beliefs should be linked with the management of commerce. His rhetoric would appear to be no less emphatic than Wilson's Preacher's: "Compromise is as impossible between the Church of Christ and the idolatry of wealth, which is the practical religion of capitalist societies, as it was between the Church and the State idolatry of the Roman Empire" (286).

What Tawney does not appreciate fully enough is that Wilson does not simply come down on the side of doctrine and churchly morality. Rather, in the play of disputation and in the afterword Wilson fully realizes the battering any simple morality suffers in the world of law and politics. Let us raise this question: if Tawney's solution is democratic socialism, what is Wilson's? "Would God England had a Cromwell, I will say no more," he exclaims in his "Dedicatory Epistle" to the Earl of Leicester (182). Thomas Cromwell's firm if ruthless administration was not unlike the executive style Wilson himself was noted for, the very style he prays Leicester to adopt. To do what? Perhaps Cromwell's dissolution of the monasteries gave Wilson an implied paragon for the decisive removal of a class or occupation. Perhaps, too, Cromwell's role as principal adviser to Henry VIII (similar to if less amatory than Leicester's to Elizabeth) in establishing a state church, in moving Henry VIII to head of the church in England and thereby giving the political world at least a nascent theocracy, might be equally implied. But if we were to tell Wilson's ghost that his prayer was literally answered when England got its Cromwell in the 1640s, we might imagine him forecasting a line from a modern poet who had himself advocated theocracy: "That is not what I meant at all. That is not it at all."[58]

The closest Wilson comes to actually advocating a union based on religious doctrine is his proposal for a sort of loose political al-

57. *The Acquisitive Society* (New York, 1920), 181.

58. The line is from T. S. Eliot's *The Love Song of J. Alfred Prufrock.* Eliot's advocacy of theocracy appears in his *The Idea of a Christian Society* (1939)—a rule not necessarily by clerics or churchmen but by rulers who "accept Christianity not simply as their own faith to guide their actions, but as the system under which they are to govern" (1982 ed., 62).

liance of Protestant nations. He offered the desideratum in a small treatise he published seven years after the appearance of his discourse on usury. That treatise begins, significantly, with a line that for us recalls Tawney/Bacon: "The chiefest care that ought to be had for the maintenance of any state or kingdom is to seek first and principally the glory of God and his righteousness to be faithfully settled everywhere . . ."[59] But Wilson's proposed alliance is limited, an international consortium constructed for purposes of mutual aid across national boundaries, to withstand papistical threat. Religion and politics were comrades in arms in the period. The extent to which they might be distinguishable, or the extent to which either has responsibility for the commercial world, may be themes of Wilson's discourse on usury but that discourse stops well short of suggesting any theocratic solution to England's problems. I discount his opening gambit, to urge a strict enforcement of recent and ancient laws prohibiting usury—a gambit which, in contrarian fashion, affirms at best half of the case. In the disputation and in its afterword no easy and ready way out of the present problems is set before us, only sermonizing, which may have only a temporary effect, and prayer, whose immediate effect is a conscious longing for an expressed ideal.

The work in sum is complex, to be enjoyed for its literary value, a minor masterpiece in rhetorical protocol, one that has perhaps more craft than subtlety. Perhaps it somehow furthered Wilson's career—or led to such rewards as the consolation prize from Elizabeth. Perhaps its forceful condemnation of usury caused the Court of High Commission to defer imprimatur—but its complication of the issues alone would be enough to do that for politicians eager to get a simple bill rapidly through Parliament. Perhaps Tawney too read the piece politically not rhetorically and like certain powerful readers in the sixteenth century had little appreciation of its complexity. That complexity I would insist lies in its form—disputation, which like paradox and litotes, brings disparate elements together, a disputation which in this case becomes suasion. And if it is its form which politically complicates matters and too easily misleads readers, it is its form which continues to make the work worthy of attention.

59. Albert J. Schmidt, "A Treatise on England's Perils, 1578," *Archiv für Reformationsgeschichte* 46 (1955): 246.

Others in tracing Wilson's career have claimed that for this deeply religious man the exile in Italy marked a turning point, from scholarship to politics. Schmidt, who makes the point most forcefully, also characterizes Wilson, with a nod toward Mair and Tawney, as a "dour" and "grave Henrician" (210–12). But these characterizations tell only part of the tale. Wilson's interest in law and politics as well as religion is present from the outset of his career as author, patent in both early books: indeed, part of my argument is that a driving and ostensibly *secular* ambition pervades the *Rhetoric*. And neither a simple dourness nor a sombre gravity distinguishes any of the books we have examined. On the contrary, I believe that what is most remarkable about this third book, on usury, is the evidence it reveals of Wilson's lively and mature humanism, a quality best seen in his use of disputation and in his assumptions about epistemology and protocol. A minor example perhaps but somewhat to my point: his afterword recalls his crucial period in Italy just at the outset of his "short, merry tale."

In this matter of lively and mature humanism, the similarities not simply with the procedures of disputation but also with *De oratore* are deeply instructive. The Preacher is Crassus, ever seeking the ideal. The Civilian is Antonius. Wilson is Cicero, always preferring the ideal but seeing himself at times most clearly in Antonius. It is not, as Medine has insisted, "the basically Christian morality of the argument" which Wilson writes to affirm[60]; it is, rather, the very means whereby humanists cast a wide net for truth and situate it finally in the practical world of affairs. Through these means, the *Discourse* shares the general intention of humanist suasion, which is always partly to affirm humanist epistemology and protocol. Nor am I attempting to dismiss the argument that a significant effect of the work may be to relocate the dispute, as others have suggested, to the realm of casuistry and individual conscience. But one very

---

60. Medine sees the possible similarities between *De oratore* and the *Discourse*, but prefers instead a view of the work as an oration, which concludes not with Wilson's afterword but with the Preacher's final speech. Thus, he finds Wilson's intention in the phrase I have quoted (Thomas Wilson, 126) and believes that Wilson's afterword was tacked on to refute any possible charges of naivete. In his introduction to his edition of Wilson's *Rhetoric*, Medine observes that the *Discourse* advances "the essentially scholastic position that money-lending at interest is immoral under any circumstances"; further, it is "an essentially medieval analysis of the economy" (7).

clear effect is Wilson's reaffirmation of the means whereby that re-
location is achieved.

The true dogmatist in Wilson's discourse is the Preacher, who
ultimately reveals himself closed to all contrary arguments. The
Lawyer and the Gromelgainer are open to ideas. So too is the Civilian. And so too is Wilson—as Tawney himself shows, if somewhat confusedly:

> But how did a humanist come to compose a work replete with citations
> from early Christian Fathers and mediaeval schoolmen? How did a fer-
> vent Protestant come to extol the canon law? How, above all, did a dip-
> lomatist, whose speciality was commercial questions, who had travelled
> in Italy, by no means an economic backwater, and who had carried
> through commercial negotiations in the financial capital of sixteenth-
> century Europe, come to treat the well-established credit system of the
> age in the tone of a mediaeval friar denouncing the deadly sin of ava-
> rice? (11)

Tawney's praise might have been clearer had he sorted out the various voices and taken account of the nature of humanist disputation.
It is the Civilian who cites the early fathers and extols canon law. It
is the Preacher who denounces in the tone of a medieval friar.[61] It is
Wilson, finally, who however much he is "in" these voices, sets before us a discourse with a conclusion made explicitly irresolute by
an afterword, in which he says:

> The world is full of sweet enticing baits, and man is made of flesh, subject
> ever to all temptation of this world. And yet shall not I wish and pray
> that all things may be well, although it be almost impossible to have
> perfection and soundness of life in all men and amongst all states? God
> forbid else, and well I know that the prayer of good men is of great force
> before God. Therefore I desire all the good true servants of God to join
> in prayer with me, that all folk may amend their lives in every vocation,
> and that the kingdom of God may come hastily amongst us, and His
> glory appear for the speedy succour of his chosen people, and perfect
> ending of all things, with most joyful triumph. (384)

Prayer is the only recourse, a Protestant recourse impelled by inner
conviction not compelled (as the Roman Priest in Wilson's "merry

---

61. In *Religion and the Rise of Capitalism*, Tawney separates the voices much more
precisely, at one point clearly attributing a line from the Civilian to Wilson himself;
see 157. See also 179, 235.

tale" was) by external authority. But the recourse is eschatological. Wilson's faith is in the world to come, where only the ideal is real. Wilson ends by echoing and affirming the point he had made earlier in his role as Civilian, that people cannot live such perfect lives as the interpreters of Scripture would have them live. But this is not to dismiss the interpreters of Scripture. Truth is scattered, between morals and politics, religion and law, the ideal and the real. And only a *via diversa* can approach it.

And so, as he said nearing the conclusion of his afterword to the loving reader, "all things are lapped up, as you see, with a joyful end. But whether it will fall out so or no hereafter, God knoweth, and not I. Therefore I shall tell you a short merry tale. . . ."

It is finally his skill as a disputer which redeems this work. That skill plus his ever-abiding sense of humor. The combination—a certain perversity of outlook and an irrepressible mirth, qualities which I find throughout Wilson's writing—marks him, I believe, as a humanist *par excellence*. The title of his *Discourse* says it best: "for the better variety and more delight of all that shall read this treatise." Both qualities, variety and delight, are affirmed, and are as deeply humanist as the optimistic epistemology and traditional protocol which are at the center of Wilson's deliberations. If Wilson was more Henrician than optimistic about the nature of men ("Men be worldly, self lovers, given for the most part to evil . . ." 384), he was surely optimistic about our interpretive powers, an optimism he found confirmed in writing by at least one early reader. The work emerges finally as a minor masterpiece of humanist suasion, an embodiment as it were of Erasmian *sermo,* that ongoing convivial conversation which is partly what the Ciceronian *perfectus orator* had become. Like all ideals, it is—for most of us—rare and elusive.

7. An End[1]

There were at least three startling events in 1995 which have bearing on my case—three "emergent occasions," our forebears might call them, in that annus mirabilis just past.[2] One was the tediously long criminal trial of O. J. Simpson for murder. Its bearing on my case lies in protocol. Any claim to the reasonableness if not rationality of a protocol that even remotely resembles courtroom procedures has surely been seriously damaged in the eyes of many, not only by the nature of that trial but also by its outcome. Second were the increasing drives toward political correctness. New assaults were made on the required reading of certain books in school curricula (*Huckleberry Finn* is perhaps the oldest tar-baby), on cultural and racial biases in our measurement of intelligence, and on the "heteropaternalistic" language of the English Bible and prayer

1. Some materials in this chapter originally appeared in my "Reinventing *Inventio*," *College English*, September 1989; the essay is reused with permission of the National Council of Teachers of English. Also see comment and response in *College English* (Oct., 1990): 686–89.

2. John Donne used "emergent occasions," meaning "significant or meaningful happenings," as part of the title of a devotional work he published in 1624. John Dryden call the year of the Great Fire, 1666, "the year of wonders," annus mirabilis, in a book by that title published in 1667. Both phrases were in common learned currency.

book. Like all assaults in the name of political correctness, the aim was to achieve change without open debate.[3]

But, third, exceeding these "emergencies" in importance at least so far as one end of my case is concerned (the one I wish to discuss in this final chapter) was the appearance of a remarkable book: *In Retrospect* by Robert S. McNamara (with Brian VanDeMark [New York]). McNamara was President Lyndon Johnson's secretary of defense and a key figure in prolonging and deepening our disastrous involvement in Vietnam. The book is a retrospective view by an old man on his greatest failure in public policy: concerning Vietnam "we were wrong," he says, "terribly wrong." The public received his book with considerable disquiet. Some furor arose over the timing of his admission (why couldn't he have realized this horrible mistake earlier, say thirty years ago?). At the same time the furor reinvigorated old protests from the 1960s over restrictions on the public's access to the very means whereby major policy decisions are reached.

His antagonist during the Vietnam years, former Senator Eugene McCarthy, came out of retirement to rebuff McNamara's mea culpa. McNamara, he argues, was duped by the quasi-formalist nature of our public debates; in particular, he was duped by the rise to power of two words which have defined those debates: *problem* and *solution*. Within the tragic limits of those terms, McCarthy argues, lay—and perhaps still lies—the deluded confidence of our policy makers. Adding to the significance of his charges, McCarthy notes that he is only echoing a critique that is now seventy years old: it was first offered in 1926 by a political observer who included in his sweep the preceding two centuries of American public debate.[4]

In delimiting the proposition, the terms *problem-solution* not only restrict the participants (only experts need apply), but they also open

3. "What is political correctness?" a German professor asked me following my lecture at a conference in Essen. He is a student of modern German reunification, an identity which heightened the irony in his subsequent comment, "The concept seems so alien to democracy."

4. Eugene McCarthy, "The Vindicator," *New Republic* (May 15, 1995): the political observer was L. P. Jacks, who according to McCarthy stated in 1926, "I am informed by philologists that the rise to power of these two words [*problem* and *solution*] as the determining terms of public debate, is an affair of the last two centuries. On the whole, the influence of these words is malignant and becoming increasingly so. They have deluded men with Messianic expectations" (14).

the way for a mechanical, almost quantifiable, resolution of the debate. McNamara, before he joined Johnson's cabinet, had a distinguished career in industry as a most efficient manager, one brilliant in dealing with numbers. He thus blended well with the kind of men who at that time were expanding and deepening our militaristic attempts to solve a certain problem usually stated as "winning the war against communism." But McNamara too seems to echo something of what would later become McCarthy's critique. At the end of his book, when he summarizes the "eleven lessons" of the Vietnam War experience, he argues that our policy makers must learn that there are "problems for which there are no immediate solutions" in "an imperfect, untidy world" (323).

The alternative is, of course, to change the terms of the proposition, to escape the "problem-solution" trap and, beyond that, to seek a new approach to the very nature of public debate itself. An important way to achieve the latter is surely to reconsider the kind of rhetorical education our students are getting. Obviously for that reconsideration I would urge if not a return to the past, at least a rethinking of our rhetorical heritage. A less-than-perfect, untidy world in which truth is not always unmistakable or likely to prevail is exactly the *prospectus* which informs the protocol of traditional rhetoric. Diversity of argument and of voice and above all contrarianism are of the essence. Furthermore, without that essence, I have tried continually to insist, rhetoric itself and rhetorical education become trivial, restricted to—as Jacques Derrida puts it—"verbality, formality, and figures of speech."[5] Of course Derrida, for whom deconstruction is all the contrarianism we need, would be happy to see rhetoric so restricted. But the restriction trivializes traditional rhetoric's possible contribution to modern education, to say nothing of its possible contribution to the nature of our public debate. That the two ends—rhetorical education and public debate—are connected would seem to go without saying.

5. Gary A. Olson, "Jacques Derrida on Rhetoric and Composition," *Journal of Advanced Composition* 10 (1990): 15. Yameng Liu has recently argued that one of the most masterful rebuttals of views like Derrida's lies in *De oratore,* wherein Crassus turns the tables on Plato and calls him a "consummate orator," thereby claiming that even a philosopher uses rhetoric; see "Disciplinary Politics and the Institutionalization of the Generic Triad in Classical Rhetoric," *College English* 57 (1995): 9–26; esp. p. 14.

Since modern rhetorical education, not public debate, has been the explicit frame of my argument, let me return to that frame, summarize, and so shape at least one end of my argument. Within that frame, I have tried to discover—invent, if you will—the protocol of traditional rhetoric. I have enclosed my "invention" within two paraphrases which were themselves "literary criticism" as I have used the term: that is, they are argumentative, intended as collateral increpations of certain oppositions to my argument. In retelling the *Phaedrus* I emphasized those Platonic features which oppose traditional rhetorical protocol as an honest mode of intellectual inquiry or discursive composition. In retelling Wilson's *Discourse upon Usury* I endeavored by means of textual and contextual analysis to emphasize what I take to be the enduring and endurable point of that work, the importance of traditional humanist-rhetorical protocol to a man, a statesman and a "lesser light" among thinkers, who in a difficult time had artfully mastered the task of "living well." Between those two pieces of literary criticism I tried, antiquarian-like, to return to the past to find, first of all, some aid in interpreting these documents and, secondarily, some answers to questions about what seems to be lacking in modern rhetoric. Cicero and Erasmus have been my guides. Their rhetorical masterpieces—*De oratore* and *De copia,* both of which have been neglected or misread in our time (the latter was also misused in its own time)—have provided the chief aids for my interpretations as well as major substance for my argument. They were useful not only because of their acknowledged importance but also because of their uniquely humanist nature as theory: they enact what they describe. For additional aid and substance I have turned to other Renaissance masterworks, in order to find the protocol at their foundation and then to explore the characteristics of that protocol and use it in interpreting the works themselves.

By these means contrarianism has become the central theme of my argument. Contrarianism, I have tried to show, animates and motivates rhetorical *inventio,* perhaps the most misunderstood feature of traditional rhetoric and, as widely acknowledged, the most deficient element in modern revivals of the art. My opposition has been present throughout—those who would deny that rhetoric's traditional mode of thought is contrarian or would deny, for that matter, that rhetoric even *has* a mode of thought. Recalling now my frame and the secondary end of my argument, I should like to concentrate the remainder of this piece on the modern rhetoric class-room.

The marriage of rhetoric and disputation, so familiar in humanist education, has become gradually dissolved, particularly in the United States. There are undoubtedly a host of causes—Ramism, the new science, even romanticism with its emphasis on "sincerity," on be-ing true to one's inner self.[6] There is another cause which I propose, though the result remains the same: debate has gradually retreated from a central position in modern rhetorical *inventio* because the im-portance of speech in education has also retreated. (As I have sug-gested throughout this text, a similar cause-effect relationship may underlie our correlative failure to understand the nature of traditional rhetorical *inventio*.)

The revival of rhetoric in American education is now over half a century old. But the *philosophical* context in which it was revived had at least three centuries to solidify. As Stephen Toulmin has recently argued, seventeenth century philosophers banished the "oral," along with the "particular," the "local," and the "timely," in order to priv-ilege arguments that no longer rested on "human facts": "From the 1630s on," Toulmin states, "Formal Logic was In, Rhetoric was Out."[7] When rhetoric returned, it had to reclaim its ground from dominant modes of disputation—this time largely silent but as be-

---

6. That American institutions owe their origins and thereby much of their cul-tural nature to Ramism was proposed a half century ago by Perry Miller (*The New England Mind: the Seventeenth Century* [New York, 1939]). It would be too simple, of course, to cast all the ills of American education on the Ramists. But Ramism, or whever it represents in its complex connections with the scientific revolution and with romanticism, is surely a cause of at least one major affliction: the overweening drive to categorize, to specialize, to claim that one discipline must not overlap an-other. The Ramists called the drive the *lex sapientia,* the law of wisdom. It found practical application in divorcing silent logic from oral rhetoric and, ultimately, in reducing rhetoric itself to simply style and oral delivery. The irony of calling this "wisdom" in the language of Cicero is stark.

7. Stephen Toulmin, "The Recovery of Practical Philosophy," *American Scholar* (Summer, 1988): 339. Toulmin's discussion of "orality" has philosophical impli-cations not directly addressed by Gerald Graff in his insightful discussion of the disappearance of America's "oratorical culture" in the nineteenth century; see *Pro-fessing Literature* (Chicago, 1987), esp. chapter 3. Moreover, as Toulmin shows in *The Abuse of Casuistry* (Berkeley, Calif., 1988), indispensable to the recovery of prac-tical reasoning might be the method of casuistry (see esp. 34–35), which was itself rooted in case law and orality.

fore utterly formalist. Currently the topics of invention are called "heuristics" in American rhetoric. But partly because we have not fully restored "the oral," we continue to slight the greatest heuristic of all, debate, or the use of the topics in disputation.

Toulmin's description of modern philosophy recalls humanist efforts to liberate dialectic. I find most insightful his listing of the "oral" first among those items banished by seventeenth century philosophers. For the oral is of the very essence in rhetoric—and the recovery of practical philosophy, which Toulmin advocates, is the recovery of forms of reasoning that are, as he puts it, "rhetorical, not geometrical." In oral argumentation, Toulmin notes, the soundness of propositions depends less upon the formal relations among them than on raising the question, "*Who* addressed this argument *to whom,* in what *forum,* and using what *examples?*" This, of course, is the true "realm of rhetoric"[8]—the realm distinguished by its orality, where Erasmus sought to place his educational and hermeneutical principles as well as the understanding of his own *philosophia christi.* But if this realm was banished from the modern philosophy which arose in the seventeenth century, it is a realm that has never been fully realized in American education, and now remains almost hopelessly fragmented.

Once "elocution"—by which we meant not style *(elocutio)* but delivery, especially the oral delivery of literature—once this discipline disappeared, and new specialties began proliferating in letters and sciences, American educationists seldom knew what to do about instruction in speaking.[9] In 1915 a union which should be indissoluble experienced divorce: the teaching of composition was distributed into two disciplines—one for writing, one for speaking, each with its own professional society. The former, the Modern Language Association, has flourished. So did the latter, at first. But over the last eighty years the speech profession has grown increasingly

8. I echo a work I admire: Chaim Perelman, *The Realm of Rhetoric,* trans. William Kluback (Notre Dame, 1982); originally published Paris, 1977, under the title *L'Empire rhétorique.* Perelman, a forensic—that is to say, legal—expert, gives little attention to the oral, however.

9. On our shores, the peculiar discipline known as "elocution" achieved a prominence unknown in France and England, where it originated. The standard work on the subject remains Karl R. Wallace, ed. *A History of Speech Education in America* (New York, 1954); see esp. chapters. 7, 8, and 9.

bewildered about how to name its own society as well as how identify its own specialty. Substantive elements of what Toulmin means
by "the oral" have undergone interdisciplinary revival in the restoration of rhetoric as a mode of composition and analysis, such as the
topics of invention and the so-called "figures of speech." Such interests are often shared between the two professions, English and
speech. But what to do in the latter profession about much of the
remainder of "the oral," actual instruction in speaking—including
above all practice in oral composition before a "live" audience—this
remains an open question, a perplexity reflected in part by the changing titles of the speech teacher's professional organization. Originally called "The National Association of Academic Teachers of Public Speaking," the organization changed its name to the "Speech Association of America" in 1956, then to the "Speech Communication
Association" in 1970, and now perhaps in the ultimate expression
of its ongoing lack of confidence, the Association continues to consider a proposal to drop "Speech" altogether from its title.[10]

The history of debating in America, especially on the University
level, follows the pattern I've just described. Initially debating was
confined to the various, largely extracurricular "literary societies"
of the 19th century. But as speech became a specialty and a discipline
apart from English, debating began to be taught and studied as a
kind of unique craft. A host of debating textbooks flooded the mar-
ket. Debating tournaments swept the country, abetted by the new
speech profession, and in some small schools the debate teams hold
a position of honor second only to athletic teams. National tournaments were—and still are—held, the most famous ones at the mili-
tary academies. Resolutions for these tournaments are decided na-
tionally each year. Though the contests are called "forensic," the
questions themselves are largely deliberative—Resolved that the Fed-
eral Government should abolish the death penalty—a conflation of
controversia and *suasoria* which seems to me natural when debating
itself is given such prominence, whether in humanist education or
in American extracurricular activities. Inevitably business got into
the act, churning out debate manuals, books of evidence pro and con
on each year's national question.

10. Cf. the brief history which appears in "Spectra," published March, 1989, by
the Speech Communication Association.

Inevitably, too, ancient charges of sophistry recurred. Forty years ago, at the very peak of debating activity in the United States, a senior member of the speech profession protested the practice of making debaters argue both sides of the question. His argument was based on the premise that "a public utterance is a public commitment" and therefore it's unethical to follow the "anachronistic" practice of overthrowing a commitment to one side in merely mouthing a commitment to the other—so certain was he that students walk in to any debate with their ethical commitments already worked out. The practice was "anachronistic," he believed, because it belongs to the older sophistic disputation of our forefathers—finding condemnation where I find sanction and assuming that sophistical practice does not, contrary to the teachings of Erasmus and Quintilian, have any bearing on moral development.[11]

Moreover, though I am gratified that the argument went nowhere, I would bring a different kind of charge against American colleagiate debating, especially the so-called "spread" debating, in which disputants conceive of arguments on either side not in terms of their impact on an audience but in terms of their position on a kind of "spread sheet" ("My objection to their Plan point II A is . . ."). Such debating is simply not rhetorical. If anything, it is rather more like dialectic, or the Scholastic disputation which provided a target for humanist reform. Like dialectic, it is less "oral"—less dependent upon circumstances, personality, consensus—than rhetorical disputation. Thus, I am not saying to the composition teacher, Get thee to a debate contest if you want to teach your students how to write or speak or think. Modern debate contests tend to be little more than formalist rituals in communication, eristic aimed at judges not juries.[12] American colleagiate debaters do not even practice good speak-

11. Richard Murphy, "The Ethics of Debating Both Sides," *Speech Teacher* 6 (1957): 1–9.

12. "Debaters, rushing to get in as much argumentation as possible, talked too fast. There was so much emphasis placed on research and evidence that one had to marry the library and sound like a bibliography to win." The description is offered by a former debater, who has made an interesting effort to apply forensic analysis as a conceptual model for critical thinking—without (here we part ways) throwing out or altering very much the structure and nature of contest debating: see Jack Perella, *The Debate Method of Critical Thinking* (Dubuque, 1987), 13. A similarly gloomy picture of British university debating was offered several years ago by George R.

ing, using rather a rapid-fire delivery which surely challenges even the judge's comprehension. These debaters, in sum, have forsaken the broadly humanistic nature of rhetorical *inventio*.

And so too have teachers of writing. Set free in 1915 of the responsibility to teach oral composition, they initially pursued a course that deflected any sustained attention whatsoever to rhetorical *inventio*. Their approach was, rather, a residue of high Victorianism with its positivistic view of sure knowledge, as two historians of rhetoric have recently claimed: since all that was important to know came from the sciences and from observation, "[i]nvention, in the classical sense of discovering probabilistic arguments, was rarely studied" and it became the job of rhetoric (or what we thought of as "rhetoric") merely "to record and transmit this knowledge with a minimum of distortion."[13] Just as for teachers of speech, so for teachers of writing disputation became a discrete specialty in the English classroom. Specifically, it became submerged—sunk, rather —within the argumentative genre, which was located with two other types (narrative and descriptive) in the hinterlands somewhere beyond the all important expository genre.

A summary of the charge I'm bringing against modern revivals of *inventio* in composition theory—oral as well as written, though for the remainder of this piece I shall concentrate on the latter—is simply this: modern revivals of *inventio* are at best partial because they have not been accompanied even on the most elementary level by the profoundly oral and profoundly contrarian protocol of traditional rhetoric, a disputatious emphasis much more readily available in Cicero than in Aristotle and currently only marginally available, at best, in composition classes outside schools of law. Thus in another way I am saying with Reed Way Dasenbrock, but without echoing his call for a "New Rhetoric," that the revival of rhetoric "is relevant; it isn't complete."[14]

Not long ago, I encountered a statement by Richard Enos in the *Rhetoric Society Quarterly* that "classical rhetoric has been, and once

Skorkowsky, Jr. "British University Debating," *Quarterly Journal of Speech* 56 (1971): 335–43.

13. Patricia Bizzell and Bruce Herzberg, eds., *The Rhetorical Tradition* (Boston, 1990), 903.

14. Reed Way Dasenbrock, "J. L. Austin and the Articulation of a New Rhetoric," *College Composition and Communication* 38 (1987): 303.

again is, a dominant theory for writing instruction."[15] I would like to believe that this is true. But in my reading I've found, with Dasenbrock, that the revival is incomplete and, to borrow a phrase from Erasmus, utterly contaminated by Aristotle. In the last fifteen years, there have been at least three important books urging the revival of classical rhetoric (as if the revolution has not yet been achieved) and at least one arguing forcibly against digging up all those old dry bones.[16] All four agree that rhetoric is the art of verbal persuasion, though all are not quite clear that argumentative discourse is of the essence in rhetorical writing. The point at issue, the *stasis,* in the argument, with three on one side and one on the other, is the flexibility of the rhetorical tradition. How adaptable is ancient rhetoric to the needs of the modern student? Not at all, argues the single work on the contra side. Ancient rhetoricians believed that truth exists and that the purpose of rhetoric is merely to verbalize it. This of course is a profound error, compounded by another error which pervades both sides. Both sides see rhetoric as a monolith, with Cicero differing little from Aristotle, and Quintilian differing little from both. As a monolith, this one is chipped and badly flawed. For a feature of the great rhetorical tradition—a feature which I would claim is essentially Ciceronian—has not been revived to any significant extent in our time. It is a feature which depends upon maintaining the vital intercon-

---

15. Richard Leo Enos, review of *Rhetoric and Praxis,* ed. Jean Dietz, *Rhetoric Society Quarterly* 17 (1987): 97. For additional material, the reader might also note the following two items. James J. Murphy offers a comprehensive survey of recent books and journals devoted wholly or in part to the restoration of rhetoric in the field of composition in his "Implications of the 'Renaissance of Rhetoric' in English Departments," *Quarterly Journal of Speech* 75 (1989): 335–43. An interesting review of the place of a related matter, *stasis,* in modern compositional theory is offered by Kathryn Rosser Raign, "Stasis Theory Revisited: An Inventional *Techne* for Empowering Students," *Focuses* 2 (Spring, 1989): 19–23.

16. The three are Robert J. Connors, Lisa S. Ede, and Andrea A. Lunsford, eds. *Essays on Classical Rhetoric and Modern Discourse* (Carbondale, Ill., 1984). Jean Dietz, ed. *Rhetoric and Praxis* (Washington, D.C., 1986). James J. Murphy, ed. *The Rhetorical Tradition and Modern Writing* (New York, 1982). Murphy, who is also a historian of rhetoric, noted in his important book on the medieval period that "the whole emphasis of both Greek and Roman rhetorical theory was on *inventio [heuresis]*"; see his *Rhetoric in the Middle Ages* (Berkeley, Calif., 1974), 218. But in discussing the rhetorical tradition and modern approaches to writing, he overlooks the vital interconnections between "heuristics" and disputation. The book opposing the revival of classical rhetoric is C. H. Knoblauch, and Lil Brannon, *Rhetorical Traditions and the Teaching of Writing* (Upper Montclair, N.J., 1984).

nections between rhetorical *inventio* and disputation, in the way and to the extent that Cicero, more than Aristotle, maintained them.[17]

A more recent entry into the dispute over the value of classical rhetoric reconceptualizes the terms of the argument while proposing aims not unlike the ones I propose. Kathleen E. Welch's book is an important effort to revive rhetoric as a mode of thinking and to reintegrate writing with speaking. To forward her effort she found it necessary to divide the scholarly universe into the bad guys (the "Heritage School," who start the history of rhetoric with Aristotle and see rhetoric as largely form and technology) and the good guys (the "Dialectical School," for whom rhetoric begins with the Sophists, of whom Plato really was, she insists, one).[18] But in spite of her compelling argument, a question remains: how shall we achieve these aims in the classroom? And beyond that another question: once these aims are achieved, what have we accomplished for our students' views of language and literature?

Surely my own argument provokes similar questions. So far I have done little more than point to Erasmus for pedagogy and Wilson for results. Let me try to be somewhat more specific.

I acknowledge that reviving Ciceronian *inventio* would require a couple of difficult undertakings, even beyond the one I suggested earlier, trying to fit a profoundly skeptical procedure into a nervously doubting age. First of all, we composition teachers would have to rid ourselves of the burden Alexander Bain imposed upon us a hundred years ago. Bain set up the laws of the four types of discourse that made the teaching of composition more formulary than inventive: expository, narrative, descriptive, and argumentative.[19] One's

---

17. True, Aristotle does mention rhetoric's function in inventing arguments on both sides of the question (1355a), but nowhere does he discuss or demonstrate, as Cicero does, the centrality of pro-con argumentation in *inventio;* see my chapter 2. Moreover, Aristotle's preference is for deliberative oratory, and he wrote his *Rhetoric* partly to correct the prevailing preference in other public speaking manuals of his time for the forensic; see 1354b.

18. Kathleen E. Welch, *The Contemporary Reception of Classical Rhetoric: Appropriations of Ancient Discourse* (Hillsdale, N.J., 1990).

19. Alexander Bain, *English Composition and Rhetoric.* New York, 1867. The trap of Bain's lessons, its ongoing influence, and its formalistic nature were vividly revealed when those founders of New Criticism, Cleanth Brooks and Robert Penn Warren, tried to write a *Modern Rhetoric* (1949) and found themselves unable to do little more with *inventio* than echo Bain's heuristic.

protocol becomes largely a recollection of the formal characteristics of each genre. We must junk those four types, because an even less than partial effort to restore *inventio* requires us to see all discourse as types of argument. Then we would have to take a second step, the more important one: we would have to see the forensic as paradigmatic of rhetorical thinking itself. If the first step has been somewhat achieved, the second one has not even been attempted (and efforts to find a New Rhetoric threaten to side-step it altogether).

Initial efforts to revive rhetoric in English departments twenty years ago did attempt to move beyond Alexander Bain and see all discourse as types of argument. The change came first in literary criticism, then in composition theory. Not quite a hundred years after Bain, Wayne Booth (in *The Rhetoric of Fiction,* Chicago, 1961) proposed that we view narrative as a type of argument and asked us to look at the novel as if it were a rhetorical act. His work was persuasive and revolutionary. Literary interpretation as the argumentative interaction of a reader with a text became a prominent hermeneutic; more than that, the act was moved to the very forefront of developments in modern rhetoric. In this way, the ancient union of rhetoric and literature, shattered for centuries, was restored, and in a positive way. In fact, it has been restored to such an extent that now the "literariness" of modern rhetoric has come in for some objection.[20] But I would take a different tack.

Perhaps because the revival of rhetoric in English departments was spurred in our age by literary critics it has slighted traditional rhetoric's forensic origins. (A similar oversight in speech departments may have been caused by that discipline's overwhelming preference for Aristotle, who among traditional rhetoricians rejected the centrality of forensic oratory.[21]) Booth, sounding much like Crassus at times in his *Vocation of a Teacher* (Chicago, 1988), argues

20. See George K. Hunter, "Rhetoric and Renaissance Drama," in *Renaissance Rhetoric,* ed. Peter Mack (New York, 1994) , esp. 104.

21. A classics seminar at Cornell in the 1920s laid the basis for Aristotelianism in early speech departments; see Raymond F. Howes, ed. *Historical Studies of Rhetoric and Rhetoricians* (Ithaca, N. Y., 1961). The heaviness of Aristotelianism was inveighed against by Edwin Black, in *Rhetorical Criticism: A Study in Method* (New York, 1965), who has recently returned to an at least moderated Aristotelianism as a critic; see his *Rhetorical Questions: Studies of Public Discourse* (Chicago, 1992). I treated some of these developments in my chapter 2. Aristotle's efforts to displace the forensic in rhetorical theory are made explicit in *Rhetoric* 1354b.

that rhetorical education is liberal education, for learning how to invent as well as how to judge arguments is learning how to think critically; ideally, the process draws on a wide variety of disciplines and so becomes a character-developing and expanding enterprise. Walter Jost, in a survey of Booth's writing, calls for a re-energizing of the *topical* mode of composition, and more explicitly than Booth allows debate a place in the scheme but without taking the step I believe is essential: making debate the conceptual model of rhetoric and actually requiring students to argue on both sides of a question.[22]

That idea has received only fleeting attention at best throughout the entire revival of rhetoric by composition theorists. In the mid 1960s, Edward Corbett, capping a movement begun by Hughes and Duhamel in composition theory, brought out his *Classical Rhetoric for the Modern Student,* in which he sought to put all discourse on an argumentative basis.[23] But Corbett is heavily Aristotelian in orientation with no more than a faint Ciceronian overlay.[24] Certainly Corbett made an extraordinarily insightful contribution to rhetoric and to composition theory. But in both he short-changed us somewhat by not giving Sophistical rhetoric its due or Ciceronian rhetoric its proper significance.

An advancement beyond Corbett's work, one that is even more antiquarian, is Winifred Bryan Horner's *Rhetoric in the Classical Tra-*

22. "Teaching the Topics: Character, Rhetoric, and Liberal Education," *Rhetoric Society Quarterly* 21 (1991): 1–16.

23. Richard E. Hughes and P. Albert Duhamel, *Rhetoric: Principles and Usage* (Englewood Cliffs, N. J., 1962). Edward P. J.Corbett, *Classical Rhetoric for the Modern Student* (New York, 1965).

24. Pro and con thinking is at least suggested, but in one place only (in "arrangement," the second part of Corbett's book, under "refutation"). And there is no indication that one should from the outset put an idea into opposing viewpoints. *Stasis* theory is present in his book, again part of the Ciceronian overlay. But it too is only briefly suggested (in the first part, on "invention"), and it is mainly associated with judicial discourse—or forensic oratory, one of the three traditional rhetorical genres—but with no indication that the forensic is either essential or paradigmatic. Too, it may be significant that in his brief appended history of rhetoric, Corbett gives no mention of the classical prominence of pro and con argumentation. It's conspicuously absent in his review of the Sophists and of Cicero, alas. Surely, if there is a feature that most profoundly distinguishes the Sophists and Cicero from other rhetoricians of their day, it is the *dissoi logoi* of the former, the *argumentum in utramque partem* of the latter.

dition (New York, 1988). Here there is plenty of room for recombining speaking with writing and for the restoration of Ciceronian *inventio*. Though she capitalizes on the former, the latter remains a missed opportunity. Horner revives the "five arts" of rhetoric, from invention to delivery, and she centers the inventive process in "exploring the subject" and "finding your thesis." She offers, in short, a setting that is a natural one for *controversia*. But disputation never rears its Janus heads, not even in a discussion of *stasis,* a process which is abstracted from the very matter—reasoning on both sides of the question—which in the classical tradition gave it meaning.

But here let me offer a further *correctio*. Even when well done debating both sides of a question, whether in a contest, in a classroom, or in private meditation, can lead merely to the self-serving contentiousness which plagues the legal profession or for that matter to the vacillation which so plagued Hamlet. For one thing, some moral truths, as the framers of our Constitution and as Cicero himself acknowledge, simply have to be taken as self-evident. For another, putting conflicting ideas together in a synthesis, particularly in a *suasory* or maieutic synthesis, the ultimate achievement of the protocol I advocate, is an extraordinarily difficult task.

But having said all that, I would nonetheless contend that at the very least reviving Ciceronian *inventio* offers the composer a different starting point, a new place to begin analysis or pre-writing. From antiquity, pro and con debating has been fundamental to rhetorical invention. If dialectic's function is to find a probable truth through formal validity, the function of rhetoric is to discern the available means of persuading people—and in both arts the ends are achieved by indifferently setting up equally probable arguments pro and con. Cicero, as I have suggested, became absorbed with the doctrine. The very last book which he wrote on the theory of rhetoric, his *Topics,* might look like a modern (or even Aristotelian) listing of the places of invention (or as a modern theorist might say, "heuristics"), but it was actually framed with a singular purpose: to make it possible for the orator to argue either side of any question. Couple that with the advice to argue both sides of all questions and these elementary tools become parts of an impartial protocol. Granted, a *speaker's* need is patent. Beginning one's composition with a kind of debate has obvious advantages for the orator, the advocate, the politician, the lawyer, who must be, like Ulysses, never at a loss. But is the starting point less advantageous for the writer?

One of the most practical efforts to reexamine and restore classical *inventio* to the English classroom is one of the three books on the "pro" side of the argument mentioned earlier, *Rhetoric and Praxis* (1986). This book clearly asserts that rhetoric is an art of "practical reasoning." It's almost equally clear that for the writers represented in this collection of essays *argumentative* discourse is the whole of rhetoric. It's much less clear whether the forensic is paradigmatic. The book was spurred by the profession's evident failures, after all our talk about a return to classical rhetoric, actually to use *inventio*: "[T]he most essential skill for developing and ordering thought for communication is rarely taught to college freshmen in a manner relevant to its use" (11). *Rhetoric and Praxis* gathers papers by distinguished rhetoricians aimed at exploring—all within an Aristotelian frame—such items as induction and deduction, the topics, the enthymeme, principles of causal explanation, and the ends of discourse. Not once is pro and con debating mentioned, though Prof. Schoeck's paper emphasizes the importance of forensic oratory and several writers are familiar with *stasis* theory. Discussion of the topics, such as the important one in Prof. Corbett's paper, seems always to overlook the purpose Cicero gave them.[25]

The precise role which pro and con debating could play in teaching writing was dramatized for me—in my imagination at least—when I reviewed a certain classroom exercise proposed in *Rhetoric and Praxis*. Prof. Hairston—who herself has written a stimulating handbook on composition—proposes in her paper that students be given the following argumentative assignment:

> . . . ask students to create a scenario that would help them develop . . . [a] paper based on science departments discriminating against women. One could do it like this: Imagine that you are a well-known woman physicist at a major state university and your department has asked you to write an article for the departmental bulletin for junior and senior

---

25. This is not to deny, however, the importance of the topics in understanding rhetoric or its history. See, for example, Michael C. Leff, "The Topics of Argumentative Invention in Latin Rhetorical Theory from Cicero to Boethius," *Rhetorica* 1 (1983): 23–44; Marc Cogan, "Rodolphus Agricola and the Semantic Revolutions of the History of Invention," *Rhetorica* 2 (1984): 163–94; and Donovan J. Ochs, "Cicero and Philosophic *Inventio*," *Rhetorical Society Quarterly* 19 (1989): 217–27.

honors students. At least half of those students are women, and you're
concerned that they may not know what to expect if they choose to go
on to graduate work in physics. (74)

Cicero—or at least Antonius and Crassus—would approach the task
much differently. Perhaps something like this. Imagine that a certain physics department—your local one, if appropriate—has been
charged with sex discrimination. Look carefully at what the charges
might be, using whatever topics seem appropriate. Too few women
on the faculty? Slow promotion of women faculty? Unfair recruit-
ment practices? Then, having gathered your evidence for the prosecution, build a case for the defense. Limited availability pools?
Women do not think early enough of a possible career in science?
Women faculty overemphasize undergraduate teaching at the expense of research and publication? Finally, having gathered your evidence for the defense, locate the *stasis:* How would you define sex
discrimination, does it exist, what harm does it cause, and to what
extent does it violate the law? (These are the four Ciceronian *stases;*
see Antonius in *De oratore,* II.xxiv-xxvi. 99–113, though as I've indicated the technique itself was more successfully used by Crassus.)
Having done this analysis, then, it seems to me, you're ready to perform the exercise the book proposes. Because, having done this analysis you no longer conceive of sex discrimination in the abstract. Like
a good humanist, you've reduced it to cases. Indeed, you may even
be prepared to write what certain humanists seemed to consider the
best form of advice, *suasion,* and, even more complicated, that mode
of suasion which consisted of a judicious and wary exfoliation of the
issues—depending, of course, on what you and your audience can
do or become.

Obviously, I have set my own sights somewhat lower than the
reformation of public debate, lower than the humanist aim of "living
well" or the Erasmian aim of *ethos.* I would seek simply an increased
richness in *inventio* through reviving disputation as a context for interpreting the principles of rhetoric. Related classroom exercises
would seem to follow of their own accord, as suggested forty years
ago by Kenneth Burke. I can hardly go beyond his practical advice:

> . . . were the earlier pedagogic practice of debating brought back into
> favor, each participant would be required, not to uphold just one position
> but to write two debates, upholding first one position and then the other.

Then, beyond this, would be a third piece, designed to be a formal transcending of the whole issue, by analyzing the sheerly verbal maneuvers involved in the placing and discussing of the issue. Such a third step would not in any sense "solve" the issue, not even in the reasonable, sociological sense of discovering that, "to an extent, both sides are right." Nor would we advise such procedures merely as training in the art of verbal combat. For though such experience could be applied thus pragmatically, the ultimate value in such verbal exercising would be its contribution toward the "suffering" of an attitude that pointed toward a distrustful admiration of all symbolism, and toward the attempt systematically to question the many symbolically-stimulated goads that are now accepted too often without question.[26]

Symbolism for Burke means all use of language. A well known lover of irony and antiquarianism, Burke in this essay avoids such terms as "nominalism" and "skepticism." Too, his "third step" invites a position similar to the one I have explored under "suasion" (though students of Burke may wish to point out that his actual goal lies in that word "transcending").

What are the chances of reviving educational disputation, of bringing back into favor "the earlier pedagogic practice of debating"? Slim, I would say, if we are speaking of oral disputation, about as slim as the chances of reviving teachers of elocution. Burke suggests, as has Erasmus, other ways whereby the procedures of disputation may be achieved (e.g., written debates, recantations, themes on disagreeable subjects). But, again, I have taken as my major task the pursuit of rhetoric's traditional protocol in the hopes that if our understanding of rhetoric would change, its possibilities in education might also change and grow. If anything I have targetted the attitudes of certain educators: those latter-day Scholastics who find a priori rules to cover every circumstance, those descendants of the Ramists who believe that rhetoric can actually be taught in handbooks, and those educators John Dewey complained about who forget that their students have bodies. But whether these attitudes can or will change hereafter, God knoweth, and not I.

Therefore I shall tell you a short merry tale. The famous Sophist Protagoras had an eager young student named Euathlus. Not only

26. Kenneth Burke, "Linguistic Approach to Problems of Education," *Modern Philosophies and Education,* the Fifty-fourth Yearbook of the National Society for the Study of Education (Chicago, 1955), 287.

was Euathlus eager, he was also wealthy, and he agreed to pay Protagoras a considerable sum for instruction in rhetoric. "In fact," said Euathlus, "I'll pay you half now, and the other half when I win my first case at law." "Agreed," said Protagoras. But, although Euathlus applied himself diligently and finished his course of studies, he kept postponing the actual trying of a case—perhaps because, Protagoras reasoned, he doesn't want to pay me the other half. So Protagoras decided to sue Euathlus for payment.

Hauling Euathlus before the judges, Protagoras said to him, "Now I've got you. For whether the judgment goes with you or against you, I'll have my money, every penny of it. For if you win, our agreement requires that you pay me the other half. A similar outcome obtains but on other grounds if *I* win, for my suit is for no more than the promised half."

Euathlus cleverly responded, "But I could easily avoid the trap you're setting, simply by hiring someone else to be my attorney. Actually, however, I prefer to plead my own case because there is no way I can lose. For if I win the case, I owe you nothing in the eyes of the law and the judgment of this court. And if you win, our agreement carries no weight, because I have not yet won my first case at law."

Wilson, who retells the tale (oddly substituting Pythagoras for Protagoras), concludes, "The Judges seeing the matter so doubtful and so hard to determine for either part [and] fearing to do amiss, left the matter raw without judgment for that time and deferred the same to another season. Thus you see that the young man being the scholar gave his master a bone to gnaw and beat him with his own rod which the master had made for his scholar's tail" (*Rule of Reason*, 213). Wilson's final remark is intended to bring the entire matter into focus as an example of a "trapping argument" *(antistrephon)* frequently used in disputation. But the implications of the story go well beyond exemplifying *antistrephon*. The tale was, moreover, a popular one in classical sources, sometimes told not about Protagoras but about Corax, the imputed founder of rhetoric.

The implications of the story, in fact, are not dissimilar to those of the famous "Cretan paradox" so brilliantly used by Wilson to bracket his logical theory. As we have seen, "All men are liars" is his example of a proposition set forth "without all ambiguity" used early in his book then echoed in its conclusion: "Epimenides, a man born in Crete, said that the people born in Crete were liars. Said he true or no?" He also concludes with another equally famous paradox, about the man who was warned in his sleep not to give credit to any of his dreams. The implications, I believe, of these stories, or argumentative tropes, when retold in a book on logic written by a humanist are clear. They're virtually the same implications the stories have when retold by the modern logician Gregory Bateson: the paradoxes impugn formalism. Where is the locus of meaning, whether in a legal contract or in a statement? In intention, character, circumstance, humanist rhetoricians would say—context, that is, or in Bateson's word, "frame."

The final point would seem to be that, particularly when we acknowledge the foolhardiness of a priori rules to cover every utterance, the extraordinary diversity of human communication becomes almost overwhelming. But that hardly distresses anyone who thinks of all uses of language as a kind of gesture, or performance. Language without parody, litotes, paradox? "Life would then," says Bateson, "be an endless interchange of stylized messages, a game with rigid rules, unrelieved by change or humor."[27]

Change and humor, variety and delight, set the conditions for "living well," the means for which, as humanists knew and know, could not be found in a handbook. As a subject to be taught "living well" is probably like the old elocution, or sophistry, or Socratic dialectic, or rhetoric: you can read about it but you can only actually learn it from other people.

27. Gregory Bateson, *Steps to an Ecology of Mind* (New York, 1972), 193.

Appendix A: Wilson's Logic and Rhetoric

In these reviews I shall quote and paraphrase Wilson (modernizing the spelling and punctuation) and try (without overusing parentheses) to make my own comments distinguishable.

The Rule of Reason, Containing the Art of Logic

This work was first published in 1551. The edition of Wilson's work which I have used is a reprint of the 1553 edition prepared by Richard S. Sprague (North-ridge, Calif., 1972).

The text opens with an "Epistle Dedicatory to King Edward VI" and two Latin poems, one written by Haddon and the other by Wilson himself. These are followed by the "Introduction."

Introduction

In the course of his introductory discussion, Wilson explains the differences between logic (by which he always means "dialectic") and sophistry (that is, false logic), and between logic and rhetoric. These differences are briefly discussed in my chapter on Wilson, wherein I also note the "logical" necessity of Wilson's inclusion of fallacies and false logic in the third section of his treatise. It is crucial to keep in mind—something not always well attended to by commentators on Wilson—that the setting and purpose of this treatise is disputation. The book is a debater's manual. There is nothing unusual about that, not for this period. What's unusual is that the work is in English—and was written by someone with clearly humanist preferences.

Wilson sets forth the primary "office" (that is, *officium,* duty) of logic in the following way: "To define the nature of every thing, to divide, to knit true arguments and unknit false" (12). That is, the primary office of this art is *analysis*—

particularly the analysis of matters called into controversy. Thus when Wilson divides logic itself into parts, it would seem natural to put *judgment* first, *invention* second (see my Figure 2):

> The first part standeth in framing of things aptly together and knitting words for the purpose accordingly, and in Latin is called *Iudicium.* / The second part consisteth in finding out matter and searching stuff agreeable to the cause, and in Latin is called *inventio.* (9)

Judgment is the logical counterpart of rhetorical *dispositio,* or arrangement; in both arts the procedure has to do with the framing of arguments.

Nonetheless, the order of the two—placing the study of arrangement *before* the study of discovery—must seem strange, at least to one of Wilson's audiences, the non-learned one with little knowledge of the long tradition of logical theory, so he offers some explanation:

> A reason is easier found than fashioned. . . . [E]very man's wit can give lightly a reason of diverse things without any learning at all, even by the instinct of nature, and yet not be able to set the same in order scholarlike, either to prove [pro] or to confute [con]. (9-10)

Iudicium is primary because it is more difficult. However, when later Wilson discusses *disputation* as the capstone of *inventio,* the discussion reveals the clearer reason why *judgment* comes first: analysis is always the first move in any debate.[1] Wilson is not talking about what we might mean by scientific inquiry or investigation. If he is talking about examining existing knowledge, the knowledge of which he speaks is that which has found its way into a dispute, a "cause," as he puts it (the word is synonymous with Cicero's *causa*). The disputant must examine the nature of the arguments that have already been or are likely to be brought to bear on the *quaestio.* Analysis is the first operation in debate and, therefore, the first formal division in Wilson's theory is:

Judgment

He begins with *questions:* the interrogatory form of the matter in dispute ("What is man?" "Is the study of Philosophy praiseworthy, or is it not?" 12). These, of course, are thesis-level questions which lurk in traditional wisdom and culture: that is, Wilson's age had traditional ways of defining "man" and traditional, if somewhat more controversial ways of deciding what was and was not "praiseworthy."

Wilson talks of how to transform the question into a declaration, or proposition, matters that might seem to belong under invention.

---

1. Wilbur Samuel Howell explores a different reason for the primacy of judgment: "This attitude [that a reason is easier found than fashioned] is a significant phenomenon in intellectual history. It really is a way of saying that subject matter presents fewer difficulties than organization, so far as composition is concerned. A society which takes such an attitude must be by implication a society that is satisfied with its traditional wisdom and knows where to find it. It must be a society that does not stress the virtues of an exhaustive examination of nature so much as the virtues of clarity in form"; *Logic and Rhetoric in England, 1500-1700* (Princeton, N.J., 1956), 23. The point is a good one but needs some qualification. The *whole* function of logic or dialectic is to prepare someone to argue well—specifically, to debate before an audience of experts, a point Howell recognizes without giving it the centrality it deserves.

The five *predicables,* or "common words," constitute the first means. These may be used to create or attempt to prove a true relationship between the subject and its predicate in a simple statement: e.g., if the subject is "man," there are five ways of predicating truth:

a. Genus   "animal"
b. Species   "Socrates"
c. Difference   "rational"
d. Property   "speaking"
e. Accident   "fear of God"

Logicians had learned from Aristotle that the perfect definition of "man" is "rational animal," a predication which places man in his genus and distinguishes him from others in that genus. It is also a predication which retrospectively justifies a "rule of reason," or any logic based on man's most significant differentia.[2] To think of Socrates as a "species" of man may only reveal how far from what we consider scientific thought this logic is. A "property" is a "natural proneness" (the prayer book of Wilson's time refers to God as a Being "whose property is always to have mercy"). An "accident" is something that may be removed without loss of "substance," without loss of something essential: e.g., the "soul" is a substance, equated among Scholastic logicians with "rational" in Aristotle's famous definition. Without his soul, man is only animal; though he is in peril of losing his soul if he loses his fear of God, until he suffers that peril the fear of God remains accidental.

Again, note that the emphasis is primarily on analysis. The logician is meant to use these predicables to examine any "is" question, or statement, and ask in effect, "Is it convertible? Is the predicate perfectly interchangeable with the subject?" Let us return to Wilson's voice:

> *Homo est animal ratione preditum, loquendi facultatem habens.* A man is a living creature endued with reason, having aptness by nature to speak. A man can not be, except he be a living creature endued with reason, and having aptness of nature to speak. [Note that this property, "to speak," is always linked with the difference, "reason"—not "thinking," which all animals may do.] The Accident notwithstanding is not necessarily spoken of the subject, but is there casually, and may be changed, as thus: *Homo est albus.* Some man is white. This Proposition may be afterward false, for he may be black, or alter his complexion some other way, so that the Accident is often altered, and another succeedeth in his room. (21)

The ten *predicaments,* or "general words," comprise the next matter. Again, by "word," Wilson is referring to verbal means of sorting ideas. Here he's looking for "words" that encompass the subject equally as well as they encompass the predicate.

---

2. By contrast, note the definition which Rorty calls the ironist's "morally relevant definition of a person": "something that can be humiliated" (*Contingency, irony, and solidarity* [Cambridge, Eng., 1989], 91). The ironist's definition would therefore require a totally different mode of argumentation from the one Wilson teaches. Irony, in Rorty's sense, is observable mainly in the responses humanists make to the failure of their own "reasonable" logic, as was seen in our discussion of Wilson, especially his discourse on usury: man may be a rational animal but reason alone is seldom enough to move his will.

If the key term in the predicables is, looking closely at the predicate, "relationship," in the predicaments the key term is "categories."[3] For now we are concerned with *classifying* both the subject and predicate. As the review of the predicables indicated, the most sensitive—that is, the trickiest when used on you in a debate—is the "accident," which an arguer might try to pass off for something essential *(Homo est albus)*. Therefore here in the predicaments the chief division is between the first, the "substance," and the others, which are all "accidents": the substance is the *sine qua non*, that without which the thing cannot be or is something else.

a. Substance	a man
b. Quantity	large
c. Quality	learned
d. Relative	son (husband, father)
e. Action	disputing
f. Passion	angry
g. When	now
h. Where	at Cambridge
i. Placement	standing
j. Clothing	caped

The list increasingly moves in the direction of rhetoric; the final items are particularly circumstantial and specific.

Wilson's most urgent advice, prefacing his discussion of the predicaments, concerns "ambiguity," the sorting out of substance from accident:

> Considering ambiguity breedeth error, most wariness ought to be used that the doubleness of no one word deceive the hearer. The cause of all controversy is either the not well understanding or else the wily using of words that in sense have double meaning. . . . If any word be used that hath a double meaning, restrain the largeness thereof and declare how you will have it taken by means whereof the fraud shall sooner be avoided, and the truth better known. (23–24)

The advice will have poignancy and relevance later, when we come to his discussion of "propositions."

Definition is the next subject: "There is nothing in all this whole art of logic more necessary for man to know than to learn diligently the definition and division of every matter that by reason may be comprehended" (37).

Division of course closely follows. The best division has two contraries (38).

Having covered these first four points under "questions" (predicables, predicaments, definition, and division) Wilson then provides a summary (43–45) explaining how to examine a question and set forth any matter plainly and with order. *Methodus* is Wilson's word for order, and by it his age meant not simply *ratio* but, increasingly, a particular kind of "method," a progression from the general to the specific—ask first whether a thing *is*, then ask about *what* it is, then inquire into its *parts*, its *causes*, *effects*, *adjuncts*, and *contraries*; finally ask whether there is an example of it, or ask which authorities attest to it (most of the "topics").

3. As Howell *(Logic and Rhetoric)* has noted, Wilson's predicaments are "equivalent to the famous ten categories analyzed in the first treatise of Aristotle's *Organon*" (19).

The second major division of *judgment* is *proposition*, which I treated at some length in my chapter 6, with an eye on Wilson's teaching about ambiguity, on his irrepressible sense of humor, and on his humanist tinkering with the elements of Scholastic logic.

Argument is the final major division: questions, propositions, then argument, by which Wilson means knitting propositions themselves into arguments.

Wilson defines an argument as "a way to prove how one thing is gathered by another, and to show that thing which is doubtful by that which is not doubtful" (56). This would seem to be, at long last, the very heart of the matter, of *judgment*. Yet the earlier material has given us the elementary tools of examining concepts and statements which at the same time, as he has shown, provide the materials of argument. Here Wilson means in particular the forms of argument, and because the emphasis is on *form* we begin to see further reasons why *judgment* and rhetorical *disposition*, "arrangement," were thought of as invoking some of the same processes:

1. Perfect syllogisms
2. Imperfect syllogisms: the enthymeme
3. Induction
4. Example
5. Sorites
6. Dilemma
7. De consequentiis: moving from antecedent to consequent too rapidly. (This near-fallacy overlaps the enthymeme and leads directly to Wilson's next section:)

Invention

Here we find again the topics, or as Wilson prefers "places." "A Place is the resting corner of an argument or else a mark which giveth warning to our memory what we may speak probably, either in one part or the other [i.e., pro or con], upon all causes that fall in question" (90).

Wilson's twenty-four places are little more than a re-listing of matters already discussed under other heads: e.g., substance, accidents, definition, predicables and predicaments. Here they are to be used more in *creating* arguments than in *analyzing* them—but this is a matter of degree only, for the one operation cannot of course be perfectly distinguished from the other. The Ramists later would indeed try to distinguish them and to compress the number of places into ten. Even later theoreticians, modern professors of writing, have attempted a further refurbishing of the topics, which they call "heuristics."

But both of these groups—the Ramists and the moderns—miss the point, which is Wilson's overriding point, about the traditional places, as emphatically shown in the next major head, the very destination of his discussion of invention, *disputation*. Wilson's long definition of the matter brings his entire book into focus:

> That is called a disputation, or reasoning of matters, when certain persons debate a cause together, and one taketh part contrary unto another, the one answering and denying, and the other still apposing [*sic*] and confirming the cause so earnestly as he can, whereupon after hard hold and long debating the truth either appeareth or else they rest both upon one point, leaving the matter to be adjudged of the hearers upon the knowledge of both their minds fully had and perceived. In all which matching and tugging together, this

would be observed that every of them keep their own standing. That is to say, the [Negative—Wilson's word is "answerer"—] must still use flat denying and shake off such light reasons as are alleged, by the help of Judgment, which is the first part of Logic, wherein are diverse rules and lessons set forth especially for that purpose. The [Affirmative—Wilson's word is "apposer"—] must fight with weapon of his wit, and still build up that which the [Negative] doth overthrow, never leaving to follow and confirm his cause till he have brought the other to some such point as he shall not well be able to avoid. And the rather to excel in this behalf, he must use the second part of Logic, which is called Invention, where he may have arguments at will, if he search the places, which are none other thing but the store house of reason and the fountain of all wisdom. (153)

In sum, *judgment* is for the Negative in the debate, *invention* for the Affirmative. And the debate doesn't need to end in the victory of one side over the other. It can, in the manner of suasion, leave "the matter to be adjudged of the hearers." The analytical work of the Negative, the primary analytical work of any debater whether seeking to attack or to defend, is, as noted earlier, another reason why *iudicium* comes first in theory.

The Places of False Conclusions, or Deceitful Reasons

The third and final section of the book is on the traps and snares of debating. The section has two divisions: fallacies (e.g., the false syllogism) and trapping arguments (e.g., the dilemma).

It was a convention of the time to append logical theory with a discussion of "sophistry," though the convention usually required justification: "To some men," Wilson says, "these places of craft that follow may seem strange, and yet even in weighty matters the wicked have derived their subtle defences from these deceitful corners." Best, then, to set forth these particular debating tactics so they "may be avoided and better known" (157). Wilson, moreover, indicates that this final section of his treatise is something far more significant than an appendix. He shows rather, in spite of his earlier teaching that logic has only two parts, that he views this third section as on a par with the first on judgment and the second on invention. This equivalence is established not only by what he says but also by his use of a certain Elizabethan typographical convention: the conclusion of each major section progresses funnel-like down the page, conventional Elizabethan typography for visually marking the end of a section. For example, section 2, on invention, concludes:

. . . but for this whole matier of aunswering to any argument, I dooe shewe my minde
at large nexte and immediately before the rehearsall, of false
conclusions, or deceiptfull argumentes, which do fol-
owe in the next page, where I speake of confu-
tacion, and therefore I surceasse to talke a-
ny ferther in this matier, least that
with double inculcacion of one
thing, I maie bryng tedi-
ousnesse vnto all
menne.[4]

---

4. Sprague, whose edition I am using, apparently failed to see the significance of the convention and did away with the funnelling effect. My version here follows the original.

At the first of this third and final part, Wilson shows his "mind at large" by pointing out—before his rehearsal of the subject (fallacies and trapping arguments)—that, having discussed formal validity, he will now discuss "deceitful arguments." His chief point, however, one reinforced by Elizabethan typography, is that this subject pertains to both sides of the debate. It spans both the Negative and the Affirmative—and, accordingly, both Judgment and Invention. Obviously, debate is, once more, the whole point of the treatise itself.

With a discussion of "trapping arguments," Wilson's book ends, its final words marching funnel-like down the page to the very last sentence: "God be praised."

The Art of Rhetoric, for the use of all such as are studious of Eloquence

The work was first published 1553. The edition I have used is Mair's (Oxford, Eng., 1909), which reprints the 1560 edition; for this choice see note 21 in my chapter 6.

Again, I have modernized the spelling and punctuation, paraphrased, and made parenthetical and bracketed remarks. Main headings are in italics. All quotations from Wilson are cited by page numbers in Mair's edition and placed in quote marks.

The text opens with four dedicatory poems in Latin. These are followed by an "Epistle Dedicatory, to the Earl of Warwick"; a "Prologue to the Reader"; and a preface entitled "Eloquence First Given by God, After Lost by Man, and Last Repaired by God Again."

The First Book

Wilson begins the text proper by defining rhetoric: "Rhetoric is a learned or rather an artificial declaration of the mind in the handling of any cause called in contention that may through reason largely be discussed" (1). Thus Wilson, following Cicero, characterizes rhetoric as a way whereby one may learn an artful ("artificial") means of speaking (later he includes writing in its purview). Again, as Wilson makes emphatically clear from the outset, rhetoric is for controversy—for causes "in contention"—a feature, I have continually insisted, that has been overlooked in modern discussions of rhetoric and attempts at its revival. Wilson also maintains a distinction he offered in the *Logic,* that rhetoric is for controversial matters that may with reason be "largely . . . discussed"—that is, presented before a mixed audience of experts and non-experts alike.

> *Its matter:* two sorts of questions
>> *Infinite* (thesis): e.g., "whether it be best to marry or to live single" (1)
>> *Definite* (hypothesis): e.g., "Whether now it be best here in England for a Priest to marry or to live single" (1).
>> "Things generally spoken without all circumstances are more proper to the Logician, who talketh of things universally without respect of person, time, or place" (2). But the orator, though focussed on circumstance, must consider both the thesis and the hypothesis.
> *Its end:* to teach, to delight, to persuade.

Wilson is often given credit for encouraging the plain style in English, through his vivid affirmations of it as something necessary to the first end, teaching:

> [A]n Orator must labor to tell his tale that the hearer may well know what he meaneth and understand him wholly, the which he shall with ease do if he utter his mind in plain words such as are usually received and tell it orderly without going about the bush. (2)

But plainness is not the major theme of Wilson's book. Indeed, as he insists, all three "ends" coincide and work best in harmony, and so must the styles associated with each. Wilson, moreover, spends most of his time discussing—and demonstrating—the importance of "delighting" one's hearers, e.g:

> [E]xcept men find delight they will not long abide: delight them, and win them, weary them and you lose them forever. And that is the reason that men commonly tary the end of a merry play and cannot abide the half hearing of a sour checking Sermon. (3)

Wilson will return to the point, in a major way, later. Note the early reference to preachers, one of Wilson's two chief examples of speakers. The other is lawyers. But he goes on to argue that rhetoric is not simply for speaking. It is for writing as well.

His next major head, rhetoric's *means of attainment* has three subdivisions: nature, art, practice. Art, he argues, is a surer guide than nature because art helps us see what we do, and therefore those that have good natural wit may be helped by art—and, of course, by practice, especially imitation of the masters of speaking and writing. This entire argument concerning nature, art, and practice is lifted from *De oratore* I.xxxii.144–148; II.xxxv.148–151. However, in this source (as in Quintilian) writing is put to the service of eloquence. For Cicero (as for Quintilian) writing is essentially a means of *achieving* eloquence, it is not necessarily a *medium* of eloquence, as it is for Wilson. Of course, the written and printed word was a culturally far more important medium in the sixteenth century. Therefore, given this not so subtle difference, it might appear that the ancients, for whom oratory was singularly eminent, could offer a more integral theory, one in which all five offices (invention, disposition, style, memory, delivery) "go together"—as Cicero, Quintilian, and Wilson himself say they must.

How, for example, could "delivery" go together with the other offices if one is producing a written or printed document? Only if, I would conjecture, one conceives of language as fundamentally *oral*. This is a conception which I believe underlies all humanist rhetoric, Wilson's most definitely included: one conceives of the written document as something being spoken by someone to someone, like all of the written examples used throughout Wilson's book, written language attempting to do the work of spoken language.[5] Part of the importance of Wilson's book, as a modern historian of language has argued, is that it maintains not simply the connections between rhetorical composition and forensic, or lawyerly, thinking but also between

---

5. Cf. Thomas Cole's definition in *The Origins of Rhetoric in Ancient Greece* (Baltimore, 1991), 1. Wayne A. Rebhorn has an interesting discussion of possible linkages between *De oratore*, Castiglione, and Wilson in the matter of delivery; see his "Baldesar Castiglione, Thomas Wilson, and the Courtly Body of Renaissance Rhetoric," *Rhetorica* 11 (1993): 241–274.

prose and speech.[6] (Moreover, that language is *not* somehow *spoken* was beginning to be a novel and controversial idea in Wilson's time.[7])

Wilson then briefly reviews *five things to be considered in an orator:* invention, disposition, elocution, memory, delivery or "utterance." For invention, he advises, one should also call on the "places of Logic," particularly whenever one seeks to teach the "truth" in proving his "cause." Wilson is not at all constrained by the overlapping of logic and rhetoric. He does not bother initially to discuss or even mention the uniquely rhetorical places; these come later. Too, he closely associates disposition, or arrangement with purpose, or intention: how you place your arguments depends upon the purpose they are meant to serve. To turn the teaching on Wilson, consider briefly the ways in which his own disposition—the apparently unorderly distribution of the five offices of this art into three books, the loose overlapping of logic and rhetoric—serves a major part of his stated intention, to show that all these offices "go together." At the same time he also shows that the art cannot be conceived of systematically. But could any profoundly oral art be so conceived, even allowing for the humanists' apparent abhorrence of system?

After these introductory remarks, Wilson begins to move more directly into *invention,* the chief subject of this first book. His first division of the subject is the *four causes:* honest, "filthy," such as speaking against "our own conscience" or withstanding "an upright truth," doubtful, that is "half honest and half unhonest," or "trifling," such as Ovid's praise of a nut or Vergil's praise of a gnat (7–8). One could add Erasmus's praise of folly, though Wilson doesn't, preferring instead to refer vaguely to some contemporary who praised a goose. These four causes are lifted from the *Rhetorica ad Herennium* I.iii.5. Philosophically troubling, and often excluded from more purely Ciceronian theory (humanists of the time, unlike their medieval predecessors, knew that the *ad Herennium* was not by Cicero), the inclusion of these causes at least underscores the argumentative perversity of the subject. Too, technically they provide an initial analysis of a matter which is usually encompassed under or closely linked with *stasis* and which is also pursued under the next implied

6. Janel M. Mueller, *The Native Tongue and the Word* (Chicago, 1984), 350. Mueller argues that "the grounding for all of Wilson's proceedings as a rhetorician" leads to his taking "a combative approach to the negative facets of his audience's psychology"—leads, that is, forward and backward to forensic oratory as the conceptual model of rhetoric. Wilson in his *Rhetoric* speaks of winning an audience, of "getting the overhand," a phraseology Mueller notes he regularly applies "not just to the opposing parties in an argument or to tactics for dealing with judges—the ordinary classical contexts—but generalizes it to represent the relation of a speaker to any hearers, or a writer to any readers" (361). Wilson's adversariness is also, Mueller believes, connected with his general Protestant sense of man's divided self—his, as Sidney put it, "infected will" and "erected wit" (372).

7. In *The Courtier,* Count Ludovico responds rather hotly to the idea that some words are better for writing, some for speaking: "[I]t is a strange matter to use those words for good in writing that are to be eschewed for naughty in every manner of speech, and to have that which is never proper in speech to be the properest way a man can use in writing. Forsomuch as (in my opinion) writing is nothing else but a manner of speech that remaineth still after a man hath spoken or (as it were) an image, or rather the life of the words"; Hoby translation (modernized), ed. Ernest Rhys (London, 1937), 50 .

heading: *[Audience]*. "[C]onsider the time, the place, the man for whom we speak, the man against whom we speak, the matter whereof we speak, and the judges before whom we speak . . . always . . . use whatsoever can be said to win the chief hearers' good will and persuade them to our purpose" (8). The judicial model invariably becomes salient in Wilson's discussion from time to time. He always speaks of rhetoric as a means of advancing one's cause, usually in disputations in courts of law. His chief example in this section is, in fact, lawyers.

One must decide, he continues in his discussion of audiences, what will serve one's cause best—establishing one's own good will before the audience or appealing to the audience's reason or emotions (i.e., *ethos, logos, pathos*), how much or how little to say, whether to emphasize confirmation or confutation. All these decisions depend on the nature of the audience. Or, rather, on the nature of the "judges," Wilson's own word.

The next division continues the judicial metaphor: *three kinds of causes, or orations*. By calling these orations "causes," Wilson risks confusion between these types and the "four causes" listed above. He means that these three causes encompass the four listed above, just as those four offered an initial classificatory analysis of the "question" (whether infinite [thesis] or definite [hypothesis]). Further, he points out that these three kinds of orations are themselves not really distinct, for any one will almost invariably perform the functions of the other—just as all center in the task of advancing a *causa*, or "case," before judges.

The *demonstrative* cause consists of praise or blame, first of a *person:* one invents through using such rhetorical places as a person's life, ancestry, upbringing. Here Wilson offers *an example of commending a noble personage:* a commendation of the "lately departed" Henry Duke of Suffolk and Lord Charles his brother. These were the Brandons, mentioned in my chapter 6, who were Wilson's students. Wilson breaks off the commendation, in order not to "renew great sorrow to many" (16), and goes on to note that the same places and oratorical parts that are used in praising a great man may be used in dispraising an evil one.

Such blatant use of a real example in a book that first appeared only two years after the death of Wilson's young students, an example which Wilson closes off by stating that the same tactics could be used in dispraising an evil person, shows the tactician's stunning removal from the principles he teaches, if it does not even tip his hand. Later we shall note another example, of comforting the boys' mother.

Praise or blame may also be assigned a person's *deed*. The topics, or places, to be used are whether the deed is honest, possible, easy, as well as such circumstances as who, what, when, and where, to be used either for praise or dispraise. Wilson then offers *an example of commending King David, for killing great Goliath.* Following the example, a brief analysis reveals the circumstantial places that were used. The example itself seems to come out of left field. However, Wilson emphasizes the patriotic nature of David's deed—he ventured his life "for the love of his Country, for the maintenance of justice, for the advancement of God's true glory, and for the quietness of all Israel" (22)—and thus the example is not removed from what I take to be the center of one of Wilson's intentions.

Finally praise or blame may be applied to a *thing,* such as virtue, vice, etc. The places of confirmation are to consider whether the thing is honest, profitable, and easy or hard to be done. Useful too, are the "places of logic": definition, cause, effects, etc.—which should probably be used first, because how can you tell if a thing is honest until you've first defined it? Next Wilson offers *an example in commendation of Justice, or true dealing* (23). The example develops the argument that justice is a law of nature given by God, on which man's law is itself predicated.

The example is a curious one for a book on rhetoric, though it grows directly out of Wilson's interest in law and his country. The example is a sermonette whose sombreness and weightiness contrast strikingly with the admission of those "trifling" causes mentioned earlier. More significantly, the example is almost totally devoid of the circumstances which in Wilson's own terms distinguish rhetorical discourse from the more abstract logical discourse. It is on an abstract thesis. It seems to have only a vague, general audience and no real occasion. Nonetheless, the piece is pervaded with ruling-class values (e.g., "no one man could long hold his own if laws were not made to restrain man's will," 26) on the side of which Wilson squarely places himself. Too, the piece lays the basis for the next example, a deliberative argument to a young man concerning law as a career.

The second cause is *deliberative:* advice-giving, including persuading or dissuading, entreating or rebuking, exhorting or dehorting, and commending or comforting. The deliberative places, where they do not simply overlap the demonstrative places, involve one in a consideration of the virtues. An example is pursued through the various places, and virtues, of *advising a young man to study the laws of England.* As I have indicated elsewhere, this sustained example offers a good glimpse of the pro-con thinking which pervades humanist rhetoric.[8] Then comes an extended, unbroken example: *an epistle to persuade a young gentleman to marry, devised by Erasmus* (the letter to Mountjoy).

Erasmus's famous letter is used to exemplify the deliberative topics—e.g., honest, profitable, pleasant, and necessary—places which Erasmus calls by name in the opening of his epistle, recurs to throughout, and concludes by summarizing. Such use would seem to second Erasmus's argument that the letter was only an exercise and meant to be instructional in the principles of composition. So it was. But as I argued in chapter 4, wrenching the letter from its context makes other issues salient, such as the importance of contextual analysis itself. Wilson does not provoke these other issues (in fact, contextual analysis becomes more important in connection with a later example). Nonetheless, the letter's anti-clerical, anti-celebate arguments seem much at home in this book, with its militantly Protestant author. More importantly, this letter, like most examples in Wilson's book, is addressed to the wealthy and powerful. Within *that* context the letter underscores Wilson's own interest in power as well as his own personal aim.

Let us note, too, that Wilson's translation of Erasmus is *lively,* it has *voice,* it sounds like someone speaking, a desideratum of the very rhetoric the humanists cherished. What I mean by that final remark can be clarified by juxtaposing Wilson's translation with the famous Toronto edition. Let us look at some of the passages which upset Church authorities:

First Erasmus:

8. In *Donne, Milton, and the End of Humanist Rhetoric* (Berkeley, Calif., 1985), 134–36.

Puella dolore victa peccavit, stultarum muliercularum, aut stultorum Monachorum impulsu sese praecipitem dedit. Tu major natu, virum te esse memineris necesse est. Illa majoribus suis commori voluit, tu ne moriantur, operam dabis. (Leclerc, I: 423 [E])

Now Toronto:

The girl [Mountjoy's sister, who had joined a nunnery upon the death of her parents] did wrong because she was overcome with grief; at the instance of foolish women or foolish monks she threw herself into it headlong. You who are the elder must remember that you are a man. She has wished to die together with her ancestors; you will make sure that they do not die. (CWE, 25: 144)

And finally Wilson:

[S]he being but a girl and overcome with sorrow for loss of her Mother took the wrong way, she cast her self down headlong and became a Nun at the earnest suit either of foolish women or else of doltish Monks. But you being much elder must evermore remember that you are a man. She would needs die together with her ancestors, you must labor that your ancestors shall not die at all. (61)

The following examples are also good illustrations of prolepses—a rhetorical figure whose efficacy depends upon the rhetorician's skill in pro-con reasoning. First Erasmus:

At ipse Christus, inquies, beatos pronunciavit, qui sese castrarunt ob regnum Dei., Non rejicio auctoritatem, sed sententiam interpretor. Primum arbitror hoc Christi dogma, ad ea tempora postissimum pertinere, quibus oportebat Ecclesiasten ab omnibus mundi negociis quam maxime expeditum esse. Cursitandum erat per omnes terras, imminebat undique persequutor. Nunc is est rerum ac temporum status, ut nusquam reperias minus inquinatam morum integritatem, quam apud conjugatos. (Leclerc, I: 419[D])

Now the Toronto edition:

"But Christ himself," you will say, "declared blessed those who became eunuchs for the kingdom of God's sake." I do not reject the authority of this statement, but I offer an interpretation of its meaning. First, I consider that this dogma of Christ pertains to those times when it was right for an ecclesiastic to be kept free as possible from all worldly affairs. He had to run about from one country to another, threatened by persecutors on all sides. But nowadays conditions and times are such that you would not find anywhere a less defiled purity of morals than among the married. (CWE, 25: 137)

Now here is Wilson's translation:

Nay, but (you will say) Christ himself hath counted them blessed, which have gelded themselves for the kingdom of God. Sir, I am content to admit the authority, but thus I expound the meaning. First, I think that this doctrine of Christ, did chiefly belong unto that time when it behoved them chiefly to be void of all cares and business of this world. They were fain to travel [the sixteenth century word is also "travail"] into all places, for the persecutors were ever ready to lay hands on them. But now the world is so that a man can find in no place the uprightness of behavior less strained than among married folk. (50)

In fact, the strength of argument to a heterosexual male seems much clearer in Wilson's translation than in Toronto's translation of Erasmus:

Hoc quod in tuo corpore vel arescit, vel magno etiam salutis periculo corrumpitur: quod in somnis elabitur, homo erat, si modo tu esses homo. (I: 420[C])

Toronto:

That which withers away within your body, or is destroyed at great risk to your health, or is ejected in sleep, would have been a human being if only you had been human. (25: 138)

And finally Wilson:

That self same thing that either withereth and drieth away in the body, or else putrifieth within thee, and so hurteth greatly thy health, yea that self same which falleth from thee in thy sleep, would have been a man if thou thy self haddest been a man. (53)

Following the letter Wilson returns to the subject of advice-giving, or deliberative, oratory by discussing *exhortation.* He lists first certain places which Erasmus advises us to use in exhortatory letters (63; cf. CWE, 25: 79). In fact, throughout this discussion Wilson must have had Erasmus's book on letter-writing at his elbow. As with Erasmus at this point in the discussion "moving pity" becomes an important topic; later Wilson will bring up the subject again, under *amplification.*

After a short excursus into *commending,* Wilson discusses *comforting* and offers *an example of comfort,* the longest (20 pp.) example in the book. Derrick finds the example imitative of Erasmus's "Declamation on Death."[9] Too, the example is most likely a "real" one, for it is one which Wilson himself claims he used to comfort the duchess of Suffolk upon the loss of her two sons. Whether letter or "declamation" the example again shows Wilson at work as a rhetorician—and, as I have argued, reveals both of his intentions in this book. Too, the piece shows us the kinds of curious moves and stances the period probably found persuasive. E.g., in one of the many examples of prolepses, Wilson argues:

But you will say, "My children might have lived longer, they died young. " Sure it is by man's estimation they might have lived longer, but had it been best for them, think you, to have continued still in this wretched world, where Vice beareth rule and Virtue is subdued, where God is neglected, his laws not observed, his word abused, and his Prophets that preach the judgment of God almost everywhere condemned? If your children were alive and by the advise of some wicked person were brought to a brothel house, where enticing harlots lived and so were in danger to commit that foul sin of whoredom, and so led from one wickedness to another, I am assured your grace would call them back with labor, and would with exhortations induce them to the fear of God and utter detestation of all sin, as you have full often heretofore done, rather fearing evil to come than knowing any open fault to be in either of them. Now then seeing God hath done the same for you himself that you would have done for them if they have lived, that is, in delivering them both from this present evil world—which I count none other then a brothel house and a life of all naughtiness—you ought to thank God highly that he hath taken away your two sons, even in their youth, being innocents both for their living and of such expectation for their [future] that almost it were not possible for them hereafter to satisfy the hope in their age which all men presently had conceived of their youth. (72–73)

9. Thomas J. Derrick, ed., *Arte of Rhetorique by Thomas Wilson* (New York, 1982), 582.

Reading that passage and similar gloomy ones "sparpled" throughout the oration, one begins to appreciate the characterization of Wilson as Henrician rather than Elizabethan, or as one whose gravity might find its counterpart in that movement rapidly becoming popular in Wilson's time, Puritanism. But to pursue that argument is to read the piece biographically, not rhetorically—to use it in a way that Wilson at the conclusion of the example urges that rhetorical matters *not* be used, flatly and literally rather than "according as the time, place, and person shall most of all require" (86). Erasmus, we recall, pressed the same point over and over. It is here that Wilson makes us aware of the importance of contextual analysis. His use of an example which might have actually been employed—perhaps even only a few months before its appearance in this book—reminds us again that we are now in the tactician's classroom. We must, and perhaps should therefore only, note his skillfulness in using popular sentiments.[10] However, as with Erasmus, the various issues have unstable if not vertiginous borders. For the case I have built concerning Wilson's intentions (in chapter 6), a vital issue is that this discourse too is addressed to the wealthy and powerful.

The final kind of cause or oration is *judicial:* "The whole burden of weighty matters and the earnest trial of all controversies rest only upon Judgment" (86). Throughout my study of humanist rhetoric, I have insisted that judicial oratory, or the trial in a court of law, is the conceptual model of that theory. Wilson, though he places this genre last in his list, nonetheless has framed his entire theory in such a way that lawyerly reasoning remains central. Review his definition of *rhetoric,* and note too what was earlier said about his use of the term *judgment* both in this book and in the *Logic.* Wagner has said, in commenting on Wilson's definition of *rhetoric,* "The words 'called in contention' need not be taken literally. The sentence following and the general content of the book indicate that Wilson does not restrict rhetoric or oratory to contentious (i.e. forensic) causes."[11] True, Wilson does not *restrict* rhetoric to the forensic mode, but I would argue that he uses the forensic as his conceptual model for all of rhetoric—as did Cicero. Increasingly throughout the discussion of judicial oratory, *wariness*—keeping an eye on the adversary through pro and con reasoning, the very quality which in the *Logic* he insisted is "ever thought great wisdom"—becomes prominent.

He discusses the doctrine of *stasis:*

---

10. That the great Haddon himself must have used a similar argument is suggested by Wilson later, in discussing figures of speech. The figure is *rogatio,* which Wilson defines as "asking other and answering ourself": "As when Doctor Haddon had comforted the Duchess of Suffolk's Grace for her children, and had said they were happily gone, because they might have fallen hereafter, and lost that worthy name, which at their death they had: at last he bringeth in the mother, speaking motherlike in her children's behalf of this sort and answereth still to her sayings. 'But all these evils whereof you speak,' quoth he [imagining the mother's argument], 'had not chanced.' 'Yet, [he responds] such things do chance.' 'Yet not always.' 'Yet full oft.' 'Yet not to all.' 'Yet to a great many.' 'Yet they had not chanced to mine.' 'Yet we know not.' 'Yet I might have hoped.' 'Yet better it had been to have feared'" (184).

11. Russell H. Wagner, "Thomas Wilson's *Arte of Rhetorique,*" *Speech Monographs* 27 (1960): 13 n.

Not only is it needful in causes of judgment to consider the scope whereunto we must level our reasons and direct our invention, but also we ought in every cause to have a respect unto some one special point and chief article, that the rather the whole drift of our doings may seem to agree with our first devised purpose. For by this means our judgment shall be framed to speak with discretion and the ignorant shall learn to perceive with profit whatever is said for his instruction. (86)

Note, too, that once more "judgment" is the orator's as well as the audience's, a linkage which further reenforces the connection between "disposition" in rhetoric and "judgment" in logic—or the similarities between compositional and interpretive procedures. Wilson covers the doctrine of *stasis* in considerable detail, drawing on *ad Herennium,* Quintilian, and *De inventione.* The point is to find the point.

And then Wilson comes down very hard on sticking to the point (87). Strictly applied, the instruction in *stasis,* finding the point and then sticking to it, could rule out the techniques of suasion. But Wilson, as we shall see, intended no such strict application.

Again, and throughout the book, lawyers become the object of several satirical and colleagial jabs: e.g., they can always find ambiguity in the law or a document— "In all this talk I except always the good lawyers," Wilson says, "and I may well spare them, for they are but a few" (96).[12] Wilson may also have had in mind a distinction between "lawyers" and "civilians." It was to the latter group that he belonged; I considered the distinction in discussing Wilson's book on usury. Here only one, fairly short, example is offered: *an example of an oration judicial, to prove by conjectures, [the murder of a wealthy farmer by a soldier].* Uniquely, the example is all pro, with no con, no *prolepses* even—kinds of wariness which, we may assume, were preparatory to this "artificial declaration of the mind" in the handling of this contentious cause. Wilson concludes this first book by discussing two *stases* unique to judicial oratory, the "legal" and the "juridical."

The second book

The first subject concerns "framing" an oration, which would *seem* to be "disposition," so much so that such a notable commentator as T. W. Baldwin has assumed that this entire second book is on disposition.[13] But Wilson is still talking about inventing "stuff" to go into the various parts of an oration, and he can't do that without explaining what those parts are. Thus, this book continues the discussion of invention, though it gives way finally to a discussion of disposition. Wilson begins by discussing the parts of orations "but especially such as are used in Judgment" (99)—that is, judicial oratory, his primary model. The parts are *entrance,* which might involve approaching the subject directly or indirectly—here Wilson shows it's possible to ignore his earlier advice, that there are times when it's wise

12. Wilson must have liked the pattern of this joke, for he uses it again in his *Discourse upon Usury:* "Excepted always, in all this my speech against women, all good women—and yet they may be spared, for they all are very few indeed, and may be easily packed up, all the whole pack of them, in a very small room" (297).

13. *Shakespere's Small Latine and Lesse Greeke* (Urbana, 1945), 2: 42. Wagner effectively answers the interpretation in "Thomas Wilson's *Art of Rhetorique,*" 17n.

to actually tell a tale of Robin Hood to win over your hearers; *narration,* the background of the case; *division* of "such principal points whereof we purpose fully to debate" (109); *proposition,* a pithy sentence or two that contains the substance of the matter; *confirmation* and *confutation,* wherein the places of logic offer much help; and *conclusion.*

Next he discusses *the figure amplification.* Amplification comes up because it is naturally related to what Wilson has said about the importance of moving the affections in the conclusion of a speech. He calls it a "figure" because, like all figures, it involves something new or strange, something unlike common talk. Yet it is not a division of style but a division of invention. For one thing, it involves *copiousness.* As to be expected Wilson makes much use of Erasmus—not only the *De copia* but, as Derrick has shown (see 599, passim.), Erasmus's treatise on preaching, *Ecclesiastes, sive de ratione concionandi.* Indeed, thoughout he makes use not only of Erasmus but also of some of Erasmus's own sources, such as, again, the *ad Herennium.* Too, here and in Book 3 he also makes use of Richard Sherry's recent (1550) book on schemes and tropes.[14] Finally, no sooner has Wilson offered a point about using the places of logic in amplifying than he reiterates the thoroughly traditional point that "the beauty of amplifying standeth most in apt moving of affections" (130).

Two further divisions are made in the subject: *of moving pity* and *of delighting the hearers and stirring them to laughter.* "Moving pity" had already been discussed. The lesson is brought back in order to juxtapose it with "delighting": "But now that I have taught men to be sorry, I will attempt again to make them merry" (134). Just previously, he had argued that amplification itself can be achieved by juxtaposing opposites, and "pity" and "delight" are precise opposites.

In this longest section of the entire book Wilson gives countless examples of humor. Perhaps one, a type beloved of Shakespeare, will suffice:

> The interpretation of a word doth oft declare a wit. As when one hath done a robbery, some will say, "It is a pity he was a handsome man." To which another made answer, "You say truth, Sir, for he hath made these shifts by his hands, and got his living with light fingering, and therefore, being handsome as you say he is, I would God he were handsomely hanged." 142)

Playing with words is an important source of humor in rhetoric, a tactic that works on an audience, certainly. But the tactic also has obvious connections with the ambiguity and irony on which rhetoric thrives and with the nominalism and *copia* that rhetoric teaches. Finally, as both Wilson and Erasmus are quick to observe, humor like all of the elements of rhetoric reminds Scholastics and all other ethereal intellectuals that people have bodies.

Wilson concludes book 2 with a discussion of *disposition.* The chief point of the discussion, made all the more striking because it comes so soon after a review of

---

14. See Derrick, *"Arte of Rhetorique,"* 603. Derrick has provided helpful notes on Wilson's sources. Although I believe that Wilson has leaned much more heavily on Cicero, the *ad Herennium,* and Quintilian than Derrick indicates, his Commentary (551–663) is an important updating of Wagner's in "Wilson and his Sources," *Quarterly Journal of Speech* 15 (1929): 530–32.

the parts of an oration, is a caution about following too closely the rules of art. Wilson's cautionary advice is reviewed in my chapter 6.

The third book

Elocution means aptly using words and framing sentences. "Style," we would say, since "elocution" came to mean something else in the late eighteenth century.

Like Crassus in *De oratore*, III, Wilson virtually equates eloquence, or the whole art of rhetoric, with style. Eytmyologically, too, there is a relationship perhaps more functional in Wilson's time than in our own: both "eloquence" and "elocution" derive from the Latin *eloquor*, meaning "to speak out"—or as Wilson might put it in a way reminiscent of part of his characterization of rhetoric itself, "to express matters at large." Eloquence is something unique to rhetoric and to rhetoric's proving ground, speaking to a mixed audience. But style and eloquence cannot be abstracted from the other offices of rhetoric, all of which "go together." Further, for both Wilson and Crassus, and Cicero, an apt and versatile style of speaking or writing is clear evidence of an eloquent composer. Like all humanists, Wilson berates the "clerks"—that is, the Scholastics—for their very lack of eloquence:

> Yea bring them to speak their mind, and enter in talk with such as are said to be learned, and you shall find in them such lack of utterance that if you judge them by their tongue and expressing of their mind, you must needs say they have no learning. Wherein me thinks they do like some rich snudges having great wealth go with their hose out at heels, their shoes out at toes, and their coats out at both elbows. (161)

There are *four parts of elocution:* plainness, aptness, composition, and exornation. It's the first part, plainness, for which Wilson has achieved some lasting fame, having been credited with virtually inventing the term "inkhorn." It is also important to note that the other three "parts of elocution" are equal in importance to plainness, though it is Wilson's insistence on using good, plain English which has garnered most fame for him in subsequent centuries.

Wilson's discussion of "exornation" leads naturally into a discussion of *figures.* Of these there are three kinds: *tropes* (e.g., metaphor), *schemes* (e.g., adding letters to words, as "He did all to berattle him" [177], or arranging sentences so that they rhyme) and *colors* (e.g., hyperbole, *rogatio,* extended similitudes, and above all examples). Wilson comments, "He that mindeth to persuade must needs be well stored with examples" (190). This is a lesson which Wilson himself has obviously taken to heart. Examples not only help us substantiate a matter and make it clear, but they also keep our audience from boredom. Wilson uses a plethora of examples, as throughout his book he "heartens" us with tales—usually "merry tales," for humor and wit are characteristic of his writing as well as important principles of the rhetoric he is teaching. The examples he discusses at this point, as part of his teaching on "colors" are drawn from history, fables, Scripture, myth. Again he leans heavily on Erasmus for his sources: *De copia, Ecclesiastes, Apophthegms, De conscribendis epistolis* (for exact references, see Derrick, *"Arte of Rhetorique,"* 646 and passim).

Amplification is brought back into the discussion once more, as part of "enriching examples by copie" (194). For me, one of the most Erasmian-sounding passages, one that seems to echo the lesson of *The Praise of Folly* while keeping in mind the rhetorical necessity to speak at large, comes under the heading "Fables":

> The multitude (as *Horace* does say) is a beast, or rather a monster that hath many heads, and therefore like unto the diversity of natures variety of invention must always be used. Talk altogether of most grave matters, or deeply search out the ground of things or use the quiddities of *Dunce* [i.e., Duns Scotus, the Scholastic nit-picker whose first name the humanists have for ever transformed into a schoolboy joke] to set forth God's mysteries, and you shall see the ignorant (I warrant you) either fall asleep or else bid you farewell. The multitude must needs be made merry, and the more foolish your talk is the more wise will they count it to be. (198)

But no sooner has the point been made than Wilson begins talking about "schemes" again, this time schemes of "sentences." It is virtually impossible to make "rational" sense of the traditional divisions of rhetorical style. Just when you think you've pinned down the difference between "trope" and "scheme," the theorist is apt to pull the rug out from under you. But such duplicity—complexity, if you will—has a function in humanist rhetoric: the point in such careful writers as Erasmus is that theoretical categories break down whenever one attempts to discuss systematically something as fluid as discourse. Style is but another manifestation of a certain habit of mind deeply intertwined with all the offices of rhetoric.

The penultimate division of this third book and the fourth office of rhetoric is *memory:* natural (e.g, people gifted with prodigious memories, like Julius Caesar) and artificial. Artificial memory is one of the more arcane offices of traditional rhetoric. It is essentially a visual and spatial art: you attempt to recall matters—the parts of your speech, or even the divisions in some piece of knowledge, like human anatomy—by distributing them into "places" in a room or building that you are thoroughly familiar with. When called upon to deliver your speech, or verbalize the knowledge you've tried to retain, you revisit that room in your mind's eye and find the elements you've "stored" therein. Too, you store that knowledge not as words but as visual images—and classical sources insisted that the more grotesque the image, the easier it is to remember. Wilson's example is appropriately, considering his classical sources, legalistic:

> My friend, whom I took ever to be an honest man, is accused of theft, of adultery, of riot, of manslaughter, and of treason. If I would keep these words in my remembrance and rehearse them in order as they were spoken, I must appoint five places, the which I had need to have so perfectly in my memory as could be possible. As for example, I will [use] these in my chamber: a door, a window, a press [i.e., a "clothes press," or freestanding closet], a bedstead, and a chimney. Now in the door I will set *Cacus* the thief, or some such notable varlet. In the window I will place *Venus*. In the press I will put *Apicius,* that famous glutton. In the bedstead I will set Richard the Third, King of England, or some notable murderer. In the chimney I will place the black Smith, or some other notable traitor. That if one repeat these places and these images twice or thrice together, no doubt though he have but a mean memory he shall carry away the words rehearsed with ease. And like as he may do with these five words, so may he do with five score, if he have places fresh in his remembrance, and do but use [accustom] himself to this trade one fortnight together. (215)[15]

15. It is little wonder that the art of memory veered over into the mystical and even the

The final division is *Pronunciation:* voice and gesture. Wilson talks briefly, and simply, about oral delivery. The subject, moreover, forces him finally to leave off discussing this art altogether. If the full range of rhetoric itself can only be suggested unsystematically in a textbook, the subject of oral delivery reveals the ultimate impossibility of capturing the whole of the art in print. "Practice," Wilson insisted at the outset, "diligent practice and earnest exercise are the only things that make men prove excellent" (4). Pronunciation, the final office which is meant to "go together" with the other four, only underscores the limitations of this book—or any book for that matter—as a complete theory of rhetoric.

Too, if Wilson has properly been credited with being "the first English writer" actually to insist on the connections between speech and prose, as Mueller observes, it should be remembered that Wilson is the first writer to speak about English prose in any extensive fashion whatsoever and that he approached it from the standpoint of traditional rhetoric, which not only includes the idea of oral delivery but assumes the primacy of speech. Wilson, sounding like members of the profession later to be named *Elocution,* from Thomas Sheridan through Henry Higgins, bemoans the state of speaking in his time; one can almost hear him complain, Why can't the English learn to speak? Theory of course has little to offer, though Wilson's entire book with its profoundly oral notion of prose lays the foundation for instruction in speech.

---

architectural. Jonathan D. Spence has a succinct and vivid review of the traditional learning about memory in *The Memory Palace of Matteo Ricci* (New York, 1983), see esp. chapter 1. The most comprehensive book on the subject remains Frances Yates's *The Art of Memory* (Chicago, 1966).

Appendix B: To Marry or
Not to Marry, That's the Question

An entire history of academic disputation could center on the question, Should one marry? Or, as it was put in Latin, Should a wife be taken? A favorite in the classroom for two millennia, the question must have appealed to students in that period, who were mainly boys and young men. It became poignant in the Renaissance, in a context of Protestant challenges to churchly teachings on priestly celibacy. The following is a brief review of certain materials this history might include.

An ducenda sit uxor? Both Quintilian (III.v.8) and Cicero describe the use of this question in education, the latter (*Orator*, xiv.46) tracking its use back to Aristotle. The exercise lay in propounding a deliberative *thesis*, arguing for or against a general question, in this case concerning the institution of marriage. The textbook tradition appears to have descended largely from the Greeks, extending from Priscian (6th century A.D.), who in effect Latinized the question in Hermogenes (2d century A.D.). Aphthonius, who also follows Hermogenes closely, wrote the most widely used *Progymnasmata* in Renaissance European education.[1]

Surely one of the cleverest contributions to the long tradition is Alberti's "Dinner Pieces" (ca. 1430), cf. "Maritus" and "Uxoria." One of the most delightful *dissasoriae* is Walter Map's epistle (ca. 1182) "Valerius to Rufinus." One of the most pointed (and therefore rhetorical) is Petrarch's letter, mentioned in my chapter 4, to Pandolfo Malatesta. And one of the most typically humanist sallies into the battle, or battles rather, is Agricola's phrasing of the question, "Ought a philosopher marry?"

In textbooks themselves, the question on marriage appears over and over again. It is alluded to so frequently, as I noted in chapter 4, that it was clearly a standard

---

1. Donald Lemen Clark, "The Rise and Fall of Progymnasmata in Sixteenth and Seventeenth Century Grammar Schools," *Speech Monographs* 19 (1952): 259–63.

one in the Renaissance classroom, whether in actual oral disputation or in the writing of declamations.

According to Foster Watson's study of English grammar schools, "declamations" on theses (called "themes" by Watson) were divided into three types: affirmative, *uxor est ducenda;* negative, *uxor non est ducenda;* and a third "moderating" between the two; he cites Richard Brinsley's consideration (in *Ludus Literarius* [1612]) that the declamation properly belongs in the University, not in the grammar school.[2] Richard Rainolde, who introduced the *progymnasmata* traditions into English literature with his *Foundacion of Rhetorike* (1563) offers a comprehensive view of the deliberative thesis ("Tully's *propositum*"), "Whether is it best to marie a wife," and offers an oration on the subject (foll. Liiij–Lix) structured by means of "objections" and "answers." In sum, the subject seemed well designed to teach the important procedures of pro-con reasoning, and beyond.

Too, the subject seemed well designed to teach another technique of rhetorical education, the compilation of commonplaces. Walter Haddon's contribution to the long tradition, for example, is in the form of two Latin poems which form a kind of commonplace book on the question. The poems are worth considering, for they show the careful balance—including, in this case, prosodic and grammatical parallelism—which must be maintained between the two sides.[3]

Uxor non est ducenda	*Uxor est ducenda*
Omnis aetatis comitem protervam,	Omnis aetatis comitem perennem,
Omnium morum sociam dolosam,	Omnium morum similem sodalem,
Omnium rerum dominam superbam	Omnium rerum dominam fidelem
Sumere durum est.	Sumere suave est.
Quae tuum secum cupiat dolorem,	Quae tuum tecum doleat dolorem,
Quae tuas risu lachrymas sugillet,	Quae suas tecum lachrymas profundat,
Quae minas, fletus, et acerba tecum	Quae iocos, risus, et amoena tecum,
Iurgia tractet.	Gaudia tractet.
Quae tuam poenam redimat salutis	Quae tuum vultum redimat salutis
Propriae lucro, pariatque prolem,	Propriae damno, parietque prolem,
Quae patris falso titulum sonabit	Quae patris nomen tenero sonabit
Ore, molestum.	Ore, iucundum.
Quae tuas iras, strepitus inanes,	Quae tuas iras, Iovis esse fulmen,
Quae tuas voces, sine mente verba,	Quae tuas voces, Iovis esse nutus,
Quae tuos Iusus, aconita dira	Quae tuos Iusus, Iovis esse nectar
Credere possit.	Credere possit.
Quae tuas muris putet esse vires,	Quae tuas Martis putet esse vires,
Quae tuos corvi putet esse cantus,	Quae tuos Phoebi putet esse cantus,
Quae tuas musas putet esse agrestis	Quae tuas musas putet esse sacras
Carmina Fauni.	Palladis artes.
Quae tuam linguam putet esse ranae,	Quae tuam linguam putet Hermis ora,
Quae tuas ursi putet esse carnes,	Quae tuam formam Veneris figuram,
Quae tuum scrophae timidae pedorem	Quae tuum sacrae Triviae pudorem

2. *The English Grammar Schools to 1660* (Cambridge, Eng., 1908), 430–34.

3. Poems 35 and 36, in *The Poetry of Walter Haddon*, ed. Charles J. Lees (The Hague, 1967), 139–41.

Iudicet esse.

Quae tibi charos Styga palude,
Quae tuos fructus Acheronte nigro,
Quae tuam vitam magis expavescat
　　　　　Manibus ipsis.
Uxor temporibus, moribus, et locis,
Naturam varie distribuit suam,
Nunquam prospiciens coniugis usibus.
Ergo si tibi vis omnia progredi,
Vitae perpetuo fac careas malo.

Iudicet esse.

Quae tuos hostes Stygia palude,
Quae tuas clades Acheronte nigro,
Quae tuum funus magis expavescat
　　　　　Manibus ipsis.
Uxor temporibus, moribus, et locis,
Naturam varie distribuit suam,
Semper prospiciens coniugis usibus.
Ergo si tibi vis omnia progredi,
Vitae perpetuo ne careas bono.

An English translation cannot quite capture the subtle balances and parallelisms of Haddon's Latin. The two poems are more strictly careful in their mirroring than Milton's *L'Allegro* and *Il Penseroso*. But the following comes close. I am indebted to John Harding for the translations.

A Wife's not to be taken

For all one's life an impudent companion,
Of all one's habits an unhappy sharer,
Over all one's possessions a prideful
　　mistress,
　　　　It's hard to take such a one.

One who may in her heart wish your
　　pain,
Who may with laughter mock your tears,

Who may engage you in threats and
　　weeping
　　　　And bitter quarrels.

Who may redeem your penalty for the
　　profit
Of her own salvation, and bear offspring
Who will with lying mouth declare their
　　father's name
　　　　Tiresome.

Who could believe your wrath to be
　　empty noise,

Your voice to be words without purpose,
Your pleasantry to be dire
　　　　Wolf's-bane.

Who may think your strength to be that
　　of a mouse,
Your songs to be those of a crow,
Your poetry to be songs
　　　　Of rustic Pan.

Who may think your tongue to be that of
　　a frog,

A Wife's to be taken

For all one's life a lasting companion,
Of all one's habits a like partner,
Over all one's possessions a faithful
　　mistress,
　　　　It's sweet to take such a one.

One who may share your grief,

Who may pour forth her tears with your
　　own.

Who may engage you in jokes and
　　laughter
　　　　And pleasant rejoicing.

Who may redeem your countenance at the
　　cost
Of her own salvation, and bear offspring
Who will with gentle lips declare their
　　father's name
　　　　Pleasant.

Who could believe your wrath to be
　　Jove's
　　　　thunderbolt,
Your voice to be Jove's command,
Your pleasantry to be Jove's
　　　　Nectar.

Who may think your strength to be that
　　of Mars,
Your songs to be those of Phoebus,
Your poetry to be the sacred arts
　　　　Of Pallas.

Who may think your tongue to be the
　　voice of Hermes,

Your flesh to be that of a bear,	Your beauty to be that of Venus,
Who may judge your modesty to be that Of a fearful sow.	Who may judge your shame to be that Of Diana.
Who may fear your loved ones more than Stygian waters,	Who may fear your enemies more than Stygian waters,
Your success more than black Acheron,	Your ruin more than black Acheron,
Your life more than Hell itself.	Your death more than Hell itself.
A wife distributes her abilities in various ways,	A wife distributes her abilities in various ways,
According to time and habit and place,	According to time and habit and place,
Never looking out for her husband's interests.	Always looking out for her husband's interests.
Therefore, if you want all things to advance in your favor,	Therefore, if you want all things to advance in your favor,
See that you lack life's lasting evil.	Do not lack life's lasting good.

Let us explore further a subject which the Haddon example has introduced: the *commonplace book,* a little written storehouse of arguments. Students of traditional rhetoric were advised to prepare these books as preparations for debating as well as for composition. One of the most famous examples which has survived from the Renaissance gives us yet another glimpse into the traditional schoolroom disputation on marriage.

In recommending that all students prepare a *"Promptuary* or Preparatory Store," Francis Bacon claimed to be following Cicero. He seems also to have had *De oratore* in mind, as the editors of both the Latin and English versions of Bacon's *De Augmentis* note—in particular II.viii. 32–4, wherein Cicero's other spokesman, Antonius, talks of delivering a prepared speech in court cases. But Bacon, unlike Cicero, argues that the "promptuary" precept should be applied

> not only to the judicial kind of oratory, but also to the deliberative and demonstrative. I would have in short all topics which there is frequent occasion to handle (whether they relate to proofs and refutations, or to persuasions and dissuasions, or to praise and blame) studied and prepared beforehand; and not only so, but the case exaggerated both ways with the utmost force of the wit, and urged unfairly, as it were, and quite beyond the truth.[4]

In other words, to get ready for *controversia* as well as *suasoria,* prepare a promptuary, listing hyperbolic arguments pro and con. The advice, as well as the interpretation of *De oratore* on which it is based, could hardly be more in line with the humanist rhetoric I have tried to describe. Bacon's own Promptuary is a virtual textbook in that rhetoric, offering examples of listings pro and con on such subjects as "unchastity," "cruelty," and even (self-reflexively, or rather in good contrarian fashion) "promptitude." The collection bears comparison with, among other works cited in my discussion, Lando's *Paradossi.* Most of the arguments, being hyperbolic, are like argumentative sallies.

4. *Works,* ed. James Spedding, Robert Leslie Ellis, and Douglas Denon Heath (London, 1875–1879), 4: 472.

Let me extend my reason for bringing up the example of Bacon. His promptuary listing of arguments on marriage (*Works*, 4: 474) as well as his essay on the subject reveal by precept and example the very core of suasion. The order of the list itself seems somewhat random and imbalanced, though each argument on each side is stated in such a way that its opposite is implied.

V. Wife and Children

For	Against
Love of his country begins in a man's own house.	He that has wife and children has given hostages to fortune.
A wife and children are a kind of discipline of humanity; whereas unmarried men are harsh and severe.	Man generates and has children; God creates and produces works.
To be without wife or children is good for a man only when he wants to run away.	The eternity of brutes is in offspring; of men, in fame, good deserts, and institutions.
He who begets not children sacrifices to death.	Domestic considerations commonly overthrow public ones.
They that are fortunate in other things are commonly unfortunate in their children; lest men should come too near the condition of Gods.	Some persons have wished for Priam's fortune, who survived all his children

Of Marriage and Single Life[5]

He that hath wife and children hath given hostages to fortune, for they are impediments to great enterprises, either of virtue or of mischief. Certainly the best works, and of greatest merit for the public, have proceeded from the unmarried or childless men, who both in affection and means have married and endowed the public. Yet it were great reason that those that have children should have greatest care of future times unto which, they know, they must transmit their dearest pledges.

Some there are who though they lead a single life yet their thoughts do end with themselves and account future times impertinences. Nay there are some other that account wife and children but as Bills of Charges. Nay more, there are some foolish rich covetous men that take a pride in having no children because they may be thought so much the richer. For perhaps they have heard some talk, "Such an one is a great rich man," and another except to it, "Yea, but he hath a great charge of children," as if it were an abatement to his riches. But the most ordinary cause of a single life is liberty, especially in certain self-pleasing and humorous minds which are so sensible of every restraint as they will go near to think their girdles and garters to be bonds and shackles. Unmarried men are best friends, best masters, best servants, but not always best subjects, for they are light to run away, and almost all fugitives are of that condition. A single life doth well with church men, for charity

5. 1625 version, from *A Harmony of the Essays, Etc. of Francis Bacon*, arr. Edward Arber (London, 1871), 265–71. I have modernized the spelling and punctuation—but see my later comment.

will hardly water the ground where it must first fill a pool. It is indifferent for judges and magistrates, for if they be facile and corrupt you shall have a servant five times worse than a wife. For soldiers I find the generals commonly in their hortatives put men in mind of their wives and children. And I think the dispising of marriage amongst the Turks maketh the vulgar soldier more base. Certainly wife and children are a kind of discipline of humanity, and single men, though they be many times more charitable because their means are less exhausted, yet on the other side they are more cruel and hard hearted (good to make severe inquisitors) because their tenderness is not so oft called upon. Grave natures, led by custom and therefore constant, are commonly loving husbands—as was said of Ulysses, *Vetulam suam praetulit Immortalitati* ["He preferred his old woman to immortality"—i.e. he preferred Penelope to Circe; see *De oratore,* I.xliii.196]. Chaste women are often proud and froward, as presuming upon the merit of their chastity. It is one of the best bonds, both of chastity and obedience in the wife if she think her husband wise, which she will never do if she find him jealous. Wives are young men's mistresses, companions for middle age, and old men's nurses. So . . . a man may have a quarrel to marry when he will. But yet, he was reputed one of the wise men that made answer to the question, "When should a man marry? "A young man not yet, an elder man not at all." It is often seen that bad husbands have very good wives, whether it be that it raiseth the price of their husband's kindness when it comes or that the wives take a pride in their [own] patience. But this never fails if the bad husbands were of their own choosing against their friends' consent, for then they will be sure to make good [i.e., never seem to repent] their own folly.

Although I endeavored to modernize Bacon's text, I found it very difficult to paragraph it, beyond the division marked in the edition I used. The reason for the difficulty may lie in the tightly-associative nature of the speaker's thoughts. The essay is, indeed, more like a soliloquy than an oration. It is dialogic but not quite public, yet another reason it does not belong among humanist suasion. The effect of the essay, however, is certainly suasory. Joel Altman describes the effect in the following way:

> What Bacon is doing is looking at marriage and the single life not simply from opposite sides of the question but also in different contexts. . . . The effect is that of a circumnavigation of the topic, which ends not offering a "stand" on marriage at all, but simply exploring its significance in the wide universe in which it exists. This accounts for its disjunctive quality: many eyes are seeing and reporting.[6]

It may not be surprising to discover that Walter Haddon married twice in his life and that Bacon waited until his mid forties to marry ("Towards his rising years, not before" said Dr. Rawley, "he entered into a married state") and had no children. But what is important about the two examples is mainly what they teach us about contrarianism. As Erasmus knew, sometimes to his sorrow and sometimes to his delight, the challenge is always to read rhetorically.

6. *Tudor Play of Mind* (Berkeley, Calif., 1978), 42.

Bibliography

Ancient and Early Modern Sources

Agricola, Rudolphus. *De inventione. Lucubrationes.* Cologne, 1539. Repr Nieuwkoop, 1967.

Alberti, Leon Battista. *Intercenales (Dinner Pieces, ca. 1430).* Trans. David Marsh. Binghamton, N.Y., 1987.

Aristotle. *Rhetoric.* Ed. and trans. George A. Kennedy: *On Rhetoric: A Theory of Civic Discourse.* Ed. George A. Kennedy. New York, 1991.

Ascham, Roger. *The Schoolmaster* (1570). Ed. Lawrence V. Ryan. Ithaca, N.Y., 1967.

———. *Toxophilus* (1545). Ed. Edward Arber. London, 1868.

Ascham, Roger. *The Whole Works of Roger Ascham.* Ed. Rev. D. Giles. 3 vols. London, 1864. Repr N.Y., 1970.

Augustine, St. *De doctrina christiana.* Vol. 32. *Corpus Christianorum, Series Latina.* Turnhout, 1962.

———. *On Christian Doctrine.* Trans. J. F. Shaw. 3rd ed. Edinburgh, 1892.

———. *Against the Academicians (Contra Academicos).* Trans. Mary Patricia Garvey. Milwaukee, 1957.

———. *De Magistro.* Ed. and trans. J. H. S. Burleigh. In *Augustine: Earlier Writings.* Philadelphia, 1953. 102–217.

Bacon, Francis. *A Harmony of the Essays, etc., of Francis Bacon.* Ed. Edward Arber. London, 1871.

———. *Complete Works.* Ed. James Spedding, Robert Leslie Ellis, and Douglas Denon Heath. 14 vols. London, 1857–1874.

Boethius. *De topicis differentiis.* Trans. Eleonore Stump. Ithaca, N.Y., 1978.

———. *In ciceronis topica.* Trans. Eleonore Stump. Ithaca, N.Y., 1988.

Brinsley, John. *A Consolation for our Grammar Schooles.* London, 1622.

Browne, Thomas. *Religio Medici* (1682). Ed. L. C. Martin. Oxford, Eng., 1964.

————. *Ludus Literarius: or, The Grammar Schoole*. London, 1612.

Bruni, Leonardo. *The Humanism of Leonardo Bruni*. Trans. and intro. Gordon Griffiths, James Hankins, and David Thompson. Binghamton, N.Y., 1987.

Castiglione, Baldassare. *The Book of the Courtier* (1561). Trans. Thomas Hoby. Repr ed. Ernest Rhys. London, 1937.

————. *The Courtier*. Trans. Friench Simpson. New York, 1980.

Cicero. *Academica*. Trans. H. Rackham. Loeb Classical Library. Cambridge, Mass., 1933.

————. *Brutus*. Trans. G. L. Hendrickson. Loeb Classical Library. Cambridge, Mass., 1939.

————. *De inventione*. Trans. H. M. Hubbell. Loeb Classical Library. Cambridge, Mass., 1949.

————. *De officiis*. Trans. Walter Miller. Loeb Classical Library. Cambridge, Mass., 1913.

————. *De oratore*. Trans. E. W. Sutton and H. Rackham. 2 vols. Loeb Classical Library. Cambridge, Mass., 1929.

————. *De partitione oratoria*. Trans. H. Rackham. Loeb Classical Library. Cambridge, Mass., 1942.

————. *Orator*. Trans. H. M. Hubbell. Loeb Classical Library. Cambridge, Mass., 1939.

————. *Paradoxa Stoicorum*. Trans. H. Rackham. Loeb Classical Library. Cambridge, Mass., 1942.

————. *Tusculan Disputations*. Trans. J. E. King. Loeb Classical Library. Cambridge, Mass. 1927.

————. *Topica*. Trans. H. M. Hubbel. Leob Classical Library. Cambridge, Mass., 1949.

[Cicero.] *Ad C. Herennium*. Trans. Harry Caplan. Loeb Classical Library. Cambridge, Mass., 1954.

Clement, Francis. *The Petie Schole with an English Orthographie*. London, 1587.

D'Ewes, Sir Simonds. *Extracts from the ms. journal of Sir Simonds D'Ewes . . . (1682)*. London, 1783.

Donne, John. *Devotions Upon Emergent Occasions* (1624). Ed. Anthony Raspa. New York, 1987.

————. *The Sermons of John Donne*. Ed. George R. Potter and Evelyn M. Simpson. 10 vols. Berkeley, Calif., 1962.

Dryden, John. *Annus Mirabilis: The Year of Wonders, 1666*. London, 1667. Repr Oxford, 1927.

Elyot, Sir Thomas. *The Education or bringinge up of children, translated oute of Plutarche*. London, 1533.

————. *The Book named The Governor* (1531). Ed. S. E. Lehmberg. London, 1962.

Erasmus. *Collected Works*. Toronto, 1974– .

————. *Colloquies*. Trans. Craig R. Thompson. Chicago, 1965.

————. *Desiderii Erasmi Roterodami opera omnia*. Ed. Jean Leclerc. 10 vols. Leiden, 1703–1706. Repr 1961–1962.

————. *Erasmus-Luther Discourse on Free Will*. Trans. Ernst F. Winter. New York, 1961.

———. *Opus epistolarum*. Ed. P. S. Allen, et al. 12 vols. Oxford, Eng., 1906–1958.

———. *Selected Writings*. Ed. John C. Olin. 3rd ed. New York, 1987.

———. *The Praise of Folly*. Trans. Clarence H. Miller. New Haven, Conn., 1979.

Fraunce, Abraham. *The Lawiers Logike*. London, 1588.

———. *The Arcadian Rhetorike* (1588). Ed. Ethel Seaton. Oxford, Eng., 1950.

Gellius, Aulus. *Attic Nights*. Trans. John C. Rolfe. 3 vols. Loeb Classical Library. Cambridge, Mass., 1948–1954.

Haddon, Walter. *Cantabrigienses, sive exhortatio ad literas* (1552). In *G. Haddoni . . . Orationes . . .* London, 1567. 109–34.

———. *The Poetry of Walter Haddon*. Ed. Charles J. Lees. The Hague, 1967.

Harvey, Gabriel. *Ciceronianus*. London, 1577.

———. *Rhetor.* London, 1577.

Hoole, Charles. *A New Discovery of the Old Art of Teaching School*. London, 1660.

Hoskins, John. *Directions for Speech and Style* (1599). Ed. Hoyt H. Hudson. Princeton, N.J., 1935.

Kempe, William. *The Education of Children in Learning*. London, 1588.

Fenner, Dudley. *The Artes of Logike and Rethorike*. London, 1584.

Lando, Ortenso. *Paradossi*. See Munday.

Lever, Ralph. *The Arte of Reason, rightly termed, Witcraft*. London, 1573.

Map, Walter. *De nugis curialium (Courtiers' Trifles, ca 1200)*. Ed. and trans. M. R. James. Oxford, Eng., 1983.

Melanchthon, Philipp. *Loci communes* (1555). Trans. Charles Leander Hill. Boston, 1944.

Milton, John. *Areopagitica*. London, 1644.

———. *Paradise Lost*. London, 1667. Rev. 1674.

More, Thomas. *Complete Works*. Ed. Louis A. Schuster et al. 14 vols. New Haven, Conn., 1963–90.

———. *Utopia (1551)*. Trans. Ralph Robynson. Ed. J. Churton Collins. Oxford, Eng., 1904.

———. *Utopia (1516)*. Repr. Leeds, Eng., 1966.

Mulcaster, Richard. *The first part of the Elementarie*. London, 1582. Montaigne, Michel de. *Complete Works*. Trans. Donald M. Frame. Stanford, Calif., 1967.

Munday, Anthony. *Defense of Contraries*. London, 1593.

Peacham, Henry. *The Garden of Eloquence*. London, 1593.

Petrarcha, Francesco. *Rerum familiarium libri, XVII–XXIV: Letters on Familiar Matters*. Trans. Aldo S. Bernardo. Baltimore, 1985.

Plato. *Phaedrus*. Trans. R. Hackforth. *Theaetetus*. Trans. F. M. Cornford. In *Plato: The Collected Dialogues*, ed. Edith Hamilton and Huntington Cairns. Princeton, N.J., 1961. 475–525; 845–919.

Puttenham, George. *The Art of English Poesy Contrived into three Books: The first of Poets and Poesy, the second of Proportion, the third of Ornament (1589)*. Ed. Gladys Doidge Willcock and Alice Walker. Cambridge, Eng. 1936.

Rainolde, Richard. *The Foundacion of Rhetorike*. London, 1563.

Quintilian. *Institutio oratoria*. Trans. H. E. Butler. 4 vols. Loeb Classical Library. London, 1920–1922.

Seneca, the Elder. *Controversiae* and *Suasoriae*. Trans. Michael Winterbottom. Loeb Classical Library. Cambridge, Mass., 1974.

Seton, John. *Dialectica* (1545) . . . *annotationibus Petri Carteri* . . . London, 1572.

Sherry, Richard. *A Treatise of Schemes and Tropes*. London, 1550.

Sidney, Philip. "An Apologie for Poetrie." In *English Literary Criticism: The Renaissance*. Ed. O. B. Hardison, Jr. New York, 1963. 99–146.

Smith, Sir Thomas. *De republica Anglorum* (1583). Repr Leeds, Eng., 1970.

Temple, William. *William Temple's Analysis of Sir Philip Sidney's Apology for Poetry (ca. 1585)*. Ed. and trans. John Webster. Binghamton, N.Y., 1984.

Udall, Nicholas, et al. *The paraphrases of Erasmus upon the newe testament eftsones conferred with the Latine and throughly corrected . . . with a perfect concordaunce diligently gathered by Nicolas Udall*. 2 vols. London, 1551–1552.

Vico, Giambattista. *On the Study Methods of our Time*. Trans. Elio Gianturco. Ithaca, N.Y., 1990.

Wilson, Thomas. *A Discourse upon Usury, by way of Dialogue and Orations* (1572). Ed. R. H. Tawney. London, 1925.

———. *"Arte of Rhetorique" by Thomas Wilson* (1553). Ed. Thomas J. Derrick. New York, 1982.

———. *The Rule of Reason conteinying the Arte of Logike* (1551). Ed. Richard S. Sprague. Northridge, Calif., 1972.

———. *The Rule of Reason conteinying the Arte of Logike*. London, 1567.

———. *Wilson's "Arte of Rhetorique"* (1580). Ed. G. H. Mair. Oxford, Eng., 1909.

———. *Arte of Rhetorique*. London, 1585.

———. *Thomas Wilson: The Art of Rhetoric* (1560). Ed. Peter E. Medine. University Park, Pa., 1994.

———. *Three Orations of Demosthenes, chief orator of the Grecians in favour of the Olynthians . . . with those his four Orations against King Philip of Macedon; most needful to be read in these dangerous days of all them that love their country's liberty and desire to take warning for their better avail*. London, 1570.

———. *A Treatise on England's Perils* (1578). In Albert J. Schmidt, *Archiv für Reformationsgeschichte* 46 (1955): 243–49.

———. With Walter Haddon. *Vita et obitus duorum fratrum Suffolciensium, Henrici et Caroli Brandoni . . .* London, 1551.

Scholarly Studies and Interpretive Works

Altman, Joel B. "'Prophetic Fury': *Othello* and the Economy of Shakespearean Reception." *Studies in the Literary Imagination* 26 (1993): 85–113.

———. *The Tudor Play of Mind: Rhetorical Inquiry and the Development of Elizabethan Drama*. Berkeley, Calif., 1979.

Augustijn, Cornelis. *Erasmus: His Life, Works, and Influence*. Trans. J. C. Grayson. Toronto, 1991.

Backman, Mark. *Sophistication: Rhetoric and the Rise of Self-Consciousness*. Woodbridge, Conn., 1991.

Bain, Alexander. *English Composition and Rhetoric*. New York, 1867.

Bainton, Roland H. *Erasmus of Christendom*. New York, 1969.

Bakhtin, Mikhail. *Problems of Dostoyevsky's Poetics.* Ed. and trans. Caryl Emerson. Minneapolis, 1984.

———. *The Dialogic Imagination.* Ed. and trans. Caryl Emerson and Michael Holquist. Austin, 1981.

Baldwin, T. W. *William Shakespere's Small Latine & Lesse Greeke.* 2 vols. Urbana, Ill., 1944.

Baron, Hans. *The Crisis of the Early Italian Renaissance: Civic Humanism and Republican Liberty in an Age of Classicism and Tyranny.* 2 vols. Princeton, N.J., 1955.

Barrett, Harold. *The Sophists.* Novato, Calif., 1987.

Barzun, Jacque. *The American University.* 2d ed. Chicago, 1993.

Bateson, Gregory. *Steps to an Ecology of Mind.* New York, 1972.

Bauer, Barbara. *Jesuitische 'ars rhetorica' im Zeitalter der Glaubenskämpfe.* Frankfurt, 1986.

Billig, Michael. *Arguing and Thinking: A Rhetorical Approach to Social Psychology.* Cambridge, Eng., 1987.

Bitzer, Lloyd F. "The Rhetorical Situation." *Philosophy and Rhetoric* 1 (1968): 1–14.

——— and Edwin Black. *The Prospect of Rhetoric.* Englewood Cliffs, N.J., 1971.

Bizzell, Patricia. "*The Praise of Folly,* The Woman Rhetor, and Post-Modern Skepticism." *Rhetoric Society Quarterly* 22 (1992): 7–17.

——— and Bruce Herzberg, eds. *The Rhetorical Tradition: Readings from Classical Times to the Present.* Boston, 1990.

Black, Edwin. *Rhetorical Criticism: A Study in Method.* New York, 1965.

———. *Rhetorical Questions: Studies of Public Discourse.* Chicago, 1992.

Bloom, Allan. *The Closing of the American Mind.* New York, 1987.

Booth, Wayne C. *The Vocation of a Teacher: Rhetorical Occasions, 1967–88.* Chicago, 1988.

———. *A Rhetoric of Irony.* Chicago, 1974.

Bouwsma, William J. "Lawyers and Early Modern Culture." *American Historical Review* 78 (1973): 303–27.

———. "Socrates and the Confusion of the Humanities." In *The American Future and the Humane Tradition.* Ed. Robert E. Hiedemann. Washington, D.C., 1982. 11–22.

Boyle, Marjorie O'Rourke. "Augustine in the Garden of Zeus: Lust, Love, and Language." *Harvard Theological Review* 83 (1990): 117–39.

———. "Folly Plus: Moria and More." *Journal of Religious History* 15 (1989): 436–47.

———. *Erasmus on Language and Method in Theology.* Toronto, 1977.

———. *Rhetoric and Reform: Erasmus's Civil Dispute with Luther.* Cambridge, Mass., 1983.

———. "Erasmus and the 'Modern' Question: Was He Semi-Pelagian?" *Archiv für Reformationsgeschichte* 75 (1984): 59–77.

———. "Fools and Schools: Scholastic Dialectic, Humanist Rhetoric; from Anselm to Erasmus." *Medievalia et Humanistica* 13 (1985): 173–95.

Braet, Antoine. "The Classical Doctrine of *status* and the Rhetorical Theory of Argumentation." *Philosophy and Rhetoric* 20 (1987): 79–93.

Brooks, Cleanth and Robert Penn Warren. *Modern Rhetoric.* New York, 1949.

Buckley, Michael J. *Motion and Motion's God: Thematic Variations in Aristotle, Cicero, Newton, and Hegel*. Princeton, N.J. , 1971.

Burgh, Ronna. *Plato's Phaedrus: A Defense of a Philosophic Art of Writing*. University, Ala., 1980.

Burke, Kenneth. *A Grammar of Motives*. Berkeley, Calif., 1969.

————. "Linguistic Approach to Problems of Education." *Modern Philosophies and Education*. Fifty-fourth Yearbook of the National Society for the Study of Education (Chicago, 1955): 259–303.

Cahn, Michael. "Reading Rhetoric Rhetorically: Isocrates and the Marketing of Insight." *Rhetorica* 7 (1989): 121–44.

Cave, Terence. *The Cornucopian Text: Problems of Writing in the French Renaissance*. Oxford, Eng., 1979.

Cheney, Lynne V. *50 Hours: A Core Curriculum for College Students*. Washington, D.C., 1989.

Clark, Donald Lemen. "The Rise and Fall of Progymnasmata in Sixteenth and Seventeenth Century Grammar Schools." *Speech Monographs* 19 (1952): 259–63.

————. *John Milton at St. Paul's School*. New York, 1948.

Cogan, Marc. "Rudolphus Agricola and the Semantic Revolutions of the History of Invention." *Rhetorica* 2 (1984): 163–94.

Cole, Thomas. *The Origins of Rhetoric in Ancient Greece*. Baltimore, 1991.

Colie, Rosalie L. *Paradoxia Epidemica: The Renaissance Tradition of Paradox*. Princeton, N.J., 1966.

Colish, Marcia L. *The Mirror of Language: A Study in the Medieval Theory of Knowledge*. Rev. ed. Lincoln, Neb., 1983.

Connors, Robert J., Lisa S. Ede, and Andrea A. Lunsford, eds. *Essays on Classical Rhetoric and Modern Discourse*. Carbondale, Ill., 1984.

Corbett, Edward P. J. *Classical Rhetoric for the Modern Student*. New York, 1965.

Costello, William T., *The Scholastic Curriculum at Early Seventeenth-Century Cambridge*. Cambridge, Mass., 1958.

Covino, William A. *The Art of Wondering: A Revisionist Return to the History of Rhetoric*. Portsmouth, N.H., 1988.

Cressy, David. *Literacy & the Social Order: Reading and Writing in Tudor and Stuart England*. Cambridge, Eng., 1980.

Curtis, Mark H. *Oxford and Cambridge in Transition 1558–1642*. Oxford, Eng., 1959.

D'Souza, Dinesh. *Illiberal Education: The Politics of Race and Sex on Campus*. New York, 1991.

Dasenbrock, Reed Way. "J. L. Austin and the Articulation of a New Rhetoric." *College Composition and Communication* 38 (1987): 291–305.

De Man, Paul. *Allegories of Reading*. New Haven, Conn., 1979.

————. *The Rhetoric of Romanticism*. New York, 1984.

Demetz, George, Thomas Greene, and William Nelson, eds. *The Disciplines of Criticism: Essays in Literary Theory, Interpretation, and History*. New Haven, Conn., 1968.

Doherty, M. J. *The Mistress-Knowledge, Sir Philip Sidney's Defence of Poesie and Literary Architectonics in the English Renaissance*. Nashville, 1991.

Dover, K. J. *Lysias and the Corpus Lysiacum*. Berkeley, Calif., 1968.

Eagleton, Terry. *Walter Benjamin: Towards a Revolutionary Criticism*. London, 1981.

Eliot, T. S. *The Idea of a Christian Society and Other Writings*. Intro. David L. Edwards. London, 1982.

Elsky, Martin. *Authorizing Words: Speech, Writing, and Print in the English Renaissance*. Ithaca, N.Y., 1989.

Enos, Richard Leo, ed. *Oral and Written Communication: Historical Approaches*. Newbury Park, Calif., 1990.

Fletcher, Harris. *The Intellectual Development of John Milton*. 2 vols. Urbana, Ill., 1961.

Freedman, Joseph S. "Cicero in Sixteenth- and Seventeeth-Century Rhetoric Instruction." *Rhetorica* 4 (1986): 227–54.

Freeman, Kathleen. *Ancilla to the pre-Socratic Philosophers*. Oxford, Eng., 1948.

Fuentes, Carlos. "Borges in Action: A Narrative Homage." *PMLA* 101 (1986): 778–87.

Gilman, Sander L. *The Parodic Sermon in European Perspective*. Wiesbaden, 1974.

Gilmore, M. P. *Humanists and Jurists*. Cambridge, Mass., 1963.

Gleason, John B. *John Colet*. Berkeley, Calif., 1989.

Goodwin, David. "Controversiae Meta-Asystatae and the New Rhetoric." *Rhetoric Society Quarterly* 19 (1989): 205–16.

Gordon, Walter M. *Humanist Play and Belief: The Seriocomic Art of Desiderius Erasmus*. Toronto, 1990.

Graff, Gerald. *Professing Literature*. Chicago, 1987.

Grafton, Anthony, and Lisa Jardine. *From Humanism to the Humanities*. Cambridge, Mass., 1986.

Grassi, Ernesto. *Rhetoric as Philosophy*. University Park, Pa., 1980.

Gray, Hannah. "Renaissance Humanism: The Pursuit of Eloquence." *Journal of the History of Ideas* 24 (1963): 497–514.

Green, Lawrence D. "Aristotelian Rhetoric, Dialectic, and the Traditions of [Antistrophe]." *Rhetorica* 8 (1990): 5–27.

Greenblatt, Stephen. *Renaissance Self-Fashioning*. Chicago, 1980.

Grendler, Paul F. *Schooling in Renaissance Italy: Literacy and Learning, 1300–1600*. Baltimore, 1989.

Guthrie, William K. *The Sophists*. Cambridge, Eng., 1971.

Hackett, M. B. *The Original Statutes of Cambridge University*. Cambridge, Eng., 1970.

Hairston, Maxine. *Successful Writing: A Rhetoric for Advanced Composition*. 3rd ed. New York, 1992.

Hardison, O. B., Jr. *English Literary Criticism: The Renaissance*. New York, 1963.

Heiserman, A. R. "Satire in the *Utopia*." *PMLA* 78 (1963): 163–74.

Hirsch, E. D. *The Schools We Need and Why We Don't Have Them*. New York, 1996.

———. *Cultural Literacy*. Boston, 1987.

Hohmann, Hanns. "The Dynamics of Stasis: Classical Rhetorical Theory and Modern Legal Argumentation." *American Journal of Jurisprudence* 34 (1989): 171–97.

Horner, Winifred Bryan. *Rhetoric in the Classical Tradition*. New York, 1988.

Howell, Wilbur Samuel. *Logic and Rhetoric in England, 1500–1700*. Princeton, N.J., 1956.

Howes, Raymond F., ed. *Historical Studies of Rhetoric and Rhetoricians*. Ithaca, N.Y., 1961.

Hughes, Richard E., and P. Albert Duhamel. *Rhetoric: Principles and Usage.* Englewood Cliffs, N.J., 1962.

Huizinga, Johan. *Erasmus and the Age of Reformation.* New York, 1924. Repr New York, 1957.

——. *Men and Ideas: History, the Middle Ages, the Renaissance.* Princeton, N.J., 1959.

Hunt, John. "Allusive Coherence in Sidney's *Apology for Poetry.*" *Studies in English Literature* 27 (1987): 1–16.

Jardine, Lisa. "The Place of Dialectic Teaching in Sixteenth-Century Cambridge. *Studies in the Renaissance* 21 (1974): 31–62.

——. *Erasmus, Man of Letters.* Princeton, N.J., 1993.

Javitch, Daniel. "Poetry and Preferment at Elizabeth's Court: Some Preliminary Observations." In *Europäische Hofkultur im 16. und 17. Jahrhundert.* Hamburg, 1981. 163–69.

——. *Poetry and Courtliness in Renaissance England.* Princeton, N.J., 1978.

Jenkins, Peter. "The Making of Mr. Major." *New York Review of Books* (April 25, 1991): 43–45.

Jonsen, Albert R., and Stephen Toulmin. *The Abuse of Casuistry: A History of Moral Reasoning.* Berkeley, Calif., 1988.

Joseph, Miriam. *Shakespeare's Use of the Arts of Language.* Ithaca, N.Y., 1947.

Jost, Walter. "Teaching the Topics: Character, Rhetoric, and Liberal Education." *Rhetoric Society Quarterly* 21 (1991): 1–16.

Kahn, Victoria. *Rhetoric, Prudence, and Skepticism in the Renaissance.* Ithaca, N.Y., 1985.

Kennedy, George A. *Classical Rhetoric and Its Christian and Secular Tradition from Ancient to Modern Times.* Chapel Hill, N.C., 1980.

Kennedy, William J. *Authorizing Petrarch.* Ithaca, N.Y., 1994.

——. *Rhetorical Norms in Renaissance Literature.* New Haven, Conn., 1978.

Kerferd, G. B. *The Sophistic Movement.* Cambridge, Eng., 1981.

Kimball, Bruce A. *Orators and Philosophers: A History of the Idea of a Liberal Education.* New York, 1986.

Kimball, Roger. *Tenured Radicals: How Politics Has Corrupted Our Higher Education.* New York, 1990.

Kinney, Arthur F. "Rhetoric as Poetic: Humanist Fiction in the Renaissance." *English Literary History* 43 (1976): 413–43.

——. *Humanist Poetics: Thought, Rhetoric, and Fiction in Sixteenth-Century England.* Amherst, Mass., 1986.

——. *Rhetoric and Poetic in Thomas More's Utopia.* UCLA *Humanita Civilitas.* Vol. 5. Malibu, Calif., 1979.

——. "Parody and Its Implications in Sydney's Defense of Poesie." *Studies in English Literature* 12 (1972): 1–20.

Kinney, Daniel. "More's Letter to Dorp: Remapping the Trivium." *Renaissance Quarterly* 34 (1981): 179–210.

Kisch, Guido. *Humanismus und Jurisprudenz: Der Kampf zwischen mos italicus und mos gallicus an der Universität Basel.* Basel, 1955.

Knoblauch, C. H., and Lil Brannon. *Rhetorical Traditions and the Teaching of Writing.* Upper Montclair, N.J., 1984.

Knox, Bernard. *The Oldest Dead White European Males.* New York, 1993.

Kristeller, Paul Oskar. "A Life of Learning." *The American Scholar* 60 (1991): 337–50.

————. *Renaissance Thought: The Classic, Scholastic, and Humanist Strains.* New York, 1961.

Lanham, Richard A. "The 'Q' Question." *South Atlantic Quarterly* 87 (1988): 653–700.

————. "Twenty Years After: Digital Decorum and Bistable Allusions." *Texte* 8/9 (1989): 63–98.

————. *The Motives of Eloquence.* New Haven, Conn., 1976.

Lechner, Joan Marie. *Renaissance Concepts of the Commonplaces.* New York, 1962.

Leff, Michael. "The Topics of Argumentative Invention in Latin Rhetorical Theory from Cicero to Boethius." *Rhetorica* 1(1983): 23–44.

Lehman, David. *Signs of the Times: Deconstruction and the Fall of Paul de Man.* New York, 1991.

Lentricchia, Frank, and Thomas McLaughlin, eds. *Critical Terms for Literary Study.* Chicago, 1990.

Lewis, C. S. *English Literature in the Sixteenth Century Excluding Drama.* Oxford, Eng., 1954.

Liu, Yameng. "Aristotle and Stasis Theory: A Re-examination." *Rhetoric Society Quarterly* 21 (1991): 53–59.

————. "Disciplinary Politics and the Institutionalization of the Generic Triad in Classical Rhetoric." *College English* 57 (1995): 9–26.

Mack, Peter, ed. *Renaissance Rhetoric.* New York, 1994.

————. *Renaissance Argument: Valla and Agricola in the Tradition of Rhetoric and Dialectic.* Leiden, 1993.

Maitland, F. W. *English Law and the Renaissance.* Cambridge, Eng., 1901.

Manschreck, Clyde Leonard. *Melanchthon the Quiet Reformer.* New York, 1958.

————. *Melanchthon on Christian Doctrine.* New York, 1965.

Margolin, Victor, ed. *Design Discourse: History/Theory/Criticism.* Chicago, 1989.

Marsh, David. *Quattrocento Dialogue: Classical Tradition and Humanist Innovation.* Cambridge, Mass., 1980.

Martz, Louis L. *Thomas More: The Search for the Inner Man.* New Haven, Conn., 1990.

May, James M. *Trials of Character: The Eloquence of Ciceronian Ethos.* Chapel Hill, N.C., 1988.

Mazzeo, J. A. *Renaissance and Seventeenth Century Studies.* New York, 1964.

McCarthy, Eugene. "The Vindicator." *New Republic* (May 15, 1995): 14.

McCarthy, Mary. *On the Contrary.* New York, 1961. Also pub. London, 1980.

McCloskey, Donald N. *The Rhetoric of Economics.* Madison, Wis., 1985.

McConica, James Kelsey. "Erasmus and the Grammar of Consent." *Scrinium Erasmianum.* Ed. Joseph Coppens. Leiden, 1969. 2:77–99.

McCutcheon, Elizabeth. "Denying the Contrary: More's Use of Litotes in the *Utopia.*" *Moreana* 31–32 (1971): 107–21.

McKeon, Richard. *Rhetoric: Essays in Invention and Discovery.* Ed. Mark Backman. Woodbridge, Conn., 1987.

McNally, James Richard. "*Dux Illa Directrixque Artium:* Rudolph Agricola's Dialectical System." *Quarterly Journal of Speech* 52 (1966): 337–47.

———. "Rudolph Agricola's *De inventione dialectica libri tres:* A Translation of Selected Chapters." *Speech Monographs* 34 1967: 393–422.

McNamara, Robert S. With Brian VanDeMark. *In Retrospect*. New York, 1995.

Medine, Peter E. *Thomas Wilson*. Boston, 1986.

Meiland, Jack W. *College Thinking*. New York, 1981.

———. "Argument as Inquiry and Argument as Persuasion." *Argumentation* 3 (1989): 185–96.

Mill, John Stuart. "Essay on Liberty" (1858). In *Harvard Classics*. Ed. Charles W. Eliot. New York, 1909. 25: 203–325.

Miller, Clarence H. "Some Medieval Elements and Structural Unity in Erasmus' *Praise of Folly*." *Renaissance Quarterly* 27 (1974): 499–511.

Miller, Perry. *The New England Mind: The Seventeenth Century*. New York, 1939.

Mooney, Michael. *Vico in the Tradition of Rhetoric*. Princeton, N.J., 1985.

Moran, Jo Ann Hoeppner. *The Growth of English Schooling 1340–1548*. Princeton, N.J., 1985.

Morson, Gary Saul. "Bakhtin and the Present Moment." *The American Scholar* (Spring 1991): 201–22.

Moss, Jean Dietz. "Dialectic and Rhetoric: Questions and Answers in the Copernican Revolution." *Argumentation* 5 (1991): 17–38.

———. "The Interplay of Science and Rhetoric in Seventeenth Century Italy." *Rhetorica* 7 (1989): 23–44.

———, ed. *Rhetoric and Praxis*. Washington, D.C., 1986.

Mueller, Janel M. *The Native Tongue and the Word*. Chicago, 1984.

Mulder, John. *The Temple of the Mind*. New York, 1969.

Müller, Wolfgang G. "Das Problem von Schein und Sein in Erasmus' *Sileni Alcibiadis* und Shakespeare's *Macbeth*." *Wolfenbütteler Renaissance Mitteilungen* 15 (April 1991): 1–18.

Murphy, James J., ed. *Renaissance Eloquence*. Berkeley, Calif., 1983.

———. "Implications of the 'Renaissance of Rhetoric' in English Departments." *Quarterly Journal of Speech* 75 (1989): 335–43.

———. *Rhetoric in the Middle Ages*. Berkeley, Calif., 1974.

———, ed. *The Rhetorical Tradition and Modern Writing*. New York, 1982.

Murphy, Richard. "The Ethics of Debating Both Sides." *Speech Teacher* 6 (1957): 1–9.

Myrick, Kenneth. *Sir Philip Sidney as a Literary Craftsman*. Cambridge, Mass., 1935.

Nadeau, Ray. "The Progymnasmata of Aphthonius." *Speech Monographs* 19 (1952): 264–85.

Neth, Michael. "Johnny One-Note." *The American Scholar* 60 (1991): 608–13.

Nietzsche, Friedrich. *Friedrich Nietzsche on Rhetoric and Language*. Ed. and trans. Sander L. Gilman, Carole Blair, and David J. Parent. Oxford, Eng., 1989.

———. *Twilight of the Idols*. Trans. R. I. Hollingdale. London, 1990.

Noonan, John. *The Scholastic Analysis of Usury*. Cambridge, Mass., 1957.

O'Malley, John W. "Grammar and rhetoric in the *pietas* of Erasmus." *Journal of Medieval and Renaissance Studies* 18 (1988): 81–98.

———. *Praise and Blame in Renaissance Rome*. Durham, N.C., 1979.

———. "Erasmus and Luther, Continuity and Discontinuity as Key to Their Conflict." *Sixteenth Century Journal* 2 (October 1974): 47–65.

———. "Erasmus and the History of Sacred Rhetoric: The Ecclesiastes of 1535." *Erasmus of Rotterdam Society Yearbook Five* (1985). 1–29.

Ochs, Donovan J. "Cicero and Philosophic *Inventio*." *Rhetoric Society Quarterly* 19 (1989): 217–27.

Olin, John C. *Christian Humanism and the Reformation, Selected Writings of Erasmus*. New York, 1987.

Olson, Gary A. "Jacques Derrida on Rhetoric and Composition." *Journal of Advanced Composition* 10 (1990): 1–21.

Ong, Walter J. *Rhetoric, Romance and Technology*. Ithaca, N.Y., 1971.

———. *Ramus, Method and the Decay of Dialogue*. Cambridge, Mass., 1958.

Orme, Nicholas. *English Schools in the Middle Ages*. London, 1973.

———. "An Early-Tudor Oxford Schoolbook." *Renaissance Quarterly* 34 (1981): 11–39.

Osmond, Rosalie. "Body and Soul Dialogues in the Seventeenth Century." *English Literary Renaissance* 4 (1974): 364–403.

Padley, G. A. *Grammatical Theory in Western Europe, 1500–1700: The Latin Tradition*. Cambridge, Eng., 1976.

Parker, Patricia, and David Quint, eds. *Literary Theory/Renaissance Texts*. Baltimore, 1986.

Perella, Jack. *The Debate Method of Critical Thinking*. Dubuque, Iowa, 1987.

Perelman, Chaim, and L. Olbrechts-Tyteca. *The New Rhetoric*. Trans. John Wilkinson and Purcell Weaver. South Bend, Ind., 1969.

Perelman, Chaim. *The Realm of Rhetoric*. Trans. William Kluback. Notre Dame, Ind., 1982. First pub Paris, 1977: *L'Empire rhétorique et Argumentation*.

Plett, Heinrich F. "Elisabethanische Hofpoetik Gesellschaftlicher Code und ästhetische Norm in Puttenhams 'Arte of English Poesie.'" In *Europäische Hofkultur im 16. und 17. Jahrhundert*. Hamburg, 1981. 41–50.

Plett, Heinrich F., ed. *Renaissance-Rhetorik: Renaissance Rhetoric*. Berlin, 1993.

Press, Gerald A. "The Subject and Structure of Augustine's *De Doctrina Christiana*." *Augustinian Studies* 11 (1980): 99–124.

Quinn, Arthur. *Figures of Speech: 60 Ways to Turn a Phrase*. Salt Lake City, 1982.

Rabil, Albert, Jr., ed. *Renaissance Humanism: Foundations, Forms, and Legacy*. Vol. 3. Philadelphia, 1988.

Raign, Kathryn Rosser. "Stasis Theory Revisited: An Inventional *Techne* for Empowering Students." *Focuses* 2 (1989): 19–26.

Rebhorn, Wayne A. "Baldesar Castiglione, Thomas Wilson, and the Courtly Body of Renaissance Rhetoric." *Rhetorica* 11 (1993): 241–74.

Reed, A. W. "Nicholas Udall and Thomas Wilson." *Review of English Studies* 1 (1925): 275–83.

Reed, Thomas L., Jr. *Medieval English Debate Poetry and the Aesthetics of Irresolution*. Columbia, Mo., 1990.

Rescher, Nicholas. *Dialectics: A Controversy-Oriented Approach to the Theory of Knowledge*. Albany, N.Y., 1977.

Rorty, Richard. *Contingency, irony, and solidarity.* Cambridge, Eng., 1989.

Rowe, J. G., and W. H. Stockdale, eds. *Florilegium Historiale: Essays Presented to Wallace K. Ferguson.* Toronto, 1971.

Ruegg, Walter. *Cicero und der Humanismus.* Zurich, 1946.

Ryle, Gilbert. "The Academy and Dialectic" and "Dialectic in the Academy." *Collected Papers.* London, 1971. 1:89–125.

Saintsbury, George. *A History of English Prose Rhythm.* London, 1912.

Schildgen, Brenda Deen. "Petrarch's Defense of Secular Letters, the Latin Fathers, and Ancient Roman Rhetoric." *Rhetorica* 11 (1993): 119–34.

———, ed. *The Rhetoric Canon.* Detroit, 1997.

Schmidt, Albert J. "A Treatise on England's Perils, 1578." *Archiv für Reformationsgeschichte* 46 (1955): 243–49.

Schmidt, Albert J. "Some Notes on Dr. Wilson and His Lincolnshire Connections." *Lincolnshire Historian* 2 (1961): 14–24.

———. "Thomas Wilson, Tudor Scholar-Statesman." *Huntington Library Quarterly* 10 (1957): 205–18 .

———. "A Household Inventory, 1581." *Proceedings of the American Philosophical Society* 101 (1957): 459–80.

———. "Thomas Wilson and the Tudor Commonwealth: An Essay in Civic Humanism." *Huntington Library Quarterly* 23 (1959): 49–60.

Schoeck, Richard J. "Sir Thomas More, Humanist and Lawyer." *University of Toronto Quarterly* 26 (1964): 1–14.

———. "Early Anglo-Saxon Studies and Legal Scholarship." *Studies in the Renaissance* 5 (1958): 102–10.

———. *Erasmus Grandescens.* Nieuwkoop, 1988.

———. "The Elizabethan Society of Antiquaries and Men of Law." *Notes & Queries* N.s. I (1954): 417–21.

Scott, Izora. *Controversies over the Imitation of Cicero as a Model for Style, and Some Phases of Their Influence on the Schools of the Renaissance.* New York, 1910.

Searle, John. "The Storm over the University." *New York Review of Books* (December 6, 1990): 34–42.

Seltzer, Amy. "Erasmus for the Sake of Argument." Diss. University of California. Berkeley, Calif., 1989.

Sharratt, Peter, ed. *French Renaissance Studies, 1540–70.* Edinburgh, 1976.

Simon, Joan. *Education and Society in Tudor England.* London, 1966.

Skorkowsky, George R., Jr. "British University Debating." *Quarterly Journal of Speech* 56 (1971): 335–43.

Slights, Camille Wells. *The Casuistical Tradition in Shakespeare, Donne, Herbert and Milton.* Princeton, N.J., 1981.

Sloan, Thomas O., and Raymond Waddington, eds. *The Rhetoric of Renaissance Poetry.* Berkeley, Calif., 1974.

Sloane, Thomas O. "Reinventing *Inventio.*" *College English* 51 (1989): 461–73.

———. "Schoolbooks and Rhetoric: Erasmus's *Copia.*" *Rhetorica* 9 (1991): 113–29.

———. *Donne, Milton, and the End of Humanist Rhetoric.* Berkeley, Calif., 1985.

Smith, Bromley. "Extracurricular Disputations: 1400–1650." *Quarterly Journal of Speech* 34 (1948): 473–76.

Snyder, Jon R. *Writing the Scene of Speaking: Theories of Dialogue in the Late Italian Renaissance*. Stanford, Calif., 1989.

Southern, R. W. *The Making of the Middle Ages*. London, 1987. First pub. 1953.

Spence, Jonathan D. *The Memory Palace of Matteo Ricci*. New York, 1983.

Sprague, Rosamund Kent. *The Older Sophists*. Columbia, S.C., 1972.

Sykes, Charles J. *Dumbing Down Our Kids*. New York, 1995.

———. *Profscam*. Washington, D.C. 1988.

Tawney, R. H. *Religion and the Rise of Capitalism*. New York, 1926.

———. *The Acquisitive Society*. New York, 1920.

Thompson, Craig R. *Schools in Tudor England*. Washington, D.C., 1959.

———. *Universities in Tudor England*. Washington, D.C., 1959.

Tinkler, John F. "Erasmus' Conversation with Luther." *Archiv für Reformationsgeschichte* 82 (1991): 59–81.

———. "Praise and Advice: Rhetorical Approaches to More's *Utopia* and Machiavelli's *The Prince*." *Sixteenth Century Journal* 19 (1988): 187–207.

———. "Renaissance Humanism and the *genera eloquentiae*." *Rhetorica* 5 (1987): 279–309.

———. "Humanism and Dialogue." *Parergon*. n.s. 6 (1988): 197–214.

Toulmin, Stephen. "The Recovery of Practical Philosophy." *The American Scholar* (Summer 1988): 337–52.

———. *The Uses of Argument*. Cambridge, Eng., 1969.

Trimpi, Wes. *Muses of One Mind*. Princeton, N.J., 1983.

Trinkaus, Charles. *In Our Image and Likeness: Humanity and Divinity in Italian Humanist Thought*. 2 vols. Chicago, 1970.

Ueding, Gert, ed. *Rhetorik zwischen den Wissenschaften*. Tübingen, 1991.

Untersteiner, Mario. *The Sophists*. Trans. Kathleen Freeman. Oxford, Eng., 1954.

Van der Poel, Marc. *De "declamatio" bij de humanisten*. Nieuwkoop, 1987.

Vickers, Brian. *In Defense of Rhetoric*. Oxford, Eng., 1988.

———. "The *Songs and Sonnets* and the Rhetoric of Hyperbole. " In *John Donne: Essays in Celebration*. Ed. A. J. Smith. London, 1972. 132–74.

Wagner, Russell H. "Wilson and His Sources." *Quarterly Journal of Speech* 15 (1929): 525–37.

———. "Thomas Wilson's *Arte of Rhetorique*." *Speech Monographs* 27 (1960): 1–32.

Walker, David M. *The Oxford Companion to Law*. Oxford, Eng., 1980.

Wallace, Karl R. "Rhetorical Exercises in Tudor Education." *Quarterly Journal of Speech* 22 (1936): 28–51.

———, ed. *A History of Speech Education in America*. New York, 1954.

Wallace, William A. "Aristotelian Science and Rhetoric in Transition: The Middle Ages and the Renaissance." *Rhetorica* 7 (1989): 7–22.

Warton, Thomas. *The History of English Poetry* (1778). Repr London, 1870.

Waswo, Richard. *Language and Meaning in the Renaissance*. Princeton, N.J., 1987.

Watson, Foster. *The English Grammar Schools to 1660: Their Curriculum and Practice*. Cambridge, Eng., 1908.

Webster, John. "Oration and Method in Sidney's *Apology:* A Contemporary's Account." *Modern Philology* 79 (1981–82): 1–15.

Welch, Kathleen E. *The Contemporary Reception of Classical Rhetoric: Appropriations of Ancient Discourse*. Hillsdale, N.J., 1990.

White, Eugene E. "Master Holdsworth and 'A Knowledge Very Useful and Necessary.'" *Quarterly Journal of Speech* 53 (1967): 1–16.

Wildermuth, Mark E. "The Rhetoric of Wilson's *Arte:* Reclaiming the Classical Heritage for English Protestants." *Philosophy and Rhetoric* 22 (1989): 43–58.

Wilson, Kenneth. *Incomplete Fictions: The Formation of English Renaissance Dialogue*. Washington, D.C., 1985.

Yates, Frances. *The Art of Memory*. Chicago, 1966.

Zadeh, Lofti, and Janusz Kacprzyk. *Fuzzy Logic for the Management of Uncertainty*. New York, 1992.

Index

On the Contrary: The Protocol of Traditional Rhetoric was composed in Bembo with Truesdell display by Brevis Press, Bethany, Connecticut; printed on 60-pound Glatfelter Natural Smooth and bound by Braun-Brumfield, Inc., Ann Arbor, Michigan; and designed and produced by Kachergis Book Design, Pittsboro, North Carolina.